Fodor's

VANCOUVER & VICTORIA

3rd Edition

Fodor's Travel Publications • New York, Toronto, London, Sydney, Auckland
www.fodors.com

FODOR'S VANCOUVER & VICTORIA

Writers: Paige Donner, Carolyn B. Heller, Chris McBeath

Editors: Mark Sullivan, Maria Hart

Production Editor: Jennifer DePrima
Maps & Illustrations: David Lindroth, Ed Jacobus, Mark Stroud, and Henry Colomb, *cartographers;* Rebecca Baer, *map editor;* William Wu, *information graphics*
Design: Fabrizio La Rocca, *creative director*; Tina Malaney, Chie Ushio, Jessica Ramirez, *designers*; Melanie Marin, *associate director of photography;* Jennifer Romains, *photo research*
Cover Photo: (Stanley Park): Heeb Photos/eStock Photo
Production Manager: Angela L. McLean

3rd Edition

ISBN 978-0-307-92932-7

ISSN 1941-0301

SPECIAL SALES

This book is available at special discounts for bulk purchases for sales promotions or premiums. Special editions, including personalized covers, excerpts of existing books, and corporate imprints, can be created in large quantities for special needs. For more information, write to Special Markets/Premium Sales, 1745 Broadway, MD 3-1, New York, NY 10019, or e-mail specialmarkets@randomhouse.com.

AN IMPORTANT TIP & AN INVITATION

Although all prices, opening times, and other details in this book are based on information supplied to us at press time, changes occur all the time in the travel world, and Fodor's cannot accept responsibility for facts that become outdated or for inadvertent errors or omissions. So **always confirm information when it matters,** especially if you're making a detour to visit a specific place. Your experiences—positive and negative—matter to us. If we have missed or misstated something, **please write to us.** Share your opinion instantly through our online feedback center at fodors.com/contact-us.

PRINTED IN SINGAPORE

10 9 8 7 6 5 4 3 2 1

CONTENTS

MAPS

ABOUT THIS GUIDE

Fodor's Ratings

Everything in this guide is worth doing—we don't cover what isn't—but exceptional sights, hotels, and restaurants are recognized with additional accolades. **Fodor's Choice** ★ indicates our top recommendations; ★ highlights places we deem highly recommended. Care to nominate a new place? Visit Fodors.com/contact-us.

Trip Costs

We list prices wherever possible to help you budget well. Hotel and restaurant price categories from **$** to **$$$$** are noted alongside each recommendation. For hotels, we include the lowest cost of a standard double room in high season. For restaurants, we cite the average price of a main course at dinner or, if dinner isn't served, at lunch. For attractions, we always list adult admission fees; discounts are usually available for children, students, and senior citizens.

Hotels

Our local writers vet every hotel to recommend the best overnights in each price category, from budget to expensive. Unless otherwise specified, you can expect private bath, phone, and TV in your room. For expanded hotel reviews, facilities, and deals visit Fodors.com.

Restaurants

Unless we state otherwise, restaurants are open for lunch and dinner daily. We mention dress code only when there's a specific requirement and reservations only when they're essential or not accepted. To make restaurant reservations, visit Fodors.com.

Credit Cards

The hotels and restaurants in this guide typically accept credit cards. If not, we'll say so.

Ratings

- ★ Fodor's Choice
- ★ Highly recommended
- Family-friendly

Listings

- Address
- Branch address
- Mailing address
- Telephone
- Fax
- Website
- E-mail
- Admission fee
- Open/closed times
- Subway
- Directions or Map coordinates

Hotels & Restaurants

- Hotel
- Number of rooms
- Meal plans
- Restaurant
- Reservations
- Dress code
- No credit cards
- Price

Other

- See also
- Take note
- Golf facilities

Experience Vancouver and Victoria

VANCOUVER & VICTORIA TODAY

Separated from the rest of the country by the Canadian Rockies, Vancouver and Victoria have always marched to a West Coast rhythm that is in many ways more similar to Seattle, Portland, and even parts of California than to their Canadian heritage. Add to this their proximity to the sea and coastal mountains and you have winters that are mild, summers that are balmy, and landscapes lush with temperate forest and gardens. Nowhere else in Canada do daffodils bloom in February! And despite Victoria's old-English facades, these are young cities with active, outdoorsy, and health-conscious populations. Residents may exude a slightly smug, laissez-faire attitude, but who can blame them? They live in a place that is consistently ranked as one of the most beautiful and livable in the world.

Today's Vancouver and Victoria . . .

. . . are booming. Ever since Vancouver hosted the World's Fair in 1986, the city had been waiting for the next big event to strut its stuff. The 2010 Winter Olympics literally reshaped the city—rapid-transit systems were expanded, infrastructure was upgraded, and Olympic venues redefined neighborhoods, upping already high real estate values to stratospheric heights (and it all happened during one of the worst global recessions). There's no doubt that the Olympics showcased the unparalleled beauty of the region and that the area will continue to prosper. Although separated from Vancouver by the Strait of Georgia, Victoria also got an economic boost from Olympic activity. Condo developments that once attracted mainly Albertans and Vancouverites to Victoria's more temperate lifestyle now have Americans, Asians, and Europeans lining up to buy. As a result, urban development is underway all along the coast, far beyond Victoria's picturesque harbor, so as foundation industries like logging continue their downward slide in many island communities, there are pockets of growth in others.

. . . are greener than ever. West Coasters are more eco-conscious than your average bear. New construction embodies eco-oriented practices from thermal heating to energy-saving fixtures; rooftop gardens add to the relatively pristine air; and recycling is a daily ritual in business and at home. The area's hotels were among the first to introduce green practices when they started installing dual-flush toilets (that's two levels of flushes, not flushing

WHAT'S HOT IN VANCOUVER AND VICTORIA TODAY

Vancouver is still basking in the afterglow from the Winter 2010 Olympics. The Olympic Village has been turned into eco-friendly housing units; the stunning convention-center expansion has transformed the downtown waterfront; and the award-winning Richmond Oval now housing two international-size ice rinks, eight gymnasiums, a 200-meter running track, and a fitness center makes the wealthy Richmond community the envy of many. The city's transit system and infrastructure also saw significant upgrades. The result? Many more Vancouverites have adopted public transit, and newly landscaped walkways and bike routes—known as greenways—have become daily commuter habits.

Gastown has risen up to be a serious contender to Yaletown in terms of hip hangout

twice) and asking guests to use linens more than once. Car pools are commonplace, bicycle lanes rule (there are about 3,500 two-wheel commuters daily), and many companies provide free bus passes to employees who give up commuting by car. To do as the locals do, be sure to carry an eco-friendly water bottle and a reusable carrying bag, and pick up your Day Pass (C$9), which is good on all the major public transportation, including SeaBus, SkyTrain, and local buses.

. . . are ethnically diverse. Although Victoria is still fairly WASPy, Vancouver's easy access to Asia-Pacific destinations has generated a great influx of Asian immigrants. News is delivered in 22 different languages; shops and ATM machines post signs in English, Mandarin, Cantonese (the Chinese are the region's largest visible minority group), Punjabi, Farsi, and even Vietnamese. Ironically, French, Canada's other official language, is rarely seen or heard except on the two Radio Canada stations. This diversity creates a cultural mosaic that comes vibrantly to life in various festivals (such as the Festival of Light) and community activities (including the Richmond Night Market) and, above all, in a range of superb restaurants.

. . . are very outdoorsy. Few cities in the world have mountains, oceans, and pristine rain forests all on their doorstep. Locals take full advantage of these options themselves, and have also realized the incredible opportunities in promoting ecotourism. Whatever your age or ability, the range of activities includes family spelunking and whale-watching excursions, stellar golf and fishing, white-knuckle rafting expeditions, and no holds-barred extreme wilderness adventures. Victoria is a popular departure point for exploring the myriad culinary and eco-adventures on Vancouver Island, while Vancouver is the gateway to sophisticated Whistler and the more rugged interior regions of B.C. It's fair to say that all this fresh air makes for an extremely health-oriented population. Fitness clubs are part and parcel of most office and residential buildings, gym memberships are valued employee benefits, and health gear outlets are plentiful. Is it any wonder that Vancouver and Victoria have some of the toughest smoking laws in Canada?

'hoods. They're both filled with trendy shops, restaurants, and bars, but tourist-oriented Gastown is spreading its wings as developers continue their conversion of seedy hotels into chic urban dwellings with must-have views. Robson Street, Vancouver's answer to Rodeo Drive, is still the place for luxury-goods shopping, but some of Vancouver's top clothing designers and trendy boutiques are in Gastown's revamped studio warehouses, in the SoMa (short for South Main Street) district, and on Kitsilano's 4th Avenue.

Victoria might be best known for its hanging flower baskets, but it's making its mark as the first city in North America to install pop-up public urinals for drunken bar patrons.

WHAT'S WHERE

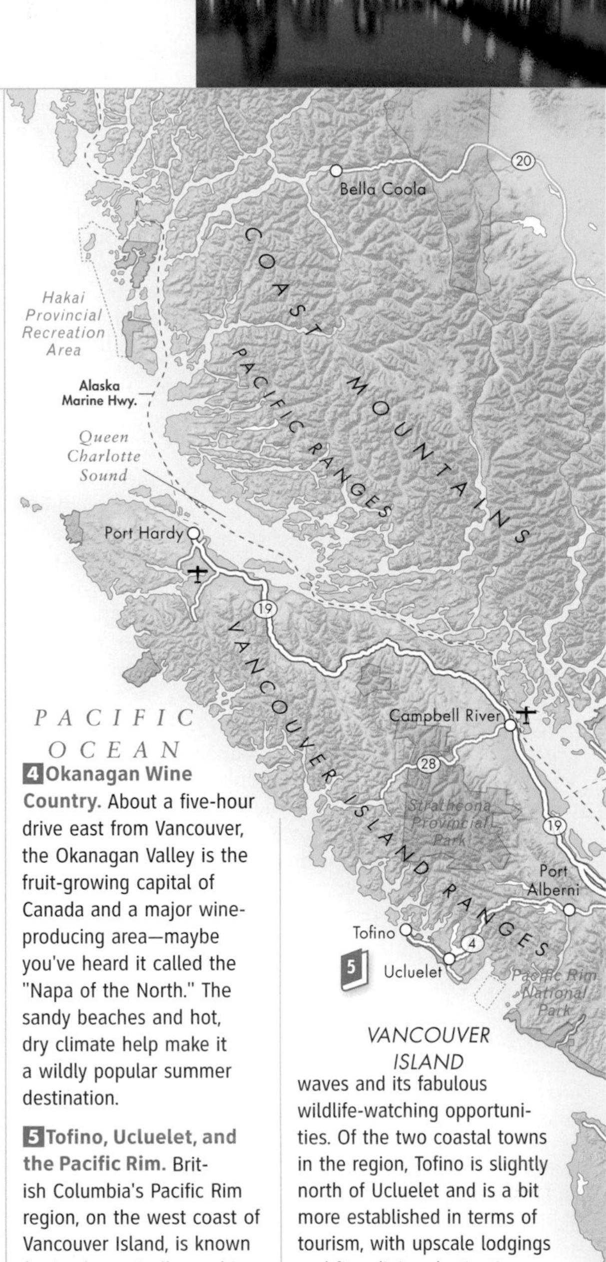

1 Vancouver. Many people argue that Vancouver is the most gorgeous city in North America and situated as it is, between mountains and water, it's hard to disagree. The Vancouver area actually covers a lot of ground, but the central core—Downtown, Gastown, Yaletown, False Creek, English Bay, Stanley Park, and Granville Island—is fairly compact. An excellent public transportation system makes getting around a snap. When in doubt, remember the mountains are to the north.

2 Victoria. At the southern tip of Vancouver Island, British Columbia's capital is a lovely, walkable city with waterfront paths, rambling gardens, fascinating museums, and splendid 19th-century architecture. In some senses remote, it's roughly midway between Vancouver and Seattle and about three hours by car and ferry from either city.

3 Whistler. Just 120 km (75 miles) north of Vancouver—about a two-hour drive along the stunning Sea-to-Sky Highway—Whistler is outdoor paradise in both winter and summer. The two mountains, Whistler and Blackcomb, are the focus of activities, and Whistler Village, at their base, is a compact mecca of lodgings, restaurants, shops, and cafés.

4 Okanagan Wine Country. About a five-hour drive east from Vancouver, the Okanagan Valley is the fruit-growing capital of Canada and a major wine-producing area—maybe you've heard it called the "Napa of the North." The sandy beaches and hot, dry climate help make it a wildly popular summer destination.

5 Tofino, Ucluelet, and the Pacific Rim. British Columbia's Pacific Rim region, on the west coast of Vancouver Island, is known for its dramatically crashing waves and its fabulous wildlife-watching opportunities. Of the two coastal towns in the region, Tofino is slightly north of Ucluelet and is a bit more established in terms of tourism, with upscale lodgings and fine-dining destinations.

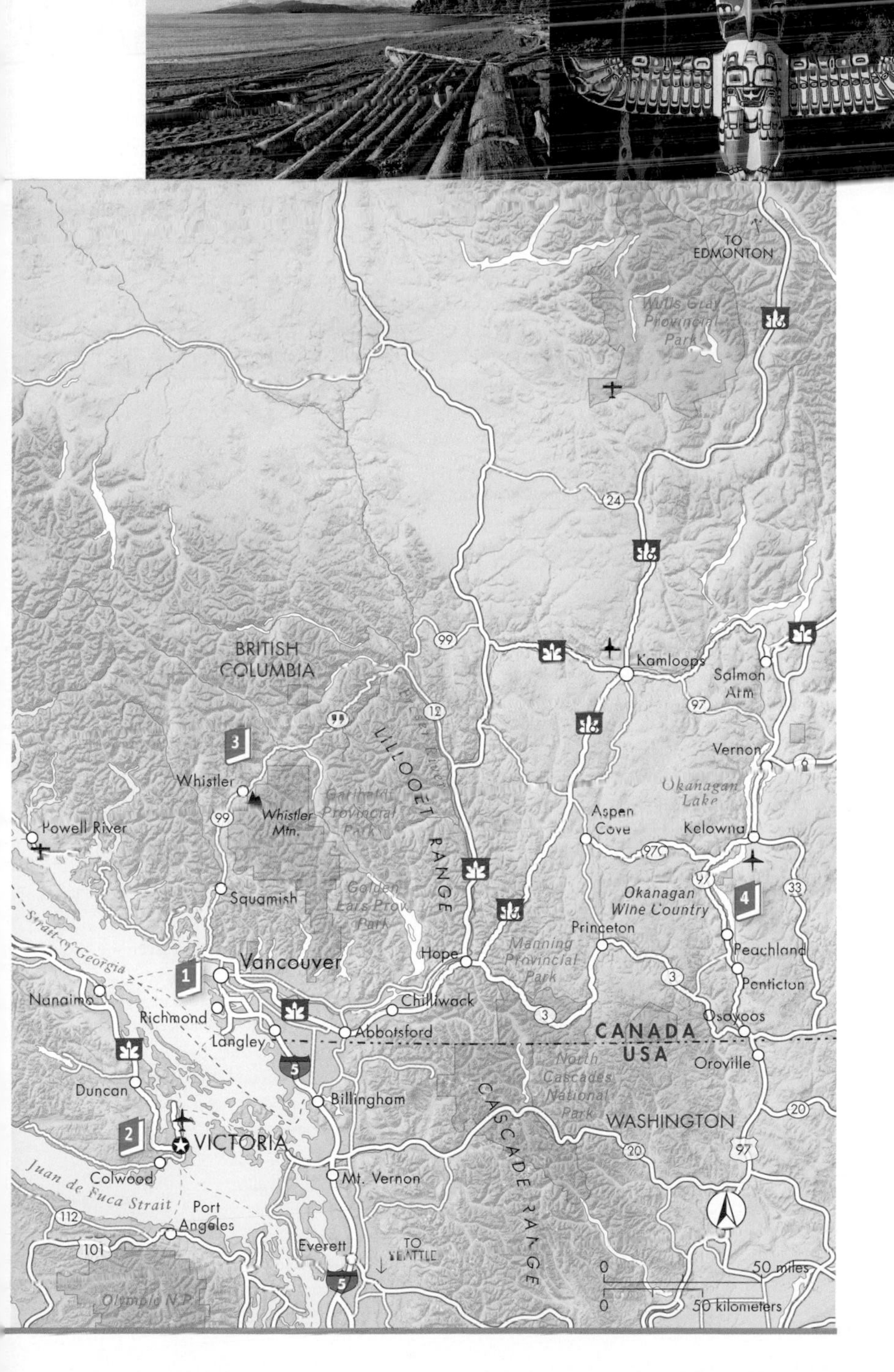

TO EDMONTON
Wells Gray Provincial Park
BRITISH COLUMBIA
Lillooet Range
Whistler
Whistler Mtn.
Garibaldi Provincial Park
Powell River
Squamish
Golden Ears Prov. Park
Strait of Georgia
Vancouver
Nanaimo
Richmond
Langley
Abbotsford
Chilliwack
Hope
Manning Provincial Park
Kamloops
Salmon Arm
Vernon
Okanagan Lake
Aspen Cove
Kelowna
Okanagan Wine Country
Princeton
Peachland
Penticton
Osoyoos
Oroville
CANADA
USA
North Cascades National Park
WASHINGTON
Cascade Range
Duncan
VICTORIA
Colwood
Juan de Fuca Strait
Port Angeles
Olympic N.P.
Billingham
Mt. Vernon
Everett
TO SEATTLE
0
50 miles
0
50 kilometers

VANCOUVER AND VICTORIA PLANNER

When to Go

Both Vancouver and Victoria are cosmopolitan, year-round destinations with an outdoor vibe that kicks into high gear whenever the sun shines.

From June to September, it seems like the entire populace of Vancouver and Victoria migrates to the beaches, parks, and hiking trails. Daffodils and cherry blossoms transform city streets from March to May. Despite the risk of rain, October's cool, crisp mornings almost invariably give way to marvelous sunshine sparkling through multicolored leaves. Come winter, expect lots of hotel and restaurant bargains, the exceptions being glorious Whistler and along Vancouver Island's westernmost coast, where storm-watching is a favorite activity.

Canadian money

U.S. dollars are widely accepted but usually at par, so carry local cash. ATMs are in abundance. Canadian currency uses one- and two-dollar coins ("loonies" and "twonies") and colorful notes for larger denominations.

Getting Here

Air Travel. There are direct flights from most major U.S. and international cities to Vancouver International Airport (YVR), with connecting services to Victoria. You can sometimes get good deals on flights to Seattle (a 2½-hour drive south) and then rent a car or take the train to Canada.

Car Travel. Interstate highway I–5 heads straight up the U.S. coast into Vancouver.

However you travel, carry a passport. Without one, even U.S. citizens might not be allowed home. That includes minors.

Getting Around

In both Victoria and Vancouver, a car can be useful for out-of-town excursions. Having one in the city is a hindrance. Parking is expensive (if it's available at your hotel, it will often be extra), and tow trucks prowl the streets looking for meter violators. Vancouver is a highly walkable city, as is downtown Victoria. Bike-rental shops are numerous, public transportation is easy to use, and there are taxis for when all else fails.

What to Pack

Layering is the best solution to the region's variable weather. And unless "swank" is on your to-do list, ditch the tie—West Coast casual means smart cotton dress pants or jeans and T-shirts. Ward off cool summer breezes with a light jacket, bring Gore-Tex for warmth in winter, and no matter what time of year it's never a bad idea to stash something waterproof. If you forget an umbrella, they're a dime a dozen at every corner store. Vancouver and Victoria are walking cities, so pack comfortable shoes.

LIKE A LOCAL

Heading out to Vancouver or Victoria? Here are a few helpful tips for appreciating this unique part of western Canada just like the locals do.

Eat Local

Supporting local producers is part of the West Coast lifestyle, so back in 2005 when two Vancouver writers originated the 100-mile diet, they didn't expect it would catch on across North America, let alone the world. Look for neighborhood farmers' markets, many of them open year-round. The renowned Granville Island Market, for example, sells such products as handcrafted island cheeses, organic meats, freshly caught fish, salmon jerky "candy," homemade jams and honey, and seasonal fresh produce.

Layer Up

Dressing for success means layering to suit the sea breezes and rain—especially rain. Local mythology says that real natives don't carry umbrellas, they just wear a lot of Gore-Tex, but reliable insider info says the locals do use their "brollies," though as elsewhere in the world, they never seem to be handy when you need them. (That probably accounts for why you can find so many inexpensive umbrellas for sale whenever it rains.) Sure, there are folks who opt for laser eye surgery to eliminate rain-splattered glasses, and certainly those multipurpose Gore-Tex overlays mean you don't have to give in to the umbrella until it really starts to pour. And chances are the locals own at least one pair of rain boots.

Love Your Lattes

West Coasters have a love–hate relationship with the ubiquitous S chain, which has an outlet—sometimes even two, as at the Robson–Thurlow intersection—on almost every street corner. Real locals, however, prefer the authenticity of Trees Organic coffee shop, the Italian coffee shops along Commercial Drive, or the award-winning creations of the champion baristas at the Caffè Artigiano outlets. Locals also like to linger over their lattes at sidewalk tables at any time of year, rain or shine.

Be Eco-Savvy

Doing your bit for the planet is integral to living like a local in Vancouver and Victoria, so rinse and recycle your cans and bottles, take a reusable bag if you're going shopping, and search out socially responsible products and companies. Lots of locals support homegrown environmental heroes such as David Suzuki, philanthropists Linda and Joel Solomon, as well as organizations such as the Western Canada Wilderness Committee.

Read the *Georgia Straight*

This once underground, now mainstream, Vancouver weekly tabloid echoes Vancouver's inner cool. Everything's here, from opinion pieces to offbeat travel articles, insightful restaurant reviews, theater schedules, and personal ads of all genres. Vancouver Is Awesome (🌐 *www.vancouverisawesome.com*) is its online brethren.

Exercise a Passion

Keeping the body healthy is a local preoccupation, as is having the wardrobe to suit the way of life, preferably purchased along Kitsilano's 4th Avenue—the mecca for sporting goods and clothing. Hike the Grouse Grind, scuba-dive Howe Sound, kayak Indian Arm (some locals even kayak to work along the Fraser River), sweat in Bikram yoga, or practice Pilates. Even visitors can partake.

VANCOUVER & VICTORIA TOP ATTRACTIONS

B

A

D

C

E

(A) Museum of Anthropology, Vancouver. The city's most spectacular museum displays art from the Pacific Northwest and around the world—dramatic totem poles and canoes; exquisite carvings of gold, silver, and argillite; and masks, tools, and textiles from many cultures.

(B) The Bill Reid Gallery, Vancouver. If First Nations heritage is your thing, be sure to visit this repository of regional art.

(C) Granville Island, Vancouver. Take the foot-passenger ferry across the inlet from downtown, and bring your appetite. This small island houses an extremely popular indoor market, a marina, theaters, restaurants, coffee shops, parks, and dozens of crafts shops and artist studios. Wander the stalls in the market, then grab a bench outside to get your fill of delicacies and the view.

(D) Dr. Sun Yat-Sen Chinese Garden, Vancouver. "Life is not measured by the number of breaths we take," according to the old saying, "but by the places and moments that take our breath away." That sentiment sums up this elegant downtown destination. It's the first authentic Ming Dynasty–style garden outside of China to incorporate symbolism and design elements from centuries-old Chinese gardens.

(E) Stanley Park, Vancouver. An afternoon in this gorgeous 1,000-acre wilderness, just blocks from downtown Vancouver, can include beaches, the ocean, the harbor, Douglas fir and cedar forests, First Nations sculptures, and a view of the North Shore Mountains. Walk, bike, picnic, or just take the trolley tour around the perimeter, but don't miss it.

(F) Whistler. With two of the longest vertical ski drops on the continent, this ski-in, ski-out village at the base of Whistler and Blackcomb mountains has enough shops, restaurants, and nightlife to fill a vacation without even hitting the slopes.

(G) Inner Harbour, Victoria. The lovely capital of British Columbia has a remarkably intimate and pedestrian-friendly downtown that wraps around the harbor. Street entertainers and crafts vendors—and lots of people—come out to stroll the waterfront walkway in summer.

(H) Butchart Gardens, Victoria. Just 20 minutes from downtown Victoria, the 55-acre Butchart Gardens was planted in a limestone quarry in 1904. Highlights include the Japanese and Italian gardens, as well as the proliferation of roses and 700 other varieties of flowers. On summer nights you can enjoy a fireworks display.

(I) Pacific Rim National Park Reserve, Vancouver Island. This park on the island's far west coast has a seemingly endless white-sand beach and hiking trails with panoramic views of the sea and rain forest. Many visitors go in the winter to witness the dramatic storms coming off the water—and to take advantage of the off-season rates. Adventurous souls can try a kayak trip out to the Broken Group Islands.

(J) Okanagan Valley. East of Vancouver, the country's "fruit basket" is no longer just "beaches and peaches." It has rapidly gained a reputation as a wine region because of the many vineyards surrounding pristine Okanagan Lake. They produce a wide range of notable varietals, including ice wines made from late-harvest grapes. The bountiful resources and gifted chefs in the area also mean the food is on par with the quality of the wines.

FLAVORS OF VANCOUVER AND VICTORIA

For an entire year, 2005–2006, one Vancouver couple ate only food that had been raised within 100 miles of their Kitsilano home. Their project became a rallying cry for the region's emerging "locavore" movement—a philosophy that's come to define the current dining scene. So what's local in Vancouver and Victoria? Seafood is a good starting point, with salmon, Dungeness crab, spot prawns, oysters, and scallops fished from B.C. waters. Locally raised pork and chicken, handcrafted cheeses, and hazelnuts round out the protein options; mushrooms, greens, and, in summer, strawberries, blueberries, and blackberries are available produce. And to drink? B.C. wines, of course.

Yet even as local ingredients are all the rage, Vancouver and Victoria continue to look for culinary inspiration beyond their borders. British Columbia is the country's gateway to the Pacific Rim, and Asian influences abound. B.C. also draws on its European roots with many chefs updating continental cuisine.

Eating Local

Eating local has become almost a religion in Vancouver restaurants, and diners across the city are benefiting from the emphasis on fresh, locally sourced products. Restaurateurs often choose from local bounty, whether it's fresh fruit from the Okanagan Valley or fish from B.C.'s coastal waters.

■ **Bishop's, Vancouver.** Before "local" became fashionable, owner John Bishop was championing seasonal eating, and his Kitsilano restaurant still emphasizes regional products.

■ **Blue Water Café, Vancouver.** Chef Frank Pabst often features underappreciated (and more abundant) varieties of seafood, many from local waters, at this fashionable Yaletown spot.

■ **Raincity Grill, Vancouver.** Another early adopter of local ingredients, this romantic restaurant near English Bay offers a 100-mile tasting menu.

■ **Refuel, Vancouver.** Chef Jane Cornborough not only cures her own bacon, but also lists on her menu the local, organic sources—from poultry farms to coffee roasters—where she obtains her ingredients.

■ **West, Vancouver.** Contemporary regional cuisine is the theme at this chic South Granville restaurant, one of the city's most innovative spots.

Drinking Local

British Columbia has a rapidly maturing wine industry, concentrated in the sunny and dry Okanagan Valley 400 km (250 miles) east of Vancouver. Vancouver Island also is a wine-producing area. In this region, many local restaurants are passionate purveyors of local wines, and wine bars pairing B.C. vino with artisanal cheeses and house-cured charcuterie are all the rage.

■ **Cru, Vancouver.** A lengthy by-the-glass list delights diners who flock to this stylish South Granville storefront for small plates and big wines.

■ **Salt Tasting Room, Vancouver.** Hidden in Gastown's historic Blood Alley, this popular spot focuses on the essentials: flavorful cheese, cured meats, and wine.

■ **Uva Wine Bar, Vancouver.** A hip downtown hangout for sipping and grazing, Uva offers plenty of local wines by the glass.

■ **Stage, Victoria.** Packed with locals, this comfortable wine bar offers Victoria's take on small plates and B.C. wines.

Asian Fine Dining

Vancouver's large population of Asian expats and immigrants has created a demand for Asian fine dining that rivals the best of Hong Kong, Shanghai, and Taipei. Homegrown chefs, such as Maenam's Angus An, are getting into the act, too. His modern Thai bistro takes Southeast Asian dishes to new levels. Locals will tell you that the real Chinese restaurants are all in the nearby community of Richmond.

■ **Kirin, Vancouver.** One branch of this stylish restaurant specializes in northern Chinese cuisine; the others serve up refined Cantonese fare.

■ **Sun Sui Wah Seafood Restaurant, Vancouver.** With locations on Main Street and in suburban Richmond, these popular spots are favorites for dim sum.

■ **Vij's, Vancouver.** This South Granville dining room is a Vancouver foodie institution and packs in the crowds for its innovative Indian creations.

■ **Glowbal Grill Steaks and Satay.** Choice cuts of steak, Indian satay, spaghetti and meatballs, seafood. Yes, it's eclectic, and it's a Yaletown institution. Soak up the local culture as you dine with your finger on the city's pulse.

■ **Tojo's, Vancouver.** Book a seat at the sushi bar, order *omakase* (chef's choice), and legendary chef Hidekazu Tojo will regale you with a parade of creative Japanese bites.

■ **Maenam, Vancouver.** Local ingredients, fresh herbs, and vibrant seasonings spice up traditional Thai dishes at this Kitsilano bistro.

European Renaissance

While Asian influences are common, recently local chefs are rediscovering European flavors, with classic French bistros, regional Italian dining rooms, and Mediterranean-style dishes taking on renewed importance.

■ **Le Crocodile, Vancouver.** A classic for French fare that's, well, classic.

■ **Mistral French Bistro, Vancouver.** The sunny flavors of Provence light up this Kitsilano bistro, even on winter's longest days.

■ **Cibo Trattoria, Vancouver.** This sleek, trendy trattoria makes Italian fare fun again.

■ **Campagnolo, Vancouver.** Take the traditional dishes of Emiglia-Romana and Piedmonte, then perk them up with organic B.C. products. The result? An out-of-the-way eatery that's worth seeking out.

Island Appetites

Much of the produce, seafood, cheese, and wine that city restaurants are serving comes from Vancouver Island or the surrounding Gulf Islands, so it's no surprise that Victoria and vicinity are developing a culture of local eating as well.

■ **Cafe Brio, Victoria.** Highlighting regional, organic fare and B.C. wines, this longtime favorite manages to be both comfortable and hip.

■ **Brasserie L'école, Victoria.** French country classics made with locally sourced provisions—what's not to love?

■ **Sooke Harbour House, Victoria environs.** If you can make one foodie side trip from Victoria, this should be it. A passionate purveyor of creative cuisine based on the freshest local ingredients, this inn-restaurant is a romantic hideaway.

WITH KIDS

Vancouver and Victoria are great places to entertain children, especially ones who like the outdoors. Check the calendar for family-oriented special events, like the Vancouver International Children's Festival in May and the Vancouver Folk Music Festival in July.

Downtown Vancouver

Allow a day to enjoy the kid-friendly activities in Stanley Park: the miniature train, aquarium, pool, water park, and beaches are great for all ages. And getting around this huge park—on a horse-drawn wagon or the free shuttle—is half the fun. Make sure you also plan a trip on the Aquabus to Granville Island, home of North America's largest free public water park and the Kids' Market, a two-story complex of toy stores and play areas. The Granville market is a great place for lunch or snacking, and even the pickiest kids will find something they like. In False Creek you can check out the interactive displays at Science World, catch an IMAX film at Canada Place, or hop a foot-passenger ferry to see one (or more) of the three kid-friendly museums at Vanier Park: the Vancouver Museum, the Maritime Museum, or the H.R. MacMillan Space Centre.

And Beyond Downtown

Outside downtown Vancouver, the North Shore is a wilderness playground. Older kids will no doubt enjoy terrifying their parents by trying to wobble the Capilano Suspension Bridge (or the Lynn Valley Suspension Bridge). The Treetops Adventure at Capilano Suspension Bridge Park and the salmon-spawning displays at the nearby Capilano Salmon Hatchery are big hits. Finish with a Skyride trip up Grouse Mountain, where you can skate or take a sleigh ride in winter, or hike and visit the bear-and-wolf refuge in summer. For a day at the beach, head west to Spanish Banks or Locarno for warm, shallow water and wide stretches of sand. Kits Beach is busier, but has a playground and a heated saltwater pool.

Don't underestimate the entertainment power of public transportation. For a few dollars, a SeaBus ride across Burrard Inlet (a larger ferry than the Granville Island Aquabus) provides a water-level view of the harbor; the same ticket gets you on an elevated SkyTrain ride across town.

Victoria

Like Vancouver, Victoria has small foot-passenger ferries zigzagging across the harbor, and Fisherman's Wharf, with its houseboats and fish-and-chips stands, is popular. Preschoolers are mesmerized by the tiny displays at Miniature World and charmed by the friendly critters at the Beacon Hill Park Petting Zoo, while older kids enjoy the Bug Zoo, the Royal BC Museum, and shopping for allowance-priced souvenirs in Chinatown. Easy hikes, bike rides, and picnics are also popular. For serious "what I did on my summer vacation" material, you can't beat a whale-watching trip. For a night out, try a movie at the IMAX theater, stargazing at the Dominion Astrophysical Observatory, or the spectacular fireworks displays on summer evenings at Butchart Gardens.

Butchart Gardens

If Victoria's Butchart Gardens is on your to-do list, you can make a full day of it by meandering through the peninsula—Sea Cider (about a 10-minute drive from the ferry and about 15 minutes from the gardens) is the place for munchies. Nearby, the Shaw Ocean Discovery Center has amazing touchy-feely exhibits to entertain everyone from 8 to 80 years old.

FREE AND ALMOST FREE

The best things in life are free and a surprising number of them are in Vancouver, Victoria, and Whistler. In fact, most of what's enjoyable in this part of the world—including beaches, parks, hiking trails, interesting architecture, great views, and fun-and-funky neighborhoods—is available free of charge.

Vancouver

In Vancouver, you can visit Stanley Park, Granville Island, Downtown, Gastown, Chinatown, and Yaletown and rarely have to open your wallet to pay admission fees—except for such worthwhile venues as the Vancouver Aquarium and the Dr. Sun Yat-Sen Garden. Granville Island's markets and galleries are all free, as are Canada Place and Stanley Park. Even the shuttle bus around Stanley Park and guided walking tours of Gastown are free.

If that's not enough, here are a few lesser-known ways to stretch those loonies and twonies:

On Tuesday evenings between 5 and 9 the Vancouver Art Gallery charges admission by donation, while the Museum of Anthropology has reduced rates. In North Vancouver, most visitors head for the fun, if pricey, Capilano Suspension Bridge. A few miles away, the equally thrilling Lynn Canyon Suspension Bridge, in Lynn Canyon Park, is absolutely free. It might be a bit of a trek, but also free on the North Shore are the Capilano Salmon Hatchery, where you can learn about the life cycle of salmon (and, in fall, watch them struggling upstream to spawn). The Lonsdale Quay Public Market is home to street entertainers, tugboats, and great city views.

Public Transit

Don't forget one of Vancouver's great unsung bargains: an off-peak, two-zone SkyTrain ticket. For just a few dollars, you can see much of the city's east side and mountains from a clean, efficient elevated train. Using the same ticket you can transfer to the SeaBus for a 15-minute ride across the harbor. The tiny foot passenger ferries across False Creek are great bargains at just a few dollars a ticket.

Victoria

In Victoria, Beacon Hill Park or any of the city's parks and beaches are free, as are most of the city's iconic buildings. A stroll through the public areas of the venerable Fairmont Empress Hotel or a guided tour of the Parliament Buildings won't cost a dime. The Inner Harbour Walk has views of Victoria's Edwardian architecture, boats and seaplanes, and great people-watching is also free. If you're there on a Sunday morning in summer, you can even watch the foot-passenger ferries perform a water ballet. Admission: a whopping C$0.

Bargains in Whistler?

Even in jet-set Whistler you can find a few bargains. In the village, you can make like the glitterati for the price of a latte: start with people-watching from a café patio, enjoy the street entertainers, then move on to a stroll through the village's half dozen or so art galleries or join a free tour at the Brewhouse. Even the village shuttle buses are free, while WAVE buses can get you pretty much anywhere in the valley for C$1.50.

GREAT ITINERARIES

See the Cities: 7–10 days

It's still possible to see Vancouver, Whistler, and Victoria, even if you just have time to hit the highlights. Start with two or three days in Vancouver, seeing Stanley Park and strolling through some neighborhoods like Granville Island, Yaletown, English Bay, Kitsilano, and Gastown. Add a day to explore the mountains and parks of the North Shore (Capilano, Grouse, or Lynn Canyon) or the museums on the city's west side before heading north to Whistler. Be sure to make the trip in daylight because the Sea-to-Sky Highway, along Howe Sound and into the Coast Mountains, is too stunning to miss. After a day or two of biking, hiking, skiing, or just shopping and café sitting in Whistler, head back down the Sea-to-Sky Highway to Horseshoe Bay, where you can board a car ferry to Nanaimo. From there, a two-hour drive south takes you to Victoria, B.C.'s lovely seaside capital, where the museums, restaurants, and shopping warrant at least two or three days of browsing. A ferry from nearby Swartz Bay will have you back in Vancouver in half a day.

Wilderness and Wildlife: 7–10 days

To get in some serious outdoors time, spend a few days in Vancouver hiking in the North Shore Mountains or kayaking in Indian Arm—then head up the Sea-to-Sky Highway, one of the world's great scenic drives, to Whistler. Here, lift-accessed hiking, mountain biking, and snowshoeing are easy ways into the backcountry. If you've ever wanted to try an outdoor sport, this is the place to do it: summer options run from golf and fishing to rafting, zip-lining, and rock climbing. And in winter, skiing is just the start. From Whistler, if you have time (it's a full day's drive each way), the Sea-to-Sky Highway continues through the mountains to link with Highway 1 to the Okanagan, where more parks, lakes, and wineries await. Otherwise, retrace your steps to Horseshoe Bay, where you can catch a ferry to Nanaimo, then make the three-hour drive across the mountains of Vancouver Island to Tofino and Ucluelet. Finish with several days of whale-watching, bear-watching, kayaking, surfing, beachcombing, and perhaps some spa time, in and around the Pacific Rim National Park Reserve.

Food and Wine: 5–10 days

So many restaurants, so many wineries, so little time! A food-and-wine tour of British Columbia would start with a couple days of browsing Vancouver's markets and specialty shops, followed by evenings in a selection of its 3,000 or so restaurants. Then you can head to the source of the bounty you've just sampled, traveling east (at five hours, Highway 5 is the quickest) to the Okanagan Valley, where more than 125 wineries line a 200-km (120-mile) string of lakes, the largest being the picturesque Okanagan Lake. The dozen vineyards around "Canada's wine capital," Oliver, known as the Golden Mile, make a good focus if you're short on time. Another option is a visit to B.C.'s "Wine Island," better known as Vancouver Island. All around Victoria, southern Vancouver Island, and the offshore Gulf Islands are home to about a dozen wineries, as well as organic produce stands, farmers' markets, cider and cheese makers, and some of B.C.'s best country inns.

FIRST NATIONS CULTURE

Home to more than 30 First Nations, each with its own language, history, and culture, B.C. has the most varied, and vibrant, range of aboriginal cultures in North America. It's also one of the best places to experience these cultures, whether in a museum, at a cultural center, or while exploring the wilderness with a First Nations guide.

Museums

Southern B.C. has several First Nations museums—in Vancouver, the Bill Reid Gallery of Northwest Coast Art is an exceptional legacy to this famous artist and includes a wide range of aboriginal art. Vancouver's Museum of Anthropology and Victoria's Royal British Columbia Museum each has a renowned collection of First Nations artifacts, from archaeological finds to modern-day works, that represent a cross section of B.C. aboriginal groups.

Cultural Centers

Another way to experience aboriginal culture is to visit one of the province's cultural centers run by First Nations people. There are several easy day-trip destinations from Vancouver, including the impressive Squamish Lil'wat Cultural Centre (🌐 *www.slcc.ca*) in Whistler and the Xá:ytem (pronounced "HAY-tum") Longhouse Interpretive Centre (🌐 *www.xaytem.ca*), about an hour east of Vancouver. On Vancouver Island, the Quw'utsun' Cultural and Conference Centre (🌐 *www.quwutsun.ca*) is an hour north of Victoria in the city of Duncan. The riverside site's cedar longhouses include the Riverwalk Café, open June to September, where you can sample traditional First Nations cuisine—perhaps some intriguingly prepared salmon or stew with bannock (unleavened bread). If you're heading east to the Okanagan, you can stop en route in Kamloops at the Secwepemc Museum and Heritage Park (🌐 *www.secwepemc.org/museum*), a traditional gathering place now home to replica homes and indigenous gardens. Also in the Okanagan, in the town of Osoyoos, is Nk'Mip Spirit of the Desert (🌐 *www.nkmipdesert.com*), a resort complex that includes North America's first aboriginal-owned (and fully operational) winery, as well as the Nk'Mip Desert Cultural Centre. Further east, in Cranbrook, the Ktunaxa Interpretive Centre (🌐 *www.ktunaxa.org*) is housed in St. Eugene Mission, a former residential school.

Powwows

To experience a powwow, check out Chilliwack's Spirit of the People Pow Wow (🌐 *www.tourismchilliwack.com*). a huge gathering of First Nations groups complete with drumming circles, dancing, traditional foods, and exhibits. Each August, Kamloops hosts the annual Kamloopa Pow Wow (🌐 *www.tourismkamloops.com*), British Columbia's biggest festival of First Nations dance.

Exploring with a First Nations guide

For more of a get-out-and-do-it kind of experience, sign up with a First Nations guide. A growing number of First Nation–owned tourism operators offer everything from kayaking to hiking to jet-boat tours, typically with traditional songs, legends, historic insights, and food (think waterfront salmon barbecues) thrown in. Experiences range from paddling a traditional oceangoing canoe near Vancouver to desert tours around Osoyoos to whale-watching near Tofino.

The Aboriginal Tourism Association of British Columbia (🌐 *www.aboriginalbc.com*) has more details about sites, tours, and experiences.

HOW TO SPEAK B.C.

"In Canada we have enough to do keeping up with two spoken languages without trying to invent slang, so we just go right ahead and use English for literature, Scotch for sermons, and American for conversation." —Stephen Leacock (1869–1944)

Canadian humorist Stephen Leacock was right: Canadians don't like to confuse visitors with obscure regional dialects. For that, we have the metric system. Still, we have our eccentricities, and a brief primer may help avoid some confusion.

Terms useful in B.C. include the words for money: loonies for the dollar coin (because of the loon that graces the coin) and twonies for the two-dollar version. British Columbians, like other Canadians, spell many things the British way (colour instead of color, for example), pronounce the letter "z" as "zed," and occasionally (okay, more than occasionally) tack an "eh?" to the end of a sentence—to turn it into a question, to invite a response, or just out of habit.

Canadianisms like toque (woolly cap) are used here, albeit less frequently given the temperate weather. What you will hear are many words for precipitation. A Vancouverite might observe that it's drizzling, spitting, pouring, or pissing down, but will avoid saying "Yup, it's raining again." That just shows a lack of imagination. Oh, and if someone does say "It's raining again, eh?" he's not asking a question; he's just inviting you to discuss the situation.

A few words are uniquely West Coast, including some derived from Coast Salish, a First Nations trading language. *Skookum*, for example, means big or powerful; *chuck* means water (as in a body of water); salt *chuck* is seawater. Chinook, which means a warm wind in Alberta, is a species of salmon in B.C. Thus you might find: "He caught a skookum chinook then chucked it right back in the salt chuck."

Probably the best sources of confusion out in B.C. are geographical. The Okanagan, and anything else not on the coast, is called "the Interior" by Vancouverites—unless it's north of, say, Williams Lake, in which case it's "Up North." There are thousands of islands in B.C., but "the Island" refers to Vancouver Island. (Many newcomers forget that Vancouver isn't on Vancouver Island; Victoria is.) The Lower Mainland is the term used to refer to Metro Vancouver, including the communities of Langley, Abbotsford, North Shore, Richmond, and even Maple Ridge and White Rock.

Food and drink offer more room for misunderstanding: order soda and you'll get soda water (Canadians drink pop). Homo milk? It's short for homogenized milk and it means whole milk. Bacon is bacon, but Canadian bacon is called back bacon in Canada. Fries are generally fries, but will be called chips if they come with fish, in which case they'll also come with vinegar.

And beer? You can just order "beer," but be prepared to discuss with the bartender your preference for lager, ale, porter, et cetera. You'll probably also be told that Canadian beer is stronger than American. This is a widely held belief that simply doesn't hold water. The alcohol levels are the same—they're just measured differently. That, and the fact that Canadian beer has more flavor, has led generations of cross-border drinkers to believe that the northern brew packs more punch. That's simply not true; it just tastes better.

2

Exploring Vancouver

WORD OF MOUTH

"Things to see in Vancouver, BC. So many! It's so beautiful. If you are active, you can hike the grouse grind, or if you prefer you can take a tram to the top. By far one of the best places to take pictures of the Vancouver skyline, stanley park, lions gate bridge, etc. It's stunning."

—RileyD

WELCOME TO VANCOUVER

TOP REASONS TO GO

★ **Stanley Park:** The views, the activities, and the natural wilderness beauty here are quintessential Vancouver.

★ **Granville Island:** Ride the mini-ferry across False Creek to the Granville Island Public Market where you can shop for delicious lunch fixings; eat outside when the weather's fine.

★ **Kitsilano beaches:** Options range from beaches with grass-edged shores to windswept stretches of sand, to cliff-side coves so private that clothing is optional.

★ **Museum of Anthropology at University of British Columbia:** The phenomenal collection of First Nations art and cultural artifacts, and the incredible backdrop, make this a must-see.

★ **Rain-forest intimacy:** Traverse the canopies at UBC Botanical Garden and Capilano Suspension Bridge Park; you can even zip-line from the treetops.

1 Downtown and the West End. The city's downtown commercial heart has the Pacific Centre Mall, most of the city's high-fashion shops, major hotels, and transit hubs. The compact layout is easy to walk and navigate, and it borders the West End, a residential neighborhood that edges beaches and Stanley Park.

2 Gastown and Chinatown. These adjoining 'hoods have been redone a bit but their ornamental architecture, nooks, and alleyways give clues to Vancouver's earliest history. Chinatown feels like a Hong Kong street market with its mishmash of exotic sights and smells.

3 Yaletown and False Creek. Colossal glass high-rises are juxtaposed against converted loft-style warehouses in this urbanely hip and happening neighborhood best known for its specialty shops and eateries.

4 Stanley Park. A rain forest with top-quality attractions, hikes, and views—all within blocks of the cosmopolitan city skyscrapers.

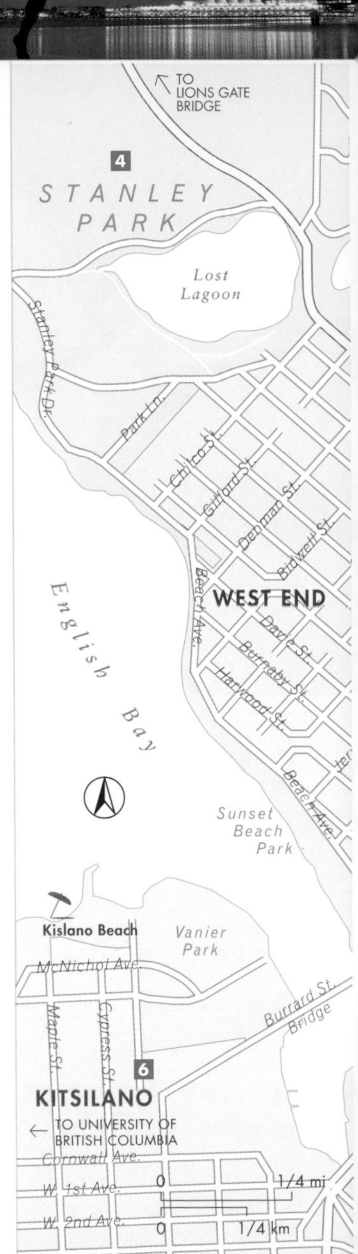

5 Granville Island. The city's most eclectic destination puts art alongside cement works alongside fresh-produce markets, with floating homes and busker entertainment to boot. Nothing disappoints.

6 The West Side and Kitsilano. This is the catchall name for the neighborhoods southwest of downtown, including the university area of Point Grey with its stunning Pacific Spirit Park; old-money Shaughnessy with its posh, seemingly multi-acre stone mansions; the busy Cambie Corridor; and trendy Kitsilano, with its boutiques, converted beach houses, hip restaurants, and terrific beaches.

7 North Shore. Across Burrard Inlet, on the North Shore, are residential and scenic West Vancouver and the more bustling North Vancouver; the mountains, your constant compass-point of reference, are the backdrop.

GETTING ORIENTED

For the most part, Vancouver central sits on a peninsula, which makes it compact and easy to explore on foot, especially since most streets are laid out on a grid system. To get your bearings, use the mountains as your "true north" and you can't go too far wrong. All the avenues, which are numbered, have east and west designations; the higher the number, the farther away from the inlet you are.

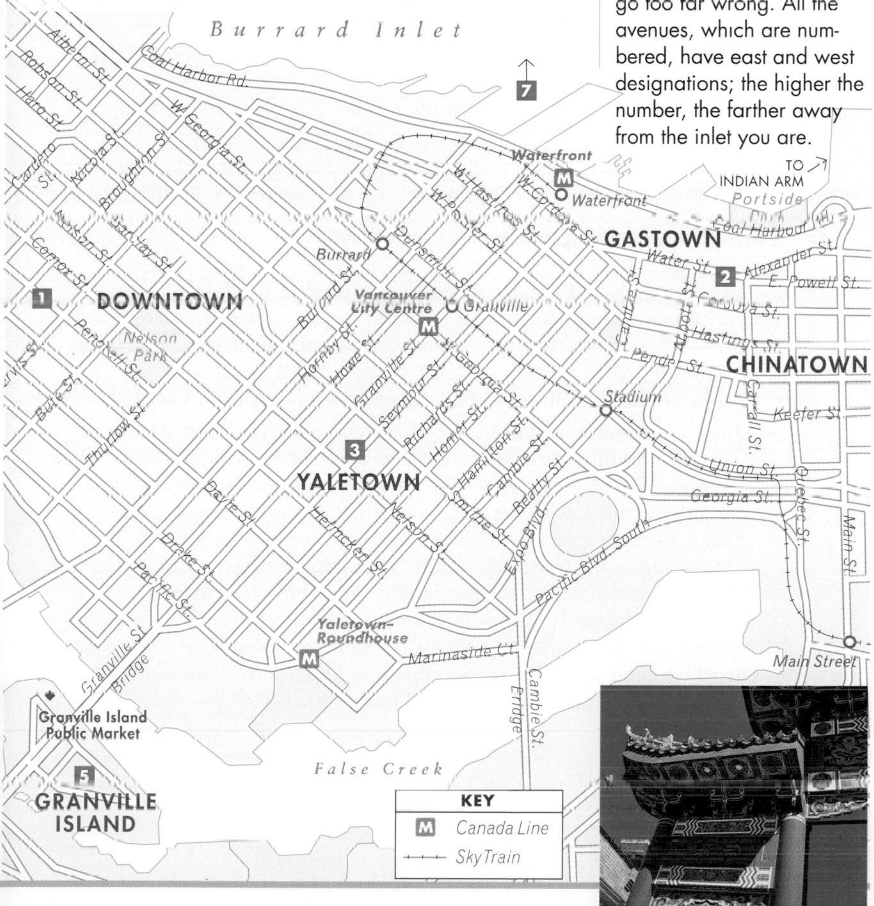

Updated by Carolyn B. Heller

Consistently ranked as one of the world's most livable cities, Vancouver lures visitors with its abundance of natural beauty, multicultural vitality, and cosmopolitan flair. The attraction is as much in the range of food choices—the fresh seafood and local produce are some of North America's best—as it is in the museums, shopping opportunities, and beaches, parks, and gardens. Indeed, the Vancouver package is a delicious juxtaposition of urban sophistication and on-your-doorstep wilderness adventure.

The mountains and seascape make Vancouver an outdoor playground for hiking, skiing, kayaking, cycling, and sailing—and so much more—while the cuisine and arts scenes are equally diverse, reflecting the makeup of Vancouver's ethnic (predominantly Asian) mosaic. Yet despite all this vibrancy, the city still exudes an easy West Coast style.

More than 8 million visitors each year come to this, Canada's third-largest metropolitan area. Because of its peninsula location, traffic flow is a contentious issue. Thankfully, Vancouver is wonderfully walkable, especially in the downtown core. The North Shore is a scoot across the harbor, and the rapid-transit system to Richmond and the airport means that staying in the more affordable 'burbs doesn't have to be synonymous with sacrificing convenience. The mild climate, exquisite natural scenery, and relaxed outdoor lifestyle keep attracting residents, and the number of visitors is increasing for the same reasons. People often get their first glimpse of Vancouver when catching an Alaskan cruise, and many return at some point to spend more time here.

CLOSE UP

Vancouver History

Vancouver's history, such as it is, remains visible to the naked eye at every corner: eras are layered east to west along the waterfront, from the origins in late-Victorian Gastown to the shiny, postmodern glass cathedrals of commerce that spread north and west.

The history of Vancouver is integrally linked with the taming of western Canada: the trappers working for the Hudson's Bay Company (the oldest retail store still operating in North America) explored the area; then the Canadian Pacific Railway, which crossed the country, chose the ramshackle site of Granville as its Pacific terminus. The coming of the railway inspired the loggers and saloon owners of Granville to incorporate as a city: on April 6, 1886, Granville Townsite, with a population of about 400, became the City of Vancouver, named after the British explorer who had toured the inlet here in 1792.

The railway, along with Canadian Pacific's fleet of clipper ships, gave Vancouver a full week's edge over the California ports in shipping tea and silk from the Orient to New York. Lumber, fish, and coal from British Columbia's hinterland—resources that are still the backbone of the provincial economy also flowed through the port to world markets. The same ships and trains brought immigrants from all corners of the earth, helping the population grow exponentially to today's 2.5 million.

PLANNING

MAKING THE MOST OF YOUR TIME

If you don't have much time in Vancouver, you'll probably still want to spend at least a half day in Stanley Park: start out early for a walk, bike, or shuttle ride through the park to see the Vancouver Aquarium Marine Science Centre, enjoy the views from Prospect Point, and stroll the seawall. If you leave the park at English Bay, you can have lunch on Denman or Robson Street, and meander past the trendy shops along Robson between Jervis and Burrard streets. Or, exit the park at Coal Harbour and follow the Seawall Walk to Canada Place, stopping for lunch at a harbor-front restaurant.

A couple of hours at the Granville Island Public Market are also a must—plan to have lunch, and, if you have time, check out the crafts stores.

Walking the downtown core is a great way to get to know the city. Start at Canada Place and head east to Gastown and Chinatown; that's a good half day. Then head north to Yaletown and travel back via Robson Street, by which time you'll have earned yourself a glass of British Columbia wine at one of Vancouver's excellent restaurants.

If you're traveling with children, make sure to check out Science World, Grouse Mountain, and the Capilano Suspension Bridge or Lynn Canyon.

For museums, adults and older children love the displays of Northwest Coast First Nations art at the Museum of Anthropology. The Bill Reid Gallery is pretty impressive, too.

RAINY-DAY ACTIVITIES

While most Vancouverites don't let a little drizzle stop them, heavier rains might inspire you to seek indoor activities. Obvious options include museums—the Museum of Anthropology at UBC is a worthwhile trek. If you're downtown, the Vancouver Art Gallery is good for an hour or two, as is the Vancouver Aquarium and Science World. Less obvious choices are the Bill Reid Gallery, the Dr. Sun Yat-Sen Classical Chinese Garden (it has covered walkways), or Granville Island Market (it's inside; you just have to get there, but then you can spend hours browsing and snacking). Lonsdale Quay is another colorful indoor market on the North Shore and getting there, via the SeaBus, is half the fun.

GETTING HERE AND AROUND

Central Vancouver is extremely walkable and the public transit system—a mix of bus, ferry, and the SkyTrain (a fully automated rail system)—is easy and efficient to use. Transfer tickets enable you to travel from one mode of transport to the other. The hop-on, hop-off Vancouver Trolley buses circle the city in a continuous loop and are a great way to see the sites—especially on a rainy day.

One note about printed Vancouver street addresses: suite numbers often appear *before* the street number, followed by a hyphen.

Contacts Vancouver Trolley ☎ *888/451-5581* 🌐 *www.vancouvertrolley.com.*

BUS AND RAPID-TRANSIT TRAVEL

TransLink, Metro Vancouver's public transport system, includes regular bus service, rapid transit (known as SkyTrain), and a 400 passenger commuter ferry (SeaBus) that connects downtown to the North Shore.

Fares are based on zones: one zone (C$2.50), two zones (C$3.75), or three zones (C$5). Travel within the Vancouver city limits is a one-zone trip; traveling between Vancouver and the North Shore or Vancouver and Richmond is two zones. Day passes (C$9, good across all zones) and discounted FareSaver tickets (sold in books of 10, at outlets such as 7-Eleven, Safeway, and London Drugs) can also be purchased. Tickets for bus travel require exact change at time of embarkation, while SkyTrain and SeaBus tickets are purchased from machines (correct change isn't necessary). Tickets, which are valid for 90 minutes and allow travel in any direction on the buses, SkyTrain, or SeaBus, must be carried with you as proof of payment.

There are three SkyTrain lines: the Expo Line and the Millennium Line share the same stations between downtown and Commercial Drive, so unless you're going east of Commercial Drive, you can use either line. Trains leave about every two to five minutes. The Canada Line travels to Richmond's commercial hub (for great shopping) and to Vancouver International Airport, a ride that's less than 30 minutes. Canada Line trains leave about every 6 to 10 minutes, more frequently during the morning and evening rush hours.

■ **TIP→** **SkyTrain is convenient for transit between downtown, B.C. Place Stadium, Pacific Central Station, Science World, and Vancouver International Airport. SeaBus is the fastest way to travel between downtown and the North Shore (there are bus connections to Capilano Suspension Bridge and Grouse Mountain).**

Contacts SkyTrain ☎ *604/953-3333* 🌐 *www.translink.ca.*
TransLink ☎ *604/953-3333* 🌐 *www.translink.ca.*

FERRY TRAVEL

Twelve-passenger ferry boats bypass busy bridges and are a key reason why you don't need a car in Vancouver. Aquabus Ferries and False Creek Ferries are private commercial enterprises that provide passenger services between key locales on either side of False Creek. Single-ride tickets range from C$2.50 to C$6.50 depending on the route; day passes are C$15. Aquabus Ferries connections include The Village (Science World and the Olympic Village), Plaza of Nations, Granville Island, Stamp's Landing, Spyglass Place, Yaletown, David Lam Park, and the Hornby Street dock. False Creek Ferries provides service between the Aquatic Centre on Beach Avenue, Granville Island, Science World, Stamp's Landing, and Vanier Park. False Creek and Aquabus ferries are not part of the TransLink system.

Contacts Aquabus Ferries ☎ *604/689-5858* 🌐 *www.theaquabus.com.*
False Creek Ferries ☎ *604/684-7781* 🌐 *www.granvilleislandferries.bc.ca.*
SeaBus ☎ *604/953-3333* 🌐 *www.translink.ca.*

TAXI TRAVEL

It can be hard to hail a cab in Vancouver. Unless you're near a hotel or find a taxi rank (designated curbside parking areas), you'll have better luck calling a taxi service. Try Black Top & Checker Cabs or Yellow Cab. Both companies allow you to book online.

Contacts Black Top & Checker Cabs ☎ *604/731-1111* 🌐 *www.btccabs.ca.*
Yellow Cab ☎ *604/681-1111* 🌐 *www.yellowcabonline.com.*

SAVING MONEY

Some attractions, like the Vancouver Art Gallery (Tues. 5–9 pm) and the Museum of Anthropology (Tues. 5–9 pm) have reduced rates or "by donation" evenings.

TOUR OPTIONS

Edible Canada. Culinary tour company Edible Canada provides guided tours of Granville Island, including a food-focused exploration of the Public Market and a combination market/shopping tour. They also run guided culinary walks around Vancouver's Chinatown, with an optional dim sum lunch. ☎ *604/558-0040, 866/272-8777* 🌐 *www.ediblecanada.com.*

DOWNTOWN AND THE WEST END

Vancouver's compact downtown juxtaposes historic architecture with gleaming brand-new buildings. Sightseeing venues include museums, galleries, and top-notch shopping, most notably along Robson Street. The harbor front, with the gleaming convention center, has a fabulous water's edge path all the way to Stanley Park, epitomizing what Vancouver is all about.

At the top of a gentle rise up from the water, the intersection of Georgia and Granville streets is considered the city's epicenter and it's always bustling with activity. Georgia Street runs east–west, past Library Square and Rogers Arena (home of the NHL's Vancouver Canucks), straight through to Stanley Park and the Lions Gate Bridge (which leads to the North Shore and on to Whistler, a two-hour drive away). North–south Granville Street is shedding its previous shabbiness and evolving into a pedestrian-friendly area of neon-lighted sidewalks, funky shops, nightclubs, and street-side cafés. There may be pockets of grunge, but the 2010 Winter Olympics spurred a renaissance that has given the street a new vitality. So, from the corner of Georgia and Granville, you'll find many key attractions within a five-minute walk, including the Vancouver Art Gallery, Robson Square, and Pacific Centre Mall.

Vancouver's landscaping adds to the city's walking appeal. In spring, flowerbeds spill over with tulips and daffodils while sea breezes scatter scented cherry blossoms throughout downtown; in summer office workers take to the beaches, parks, and urban courtyards for picnic lunches and laptop meetings. The West End has the prettiest streetscapes and harks back to the early 1930s when it housed the affluent middle class: trees are plentiful, gardens are lushly planted, and homes and apartment buildings exude the character of that era. Even in winter the West End makes for an idyllic walk. On rainy days, many downtown buildings have overhangs, so that you don't have to get as wet as the weather.

TOP ATTRACTIONS

WASSERMAN'S BEAT

At the northwest corner of Georgia and Hornby streets, an area once filled with nightclubs, there is a yellow street sign that says "Wasserman's Beat." Most passersby have no idea what this means, but we'll fill you in: the sign recalls Jack Wasserman, a high-society reporter of the '50s and '60s whose most famous celebrity scoop was the death of 50-year-old Errol Flynn, who had a heart attack in a West End apartment in 1959 while traveling with his 15-year-old girlfriend.

Fodor's Choice ★ **Bill Reid Gallery.** Vancouver's newest aboriginal art gallery, named after one of B.C.'s pre-eminent artists, Bill Reid (1920–98), is as much a legacy of his works as it is a showcase of current artists. Displays include wood carvings, jewelry, print, and sculpture. The gallery may be small but its expansive offerings often include artist talks and other public programs. Bill Reid is best known for his bronze statue, "The Spirit of Haida Gwaii, The Jade Canoe"—measuring 12 feet by 20 feet; the original is an iconic meeting place at the Vancouver International Airport, and its image is on the back of the Canadian $20 bill. ✉ *639 Hornby St., Downtown* ☎ *604/682–3455* 🌐 *www.billreidgallery.ca* 🎟 *C$10* ⏲ *Open Wed.–Sun. 11–5.*

★ **Canada Place.** Extending four city blocks (about a mile and a half) north into Burrard Inlet, this complex (once a cargo pier) mimics the style and size of a luxury ocean liner, with exterior esplanades. The Teflon-coated fiberglass roof, shaped like five sails (the material was invented by NASA and once used in astronaut space suits), has become a Vancouver skyline landmark. Home to Vancouver's main cruise-ship terminal, Canada Place can accommodate up to four luxury liners at once. Follow the **Canadian Trail** on the west side of the building with displays about the country's provinces and territories; with your smart phone or other device, you can access multimedia content along the trail (there's free Wi Fi). Also check out the **War of 1812 Experience**, commemorating the bicentennial of this conflict. Canada Place is also home to the luxurious **Pan Pacific Hotel** and the East Building of the **Vancouver Convention Centre** (☎ *604/689–8232*); you can follow the outdoor walkways across the plazas to the Convention Centre's even-more-impressive window-lined West Building. The waterfront promenades, which wind all the way to Stanley Park, present spectacular vantage points to view Burrard Inlet and the North Shore Mountains; plaques posted at intervals offer historical information about the city and its waterfront. At the north end of the complex, at the **Port Authority Interpretive Centre** (☎ *604/665–9179* 🎟 *Free* ⏲ *Weekdays 9–4*), you can catch a video about the workings of the port, see some historic images of Vancouver's waterfront, or try your hand at a virtual container-loading game. ✉ *999 Canada Place Way, Downtown* ☎ *604/775–7200* 🌐 *www.canadaplace.ca.*

Christ Church Cathedral. Built between 1889 and 1895, this is oldest church in Vancouver. Constructed in the Gothic style, the Anglican church looks like the parish church of an English village from the outside, though underneath the sandstone-clad exterior it's made of Douglas fir from what is now south Vancouver. The 32 stained-glass windows depict Old and New Testament scenes, often set against Vancouver landmarks (St. Nicholas presiding over the Lions Gate Bridge, for example). The building's excellent acoustics enhance the choral evensong and carols frequently sung here. Gregorian chants are performed every Sunday evening at 9:30 pm. ✉ *690 Burrard St., Downtown* ☎ *604/682–3848* 🌐 *www.cathedral.vancouver.bc.ca* ⏲ *Open weekdays 10–4. Services Sun. at 8 am, 10:30 am; weekdays at 12:10 pm.*

★ **Marine Building.** Inspired by New York's Chrysler Building, the terracotta bas-reliefs on this 21-story, 1930s art-deco structure depict the history of transportation—airships, steamships, locomotives, and submarines—as well as Mayan and Egyptian motifs and images of marine life. Step inside for a look at the beautifully restored interior, then walk to the corner of Hastings and Hornby streets for the best view of the building. It serves as the headquarters of the *Daily Planet* in the TV show *Smallville.* ✉ *355 Burrard St., Downtown.*

QUICK BITES

Bella Gelateria. A tiny shop tucked into a corner of the Fairmont Pacific Rim Hotel building, Bella Gelateria makes its *gelato* the old-fashioned Italian way, whipping up a changing selection of 24 flavors daily from fresh natural ingredients. These treats don't come cheap, but they sure are delectable. ✉ *1001 W. Cordova St., Downtown* ☎ *604/569–1010* 🌐 *www.bellagelateria.com.*

Olympic Cauldron. A four-pronged sculpture towering more than 30 feet, this structure can be found adjacent to the Vancouver Convention Centre's West Building. In 2010 when Vancouver hosted the Winter Olympic and Paralympic Games, it burned with the Olympic flame. It's relit occasionally, for Canada Day and other special events. The Cauldron overlooks the Burrard Inlet on Jack Poole Plaza, which is named for the Canadian businessman who led the bid to bring the Olympics to Vancouver. Sadly, Poole died of cancer just one day after the flame for the Olympic torch relay was lit in Olympia, Greece, at the start of its journey to Vancouver. ✉ *Foot of Thurlow St., at Canada Pl., Downtown.*

Robson Street. Robson, Vancouver's busiest shopping street, is lined with see-and-be-seen sidewalk cafés, chain stores, and high-end boutiques. The street, which links downtown to the West End, is particularly lively between Jervis and Burrard streets and stays that way into the evening with buskers and entertainers. 🌐 *www.robsonstreet.ca.*

Vancouver Art Gallery. Painter Emily Carr's haunting evocations of the British Columbian hinterland are among the attractions at western Canada's largest art gallery. Carr (1871–1945), a grocer's daughter from Victoria, fell in love with the wilderness around her and shocked middle-class Victorian society by running off to paint it. Her work accentuates the mysticism and the danger of B.C.'s wilderness, and records the diminishing presence of native cultures during that era (there's something of a renaissance now). The gallery, which also hosts touring historical and contemporary exhibitions, is housed in a 1911 courthouse that Canadian architect Arthur Erickson redesigned in the

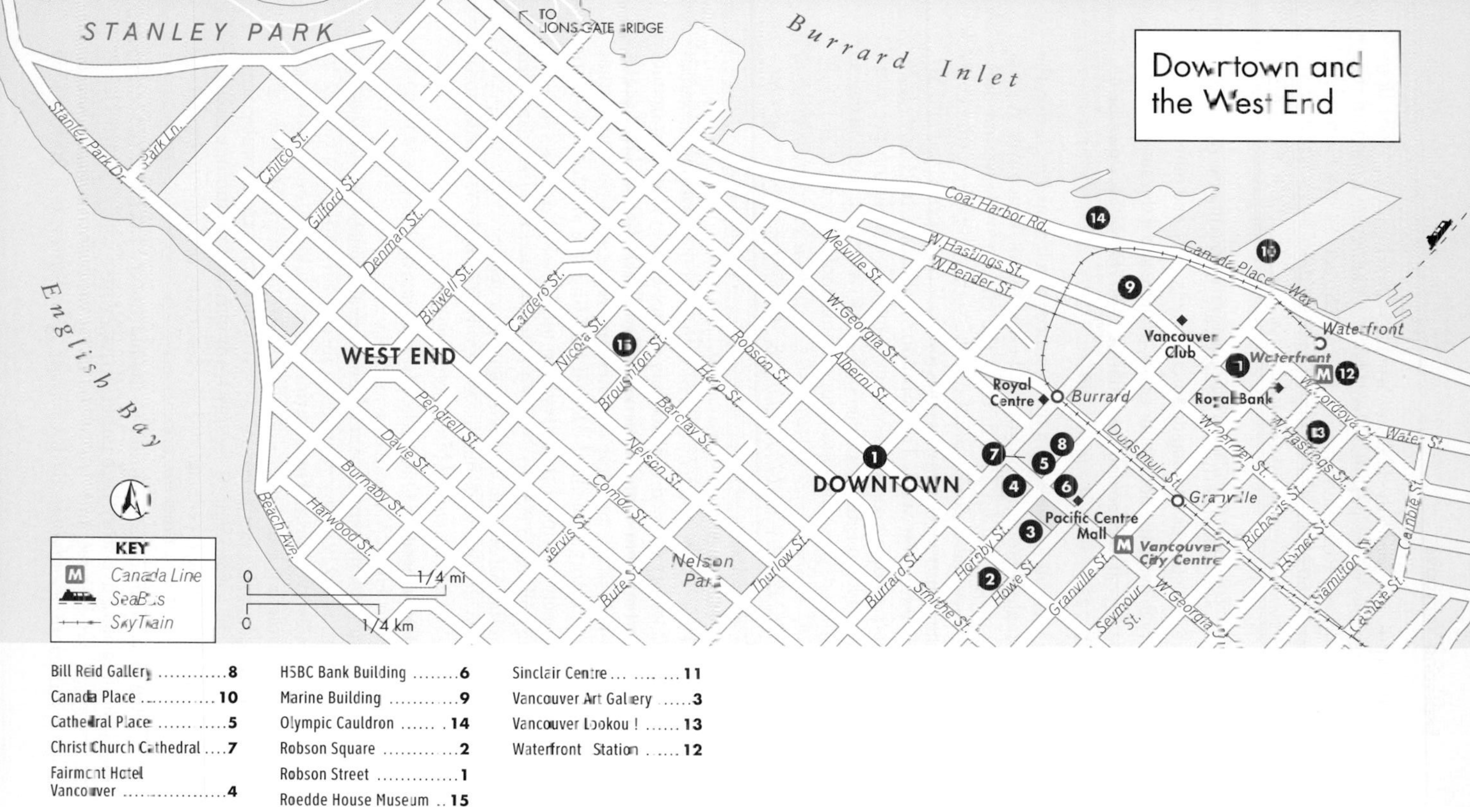

Bill Reid Gallery 8	HSBC Bank Building 6	Sinclair Centre 11
Canada Place 10	Marine Building 9	Vancouver Art Gallery 3
Cathedral Place 5	Olympic Cauldron 14	Vancouver Lookout 13
Christ Church Cathedral 7	Robson Square 2	Waterfront Station 12
Fairmont Hotel Vancouver 4	Robson Street 1	
	Roedde House Museum ..15	

early 1980s as part of the Robson Square redevelopment. Stone lions guard the steps to the parklike Georgia Street side; the main entrance is accessed from Robson Square or Hornby Street. ✉ *750 Hornby St., Downtown* ☎ *604/662–4719* 🌐 *www.vanartgallery.bc.ca* *C$19.50; higher for some exhibits; by donation Tues. 5–9* ⏲ *Open Wed.–Mon. 10–5:30, Tues. 10–9.*

QUICK BITES

Gallery Café. The culinary artists at Gallery Café (inside the Vancouver Art Gallery) create delicious homemade soups, salads, pies, and other sinful desserts. Try to avoid the noon-hour crush, though, and if the sun is shining, opt for a patio seat overlooking the square. ✉ ***750 Hornby St., Downtown*** ☎ ***604/688–2233*** 🌐 ***www.thegallerycafe.ca.***

Vancouver Lookout! Resembling a flying saucer stuck atop a high-rise, the 553-foot-high lookout has one of the best views of Vancouver. A glass elevator whizzes you up 50 stories to the circular observation deck, where knowledgeable guides point out the sights and give a tour every hour on the hour. On a clear day you can see Vancouver Island and Mt. Baker in Washington State. The top-floor restaurant (*604/669–2220, www.topofvancouver.com*) makes one complete revolution per hour; the elevator ride up is free for diners. **■TIP→ Tickets are good all day, so you can visit in daytime and return for another look after dark.** ✉ *555 W. Hastings St., Downtown* ☎ *604/689–0421* 🌐 *www.vancouverlookout.com* *C$15* ⏲ *May–mid-Oct., daily 8:30 am–10:30 pm; mid-Oct.–Apr., daily 9–9.*

WORTH NOTING

Cathedral Place. One of Vancouver's most handsome postmodern buildings, the 23-story Cathedral Place has a faux-copper roof that mimics that of the Fairmont Hotel Vancouver nearby. The three large sculptures of nurses at the building's corners are replicas of the statues that adorned the Georgia Medical–Dental Building, the art-deco structure that previously occupied this site. Step into the lobby to see another interesting sculpture: Robert Studer's *Navigational Device*, suspended high up on the north wall. The small garden courtyard is an unexpected respite from downtown's bustle. ✉ *925 W. Georgia St., Downtown* ☎ *604/669–3312* 🌐 *www.925westgeorgia.com.*

Fairmont Hotel Vancouver. One of the last railway-built hotels in Canada, the Fairmont Hotel Vancouver was designed in the château style, its architectural details reminiscent of a medieval French castle. Construction began in 1929 and wrapped up just in time for King George VI of England's 1939 visit. The exterior of the building, one of the most recognizable in Vancouver's skyline, has carvings of malevolent-looking gargoyles at the corners, native chiefs on the Hornby Street side, and an assortment of figures from classical mythology decorating the building's facade. ✉ *900 W. Georgia St., Downtown* ☎ *604/684–3131* 🌐 *www.fairmont.com.*

HSBC Bank Building. Kitty-corner to the Fairmont Hotel Vancouver, this building has a five-story-high public atrium with a café, regularly changing art exhibitions, and one of the city's more intriguing public-art installations: *Pendulum*, by B.C. artist Alan Storey, is a 90-foot-long

Robson Square, in front of the Vancouver Art Gallery, is a downtown focal point; there's a skating rink here in winter.

hollow aluminum sculpture that arcs hypnotically overhead. ✉ *885 W. Georgia St., Downtown* ☎ *604/525–4722.*

Robson Square. Architect Arthur Erickson designed this refurbished plaza to be *the* gathering place of downtown Vancouver, although its below-street-level access makes it a bit of a secret. Landscaped walkways connect the Vancouver Art Gallery, government offices, and law courts at street level while the lower level houses a University of British Columbia satellite campus and bookstore. In winter, there's also a covered, outdoor, public ice-skating rink; in summer the rink becomes a dance floor for weekly (free) salsa sessions. Political protests and impromptu demonstrations take place on the grandiose gallery stairs facing Georgia Street, a tradition that dates from the days when the building was a courthouse. ✉ *Bordered by Howe, Hornby, Robson, and Smithe Sts., Downtown.*

OFF THE BEATEN PATH

Roedde House Museum. Two blocks south of Robson Street is the Roedde (pronounced *roh*-dee) House Museum, an 1893 house in the Queen Anne Revival style, set among Victorian-style gardens. Tours of the restored, antiques-furnished interior take about an hour. On Sunday, tours are followed by tea and cookies. The gardens (free) can be visited anytime. ✉ *1415 Barclay St., between Broughton and Nicola Sts., West End* ☎ *604/684–7040* 🌐 *www.roeddehouse.org* 🎫 *C$5; Sun. C$6, including tea* ⏲ *Open Tues.–Sun. 1–4.*

Sinclair Centre. Vancouver architect Richard Henriquez knitted four buildings together into Sinclair Centre, an office–retail complex that takes up an entire city block between Cordova and Hastings, and Howe and Granville streets. Inside are high-end designer-clothing shops, federal government offices, and a number of fast-food outlets. The two Hastings Street buildings—the 1910 **Post Office,** which has an elegant clock tower, and the 1911 **Winch Building**—are linked with the 1937 **Post Office Extension** and the 1913 **Customs Examining Warehouse** to the north. As part of a meticulous restoration in the mid-1980s, the Post Office facade was moved to the Granville Street side of the complex. The original clockwork from the old clock tower is on display inside, on the upper level of the arcade. ✉ *757 W. Hastings St., Downtown* ☎ *604/488–0672* 🌐 *www.sinclaircentre.com.*

Waterfront Station. This former Canadian Pacific Railway passenger terminal was built between 1912 and 1914 as the western terminus for Canada's transcontinental railway. After Canada's two major railways shifted their focus away from passenger service, the station became obsolete, but a 1978 renovation turned it into an office–retail complex and depot for SkyTrain, SeaBus, and West Coast Express (suburban commuter rail) passengers. In the main concourse, murals up near the ceiling depict the scenery travelers once saw on journeys across Canada. This is where you catch the SeaBus for the 13-minute trip across the harbor to the waterfront public market at Lonsdale Quay in North Vancouver. ✉ *601 W. Cordova St., Downtown* ☎ *604/953–3333 SeaBus and SkyTrain, 604/488–8906, 800/570–7245 West Coast Express.*

2

GASTOWN AND CHINATOWN

Gastown and Chinatown are favorite destinations for visitors and residents alike. Gastown is fast becoming the new Yaletown as überhip stores, ad agencies, and restaurants take over refurbished brick warehouses. Chinatown's array of produce stalls and curious alleyways make it look as if they're resisting gentrification, but inside many of the historic buildings are getting a new lease on life.

Gastown is best known for its cobblestone streets, Victorian era–style streetlamps and an overabundance of souvenir shops from tacky to tasteful. Nicknamed for the garrulous ("Gassy") Jack Deighton who opened his saloon where his statue now stands on Maple Tree Square, this is where Vancouver originated. A fire burned the fledgling community to the ground in 1886, but it was quickly resurrected. By the time the first transcontinental train arrived less than a year later, in May 1887, Vancouver had become an important transfer point for trade with the Far East and a stopping point for those en route to the gold rushes. The waterfront was crowded with hotels, warehouses, brothels, and dozens of saloons—place names such as Gaoler's Mews and Blood Alley can only hint to those early rough-and-tumble days. As commerce shifted toward Hastings Street and the Depression took its toll, though, Gastown fell into general neglect: hotels were converted into low-rent rooming houses and "the Downtown Eastside," which includes Chinatown, gradually earned the reputation as having the poorest demographic in the country.

In 1971, the Gastown area was declared a historic district and it became the focus of a huge revitalization effort. Warehouses that once lined the shorefront were remodeled to house boutiques, cafés, loft apartments, and shops. Gastown became a visitor destination once again and today also attracts hip professional residents, and gentrification is extending into Chinatown.

As for Chinatown, it still has a completely distinct vibe, and although a large percentage of Vancouver's Chinese community has shifted to suburban Richmond, there's still a wonderful buzz of authenticity in the open-front markets, bakeries, and herbalist and import shops. Street signs are in Chinese lettering, streetlights look like lanterns topped with decorative dragons, and much of the architecture is patterned on that of Guangzhou (Canton).

NIGHT MARKET

If you're in the area in summer on a Friday, Saturday, or Sunday, check out Chinatown's bustling Night Market for food and tchotchkes: Keefer Street, between Main and Columbia, is closed to traffic from 6 to 11 pm.

GETTING HERE AND AROUND

Getting to Gastown is easy: head for the waterfront. It's just east of Waterfront Station. Allow about an hour to explore Gastown—that's without shopping too much. Then, if you have time, continue on to Chinatown, where you could spend an hour just wandering around, checking out the architecture and exotic wares; add at least an hour if you also want to visit the Dr. Sun Yat-Sen Classical Chinese Garden.

Be aware that you might come across one or two seedy corners: it's all pretty safe by day, but you might prefer to cab it at night. The No. 19 Metrotown and No. 22 Knight buses travel east to Chinatown from stops along West Pender Street; the No. 3 Main and No. 8 Fraser serve Gastown and Chinatown from Cordova and Seymour near Waterfront Station. The Stadium SkyTrain station is a five-minute walk from Chinatown. From the station head down the Keefer Street steps, and turn left at Abbott Street. This will take you to Pender Street and the Millennium Gate.

Another option is to follow the Silk Road Walking Tour, a self-guided route marked with colorful banners. It starts at the Vancouver Public Library downtown and leads north and east to the main attractions in Chinatown, before the banners lead you back to the library.

TOP ATTRACTIONS

★ **Dr. Sun Yat-Sen Chinese Garden.** The first authentic Ming Dynasty–style garden outside China, this small garden was built in 1986 by 52 Chinese artisans from Suzhou. It incorporates design elements and traditional materials from several of Suzhou's centuries-old private gardens. No power tools, screws, or nails were used in the construction. Guided tours (45 minutes long), included in the ticket price, are conducted on the hour between mid-June and the end of August (call ahead or check the website for off-season tour times); tours are valuable for understanding the philosophy and symbolism that are central to the garden's design. A concert series, including classical, Asian, world, jazz, and sacred music, plays on Friday evenings in July, August, and early September. The free public park next door is also designed as a traditional Chinese garden. ■ **TIP→ Covered walkways make this a good rainy-day choice.** ✉ *578 Carrall St., Chinatown* ☎ *604/662–3207* 🌐 *www.vancouverchinesegarden.com* 🎫 *C$12* ⏲ *Open May–mid-June and Sept., daily 10–6; mid-June–Aug., daily 9:30–7; Oct., daily 10–4:30; Nov.–Apr., Tues.–Sun. 10–4:30.*

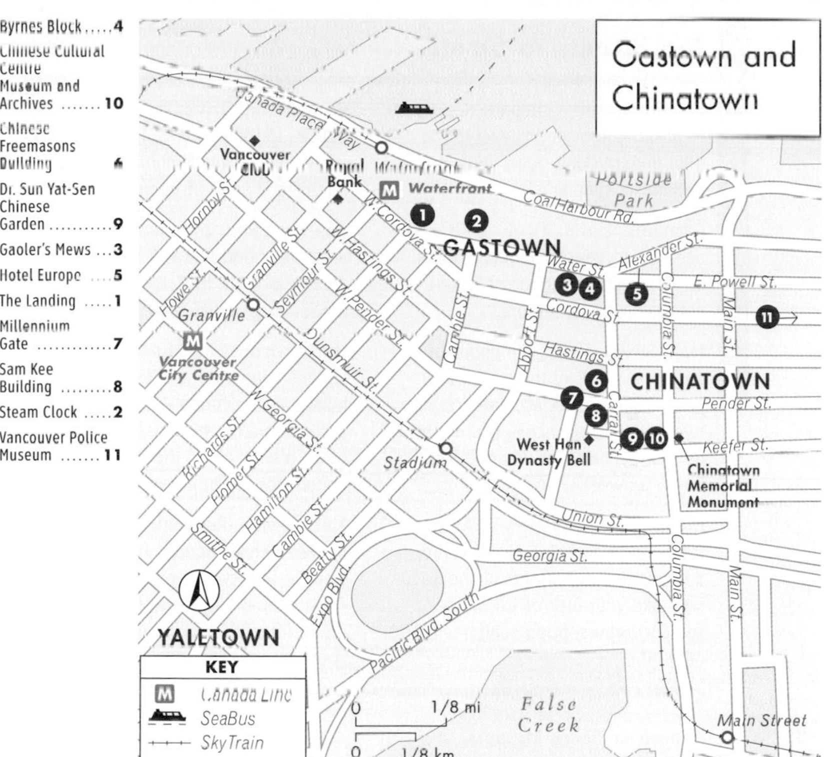

Gaoler's Mews. Once the site of the city's first civic buildings—the constable's cabin and customs house, and a two-cell log jail—this atmospheric brick-paved courtyard is home to cafés, offices, and the contemporary restaurant Boneta. ✉ *Behind, 12 Water St., Gastown.*

Hotel Europe. Once billed as the best hotel in the city, this 1908 flatiron building is one of the world's finest examples of triangular architecture. Now used for government-subsidized housing and not open to the public, the hotel still has its original Italian tile work and lead-glass windows. The glass tiles in the sidewalk on Alexander Street were the former "skylight" for an underground saloon. ✉ *43 Powell St., Gastown.*

Steam Clock. An underground steam system, which also heats many local buildings, supplies the world's first steam clock—possibly Vancouver's most-photographed attraction. On the quarter hour a steam whistle rings out the Westminster chimes, and on the hour a huge cloud of steam spews from the apparatus. The ingenious design, based on an 1875 mechanism, was built in 1977 by Ray Saunders of Landmark Clocks (at 123 Cambie Street) to commemorate the community effort that saved Gastown from demolition. ✉ *Water St., at Cambie St., Gastown.*

CLOSE UP

Top Streets to Stroll

Robson Street: A shopaholic's dream come true, Robson has everything from finger-licking-good fudge to fashionista shopping.

Granville Island: It's always a voyage of discovery for fabulous local art, foodstuffs, boutique shops, street entertainment, and more.

Main Street: This is the undisputed antiques capital of the city, where you'll also find folk art, fine art, and retro 1950s appliances—you might not be in the market for any of it, but it's fun to browse.

Chinatown: The variety of Asian treats and delicacies along Keefer and East Pender streets is spectacular—take your pick of exotic teas, sea cucumbers, dried seahorses, and nifty gifts.

Commercial Drive: From the coffeehouses to the cantinas, The Drive has a healthy serving of cultural cool with an eclectic array of people and shops.

The West End: This pleasing, tree-lined neighborhood is a refreshing change of pace from the urban commotion steps away.

Harbor-front Shoreline: With the water's edge on one side and glassy, million-dollar condo developments and commercial high-rises on the other, a walk along the harbor front epitomizes the future of this city.

Marina-side: Residents of Yaletown's intense-density condos flock to this walking and cycling path around False Creek. Combine your walk with a ride on an Aquabus ferry if time is short or your feet get weary.

OFF THE BEATEN PATH

Vancouver Police Museum. It's not in the best neighborhood, and its morgue and autopsy areas may be off-putting to some, but this museum provides an absorbing glimpse into the history of the Vancouver police and the city's criminal underside. Firearms and counterfeit money are on exhibit, as are clues from some of the region's unsolved crimes: one of the more compelling mysteries, "Babes in the Woods," is about two children whose remains were found in Stanley Park in the 1950s. ✉ *240 E. Cordova St., Gastown/Chinatown* ☎ *604/665–3346* 🌐 *www.vancouverpolicemuseum.ca* 🎫 *C$10* ⏲ *Tues.–Sat. 9–5.*

WORTH NOTING

Byrnes Block. George Byrnes constructed Vancouver's oldest brick building on the site of Gassy Jack Deighton's second saloon after the 1886 Great Fire, which wiped out most of the fledgling settlement of Vancouver. It now houses shops and offices, but for a while this two-story building was Vancouver's top luxury hotel, the Alhambra Hotel, charging a dollar a night. The site of Deighton's original saloon, east of the Byrnes Block where his statue now stands, is the zero point from which all Vancouver street addresses start. ✉ *2 Water St., Gastown.*

Chinese Cultural Centre Museum and Archives. The Chinese have a rich, grueling, and enduring history in British Columbia, and it's well represented in this Ming Dynasty–style facility. The art gallery upstairs hosts traveling exhibits by Chinese and Canadian artists, and an on-site military museum recalls the role of Chinese Canadians in the last two world wars. Across the street is the Chinatown Memorial Monument, commemorating the Chinese-Canadian community's contribution to the city, province, and country. The monument, shaped in the Chinese character "zhong," symbolizing moderation and harmony, is flanked by bronze statues of a railroad worker and a World War II soldier. ✉ *555 Columbia St., Chinatown* ☎ *604/658–8880* 🌐 *www.cccvan.com* 🎫 *C$5.50, Tues. by donation* 🕓 *Open Tues.–Sun. 11–5.*

Chinese Freemasons Building. Two completely different facades distinguish this structure on the northwest corner of Pender and Carrall streets. The side facing Pender represents a fine example of Cantonese recessed balconies. The Carrall Street side displays the standard Victorian style common throughout the British Empire. Dr. Sun Yat-Sen hid in this building for months from agents of the Manchu Dynasty while he raised funds for its overthrow, which he accomplished in 1911. ✉ *3 W. Pender St., Chinatown.*

The Landing. Built in 1905 with gold-rush money, this elegantly renovated brick warehouse now houses offices, shops, and Steamworks, a popular brewpub *(⇨ see the review in the Nightlife chapter)*. From the oversized bay window at the rear of the lobby you can appreciate where the shoreline was 100 years ago, as well as enjoy terrific views of Burrard Inlet and the North Shore Mountains. ✉ *375 Water St., Gastown.*

Millennium Gate. This four pillar, three-story high, brightly painted arch spanning Pender Street was erected in 2002 to mark the millennium and commemorate the Chinese community's role in Vancouver's history. The gate incorporates both Eastern and Western symbols, and both traditional and modern Chinese themes. Just east of the Millennium Gate, a right turn will take you into Shanghai Alley. Also known as Chinatown Heritage Alley, this was the site of the first Chinese settlement in the Vancouver area. By 1890 Shanghai Alley and neighboring Canton Alley were home to about 1,000 Chinese residents. At the end of the alley is a replica of the West Han Dynasty Bell, a gift to Vancouver from the city of Guangzhou, China. Surrounding the bell is a series of panels relaying some of the area's early history. ✉ *Pender St., Chinatown.*

Sam Kee Building. *Ripley's Believe It or Not!* recognizes this 6-foot-wide structure as the narrowest office building in the world. In 1913, after the city confiscated most of the then-owner's land to widen Pender Street, he built a store on what was left, in protest. Customers had to be served through the windows. These days the building houses an insurance agency, whose employees make do within the 4-foot-10-inch-wide interior. The glass panes in the sidewalk on Pender Street once provided light for Chinatown's public baths, which, in the early 20th century, were in the basement here. The presence of this and other underground sites has fueled rumors that Chinatown and Gastown were connected by tunnels, enabling residents of the latter to anonymously enjoy the vices of the former. No such tunnels have been found, however. ✉ *8 W. Pender St., Chinatown.*

DID YOU KNOW?

Gastown's steam clock is one of the Vancouver's most famous landmarks. Rather than bells, a steam whistle sounds on the quarter hour.

321
BORGO ANTICO
& GEMS

YALETOWN AND FALSE CREEK

Back around 1985–86 the B.C. provincial government cleaned up a derelict industrial site on the north shore of False Creek, built a world's fair, and invited everyone; 20 million people showed up for Expo '86. Now, the site of the fair, Yaletown, has become one of the largest and most densely populated urban-redevelopment projects in North America. It's one of the city's most fashionable neighborhoods, and the Victorian-brick loading docks have become terraces for cappuccino bars and trendy restaurants.

First settled by railroad workers who followed the newly laid tracks from the town of Yale in the Fraser Canyon, Yaletown in the 1880s and '90s was probably the most lawless place in Canada: it was so far into the woods that the Royal Canadian Mounted Police complained they couldn't patrol it. The area—which also has brewpubs, day spas, retail and wholesale fashion outlets, and shops selling upscale home decor—makes the most of its waterfront location, with a seaside walk and cycle path that completely encircles False Creek.

GETTING HERE AND AROUND

Parking is tight in Yaletown; your best bet is the lot at Library Square nearby. It's easy to walk here from downtown, though, and there's a Yaletown stop on the Canada Line. You can also set sail for Yaletown aboard the False Creek and Aquabus ferries (☎ *604/689–5858*), which run every 15 minutes from 7 am to 10 pm between Granville Island, Science World, Yaletown, and the south shore of False Creek.

TOP ATTRACTIONS

Science World. In a gigantic shiny dome built over the Omnimax theater, this hands-on science center encourages children to participate in interactive exhibits and demonstrations about the natural world,

B.C. Sports Hall of Fame and Museum 3
Contemporary Art Gallery 2
Library Square 1
Science World ...4

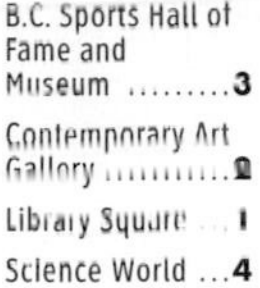

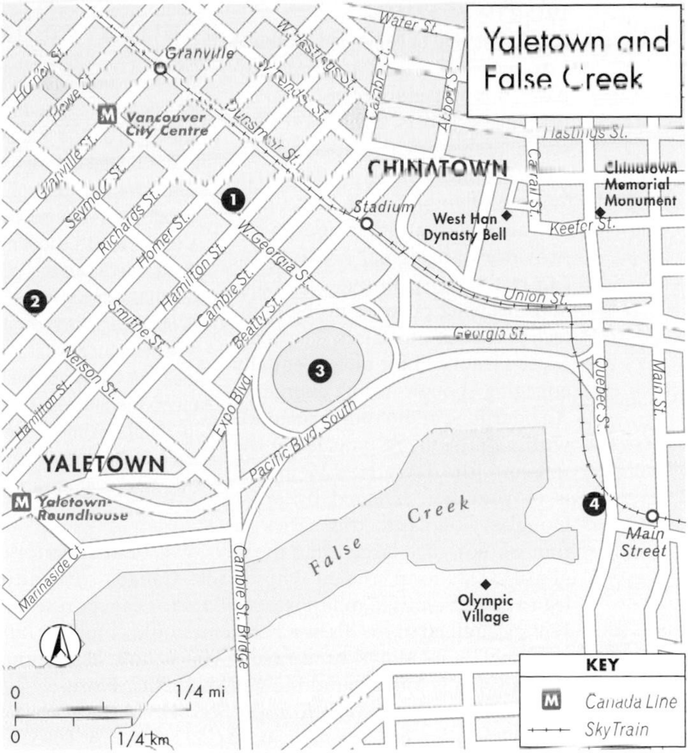

the human body, and other science topics. Exhibits change throughout the year, so there's always something new to see. Adjacent to the museum, the Ken Spencer Science Park is an outdoor exhibit area focusing on environmental issues. It's an easy walk (and mini-ferry ride) from Yaletown; the Main Street/Science World SkyTrain station is on its doorstep, and there's plenty of parking. ✉ *1455 Quebec St., False Creek* ☎ *604/443–7440* 🌐 *www.scienceworld.bc.ca* *C$23.50 Science World, C$29 Science World and Omnimax theater* ⏲ *July–Labor Day, daily 10–6; Sept.–June, weekdays 10–5, weekends 10–6.*

QUICK BITES

Urban Fare. **Open daily 6 am–10 pm, this large colorful grocery store is a popular destination for gastronomes. Here you'll find food products from across B.C. and around the world. You can sample the wares at the café or purchase a take-out snack to eat at the water's edge overlooking an idyllic marina. Additional Urban Fare outlets are at Coal Harbour (Bute Street) and on Alberni Street next to the posh Shangri-La Hotel.** ✉ ***177 Davie St., Yaletown*** ☎ ***604/975–7550*** 🌐 ***www.urbanfare.com.***

WORTH NOTING

B.C. Sports Hall of Fame and Museum. Inside the B.C. Place Stadium complex, this museum celebrates the province's sports achievers in a series of historical displays. One gallery commemorates the 2010 Winter Olympics that were held in Vancouver; another honors the province's aboriginal artists. You can test your sprinting, climbing, and throwing prowess in the high-tech participation gallery. The Scavenger History Hunt quiz is equally engaging though not as energetic. An hour-long audio tour is included with admission. As you leave the museum, the Terry Fox Memorial is to your left. Created by artist Douglas Coupland, this series of four statues, each larger than the next, was built in honor of Terry Fox (1958–81), a local student whose cross-Canada run—after he lost his leg to cancer—raised millions of dollars for cancer research. Although Fox succumbed to the disease before he could complete his "Marathon of Hope," a memorial fund-raising run is now held annually in cities across Canada and around the world. ✉ *B.C. Place, 777 Pacific Blvd. S, Gate A, at Beatty and Robson Sts., Downtown* ☎ *604/647–7414* 🌐 *www.bcsportshalloffame.com* 🎟 *C$15* 🕐 *Daily 10–5.*

HOLLYWOOD NORTH

You may have already heard that it's cheaper to film movies and television shows in Canada than in the United States. As a result, Vancouver has been the stand-in for all sorts of American cities. For a list of what's shooting around town, check out the BC Film Commission website (🌐 *www.bcfilmcommission.com*). You'll get a heads-up on what celebrities to look out for as you wander about town. The movie *2012* (released in 2009) was the biggest mega-million-dollar movie ever shot in the Vancouver environs.

Contemporary Art Gallery. On the lobby level of a modern apartment tower, this small nonprofit public gallery has regularly changing exhibits of contemporary local and international visual art. Events include artists' talks, lectures, and tours. ✉ *555 Nelson St., Downtown* ☎ *604/681–2700* 🌐 *www.contemporaryartgallery.ca* 🎟 *By donation* 🕐 *Tues.–Sun. noon–6.*

Library Square. The spiraling library building, open plazas, and lofty atrium of Library Square, completed in the mid-1990s, were built to evoke images of the Colosseum in Rome. A high-tech public library is the core of the structure; the outer edge of the spiral houses cafés and fast-food outlets. ✉ *350 W. Georgia St., Downtown* ☎ *604/331–3603* 🌐 *www.vpl.ca* 🕐 *Open Mon.–Thurs. 10–9, Fri. and Sat. 10–6, Sun. 12–5.*

CLOSE UP

2

Vancouver's Olympic Legacy

The 2010 Winter Olympic Games, hosted in Vancouver and the nearby town of Whistler, may be long over, but you can still catch some of that Olympic spirit. At several locations around the region, there is evidence of the Games.

Olympic Cauldron. The Olympic flame burned in this landmark on the downtown waterfront, adjacent to the Vancouver Convention Centre. These days, the cauldron is lit only on special occasions, but you can still wander around this impressive towering sculpture. ✉ *Foot of Thurlow St.*

Olympic Village. During the Games, Olympic athletes stayed in a collection of new residential buildings on the southeast shore of False Creek, not far from Science World. They're now a mix of condominiums and rental apartments. With the exception of the Creekside Community Centre, which houses a public fitness facility, the buildings themselves are not open to the public, but the waterfront setting, with views of the city, is spectacular.

Hillcrest Centre. Home to the 2010 Olympic curling events, this complex near Queen Elizabeth Park is one of the city's newest community centers, with indoor and outdoor pools, a skating rink, a fitness center, and a branch of the public library. ✉ *4575 Clancy Loranger Way (Ontario St., at 30th Ave.)* ☎ *604/257–8680* 🌐 *www.hillcrestcentre.ca.*

Richmond Olympic Oval. Olympic speed skaters circled the tracks at this riverfront complex in suburban Richmond. It's now a massive 23,000-square-foot fitness facility, offering exercise equipment; two Olympic-size skating rinks; basketball, volleyball, and badminton courts; running tracks; indoor rowing; and more. You can purchase a one-day pass to use the facility for C$16.50. ✉ *6111 River Rd., Richmond* ☎ *778/296–1400* 🌐 *www.richmondoval.ca.*

STANLEY PARK

Fodor's Choice ★

A 1,000-acre wilderness park, only blocks from the downtown section of a major city, is a rare treasure. Vancouverites use it, protect it, and love it with such zeal that when it was proposed that the 120-year-old Hollow Tree be axed due to safety concerns, citizens rallied, raised funds, and literally engineered its salvation.

The fact that Stanley Park is so close to the city is actually all thanks to the Americans—sort of! In the 1860s, because of a threat of American invasion, this oceanfront peninsula was designated a military reserve, though it was never needed. When the City of Vancouver was incorporated in 1886, the council's first act was to request the land be set aside as a park. Permission was granted two years later and the grounds were named Stanley Park after Lord Stanley, then governor general of Canada. The only military vestige is Deadman's Island, a former burial ground for local Salish First Nations people and early settlers; the small naval installation here, HMCS *Discovery,* is not open to the public.

Vancouverites make use of it fervently to cycle, walk, jog, Rollerblade, play cricket and tennis, and enjoy outdoor art shows and theater performances alongside attractions such as the renowned aquarium and Klahowya Village, a summer aboriginal cultural village.

When a storm swept across the park's shores in December 2006, it destroyed close to 10,000 trees as well as parts of the perimeter seawall. Locals contributed thousands of dollars to the clean-up and replanting effort in addition to the monies set aside by local authorities. The storm's silver lining was that it cleared some dead-wood areas, making room for the reintroduction of many of the park's original species of trees. It also gave rise to an unusual ecological arts program in which ephemeral sculptures have been placed in various outdoor locations. Made of natural and organic materials, the elements are constantly changing the look of each piece which, over the course of its 24-month "display period," will decay and return to the earth.

2

GETTING HERE AND AROUND

If you're driving to Stanley Park, head northwest on Georgia Street from downtown. Parking is available at or near all the major attractions; one ticket (C$10 April–September, C$5 October–March) allows you to park all day and to move between lots. Tickets are purchased from automated dispensers in lots and should be displayed on your dashboard.

If you're taking public transit, catch Bus 19 "Stanley Park" along West Pender Street downtown; it runs to the park bus loop, which is within walking distance of the aquarium and Klahowya Village. You can also catch North Vancouver Bus 240 or 246 from anywhere on West Georgia Street to the park entrance at Georgia and Chilco streets, or a Robson Bus 5 to Robson and Denman streets, where there are a number of bicycle-rental outlets.

There is no public transit around or within the park; you can bike, walk, drive, or take the privately run park shuttle to reach the main attractions.

Stanley Park Shuttle. The Vancouver Trolley Company runs the hop-on/hop-off Stanley Park Shuttle, a narrated tour within the park that provides frequent (every 15 minutes) transportation to 15 major park sights. The shuttle operates from June to early September between 11 am and 6:30 pm. Pick it up on Pipeline Road, near the Georgia Street park entrance. ☎ *604/801–5515* 🌐 *www.vancouvertrolley.com* 🎫 *C$10.*

TOURS

Lost Lagoon Nature House. For information about guided nature walks in the park, contact the Lost Lagoon Nature House on the south shore of Lost Lagoon, at the foot of Alberni Street. In July and August, the Nature House is open 10 am to 5 pm Tuesday through Sunday; from September through June, it's open Saturday and Sunday only, 10 am to 4 pm. ☎ *604/257–8544* 🌐 *www.stanleyparkecology.ca.*

TOP ATTRACTIONS

Klahowya Village. Celebrating the cultures of the First Nations whose historical territory encompasses parts of Stanley Park, this aboriginal village is staffed by First Nations artisans and performers who demonstrate carving, weaving, and other crafts, perform traditional dances, and hold storytelling sessions to narrate aboriginal legends. You can take a ride on the "Spirit Catcher" train, the child-size steam train that chugs through the woods, and sample aboriginal foods in the Raven's Landing café. The village is a short walk from the Stanley Park bus loop, the terminus for Bus 19 from downtown; the park shuttle stops nearby as well. ✉ *Off Pipeline Rd., Stanley Park* ☎ *604/921–1070* 🌐 *www.aboriginalbc.com/Klahowya-Village* 🎫 *Village free, Spirit Catcher train C$10* ⏲ *Mid-June–early Sept., daily 10–6.*

Prospect Point. At 211 feet, Prospect Point is the highest point in the park and provides striking views of the Lions Gate Bridge (watch for cruise ships passing below), the North Shore, and Burrard Inlet. There's also a year-round souvenir shop, a snack bar with terrific ice cream, and a restaurant. From the seawall, you can see where cormorants build their seaweed nests along the cliff ledges.

DID YOU KNOW?

The view from Stanley Park out over the marina and Coal Harbour shows just how close this fabulous 1,000-plus-acre park is to downtown.

Klahowya Village 7
Lumberman's Arch 4
Miniature Railway 6
Nine O'Clock Gun 3
Prospect Point 8
Seawall 1
Second Beach 10
Siwash Rock 9
Totem poles 2
Vancouver Aquarium Marine Science Centre 5

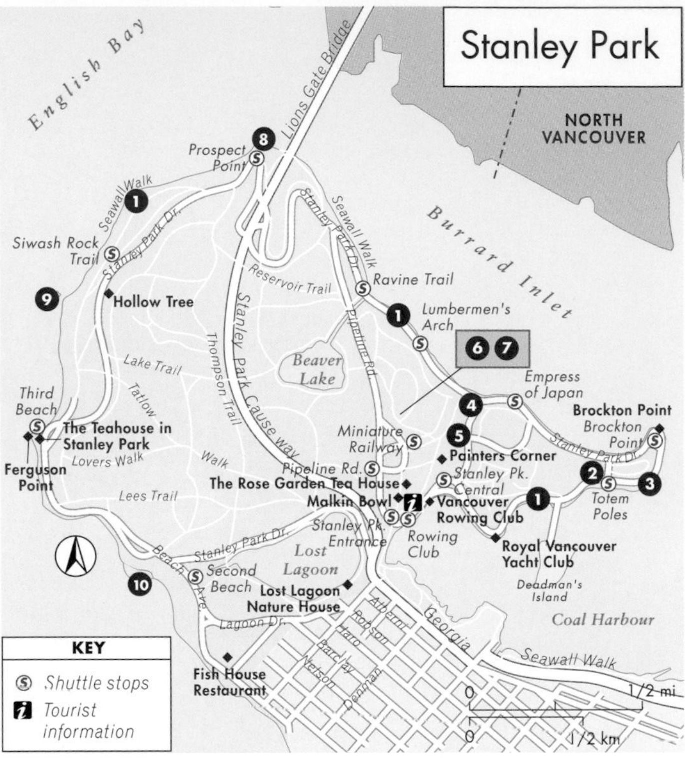

Fodor's Choice ★ **Seawall.** The seawall path, a 9-km (5½-mile) paved shoreline route popular with walkers, cyclists, and in-line skaters, is one of several car-free zones within the park. If you have the time (about a half day) and the energy, strolling the entire seawall is an exhilarating experience. It extends an additional mile east past the marinas, cafés, and waterfront condominiums of Coal Harbour to Canada Place downtown, so you could start your walk or ride from there. From the south side of the park, the seawall continues for another 28 km (17 mile) along Vancouver's waterfront, to the University of British Columbia, allowing for a pleasant, if ambitious, day's bike ride. Along the seawall, cyclists must wear helmets and stay on their side of the path. Within Stanley Park, cyclists must ride in a counterclockwise direction.

The seawall can get crowded on summer weekends, but inside the park is a 28-km (17-mile) network of peaceful walking and cycling paths through old- and second-growth forest. The wheelchair-accessible Beaver Lake Interpretive Trail is a good choice if you're interested in park ecology. Take a map—they're available at the park-information booth and many of the concession stands—and don't go into the woods alone or after dusk.

Totem poles. Totem poles are an important art form among native peoples of British Columbia's coast. These nine poles—eight carved in the latter half of the 20th century, and one created in 2009—include replicas of poles originally brought to the park from the north coast in the 1920s, as well as poles carved specifically for the park by First Nations artists. The styles represent a cross-section of B.C. native groups, including the Kwakwaka'wakw, Haida, and Nisga'a. The combination of carved animals, fish, birds, and mythological creatures represents clan history. An visitor center near the site has a snack bar, a gift shop, and information about B.C.'s First Nations. ✉ *Brockton Point.*

Vancouver Aquarium Marine Science Centre. ★ Massive pools with windows below water level let you come face to face with beluga whales, sea otters, sea lions, dolphins, and harbor seals at this research and educational facility. In the Amazon rainforest gallery you can walk through a jungle populated with piranhas, caimans, and tropical birds; in summer, you'll be surrounded by hundreds of free-flying butterflies. Other displays, many with hands-on features for kids, show the underwater life of coastal British Columbia and the Canadian Arctic. A Tropic Zone is home to exotic freshwater and saltwater life, including clown fish, moray eels, and black-tip reef sharks. Beluga whale, sea lion, and dolphin shows, as well as dive shows (where divers swim with aquatic life, including sharks) are held daily. Make sure to check out the "4-D" film experience; it's a multisensory show that puts mist, smell, and wind into the 3-D equation. For an extra fee, you can help the trainers feed and train the animals. There's also a café and a gift shop. Be prepared for lines on weekends and school holidays. **■ TIP→ In summer, the quietest time to visit is before 11 am or after 4 pm; in other seasons, there are fewer crowds before noon or after 2 pm.** ✉ *845 Avison Way, Stanley Park* ☎ *604/659–3474* 🌐 *www.vanaqua.org* 🎫 *C$27* ⏲ *Open July–Labor Day, daily 9:30–7; Labor Day–June, daily 9:30–5:30.*

WORTH NOTING

Lumberman's Arch. Made of one massive log, this archway, erected in 1952, is dedicated to the workers in Vancouver's first industry. Beside the arch is an asphalt path that leads back to Lost Lagoon and the Vancouver Aquarium. There's a picnic area, a snack bar, and small beach here, too. The Variety Kids Water Park is across the road.

Miniature Railway. A child-size steam train takes kids and adults on a ride through the woods. In summer, the railway operates as the "Spirit Catcher," a First Nations–themed excursion as part of the Klahowya Aboriginal Village. Halloween displays draw crowds throughout October for the annual "Ghost Train," and at Christmas an elaborate light display illuminates the route during "Bright Nights." ✉ *Off Pipeline Rd., Stanley Park* ☎ *604/257–8531* 🎫 *Miniature Railway: C$6.25, C$3.13 children; Special events (Spirit Catcher, Ghost Train, Bright Nights): C$10–C$8, C$8–C$5 children* ⏲ *Miniature Railway May–mid-June, Sat.–Sun. 11–4; Spirit Catcher mid-June–early Sept., daily 10–4; Ghost Train Oct., Sun.–Thurs. 6–10 pm, Fri.–Sat. 6–11 pm; Bright Nights Dec., Sun.–Thurs. 6–10 pm, Fri.–Sat. 6–11 pm; call for off-season hours.*

CLOSE UP

A Tour of Stanley Park

Stanley Park Drive circles the park, often parallel to the **Seawall walking/cycling path.** If you're walking or cycling, start at the foot of Alberni Street, beside Lost Lagoon. Go through the underpass and veer right, following the cycle-path markings, to the seawall.

Whichever route you travel, the old wooden structure that you pass on your right is the Vancouver Rowing Club, a private athletic club established in 1903. Ahead and to your left is a parking lot, an information booth, and a turnoff to the aquarium and Painters Circle, where artists sell their work. A Salmon Demonstration Stream near the information booth presents facts about the life cycle of the fish.

Continue along past the Royal Vancouver Yacht Club, and after ½ km (¼ mile) you'll reach the causeway to Deadman's Island. The **totem poles,** a bit farther down Stanley Park Drive and on your left, are a popular photo stop. The **Nine O'Clock Gun** is ahead at the water's edge, just past the sign for Hallelujah Point. Brockton Point and its small lighthouse and foghorn are to the north. Brockton Oval, where you can catch a rugby game in winter or cricket in summer, is on your left. On the water side, watch for the *Girl in a Wetsuit,* a sculpture that mimics Copenhagen's *Little Mermaid.* A little farther along the seashore stands a replica of the dragon-shaped figurehead from the SS *Empress of Japan,* which plied these waters between 1891 and 1922.

Lumbermen's Arch, a log archway, is at km 3 (mile 2) of the drive. There's a picnic area, a snack bar, and a small beach. The Variety Kids Water Park, across the road, is a big draw in summer. Cyclists and walkers can turn off here for a shortcut back to the **Vancouver Aquarium, Klahowya Village and the Miniature Railway,** and the park entrance.

At the Lions Gate Bridge: cyclists go under the bridge, past **Prospect Point**; drivers go over the bridge to a viewpoint–café at the top of Prospect Point. Both routes continue to the English Bay side of the park and its beaches. Keep an eye open for the Hollow Tree. The imposing monolith offshore (not visible from the road) is **Siwash Rock,** the focus of a native legend. Continue to the swimming area and snack bar at Third Beach, then the heated pool at **Second Beach.** If you're walking or cycling, you can shortcut from here back to Lost Lagoon by taking the perpendicular path behind the pool that cuts into the park. Either footbridge ahead leads to a path along the south side of the lagoon that will take you to Alberni and Georgia streets. If you continue along the seawall from Second Beach, you'll emerge into a residential part of the West End.

Nine O'Clock Gun. This cannonlike apparatus by the water was installed in 1890 to alert fishermen to a curfew ending weekend fishing. Now it signals 9 o'clock every night.

An underwater view of a beluga whale at the Vancouver Aquarium.

QUICK BITES

Stanley's Park Bar and Grill. In a 1911 manor house, this bar and grill is a family-friendly veranda serving burgers, fish, soups, and salads. Open May through September, it overlooks the Rose Garden and is near the Malkin Bowl, where outdoor theater and concerts are held in summer. There's also a gift and souvenir shop. ☎ ***604/602–3088*** 🌐 ***www.stanleyparkpavilion.com.***

Second Beach. The 50-meter pool here, with lifeguards and waterslides, is a popular spot in summer; the beach has a playground and covered picnic areas. If you like romantic beachside sunsets, you'll want to come here with your sweetheart. ☎ *604/257–8371 summer only* 🌐 *www.vancouver.ca/parks/* *Free beach, C$5.36 pool* *Pool mid-May–mid-June, weekdays noon–8:45, weekends 10–8:45; mid-June–early Aug., daily 10–8:45; early Aug.–early Sept., daily 10–8:30.*

Siwash Rock. According to a local First Nations legend, this 50-foot-high offshore promontory is a monument to a man who was turned into stone as a reward for his unselfishness. The rock is visible from the seawall; if you're driving, you need to park and take a short path through the woods. (Watch for the Hollow Tree nearby. This centuries-old 56-foot-wide burnt cedar stump has shrunk over the years but still gives an idea of how large some of the old-growth trees can be.)

GRANVILLE ISLAND

Fodor's Choice ★

The creative redevelopment of this former industrial wasteland vies with Stanley Park as the city's top attraction. An active cement works remains at its heart and is oddly complemented with a thriving diversity of artist studios, performing arts spaces, an indoor food market, specialty shops, and a jammed-to-the-gills marina. There's not a chain store or designer label in sight.

In the early 20th century False Creek was dredged for better access to the sawmills that lined the shore, and the sludge was heaped onto a sandbar that grew large enough to house much-needed industrial and logging-equipment plants. Although business thrived in the 1920s, most fell into derelict status by the '60s. In the early '70s, though, the federal government came up with a creative plan to redevelop the island with a public market, marine activities, and artisans' studios. The refurbished Granville Island opened to the public in 1979 and was an immediate hit with locals and visitors alike.

Explore Granville Island at your leisure but try to plan your expedition over a meal, since the market is an excellent place for lunch, snacks, and shopping. The buildings behind the market are as diverse as the island's main attractions and house all sorts of crafts shops. The waterside boardwalk behind the Arts Club and around the Creekhouse building will bring you to Ocean Art Works, an open-sided longhouse-style structure where you can watch First Nations artists at work. Be sure to visit the free contemporary galleries beside the covered walkway to Sea Village, one of the few houseboat communities in Vancouver. Other nooks and alleys to note are Ron Basford Park, a natural amphitheater for outdoor performances, and Railspur Alley, home to about a dozen studios and galleries that produce everything from jewelry to leather work and sake. Granville Island is also a venue for Vancouver's many performing arts festivals—and a great place to catch top-quality street entertainment at any time.

Though the 35-acre island is now technically a peninsula, connected years ago by landfill to the south shore of False Creek, it still feels like an island with its own distinct character.

GETTING HERE AND AROUND

The mini Aquabus ferries are a favorite way to get to Granville Island (it's about a two minute ride); they depart from the south end of Hornby Street, a 15-minute walk from downtown Vancouver. The Aquabus delivers passengers across False Creek to the Granville Island Public Market *(see below)*. The larger False Creek ferries leave every five minutes for Granville Island from a dock behind the Vancouver Aquatic Centre, on Beach Avenue. Still another option is to take a 10-minute ride on a TransLink bus: from Waterfront Station or stops on Granville Street, take False Creek South Bus 50 to the edge of the island. Several other Granville Street buses, including 4 UBC, 7 Dunbar, 10 Granville, 14 UBC, and 16 Arbutus, stop at West 5th Avenue and Granville Street, a few minutes' walk from the island. The market is a short walk from the bus, ferry, or tram stop. Come by public transit if you can, since the island's narrow roadways get clogged with traffic. If you do drive, parking is free for up to three hours (although free spots can be hard to find, particularly on busy summer days); paid parking is available in several island garages.

TIMING

If your schedule is tight, you can tour Granville Island in two to three hours. If you like to shop you could spend a full day.

TOP ATTRACTIONS

Fodor's Choice ★ **Granville Island Public Market.** Dozens of stalls in this 50,000-square-foot building sell locally grown fruits and vegetables direct from the farm and other produce from farther afield; others stock crafts, chocolates, cheese, fish, meat, flowers, and exotic foods. On Thursdays in summer, farmers sell fruit and vegetables from trucks outside. At the north end of the market, you can pick up a snack, lunch, or coffee from one of the many prepared-food vendors. The Market Courtyard, on the waterside, is a good place to catch street entertainers—be prepared to get roped into the action, if only to check the padlocks of an escape artist's gear. Weekends can get madly busy. ✉ *1689 Johnston St.* ☎ *604/666–5784* 🌐 *www.granvilleisland.com* ⏲ *Open daily 9–7.*

WORTH NOTING

Emily Carr University of Art+Design. The university's three main buildings—tin-plated structures formerly used for industrial purposes—were renovated in the 1970s. The Charles H. Scott Gallery to the right of the main entrance hosts contemporary exhibitions in various media. Two other galleries showcase student work. Note that there isn't any Emily Carr work on display here; the building is simply named in her honor. ✉ *1399 Johnston St.* ☎ *604/844–3800* 🌐 *www.ecuad.ca* 🎫 *Free* ⏲ *Open weekdays noon–5, weekends 10–5.*

Granville Island Brewing. Tours of Canada's first modern microbrewery last about 45 minutes and include tastes of three brews. ✉ *1441 Cartwright St.* ☎ *604/687–2739* 🌐 *www.gib.ca* 🎫 *C$9.75* ⏲ *Store open daily 10–9; tours mid-May–early Sept. daily at 11 am, noon, 3 pm, 4 pm, and 5 pm, early Sept.–mid-May daily at noon, 2 pm, and 4 pm.*

Emily Carr University of Art+Design **6**
Granville Island Brewing **3**
Granville Island Public Market **1**
Granville Island Water Park **5**
Kids Market **4**
Net Loft **2**

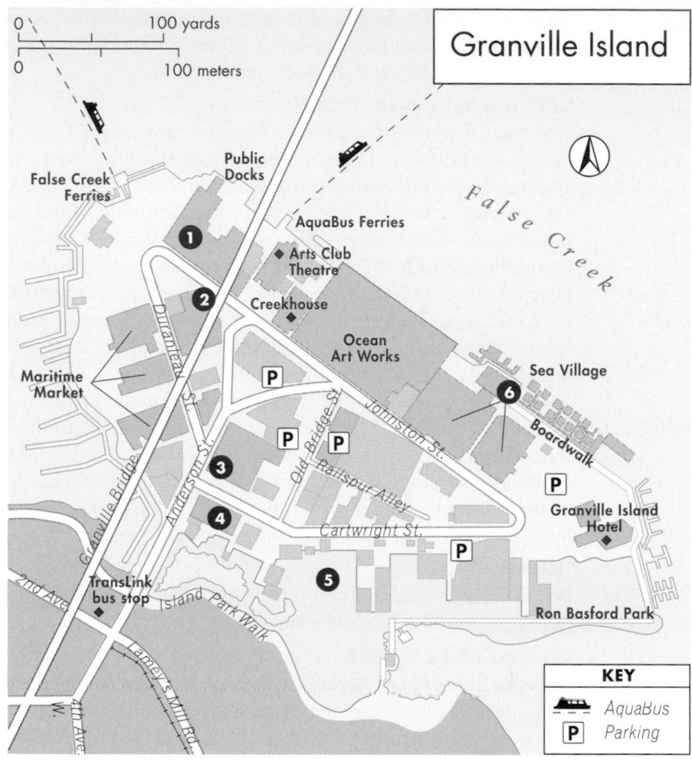

Granville Island Water Park. North America's largest, free public water park has slides, pipes, and sprinklers for children to run through. There's a grassy patch for picnics, and clean washrooms are at the adjacent community center. *1318 Cartwright St.* *604/257–8195* *www.vancouver.ca/parks* *Free* *Mid-May–Labor Day, daily 10–6; slides open mid-June.*

Kids Market. A converted factory warehouse sets the stage for a slice of kids' heaven on Granville Island. The Kids' Market has an indoor play area and two floors of small shops that sell all kinds of toys, magic gear, books, and other fun stuff. *1496 Cartwright St.* *604/689–8447* *www.kidsmarket.ca* *Open daily 10–6.*

Net Loft. A former loft where fishermen used to dry their nets, this blue-and-red building includes a bookstore, a café, and a collection of high-quality boutiques selling imported and locally made crafts, exotic fabrics, handmade paper, and First Nations art. *1666 Johnston St.* *No phone* *Open daily 10–7.*

DID YOU KNOW?

Cooking demonstrations are part of the fun at Granville market, where you can also shop for produce, baked goods, and prepared foods.

THE WEST SIDE AND KITSILANO

Once a hippie haven, Kitsilano has gone upmarket. Distinctive homes and specialty shopping now make up some of the country's most expensive few square miles of real estate. The West Side has the city's best gardens and natural sights; "Kits," however, is really where all the action is.

Leave downtown via Burrard, Granville, or Cambie Street bridge and you'll be on the West Side, an area of diverse neighborhoods just south of the downtown core. Any reference to "the West Side" usually has moneyed connotations, as in South Granville's chic galleries and upscale shopping, the old-family mansions of Shaughnessy, the tony university district, and even the up-and-coming area surrounding Cambie Street. The West Side is the antithesis of the city's funkier, lower-income East Side. Some of Vancouver's best gardens, natural sights, and museums, including the renowned Museum of Anthropology on the campus of the University of British Columbia, are south of downtown Vancouver. Established in 1908, UBC is the city's main university campus with a student population of approximately 46,000. The university is where you'll also find the Chan Centre for the Performing Arts *(⇨ See the Nightlife and Performing Arts chapter)*, the Botanical Gardens, and Pacific Spirit Regional Park—the latter, although it can't compare with Stanley Park, is where the locals go for meandering forested trails that put you in touch with nature. Except during rush hour, it takes about 30 minutes to drive and 30–40 minutes to travel by bus from downtown to the University of British Columbia.

The beachfront district of Kitsilano (popularly known as Kits) is among the trendiest of Canadian neighborhoods. Originally inhabited by the Squamish people, whose Chief Khahtsahlanough gave the area its name, Kitsilano began to attract day-trippers from Vancouver in the early part of the 20th century. Some stayed and built lavish waterfront mansions; others built simpler Craftsman-style houses farther up the slope. After a period of decline in the mid-20th century, Kits became a haven for hippies and their yuppie offspring who have since restored many of the wood-frame houses, and the neighborhood is once again chic. Kitsilano is home to three museums, some fashionable shops, and popular pubs and cafés. Kits has hidden treasures, too: rare boats moored at Heritage Harbour, stately mansions on forested lots, and, all along the waterfront, quiet coves and shady paths within a stone's throw of Canada's liveliest beach. Vanier Park, the grassy beachside setting for three museums and the best kite-flying venue in Vancouver, is the logical gateway to Kits. Every summer, it also hosts the Children's Festival, and Bard on the Beach theater—both presented under billowing tents. Because Vanier Park is home to three indoor attractions, it's also a great rainy-day activity center.

GETTING HERE AND AROUND

Individual attractions on the West Side are easily reached by TransLink buses, but a car makes things easier, especially if you want to see more than one of these sites in a day.

The most enjoyable way to get to Kitsilano is by a False Creek ferry from Granville Island or from the dock behind the Vancouver Aquatic Centre, on Beach Avenue. The ferries dock at Heritage Harbour in Kitsilano, behind the Vancouver Maritime Museum. You can also walk or cycle the 1 km (½ mile) or so along the waterfront pathway from Granville Island (leave the island by Anderson Street and keep to your right along the waterfront, following the Seaside Bike Path signs). If you prefer to come by road, drive over the Burrard Street Bridge, turn right at Chestnut Street, and park in either of the museum parking lots; or take Bus 2, or 22, traveling south on Burrard Street downtown, get off at Cypress Street and Cornwall Avenue, and walk over to the park.

TOP ATTRACTIONS

Fodor'sChoice ★ **Museum of Anthropology.** Part of the University of British Columbia, the MOA has one of the world's leading collections of Northwest Coast First Nations art. The Great Hall displays dramatic cedar poles, bentwood boxes, and canoes adorned with traditional Northwest Coast–painted designs. On clear days, the gallery's 50-foot-tall windows reveal a striking backdrop of mountains and sea. Another highlight is the work of the late Bill Reid, one of Canada's most respected Haida artists. In *The Raven and the First Men* (1980), carved in yellow cedar, he tells a Haida story of creation. Reid's gold-and-silver jewelry work is also on display, as are exquisite carvings of gold, silver, and argillite (a black shale found on Haida Gwaii, also known as the Queen Charlotte Islands) by other First Nations artists. The museum's visible storage section displays, in drawers and cases, contain thousands of examples of tools, textiles, masks, and other artifacts from around the world. The Koerner Ceramics Gallery contains 600 pieces from 15th- to 19th-century Europe. Behind the museum are two Haida houses, set on the cliff over the water. Free guided tours—given several times daily (call to confirm times)—are immensely informative. For an extra C$5 you can rent a VUEguide, an electronic device that senses where you are in the museum and shows relevant artist interviews, archival footage, and photographs of the artifacts in their original contexts, on a hand-held screen. Arthur Erickson designed the cliff-top structure that houses the MOA, which also has an excellent book and fine-art shop and a café. To

SAVING MONEY AT UBC

If you're planning to visit several of the attractions at the University of British Columbia, consider purchasing a **UBC Museums and Gardens Pass** ($33). It includes admission to the Museum of Anthropology, UBC Botanical Garden, Nitobe Memorial Garden, and Beaty Biodiversity Museum. There's also a family version of the pass ($85) that covers two adults and up to four children under 18. The pass doesn't include the Greenheart Canopy Walkway, but it does give you ten percent off walkway tickets. Passes are valid for six months, so you don't need to squeeze all your sightseeing into one day. Purchase the pass at any of the participating attractions.

reach the museum by transit, take any UBC-bound bus from Granville Street downtown to the university bus loop, a 10-minute walk from the museum. ■ **TIP➜ Pay parking is available in the Rose Garden parking lot, across Marine Drive from the museum.** ✉ *University of British Columbia, 6393 N.W. Marine Dr., Point Grey* ☎ *604/822–5087* 🌐 *www.moa.ubc.ca* *C$16.75, Tues. 5–9 C$9* ⏲ *Late May–mid-Oct., Tues. 10–9, Wed.–Mon. 10–5; mid-Oct.–late May, Tues. 10–9, Wed.–Sun. 10–5.*

Nitobe Memorial Garden. Opened in 1960 in memory of Japanese scholar and diplomat Dr. Inazo Nitobe (1862–1933), this 2½-acre walled garden, which includes a pond, a stream with a small waterfall, and a ceremonial teahouse, is considered one of the most authentic Japanese tea and strolling gardens outside Japan. Designed by Professor Kannosuke Mori of Japan's Chiba University, the garden incorporates many native British Columbia trees and shrubs, pruned and trained Japanese style, and interplanted with Japanese maples and flowering shrubs. The circular path around the park symbolizes the cycle of life and provides a tranquil view from every direction. Cherry blossoms are the highlight in April and May, and in June the irises are magnificent. Because the garden is so exotic, it's worth renting an audio guide. ■ **TIP➜ Japanese tea ceremonies are held the last Saturday of every month, May through September; call 604/939-7749 for reservations.** ✉ *University of British Columbia, 1895 Lower Mall, Point Grey* ☎ *604/822–6038* 🌐 *www.botanicalgarden.ubc.ca/nitobe* *C$6 Apr.–Oct.; C$12 includes admission to the UBC Botanical Gardens; by donation Nov.–Mar.* ⏲ *Apr.–Oct., daily 9:30–5; Nov.–Mar., weekdays 10–2.*

EN ROUTE

Old Hastings Mill Store Museum. Vancouver's first store and oldest building was built in 1865 at the foot of Dunlevy Street in Gastown and moved to this seaside spot near the Royal Vancouver Yacht Club in 1930. It's a little wooden structure at the corner of Point Grey Road and Alma Street—west of Kitsilano en route to UBC—and is the only building to predate the 1886 Great Fire. The site is now a museum with displays of First Nations artifacts and pioneer household goods. ✉ *1575 Alma St., Point Grey* ☎ *604/734–1212* 🌐 *hastings-mill-museum.ca* *By donation* ⏲ *Open mid-June–mid-Sept., Tues.–Sun. 1–4; mid-Sept.–mid-Dec. and Feb.–mid-June, weekends 1–4.*

Part of the attraction of the Museum of Anthropology is the exhibits outside the museum, on the cliffs overlooking the water.

Queen Elizabeth Park. At the highest point in the city, showcasing 360-degree views of downtown, this 52-hectare (130-acre) park has lavish sunken gardens (in a former stone quarry), a rose garden, and an abundance of grassy picnicking spots. Other park facilities include 18 tennis courts, pitch and putt (an 18-hole putting green), and a restaurant. On summer evenings there's free outdoor dancing on the Plaza—everything from Scottish country dance to salsa, for all ages and levels. In the **Bloedel Conservatory** you can see tropical and desert plants and 100 species of free-flying tropical birds in a glass geodesic dome—the perfect place to be on a rainy day. To reach the park by public transportation, take the Canada Line to King Edward station; from there, it's a six-block walk to the edge of the park (and a hike up the hill to appreciate the views). Cambie Bus 15, which runs south along Cambie Street from the Olympic Village SkyTrain station, will drop you a little closer, at the corner of 33rd and Cambie. **TIP→ Park activities make for a great family excursion, and unlike Stanley Park with its acres of rain forest, Queen Elizabeth Park is all about the flowers.** *Cambie St. and 33rd Ave., Cambie Corridor 604/257–8584 www.vancouver.ca/parks Conservatory C$5 Park daily year-round; Conservatory May–mid-Sept., weekdays 9–8, weekends 10–9; mid-Sept.–Apr., daily 10–5.*

★ **University of British Columbia Botanical Garden.** Ten thousand trees, shrubs, and rare plants from around the world thrive on this 70-acre research site on the university campus, which edges on Pacific Spirit Park. The complex feels as far away from the city as you can get, with forested walkways through an Asian garden, a garden of medicinal plants, and an alpine garden with some of the world's rarest plants. A Walk in the

Woods is a 20-minute loop that takes you through more than 1,000 species of coastal plant life. The garden gift store is one of the best of its kind. One-hour guided tours, free with garden admission, are offered on certain days; call or check the website for schedule.

A thrilling way to explore the garden, the 308-meter-long (1,010-foot-long) **Greenheart Canopy Walkway** (✉ *Point Grey* ☎ *604/822–4208* 🎫 *C$20, including admission to the main UBC Botanical Garden*) is a swaying network of suspended bridges, weaving a trail between gargantuan cedars and hemlocks. Along the way, you stop off on eight platforms in the trees, each more than 15 meters (49 feet) high, while an additional two-story viewing platform tops a free-standing tower more than 22 meters (72 feet) in the air. Visits to the walkway are by 45-minute guided tour, where you learn about the forest, local wildlife, environmental issues, and First Nations traditions; call or check the website for seasonal tour schedules. The walkway is open year-round and is a great adventure for kids; just note that small children must either be able to walk on their own or be carried in a child backpack or other carrier (strollers aren't permitted). ✉ *6804 S.W. Marine Dr., Point Grey* ☎ *604/822–4208* 🌐 *www.ubcbotanicalgarden.org* 🎫 *C$8; C$12 includes admission to Nitobe Memorial Garden; C$20 includes Greenheart Canopy Walkway; C$24 includes Nitobe Memorial Garden and Greenheart Canopy Walkway* ⏲ *Daily 9:30–5.*

★ **VanDusen Botanical Garden.** An Elizabethan maze, a formal rose garden, a meditation garden, and a collection of Canadian heritage plants are among the many themed displays at this 55-acre site. The collections include flora from every continent and many rare and endangered species. The Phyllis Bentall Garden area features hybrid water lilies and carnivorous plants (a hit with kids). From mid-May to early June the Laburnum Walk forms a canopy of gold; in August and September the wildflower meadow is in bloom. The garden is also home to five lakes, a garden shop, a library, and the Truffles Fine Foods Café (serving breakfast, lunch, and afternoon tea). It hosts special events throughout the year, including an outdoor flower and garden show, a large outdoor vintage-car exhibit, and a spectacular Christmas-theme Festival of Lights every December (daily 4:30–9 pm). From downtown, catch the Oak Bus 17 directly to the garden entrance. Queen Elizabeth Park is a 1-km (½-mile) walk away, along West 37th Avenue. ■ **TIP→ Because this was once a golf course, pathways make this garden extremely wheelchair accessible.** ✉ *5251 Oak St., at W. 37th Ave., Shaughnessy* ☎ *604/257–8335 garden, 604/267–4966 restaurant* 🌐 *www.vandusengarden.org* 🎫 *C$10.75 Apr.–Sept.; C$7.75 Oct.–Mar.* ⏲ *June–Aug., daily 9 am–8:30 pm; Sept.–May, daily from 10 am (call for seasonal closing times).*

WORTH NOTING

Beaty Biodiversity Museum. If you can imagine a vast underground library, but instead of books, the stacks are filled with bones, fossils, and preserved lizards, then you can begin to imagine this modern museum on the U.B.C. campus that exhibits more than two million specimens from the university's natural-history collections. The most striking attraction hangs in the entrance atrium: a 25-meter-long (82-foot-long) skeleton of a blue whale—the largest on view in Canada. On the lower level, you'll find scads of animal skulls, taxidermied birds, and other creatures displayed through glass windows (many of which are at kids' eye level). In the interactive Discovery Lab, you can play scientist yourself; you might compare the claws of different birds or examine animal poop under a microscope. There's also a family space stocked with books, art supplies, and kid-size furniture. To find the museum from the university bus loop, walk west to the Main Mall and turn left; the museum is just south of University Boulevard. ✉ *University of British Columbia, 2212 Main Mall, Point Grey* ☎ *604/827–4955* 🌐 *www.beatymuseum.ubc.ca* 🎫 *C$12* ⏲ *Tues.–Sun. 10–5.*

WHAT IS THAT?

The massive white-and-yellow contraption behind the Maritime Museum is the *Ben Franklin* submersible. It looks like something a Jules Verne character would put to sea but was actually built in 1968 as a marine research tool to, among other things, chart the Gulf Stream. A more fascinating claim to fame is that it was once the largest of its kind in America and was instructional for NASA: the information about how people lived in such close quarters for extended periods of time provided preliminary research data on the dynamics of living aboard a space station.

2

H.R. MacMillan Space Centre. The interactive exhibits and high-tech learning systems at this museum include a Virtual Voyages ride, where visitors can take a simulated space journey (definitely not for those afraid of flying); GroundStation Canada, showcasing Canada's achievements in space; and the Cosmic Courtyard, full of hands-on space-oriented exhibits including a moon rock and a computer program that shows what you would look like as an alien. You can catch daytime astronomy shows or evening music-and-laser shows at the **H. R. MacMillan Planetarium.** When the sky is clear, the ½ meter telescope at the **Gordon MacMillan Southam Observatory** (☎ *604/738–2855*) is focused on whatever stars or planets are worth watching that night. Admission to the observatory is by donation, and it's open year-round Saturday evenings, from 8 to 11, weather permitting. ✉ *Vanier Park, 1100 Chestnut St., Kitsilano* ☎ *604/738–7827* 🌐 *www.spacecentre.ca* 🎫 *C$15* ⏲ *Open July–Aug., daily 10–5; Sept.–June, Mon.–Fri. 10–3, Sat. 10–5, Sun. noon–5.*

Kitsilano Beach. Picnic sites, a playground, tennis courts, beach volleyball, a restaurant, take-out concessions, Vancouver's biggest outdoor pool (open May to September), and some fine people-watching can all be found at Kits Beach. Inland from the pool, the **Kitsilano Showboat,** an outdoor amphitheater, hosts free music and dance performances in summer. ✉ *2305 Cornwall Ave., Kitsilano* ☎ *604/731–0011 Pool (summer only)* 🌐 *www.vancouver.ca/parks* 🎫 *Beach free, pool C$5.36* ⏲ *Pool open late May–mid-June, weekdays noon–8:45, weekends 9–8:45; mid-June–early Aug., weekdays 7 am–8:15 pm, weekends 9–8:45; early Aug.–mid-Sept., weekdays 7 am–sunset weekends 9 am–sunset.*

NEED A BREAK?

The Boathouse on Kits Beach. Just steps from the sand, the Boathouse on Kits Beach serves lunch, dinner, and weekend brunch inside and on its big ocean-view deck. There's also a take-out concession at the same site. ✉ ***1305 Arbutus St.*** ☎ ***604/738–5487*** 🌐 ***www.boathouserestaurants.ca.***

BATHING SUIT, OR NOT?

Wreck Beach, Vancouver's only clothing-optional beach, lies at the bottom of the cliffs on the most western point of Point Grey, on the UBC campus. Its bohemian hippie atmosphere isn't for everyone, but its seclusion is a haven for unlicensed vendors selling pot, vodka-soaked watermelon, pizza by the slice, and sandwiches. People are generally typically respectful, and driftwood "sculptures" create cozy resting spots along the sandy beach.

Vancouver Maritime Museum. About a third of this museum has been turned over to kids, with touchable displays offering a chance to drive a tug, maneuver an underwater robot, or dress up as a seafarer. Toddlers and school-age children can work the hands-on displays in Pirates' Cove and the Children's Maritime Discovery Centre. The museum also has an extensive collection of model ships and is the last moorage for the RCMP *Arctic St. Roch*, the first ship to sail in both directions through the treacherous Northwest Passage and the first to circumnavigate North America. While you're here, take a moment to look at the 100-foot-tall replica Kwakiutl totem pole in front of the museum. ✉ *Vanier Park, 1905 Ogden Ave., north end of Cypress St., Kitsilano* ☎ *604/257–8300* 🌐 *www.vancouvermaritimemuseum.com* *C$11* *Open mid-May–Labor Day, daily 10–5; Labor Day–mid-May, Tues.–Sat. 10–5, Sun. noon–5.*

Museum of Vancouver. Vancouver's short-but-funky history comes to life at this seaside museum. The war-years gallery remembers some poignant episodes involving the Japanese internment, as well as local stories of the war effort. The 1950s Gallery has a 1955 Ford Fairlane Victoria and a Seeburg Select-o-Matic jukebox. The 1960s-theme Revolution Gallery revisits the city's days as the hippie capital of Canada: visitors can hear local bands from the '60s and poke around a re-created communal house. The museum regularly mounts intriguing temporary exhibits and hosts lectures and other public events. ✉ *Vanier Park, 1100 Chestnut St., Kitsilano* ☎ *604/736–4431* 🌐 *www.museumofvancouver.com* *C$12* *July–Aug., Fri.–Wed. 10–5, Thurs. 10–8; Sept.–June, Tues., Wed., and Fri.–Sun. 10–5, Thurs. 10–8.*

2

NORTH SHORE

The North Shore and its star attractions—the Capilano Suspension Bridge, Grouse Mountain, Lonsdale Quay, and, farther east, the lovely hamlet of Deep Cove—are just a short trip from downtown Vancouver.

The North Shore is where to come to kayak up fjords, and hike, ski, and explore mountainous terrain with large swaths of forest. Posh "West Van," as the locals call the North Shore suburb of West Vancouver, has retained its well-heeled character from the time when the Guinness family developed the area in the 1930s, and it's a network of English style, winding country roads, and multimillion-dollar homes. West Van is en route to the Horseshoe Bay ferry terminal for ferries to Vancouver Island, the Sea-to-Sky Whistler Highway, and Cypress Mountain, which hosted the Olympic freestyle skiing and snowboard competitions. If you have a car, you can drive to the top for spectacular vistas of Vancouver and beyond. Unlike Grouse Mountain, the views here are free. North Vancouver to the east is more commercial in nature, including tourist havens of Grouse and Capilano.

GETTING HERE AND AROUND

From downtown, drive west down Georgia Street to Stanley Park and across the Lions Gate Bridge to North Vancouver. Stay in the right lane, take the North Vancouver exit, and then turn left onto Capilano Road. In about 2 km (1 mile), you come to the Capilano Suspension Bridge. A few hundred yards up Capilano Road, on the left, is the entrance to Capilano River Regional Park. About 1½ km (1 mile) along the park access road you'll find the Capilano Salmon Hatchery. Returning to Capilano Road and continuing north, you'll reach Cleveland Dam (also part of the park), where you can stop for great mountain views. As you continue north, Capilano Road becomes Nancy Greene Way, which ends at the base of Grouse Mountain.

If you don't have a car, you can take the SeaBus from Waterfront Station to Lonsdale Quay and then catch a Grouse Mountain Bus 236. This stops at the Capilano Suspension Bridge and near the Salmon Hatchery on its way to the base of Grouse Mountain. It's an easy trip, but if you only have the Capilano Suspension Bridge on your agenda, take advantage of its complimentary shuttle from downtown.

TIMING

You need at least a half day to see the sights around the North Shore; allow a full day if you want to hike at Grouse Mountain or Capilano River Regional Park, or include a meandering drive through West Vancouver. You'll literally pass the entrance of the Capilano Bridge en route to Grouse Mountain, so it makes sense to do both. To save time, avoid crossing the Lions Gate Bridge during weekday rush hours (about 7–9 am and 3–6 pm). Note that there's also a suspension bridge—which is toll-free—at Lynn Canyon, though many opt for the more well-known Capilano Suspension Bridge.

TOP ATTRACTIONS

Fodor's Choice ★ **Capilano Suspension Bridge.** At Vancouver's oldest tourist attraction (the original bridge was built in 1889), you can get a taste of rain-forest scenery and test your mettle on the swaying, 450-foot cedar-plank suspension bridge that hangs 230 feet above the rushing Capilano River. Across the bridge is the Treetops Adventure, where you can walk along 650 feet of cable bridges suspended among the trees. If you're even braver, you can follow the **Cliffwalk,** a series of narrow cantilevered bridges and walkways hanging out over the edge of the canyon. Without crossing the bridge, you can enjoy the site's viewing decks, nature trails, totem park, and carving center (where you can watch First Nations carvers at work), as well as history and forestry exhibits, a massive gift shop in the original 1911 teahouse, and a restaurant. May through October, guides in 19th-century costumes conduct free tours on themes related to history, nature, or ecology, while fiddle bands, First Nations dancers, and other entertainers keep things lively. In December, more than 250,000 lights illuminate the canyon during the Canyon Lights winter celebration. **■ TIP→ Catch the attraction's free shuttle service from Canada Place; it also stops along Burrard and Robson streets.** ✉ *3735 Capilano Rd., North Vancouver* ☎ *604/985–7474* 🌐 *www.capbridge.com* *C$34.95* *May–Labor Day, daily 8:30–8; Nov.–Mar., daily 9–5; Sept., Oct., and Apr.–mid-May call for hrs.*

★ **Grouse Mountain.** North America's largest aerial tramway, the **Skyride** is a great way to take in the city, sea, and mountain vistas (be sure to pick a clear day or evening). The Skyride makes the 2-km (1-mile) climb to the peak of Grouse Mountain every 15 minutes. Once at the top you can watch a half-hour video presentation at the Theatre in the Sky (it's included with your Skyride ticket). Other mountaintop activities include, in summer, lumberjack shows, chairlift rides, walking tours, hiking, falconry demonstrations, and a chance to visit the grizzly bears and gray wolves in the mountain's wildlife refuge. For an extra fee you can also try zip-lining and tandem paragliding, tour the wind turbine that tops the mountain, or take a helicopter flight. In winter you can ski, snowshoe, snowboard, ice-skate on a mountaintop pond, or take Sno-Cat-drawn sleigh rides. A stone-and-cedar lodge is home to snack shops, a pub-style bistro, and a high-end restaurant, with expansive city views. ■ **TIP→ The Grouse Grind—a hiking trail up the face of the mountain—is one of the best workouts on the North Shore. Depending on your fitness level, allow between 40 minutes and two hours to complete it (90 minutes is an average time). Then you can take the Skyride down. The BCMC trail is a less crowded, slightly longer alternative.** *(⇨ See the Vancouver Outdoors chapter for more info.)* ✉ *6400 Nancy Greene Way, North Vancouver* ☎ *604/980–9311* 🌐 *www.grousemountain.com* 🎟 *Skyride and many activities C$39.95* ⏱ *Daily 9 am–10 pm.*

WORTH NOTING

Capilano River Regional Park. The park has hiking trails and footbridges over the Capilano River, where it cuts through a dramatic gorge. At the park's **Capilano Salmon Hatchery** *(4500 Capilano Park Rd., 604/666–1790)*, viewing areas and exhibits illustrate the life cycle of the salmon. The best time to see the salmon run is between July and November. **The Cleveland Dam** *(Capilano Rd., about 1½ km [1 mile] past main park entrance)* is at the north end of the park. Built in 1954 and named for Dr. E. A. Cleveland, a former chief commissioner of the Greater Vancouver Water District, it dams the Capilano River to create the 5½-km-long (3½-mile-long) Capilano Reservoir. A hundred yards from the parking lot, you can walk across the top of the dam to enjoy striking views of the reservoir and mountains behind it. The two sharp peaks to the west are the Lions, for which the Lions Gate Bridge is named. ✉ *Capilano Rd., North Vancouver* ☎ *604/224–5739* 🌐 *www.metrovancouver.org/services/parks_lscr/regionalparks/pages/capilanoriver.aspx* 🎟 *Free* ⏱ *Park daily 8–dusk. Hatchery June–Aug., daily 8–8; May and Sept., daily 8–7; Apr. and Oct., daily 8–4:45; Nov.–Mar., daily 8–4.*

International Buddhist Temple. You don't have to be a Buddhist to appreciate the intricate workmanship of traditional Chinese art and culture inside this magnificent Buddhist temple, one of the most exquisite examples of Chinese palatial architecture in North America. Amid the peace and tranquility, the temple holds regular Buddhist ceremonies, lectures, and meditation classes, and conducts tea ceremonies. There is also a renowned bonsai garden, resource library, and museum on the grounds, as well as a cafeteria that serves vegetarian lunches. Because of the sacred nature of the temple, photography is restricted to outside areas. To reach the temple by public transit, take the Canada Line to Brighouse Station, then catch Bus 403 to the temple. ✉ *9160 Steveston Hwy., between No. 3 and No. 4 Rds., Richmond* ☎ *604/274–2822* 🌐 *www.buddhisttemple.ca* 🎟 *C$2 suggested donation* ⏱ *Daily 9:30–5:30.*

Gulf of Georgia Cannery National Historic Site. At the mouth of the Fraser River, this cannery grew from a single salmon canning line in 1894 to the second-largest cannery in the province. Through the years, its fortunes rose and fell, impacted by the landslide at Hells Gate, the onset of the Depression, and World War II, when much of its activities turned to canning herring for wartime consumption by troops and civilians. Designated a Federal Heritage site in 1987, the cannery now operates as a West Coast fishing industry museum with ongoing interpretive

DID YOU KNOW?

The 450-foot-long cedar-plank Capilano Suspension Bridge hangs 230 feet above the rushing Capilano River and makes for an exhilarating walk in the woods.

2

SUBURBAN RICHMOND'S CHINATOWN

Vancouver's city-center Chinatown is its "old" Chinatown, originally settled in the late 1800s, primarily by immigrants who came seeking work in the region's canneries or on the railroads. Beginning in the 1970s, however, the demographics of Vancouver's Chinese community began to change. Increasingly, the Chinese immigrants who settled in Vancouver were well-to-do professionals from Hong Kong and Taiwan, and many of these immigrants avoided the working-class downtown Chinatown, taking up residence elsewhere in the Vancouver region. In particular, the suburban community of Richmond, a suburb just south of Vancouver and home to the city's airport, became a popular destination for these new emigrés. Today, with a population that is more than 60 percent Asian, Richmond has become Vancouver's "new" Chinatown.

SkyTrain's Canada Line will take you right up to Richmond, where you can explore Asian-style shopping centers—it's almost like being in Hong Kong—and sample the vast number of restaurants serving authentic fare from across China and elsewhere in Asia. *www.tourismrichmond.com.*

programs and tours. You can check out the canning line, learn more about the B.C.'s fishing industry, and explore the heritage of the various ethnic groups who worked at the cannery. The cannery is located in the Richmond neighborhood of Steveston, where you can also explore the waterfront, stop for fish 'n' chips, or head out on a whale-watching excursion. Steveston is a 35- to 40-minute drive from downtown Vancouver; by public transit, take the Canada Line to Brighouse Station, then change to Bus 401, 402, or 407. *12138 Fourth Ave., Richmond 604/664–9009 www.pc.gc.ca/gulfofgeorgiacannery C$7.80 Daily 10–5.*

OFF THE BEATEN PATH

Lynn Canyon Park. With a steep canyon landscape, a temperate rain forest complete with waterfalls, and a suspension bridge that opened in 1912, 166½ feet above raging Lynn Creek, this 616-acre park provides thrills to go with its scenic views. The on-site Ecology Centre distributes maps of area hiking trails, waterfalls, and pools as well as information about the local flora and fauna. There's also a gift shop and a café here. To get to the park, take the Lions Gate Bridge and Capilano Road, go east on Highway 1, take the Lynn Valley Road exit, and turn right on Peters Road. From downtown Vancouver, you can take the SeaBus to Lonsdale Quay, then Bus 228 or 229 from the quay; both stop near the park. *3663 Park Rd., at end of Peters Rd., North Vancouver 604/990–3755 Ecology Centre, 604/984–9311 café www.dnv.org/ecology Ecology Centre by donation, suspension bridge free Park daily, dawn–dusk; Ecology Centre June–Sept., daily 10–5; Oct.–May, weekdays 10–5, weekends noon–4.*

Lonsdale Quay. Stalls selling fresh produce and ready-to-eat food fill the lower level of this popular indoor seaside market; upstairs are boutiques, toy stores, and a kids' play area. Outside you can wander the quay, admire the fishing boats and tugs moored here, and enjoy the views of the downtown skyline across the water. You'll also see a number of old dry docks and canneries finding fresh leases on life as modish condominiums. The **SeaBus foot-passenger ferry** (☏ *604/953–3333* ⊕ *www.translink.bc.ca*), part of the city's public transit system, leaves the quay every 15 to 30 minutes for the 13-minute ride to Waterfront Station downtown. ■ **TIP→** This is a great rainy-day activity. ✉ *123 Carrie Cates Ct., at foot of Lonsdale Ave.* ☏ *604/985–6261* ⊕ *www.lonsdalequay.com* 🎟 *Free* ⏲ *Daily 9–7.*

3

Vancouver Outdoors and Sports

WORD OF MOUTH

"If you go whalewatching out of Vancouver, two of the companies are located out of Steveston. It's a nice daytrip destination for something completely different from Vancouver."

—Carmanah

By Paige Donner

Blessed with a mild climate, fabulous natural setting, and excellent public-use facilities, Vancouverites, unsurprisingly, are an outdoorsy lot. It's not uncommon for locals to commute to work by foot or bike and, after hours, they're as likely to hit the water, trails, ski slopes, or beach volleyball courts as the bars or nightclubs.

Exceptional for North American cities, the downtown peninsula of Vancouver is entirely encircled by a seawall along which you can walk, in-line skate, cycle, or otherwise propel yourself for more than 22 km (13 miles), with plenty of picturesque jumping on and off points. It's so popular that it qualifies as an, albeit unofficial, national treasure. There are places along the route where you can rent a bike, skate, canoe, or kayak, or simply go for a swim. Top-rated skiing, snowboarding, mountain biking, fishing, diving, and golf are just minutes away.

You'll find rental equipment and tour operators in Vancouver for every imaginable outdoor activity, from tandem mountain bikes for Stanley Park trails to fly-fishing rods for English Bay. You'll find yoga studios around every corner and hiking trails that seem to materialize just at the end of the road. Hotel concierges can recommend the best wilderness trails just as easily as they can top sushi spots. And don't forget there are eight public ice rinks, eight public skateboard parks, and 180 public tennis courts all within Vancouver city.

PLANNER

TOP OUTDOORS EXPERIENCES

Walk or bike the Seawall: The 10-km (6.2-mile) paved path around Stanley Park is a civilized entrée into the coastal habitat where forest meets sea. The entire 22-km (13.6-mile) Seawall circles the city and is great for biking.

Hike the Grouse Grind: This two-hour climb up Grouse Mountain is a local rite of passage. The city and ocean views from the top are stunning. You can take the gondola back down, or both up and down and do your hiking along the trails up top such as to Goat Mountain.

White-water kayak the Capilano River: It's a serious tumble along canyons, through rain forest, and over rocks and rapids.

Play volleyball at Kits Beach: Vancouverites play a mean game of beach volleyball. Listen for the shouts of "good kill" on weekends from late spring to fall.

Kayak Indian Arm: Barely 30 minutes from downtown, the North Shore's fjordic landscape is stunning and best appreciated under paddle power.

WHEN TO DO IT

Vancouver has a moderate climate, with temperatures rarely exceeding 90°F or falling below freezing for sustained periods, though winter storms that blend relentless rain with 40°F days can feel colder than the Canadian Rockies. Whatever you're doing, wearing layers is key, as a downpour may abruptly turn into a 60-minute sun break, or marine air can bring a sudden chill to a July day.

Year-round: If Vancouverites postponed jogging, biking, or golfing because of a bit of rain, they'd get outside only half the time (Vancouver's annual rainfall is 43.9 inches, compared to Seattle's 36.2 inches). Visitors are encouraged to venture out in all but the worst rainstorm to participate in adventure, whether crossing the Capilano Suspension Bridge, hiking in Stanley Park, or kayaking on False Creek. Though water temps in Georgia Strait hardly vary from summer to winter, visibility improves significantly from December to March in what Jacques Cousteau declared the second-best scuba location in the world. Sportfishing and most wilderness tours take place year-round; you should check with operators for peak migration periods of sea mammals and birds.

Summer: True summer weather starts late in Vancouver, around Canada Day (July 1), but warm temperatures and sunshine persist into October. The beach scene is popular when the weather's good.

Winter: Most cities boast plenty of parks, but how many can claim three ski areas within the city limits? Welcome to the North Shore, where Cypress Mountain hosted the 2010 Olympic snowboard and freestyle ski events. February often offers so many sunny days that a T-shirt and jeans are the preferred ski clothes. The winter-sports season starts in November and runs through March—in addition to skiing and boarding, snowshoeing and dogsledding, too, are popular options.

GEAR

Mountain Equipment Co-op. Something of a local institution, Mountain Equipment Co-op is a veritable outdoor-lovers' emporium with every kind of gear imaginable, as well as rentals, books and maps, and information from people in the know. There's a one-time C$5 membership fee. ✉ *130 W. Broadway, Fairview* ☎ *604/872–7858* 🌐 *www.mec.ca.*

SPECIAL EVENTS

The Bank of Montreal Marathon is early May; the Scotiabank Half-Marathon and 5K are in June; the popular 10K Vancouver Sun Run is mid-April. And every New Year's Day since 1920, thousands of Vancouverites plunge into the frigid waters at English Bay beach—often in costume for the Polar Bear Swim.

BEACHES

Greater Vancouver is well endowed with beaches—from the pebbly coves of West Vancouver to a vast tableau of sand at Spanish Banks—but the waters are decidedly cool, even in summer, and, aside from the kids and the intrepid, the preferred activity is sunbathing. That said, the city provides several exceptional outdoor pools—right smack on the ocean. The most spectacular is Kitsilano Pool, where you can gander up at the North Shore Mountains while swimming lengths in this heated saltwater pool or splashing in its shallows. Beaches at Kitsilano, Spanish Banks, and nearby Locarno are popular beach-volleyball venues. At the city's historic beach and round-the-clock social venue, English Bay, you can swim, rent a kayak, or simply stroll with an ice cream cone and people-watch. Vancouver is also known for its clothing-optional beaches, the most celebrated being Wreck Beach, which reflects the city's cosmopolitan perspective.

All city beaches have lifeguards, washrooms, concession stands, and most have paid parking. Liquor and smoking are prohibited in parks and on beaches. With a few exceptions, dogs are not permitted on beaches.

Ambleside Park and Beach. West of the Lions Gate Bridge, this long stretch of sand is West Vancouver's most popular beach. There are tennis courts, volleyball nets, and a pool in the summer. This hidden gem of a beach area is just off Marine Drive at the foot of 13th Street. There are superb views of Stanley Park from all along the Seawalk. There's also a huge off-leash area for dogs. **Amenities**: food and drink; showers; toilets. **Best for:** sunrise; swimming; walking. ✉ *Argyle Ave. and 13th St., West Vancouver* 🌐 *www.vancouver.ca/parks/rec/beaches.*

English Bay Beach. The city's best-known beach, English Bay, lies just to the east of Stanley Park's southern entrance. A long stretch of sable sand, a waterslide, volleyball courts, kayak rentals, and street performers keep things interesting all summer. Known locally for being gay friendly, it draws a diverse crowd. **Amenities:** food and drink; lifeguards; parking (fee); toilets; water sports. **Best for:** partiers; sunset; swimming; walking. ✉ *1791 Beach Ave., between Gilford and Bidwell Sts., English Bay* ☎ *604/665–3424* 🌐 *www.vancouver.ca/parks/rec/beaches.*

Jericho Beach. Home of the Jericho Sailing Centre, this Point Grey destination is popular for windsurfing, especially at the western end. Swimmers can use the eastern section, where the expansive sands invite sunbathing. **Amenities:** food and drink; lifeguards; parking (fee); toilets; water sports. **Best for:** swimming; walking; windsurfing. ✉ *1300 Discovery St., West Point Grey* 🌐 *www.vancouver.ca/parks/rec/beaches.*

Fodor's Choice ★ **Kitsilano Beach.** West of the southern end of the Burrard Bridge, Kits Beach is the city's busiest beach—in-line skaters, volleyball players, and sleek young people are ever present. Facilities include a playground, restaurant, concession stand, and tennis courts. It's also good for windsurfing. **Kitsilano Pool** is here: at 137 meters (445 feet), it's the longest pool in Canada and one of the few heated saltwater pools in the world. **Amenities:** food and drink; lifeguards; parking (fee); toilets. **Best for:**

Beaches might not be the first thing you think of in Vancouver, but in summer Kits Beach and English Bay are hot spots.

sunrise; sunset; swimming; walking. ✉ *2305 Cornwall Ave., Kitsilano* ☎ *604/731–0011* 🌐 *www.vancouver.ca/parks/rec/beaches.*

Spanish Banks Beach. **Spanish Banks** and **Locarno** beaches begin at the start of Northwest Marine Drive and offer huge expanses of sunbathing sand backed by wide lawns full of picnic tables and, in areas, tall evergreens that offer shade. The shallow water, warmed slightly by sun and sand, is good for swimming. Farther out, toward Spanish Bank Extension, the beach becomes less crowded. Spanish Bank West and Locarno beaches are designated "quiet beaches." **Amenities:** food and drink; lifeguards; parking (free); toilets; water sports. **Best for:** swimming; walking; windsurfing. ✉ *NW Marine Drive, West of Tolmie Street, West Point Grey.*

Stanley Park. There are two fine beaches accessed from Stanley Park. The most popular with families is **Second Beach,** which has a small sandy area, a playground, and a large heated pool with a slide. **Third Beach** is a little quieter than the other central beaches. It has a larger stretch of sand, fairly warm water, and great sunset views. It's a popular evening picnic spot. **Amenities:** food and drink; lifeguards; parking (fee); toilets. **Best for:** sunset; swimming; walking. ✉ *8001 Stanley Park Dr.* 🌐 *www.vancouver.ca/parks/rec/beaches.*

Sunset Beach. Farther along Beach Avenue towards the Burrard Bridge, Sunset Beach, between Thurlow and Bute streets, is too close to the downtown core for clean, safe swimming, but is a great spot for an evening stroll, as well as taking your dog for a (off-leash optional) walk. It's also a "quiet" beach. You can catch a ferry to Granville Island here, or swim at the Vancouver Aquatic Centre, a public indoor pool and fitness center. **Amenities:** food and drink; lifeguards; parking (fee); toilets. **Best for:** sunset; walking. ✉ *Beach Ave. and Bute St., between Bute and Thurlow Sts. along Beach Ave., English Bay* ☎ *311.*

Trout Lake Beach. The only freshwater lake in the center of Vancouver, Trout Lake's sandy beach has a swimming raft and places to launch small kayaks. There's a designated off-leash area for dogs at the north end of the lake. Family picnics are popular here. **Amenities:** food and drink; lifeguards; parking (free); toilets. **Best for:** swimming; walking. ✉ *2120 E. 19th Ave., off Victoria Dr., Kensington-Cedar Cottage* ☎ *604/738–8535* 🌐 *www.vancouver.ca/parks/rec/beaches.*

Whytecliff Park. West Vancouver residents are fond of leaping from the cliffs along this rocky beach for a quick, cheap thrill. This calm cove is usually good for swimming and sunset-watching. Also along the north side of Burrard Inlet in West Vancouver are dozens of coveted retreats for in-the-know beach-seekers, including (from west to east) **Kew Beach, Caulfield Cove, Sandy Cove, West Bay,** and **Dundarave.** East of Marine Drive is a designated off-leash area for well-behaved dogs. **Amenities:** food and drink; parking (fee); toilets. **Best for:** sunset; swimming; walking. ✉ *7000 Marine Dr., west of Horseshoe Bay, West Vancouver* ☎ *604/925–7000* 🌐 *www.westvancouver.ca.*

Wreck Beach. Canada's largest clothing-optional beach is reached via a steep trail and flight of stairs from Gate 6, off Marine Drive. This 6-km-long (4-mile-long) wilderness beach, managed by a team of volunteers, has a delightfully anarchic culture. The driftwood is tangled, bathing suits are optional, and at Vendors Row, below Trail 6, you can buy an array of food, including pizza, homemade sandwiches, and buffalo burgers. You can get a pedicure, massage, or haircut; buy handmade jewelry; or indulge in a cocktail. Up to 14,000 people might visit this sandy beach on a summer weekend. There are no lifeguards. **Amenities:** food and drink. **Best for:** partiers; nudists; swimming; walking. ✉ *University of British Columbia Campus, Marine Dr.* 🌐 *www.wreckbeach.org.*

CYCLING

Although Vancouver has always sported a bike-friendly culture, the 2011 Vancouver Downtown Separated Bike Lanes program made biking even easier. This system of bike lanes protects cyclists by placing a barrier between them and traffic. Look for the lanes downtown, especially along Hornsby Street and Dunsmuir Street. These lanes are in addition to the 16 interconnected bikeways, identified by green bicycle signs, that the city introduced in time for hosting the Olympics.

Vancouver cycling routes connect with those in nearby communities. Most routes do share the road with cars, but they're safe and include cyclist-activated signals and other bike-friendly measures. Many TransLink buses have bike racks, and bikes are welcome on the SeaBus and on the SkyTrain at off-peak times. Aquabus Ferries transport bikes and riders across False Creek. If cycling is a key component of your visit, check online with the Vancouver Area Cycling Coalition (🌐 *www.vacc.bc.ca*).

There are detailed maps and other information on the website operated by the City of Vancouver (⊕ *www.vancouver.ca/engsvcs/transport/cycling*). Cycling maps are also available from most bike shops and bike-rental outlets. Helmets are required by law, and a sturdy lock is essential.

Seaside Trek. Mostly on paved bike paths, the 9-mile Seaside Trek starts in English Bay and ends at the University of British Columbia, passing through False Creek along the way. ✉ *Beach Ave. at Gilford St., English Bay.*

Fodor's Choice ★ **Stanley Park Seaside Route.** Vancouver's most popular bike path is the 6½-mile Stanley Park Seaside Route, which follows the perimeter of Stanley Park, hugging the harbor along the way. From here, the views of Lion's Gate Bridge and the mountains to the north are breathtaking. This path converges with the Seaside Trek if you feel like making a day of it. ■ **TIP→ Rent your bike near the entrance to Stanley Park, as there are no rentals once you're inside.** ✉ *W. Georgia St. and Stanley Park Dr., Stanley Park* ☎ *604/873–7526* ⊕ *www.vancouver.ca/engsvcs/transport/cycling.*

BIKE RENTALS

Most bike-rental outlets also rent Rollerblades and jogging strollers. Cycling helmets, a legal requirement in Vancouver, come with the rentals. Locks and maps are also normally supplied.

Bayshore Bike Rentals. If you're starting your ride near Stanley Park, try this friendly store. It has a wide range of bikes as well as baby joggers and bike trailers. ✉ *745 Denman St., West End* ☎ *604/688–2453* ⊕ *www.bayshorebikerentals.ca.*

Reckless Bike Stores. This outfit rents bikes on the Yaletown section of the Seaside Bicycle Route. To explore Granville Island, check out the branch at 1810 Fir Street in Kitsilano. ✉ *110 Davie St., Yaletown* ☎ *604/648–2600* ⊕ *www.reckless.ca* ✉ *1810 Fir St., at 2nd Ave., Kitsilano* ☎ *604/731–2420* ⊕ *www.reckless.ca.*

Spokes Bicycle Rentals. Located near Stanley Park, Spokes has a wide selection of mountain bikes, tandem bikes, and children's bikes. Everything from hourly to weekly rentals is available. Helmets, locks, and route maps are complimentary. ✉ *1798 W. Georgia St., West End* ☎ *604/688–5141* ⊕ *www.spokesbicyclerentals.com.*

MOUNTAIN BIKING

Mountain biking may be a worldwide phenomenon, but its most radical expression, known as free-riding, was born in the 1990s on the steep-and-rugged North Shore Mountains. Here, the mostly young thrill-seekers ride ultra-heavy-duty bikes through gnarly forests, along log-strewn trails, over rocky precipices, and down stony stream beds (not to mention along obstacles like planks and teeter-totters)—and live to tell about it. This anarchic culture can be explored at the website operated by North Shore Mountain Biking (⊕ *www.nsmb.com*).

Lower Seymour Conservation Reserve. Nestled into the precipitous North Shore Mountains, this reserve has 25 km (15.5 miles) of challenging rain-forest trails through alpine meadows, forested slopes, and river flood plains. The meandering **Seymour Valley Trailway** is a 10-km (6-mile) paved pathway, suitable for cyclists, in-line skaters, baby strollers, and wheelchairs. Other trails, like Corkscrew and Salvation, are classified as advanced or even extreme. ✉ *End of Lillooet Rd., North Vancouver* ☎ *604/432–6286* 🌐 *www.metrovancouver.org.*

Pacific Spirit Regional Park. Beautifully sited on the Point Grey peninsula on Vancouver's west side, Pacific Spirit sits close to the University of British Columbia. Open year-round from dawn to dusk, it includes 38 km (23.5 miles) of trails for cycling and horseback riding. ✉ *4915 W. 16th Ave., Point Grey* ☎ *604/224–5739* 🌐 *www.greatervancouverparks.com.*

MOUNTAIN BIKE RENTALS

Cove Bike Shop. In the village of Deep Cove on Indian Arm, the Cove Bike Shop pioneered the design and construction of mountain bikes for this punishing terrain. Given the huge insurance costs, it's the only bike shop that rents them. Bikes of all types and sizes are available from March through October. ✉ *1389 Main St., North Vancouver* ☎ *604/929–2222* 🌐 *www.covebike.com.*

DIVING

The rugged coastline of southwestern British Columbia offers excellent and varied diving with vistas of below surface sheer rock walls and thick plots of plumose anemones. From late summer through winter, when water clarity is best and allows visibility of up to 100 feet, the region delivers some of the most spectacular temperate-water (avg. mid-40 F) diving in the world, including sightings of the North Pacific Giant Octopus. Dry suits are imperative.

Rowand's Reef Scuba Shop. On Granville Island, this PADI-certified scuba and snorkeling business specializes in year-round diving trips to Howe Sound. Courses are also available. ✉ *1512 Duranleau St., Granville Island* ☎ *604/669–3483* 🌐 *www.rowandsreef.com.*

ECOTOURS AND WILDLIFE VIEWING

Given a temperate climate and forest, mountain, and marine environments teeming with life, it's no surprise that wildlife-watching is an important pastime and growing business in and around Vancouver. Many people walk the ocean foreshores or park and mountain trails, binoculars or scopes in hand, looking for exceptional or rare birds. Others venture onto the water to see seals, sea lions, and whales—as well as the birds that inhabit the maritime world.

Sewell's Marina. This marina near the protected waters of Howe Sound runs year-round, two-hour ecotours of the surrounding marine and coastal mountain habitat. Sightings range from swimming seals to soaring eagles. High-speed rigid inflatable hulls are used. ✉ *6409 Bay St., Horseshoe Bay, West Vancouver* ☎ *604/921–3474* 🌐 *www.sewellsmarina.com.*

Whale-watching tours—humpbacks, minkes, orcas—from Vancouver (or Victoria) are popular.

BIRD- AND EAGLE-WATCHING

Brackendale Eagles Provincial Park. Between mid-November and mid-February, the world's largest concentration of bald eagles gathers to feed on salmon at Brackendale Eagles Provincial Park, about an hour north of Vancouver on the scenic Sea-to-Sky Highway. **■ TIP→ The Brackendale Art Gallery has a teahouse that's a good place to stop along the way.** ✉ *Government Rd., off Hwy. 99, Brackendale.*

Canadian Outback Adventures. This outfit runs "eagle safari" trips that allow you to watch and photograph eagles from a slow-moving raft on the Cheakamus River. Transportation from Vancouver is available. ✉ *332 East Esplanade, North Vancouver* ☎ *604/921–7250, 800/565–8735* 🌐 *www.canadianoutback.com.*

George C. Reifel Migratory Bird Sanctuary. More than 260 species of migratory birds visit this 850-acre site on Westham Island, about an hour south of Vancouver. A seasonal highlight is the arrival of an estimated 80,000 Lesser Snow Geese in the late fall. ✉ *5191 Robertson Rd., Delta* ☎ *604/946–6980* 🌐 *www.reifelbirdsanctuary.com* 🎫 *C$4* 🕘 *Daily 9–4.*

Vancouver All-Terrain Adventures. Day trips to Brackendale include pickup in Vancouver in a four-wheel drive, and an option to watch the eagles by raft or horseback. ✉ *375 West 2nd Ave., Olympic Village* ☎ *778/371–7830, 888/754–5601* 🌐 *www.all-terrain.com.*

SEA LION–VIEWING

In April and early May thousands of male California sea lions and larger Steller sea lions settle on rocks near the mouth of the Fraser River to feed on the eulachon, a member of the smelt family. Sightseeing boats make the short trip from Steveston into the estuary.

Steveston Seabreeze Adventures. From docks in Steveston village in Richmond, south of Vancouver, Seabreeze motors into the sea lion's natural habitat. During the autumn bird migratory season, Seabreeze also takes bird-watchers by boat along the Fraser Estuary to the Reifel Bird Sanctuary on Westham Island. ✉ *12551 No. 1 Rd., Richmond* ☎ *604/272–7200* 🌐 *www.seabreezeadventures.ca.*

WHALE-WATCHING

Between April and October pods of orca whales travel through the Strait of Georgia, near Vancouver. The area is also home to harbor seals, elephant seals, bald eagles, minke whales, porpoises, and a wealth of birdlife. Other migrating whales include humpbacks and grays.

Lotus Land Tours. High-speed covered boats take you out to watch for whales and other wildlife in the Strait of Georgia. The five-hour cruise costs C$175 per adult and includes lunch and a pickup anywhere in Vancouver. The company also offers kayaking tours in Indian Arm and the Gulf Islands, as well as white-water rafting trips on the Elaho and Squamish rivers. ✉ *1251 Cardero St., West End* ☎ *604/684–4922, 800/528–3531* 🌐 *www.lotuslandtours.com.*

Prince of Whales. This established Victoria operator runs four-hour trips from Vancouver's downtown waterfront (near Waterfront Station) across the Georgia Strait in season. ✉ *812 Wharf St., Victoria* ☎ *888/383–4884* 🌐 *www.princeofwhales.com.*

Wild Whales Vancouver. Boats leave Granville Island in search of orca pods in the Georgia Strait, often traveling as far as Victoria. Rates are C$125 for a three to seven-hour trip in either an open or glass-domed boat. Each boat leaves once daily, April through October, conditions permitting. ✉ *1806 Mast Tower Rd., Granville Island* ☎ *604/699–2011* 🌐 *www.whalesvancouver.ca.*

FISHING

You can fish for salmon all year in coastal British Columbia, weather and marine conditions permitting. Halibut, at 50 pounds and heavier, is the area's other trophy fish. Charters ply waters between the Capilano River mouth in Burrard Inlet and the outer Georgia Strait and Gulf Islands. Your fishing license can be purchased from the boat rental or tour operator.

Bonnie Lee Fishing Charters. From moorings in the Granville Island Maritime Market, this company runs five-hour fishing trips into Burrard Inlet and the Georgia Strait year-round. Guided outings start at C$395 per person. ✉ *104–1676 Duranleau St., Granville Island* ☎ *604/290–7447* 🌐 *www.bonnielee.com.*

GOLF

Vancouver-area golf courses offer golfing with great scenery. Most are open year-round. Three championship golf courses are operated by the city, meaning they are more affordable. To reserve up to 30 days in advance, contact the Vancouver Board of Parks and Recreation (🌐 *www.vancouver.ca/parks/golf*).

Just want to practice? Pitch & Putt courses are 18-hole putting greens that are perfect for beginner golfers. The best one is near the entrance to Stanley Park, next to a spectacular rhododendron garden. A round costs C$12.95.

Fodor's Choice ★ **Fraserview Golf Course.** The most celebrated of Vancouver's public courses, the 18-hole Fraserview Golf Course sits on 225 heavily wooded acres overlooking the Fraser River. It has a tree-lined fairway, a driving range, and a lovely clubhouse. There's a golf institute staffed with instructors who teach players of all levels. Golf carts are available on a first-come, first-served basis. ✉ *7800 Vivian Dr., South Vancouver* ☎ *604/257–6923, 604/280–1818 advance bookings* 🌐 *www.vancouver.ca/parks/golf* *18 holes. 6,700 yds. Par 72. Greens Fee: C$35* ☞ *Driving range, putting green, pitching area, golf carts, rental clubs, pro-shop, golf academy/lessons.*

3

Langara Golf Course. Its central location and highly walkable green are two features that make the public Langara Golf Course a great golf getaway, even if you have only part of a day. There's a clubhouse with large-screen TVs tuned to the day's sporting events, and plenty of free parking. The greens fees are about half the price of its more celebrated sister course, the Fraserview Golf Course. It does not, however, have a driving range. ✉ *6706 Alberta St., South Vancouver* ☎ *604/713–1816* 🌐 *www.vancouver.ca/parks/golf* *Putting green, pitching area, golf carts, pull carts, rental clubs, pro-shop, restaurant, bar* ☞ *18 holes. 6,261 yds. Par 71. Greens Fee: C$25.*

Last Minute Golf. For advance tee time bookings at about 20 Vancouver-area courses, or for a spur-of-the-moment game, call Last Minute Golf. The company matches golfers and courses, sometimes at substantial greens-fee discounts. ☎ *604/878–1833, 800/684–6344* 🌐 *www.lastminutegolfbc.com.*

McCleery Golf Course. Want to practice your putting and driving? With its expansive greens, the McCleery Golf Course is the best place in Vancouver. The public course is located on the north banks of the Fraser River and has the best views from the 9th and 18th greens. There's also an on-site golf academy particularly geared toward less experienced golfers. ✉ *7188 MacDonald St., South Vancouver* ☎ *604/257–8191* 🌐 *www.vancouver.ca/parks/golf* *18 holes. 6,527 yds. Par 72. Greens Fee: C$25* ☞ *Driving range, putting green, pitching area, golf carts, pull carts, rental clubs, pro-shop, golf academy/lessons, restaurant, bar.*

Northlands Golf Course. Just 20 minutes from downtown, Northlands may be Vancouver's best-kept secret. Douglas firs line the fairways, which make it feel like a course at Whistler or Vancouver Island. The public course's greens and fairways are well maintained. ✉ *3400 Anne Macdonald Way, North Vancouver* ☎ *604/280–1111* 🌐 *www.golfnorthlands.com* *18 holes. 6,504 yds. Par 72. Greesn Fee: C$70* ☞ *Golf carts, pull carts, caddies, rental clubs, pro-shop, restaurant, bar.*

Northview Golf and Country Club. In the rolling terrain southeast of Vancouver, this lovely golf club is home to two Arnold Palmer–designed courses. The Ridge Course crosses meandering streams, while the Canal

Course has wide fairways and undulating greens. An optional cart at either course costs C$36. There's a strict dress code: no jeans or T-shirts allowed. ✉ *6857 168th St., Surrey* ☎ *604/576–4653, 888/574–2211* 🌐 *www.northviewgolf.com* *Ridge Course: 18 holes. 6,900 yds. Par 72. Greens Fee: C$58. Canal Course: 18 holes. 7,100 yds. Par 72. Greens Fee: C$48* ☞ *Driving range, putting green, golf carts, pull carts, caddies, rental clubs, pro-shop, golf academy/lessons, restaurant, bar.*

Seymour Golf and Country Club. This semiprivate course's fairways wind around towering old-growth fir and cedar trees at the foot of Mt. Seymour. It's open to the public on Monday and Friday, and has a fairly strict dress code. ✉ *3723 Mt. Seymour Pkwy., North Vancouver* ☎ *604/929–2611* 🌐 *www.seymourgolf.com* *18 holes. 6.291 yds. Par 72. Greens Fee: C$78* ☞ *Driving range, putting green, golf carts, pull carts, caddies, rental clubs, pro-shop, golf academy/lessons, restaurant, bar.*

University Golf Club. On the Point Grey peninsula, this challenging 1929 course includes a clubhouse and restaurant and is home to the British Columbia Golf Museum. The course's narrow fairways, lined with old-growth trees, appeals to golfers of all skill levels. ✉ *5185 University Blvd., Point Grey* ☎ *604/224–1818* 🌐 *www.universitygolf.com* *18 holes. 6560 yds. Par 71. Green Fee: C$67* ☞ *Driving range, putting green, pitching area, golf carts, caddies, rental clubs, pro-shop, golf academy/lessons, restaurant, bar.*

Westwood Plateau Golf and Country Club. This well-manicured course is located just east of the city. In addition to a pro shop and other amenities, the club has a restaurant that's open seasonally. The 9-hole executive course includes a driving range. The courses are open April to October. ✉ *3251 Plateau Blvd., Coquitlam* ☎ *604/552–0777, 604/945–4007* 🌐 *www.westwoodplateaugolf.com* *18 holes. 6,770 yds. Par 72. Greens Fee: C$125* ☞ *Driving range, golf carts, pull carts, caddies, rental clubs, pro-shop, golf academy/lessons, restaurant, bar.*

HEALTH, FITNESS, AND YOGA

Vancouver embraces health and wellness. Public and private gyms are well patronized. There are myriad martial arts, yoga, and Pilates classes offered around the city. If you're craving a fitness fix, you'll easily find something that suits you.

Bentall Centre Athletic Club. Specializing in squash, the Bentall Centre also has racquetball courts and weight and cardio gyms. Aerobics and yoga classes are given as well. The drop-in fee is C$15, and you can also call ahead for a free one-day pass. ✉ *4 Bentall Centre, 1055 Dunsmuir St., Downtown* ☎ *604/689–4424* 🌐 *www.bentallcentreathleticclub.com.*

Coal Harbour Community Centre. Operated by the Vancouver Board of Parks and Recreation, this ultramodern facility is shaped like a ship. On the Coal Harbour seawall, it's conveniently close to downtown hotels and has a fitness center with drop-in classes that cost around C$15. ✉ *480 Broughton St., West End* ☎ *604/718–8222* 🌐 *www.westendcc.ca.*

★ **Richmond Olympic Oval.** For the 2010 Olympic Games, the neighborhood of Richmond received this speed-skating oval along the Fraser River. The

CLOSE UP

Sea 'n' Ski

Given the proximity of water to mountain or bike path to swimming pool, and the ease of getting around by bike, bus, car, ferry, or even in-line skates, it's definitely possible to undertake two or more outdoor activities in a single day. Cross-trainers, this is the place for you.

If you're going to multitask, though, it's a good idea to plan ahead, and if you need to rent equipment, do so in advance. In the interest of making the most of your time, and ensuring your safety, download maps and other descriptive information you may need. If you're venturing off the beaten path, be sure you're dressed suitably, have emergency food and gear, and leave notification of where you're headed and when you'll return.

And you're off. The possibilities are almost endless, but here are some pointers for combining activities:

Kayaking in False Creek: The waters are usually tranquil in early morning so it's a good time to savor the pleasures of traveling at sea level.

Jogging around Stanley Park: Early-morning joggers have the seawall pretty much to themselves.

Swimming in Kitsilano Pool: Early morning is considered by many to be the best time to hit the lanes at the heated saltwater pool.

Cycling the Greenway: By midmorning, all but the city's major arterial streets should be relatively calm. This may be the time to cycle the network of bicycle routes.

Fishing or wildlife-watching: In all but the worst weather, you can rent a boat for a few hours spent in pursuit of salmon, or join a tour in search of whales, sea lions, or eagles.

Tennis or beach volleyball: Late afternoon is a good time to head to Kitsilano Beach for a volleyball game, or to Stanley Park, or one of the other 180 tennis courts in Vancouver, for a game of tennis.

Golf at Fraserview: A warm summer evening is the ideal time to golf at the most celebrated of the city's three public golf courses—all of which lie on the city's south-facing slope.

Night skiing at Grouse: On a crisp winter night, there's no better place to be than on the slopes of Grouse Mountain. The canopy of stars will glitter, while below, the city dazzles.

facility, with a gorgeous glass-and-steel design, contains Olympic-size ice rinks, six basketball courts, and a huge fitness center. It's a 15-minute walk from the Canada Line. Day passes cost C$16.50. ✉ *6111 River Rd., Richmond* ☎ *778/296–1400* 🌐 *www.richmondoval.ca.*

Robert Lee YMCA. Completely renovated in 2010, this downtown YMCA has the latest in fitness facilities—an indoor pool, sports courts, and yoga areas. ✉ *955 Burrard St., Downtown* ☎ *604/689–9622* 🌐 *www.robertleeymca.ca.*

Semperviva Yoga Studios. Based in Kitsilano, this major yoga operator runs four studios—including one called the Sea Studio in a former fish factory on Granville Island overlooking False Creek. The drop-in fee is C$16. ✉ *Pier 32 Bldg., 1333 Johnston St., Granville Island* ☎ *604/739–1958* 🌐 *www.semperviva.com.*

3

Vancouver Olympic Centre. Every visitor to Canada should consider experiencing curling at least once—it's the country's national pastime. At this sports facility, built for the 2010 Olympics, you can push off the "hack" to toss the 42-pound rock over the "pebbles" in hopes of at least a "biter." Renovated in 2011, the facility also has an indoor/outdoor aquatic center. ✉ *4575 Clancy Loranger Way, Riley Park* ☎ *604/873–7000* 🌐 *www.vancouver.ca/parks/info/2010olympics/hillcrest.htm.*

YWCA. With three weight rooms (one reserved for women), an ozone pool, cardio room, hot tub and steam room, and aerobics and yoga classes, the YWCA has it all. The day rate is C$16. ✉ *535 Hornby St., Downtown* ☎ *604/895–5766* 🌐 *www.ywcahealthandfitness.com.*

HIKING

With its expansive landscape of mountains, inlets, alpine lakes, and approachable glaciers, as well as low-lying rivers, hills, dikes, and meadows, southwestern British Columbia is a hiker's paradise. That said, areas and trails should be approached with physical ability and stamina in mind. The North Shore Mountains, for example, may appear benign, but this is a vast and rugged territory filled with natural pitfalls and occasionally hostile wildlife, and you should exercise great caution. The Baden-Powell Trail is a roughly 48-km (30-mile) trail for only the ablest hikers; it extends the entire length of the North Shore Mountains, from Horseshoe Bay to Deep Cove, passing through both Cypress Provincial Park and Mount Seymour Provincial Park. Every year, hikers wander off clearly marked trails, or outside well-posted public areas, with tragic results. If you're heading into the mountains, hike with a companion, pack warm clothes (even in summer), and extra food and water, and leave word of your route and the time you expect to return. Remember that weather can change quickly in the mountains.

Environment Canada. It's always a good idea to check the weather forecast with Environment Canada. 🌐 *www.weatheroffice.gc.ca.*

In addition to the Mountain Equipment Co-op, there are several places around town for good books, maps, and advice.

International Travel Maps & Books. The well-regarded International Travel Maps & Books publishes its own maps, and is also the local distributor for the Canada Map Office, stocking federally made topographic maps and charts of the region. ✉ *12300 Bridgeport Rd., Richmond* ☎ *604/273–1400* 🌐 *www.itmb.ca.*

Wanderlust. A major supplier of goods and gear for travelers, Wanderlust has a well-stocked section of maps and guidebooks. ✉ *1929 W. 4th Ave., Kitsilano* ☎ *604/739–2182* 🌐 *www.wanderlustore.com.*

PARKS AND RESERVES

Fodor's Choice ★ **Capilano River Regional Park.** This small but spectacular park is where you'll find old-growth fir trees approaching 61 meters (200 feet). In addition to 26 km (16 miles) of hiking trails in and around Capilano Canyon, there are a dramatic suspension bridge and a salmon hatchery that's open to the public. The park is at the end of Capilano Park

Road in North Vancouver. ✉ *4063–4077 Capilano Park Rd., North Vancouver* ☎ *604/224–5739* 🌐 *www.metrovancouver.org.*

Cultus Lake Provincial Park. About 11 km (7 miles) southwest of Chilliwack is Cultus Lake, known for its great fishing and water sports. All five types of salmon live here, as well as rainbow, steelhead, and cutthroat trout. In summer, a free fishing camp for kids under 16 is offered by the Freshwater Fisheries Society of British Columbia. There are also waterskiing, windsurfing, and swimming, as well as hiking. The Cascade Mountains, where you'll find Cultus Lake, are about an hour and a half east of Vancouver. ✉ *4150 Columbia Valley Hwy., off Hwy. 1, Cultus Lake* ☎ *604/858–7241.*

Cypress Provincial Park. This 3,012-hectare (7,442-acre) park sprawls above Howe Sound, embracing the Strachan, Black, and Hollyburn mountains. On a clear day you can see Mt. Baker (in Washington State) and Vancouver Island. While the park includes a commercial ski and biking area operated by Cypress Bowl Resorts, much of the terrain is a public hiking paradise (bikes are permitted on roadways, but not on hiking trails). This is backcountry, though, and only experienced hikers should attempt the more remote routes, including the Baden-Powell and Howe Sound Crest trails, which traverse this mountain region. ✉ *Cypress Bowl Rd., off Hwy. 1, West Vancouver* ☎ *604/926–5612* 🌐 *www.env.gov.bc.ca.*

Garibaldi Provincial Park. About 97 km (60 miles) north of Vancouver, Garibaldi Provincial Park is a serious hiker's dream. You can't miss it: the 8,786-foot (2,678-m) peak of Mount Garibaldi kisses the heavens just north of Squamish. Alpine meadows and wildlife viewing await you on trails leading to Black Tusk, Diamond Head, Cheakamus Lake, Elfin Lakes, and Singing Pass. Mountain goat and bald eagles are found throughout the park. If you venture into the Red Heather area, also be prepared for black bears. This is truly one of Canada's most spectacular wildernesses, and being easily accessible from Vancouver makes it even more appealing. A compass is mandatory, as are food and water, rain gear, a flashlight, and a first aid kit. There are also two medium to advanced mountain bike trails. Take seriously the glacier hazards and avalanche warnings. Snow tires are necessary in winter. ✉ *Hwy. 99, between Squamish and Pemberton, Squamish-Lillooet* ☎ *800/689–9025.*

Golden Ears Provincial Park. Hiking, horseback riding, and swimming in Alouette Lake are popular pastimes in Golden Ears Provincial Park. There are also windsurfing, waterskiing, boating, and fishing in these traditional lands of the Coast Salish and Interior Salish First Nations peoples. When it was split off from Garibaldi Provincial Park in 1927, Golden Ears earned its name from the twin peaks of Mount Blanshard. Binoculars come in handy for wildlife viewing like beaver, deer, mountain goat. ⚠ **Be on your guard, as there are frequent black bear sightings.** ✉ *Fern Crescent Rd., Maple Ridge* ☎ *604/466–8325.*

★ **Grouse Mountain.** Vancouver's most famous, or infamous, hiking route, the Grind, is a 2.9-km (1.8-mile) climb straight up 2,500 vertical feet to the top of Grouse Mountain. Thousands do it annually, but climbers are advised to be very experienced and in excellent physical condition. The route is open daily, 6:30 am to 7:30 pm, from spring through autumn (conditions permitting). Or you can take the Grouse Mountain Skyride to the top 365 days a year; a round-trip ticket is C$39.95. There are additional hiking trails accessible from the gondola, including the Goat Mountain Trail, which can take you even farther up. At the ski resort, drop-in ski and snowboard lessons are C$125, including lift and equipment rental. ✉ *6400 Nancy Greene Way, North Vancouver* ☎ *604/980–9311* 🌐 *www.grousemountain.com.*

Indian Arm Provincial Park. This somewhat remote region of rugged mountains, alpine lakes, vigorous creeks, and the 150-foot-high Granite Falls lies just east of Vancouver along an 18-km (11-mile) fjord called Indian Arm. The park is co-managed by the Tsleil-Waututh Nation, who have lived here since "time out of mind." There's boating, kayaking, scuba diving, and fishing, as well as excellent hiking opportunities through old-growth forests. Most trails are steep and are not for novices. Downloadable maps are available at 🌐 *vancouver.ca/maps.htm.* At this writing the access road was closed, making the park accessible only by boat. ✉ *On the eastern and western shores of Indian Arm, North Vancouver* ☎ *604/990–3800.*

★ **Lighthouse Park.** This 75-hectare (185-acre) wilderness wraps around the historic lighthouse at Point Atkinson, where Howe Sound meets Burrard Inlet in the municipality of West Vancouver. A bank of soaring granite (popular for picnicking) shapes the foreshore, while the interior is an undulating terrain of mostly Douglas fir, arbutus, and rich undergrowth. Three miles of trails, from easy to challenging, bring you close to the birds and other wildlife. ✉ *Beacon La., off Marine Dr., West Vancouver* ☎ *604/925–7200* 🌐 *www.westvancouver.ca.*

Lower Seymour Conservation Reserve. This 5,668-hectare (14,000-acre) reserve includes 25 km (15.5 mi) of hiking trails, some steep and challenging. ✉ *End of Lillooet Rd., North Vancouver* ☎ *604/432–6286.*

Mount Seymour Provincial Park. Located 30 minutes from downtown Vancouver, this 3,508-hectare (14,683-acre) wilderness park offers 14 hiking trails of varying length and difficulty and spectacular views of the Lower Mainland. Warm clothing—and caution—are advised. Routes include access to the Baden-Powell Trail, which continues northwest to Horseshoe Bay. You can also hike 3.2 km (just under 2 miles) down to Deep Cove on Indian Arm. In winter, the trails are used for snowshoeing, and there's a supervised snow play area. ✉ *Mount Seymour Rd., off Seymour Pkwy., North Vancouver* 🌐 *www.env.gov.bc.ca.*

Pacific Spirit Regional Park. A 763-hectare (1,185-acre) forest, Pacific Spirit has 54 km (33 miels) of walking and hiking trails around Point Grey. It sits on Vancouver's west side, close to the University of British Columbia. Open dawn to dusk year-round, it provide access to beaches on Burrard Inlet and Georgia Strait. ✉ *4915 W. 16th Ave.* ☎ *604/224–5739* 🌐 *www.metrovancouver.org.*

The hike up Grouse Mountain is no easy feat, but the views from the top, and from Goat Mountain, slightly farther up, are breathtaking. Or you can always take the Skyride (gondola).

Fodor's Choice ★ **Stanley Park.** With its moderate walking and easy hiking paths, it's no wonder that Stanley Park attracts 8 million visitors annually. The most picturesque route is the 8.8-km (5½-mile) seawall around its perimeter, but the 1,000-acre park also offers 27 km (167 miles) of well-maintained trails through the coniferous forest, including patches of old growth forest. Here you'll experience a true rain forest and spot birds and small mammals. An easy interior trail runs around Lost Lagoon, and Beaver Lake is a popular destination. Vancouver Aquarium's beluga whales are not to be missed. ✉ *Northern end of Georgia St.* ☎ *604/602–3088* 🌐 *www.vancouver.ca/parks/parks/stanley.*

GUIDED HIKES

Novice hikers and serious walkers can join guided trips or do self-guided walks of varying approach and difficulty. Grouse Mountain hosts several daily "eco-walks" along easy, meandering paths. Discussion of flora and fauna and a visit to the Refuge for Endangered Wildlife is included. They're free with admission to Grouse Mountain Skyride.

Rockwood Adventures. This company gives guided walks of rain forest or coastal terrain, including Lighthouse Park, Lynn and Capilano canyons, and Bowen Island in Howe Sound. It also offers walking tours of Vancouver with an emphasis on wine and food. ✉ *6578 Acorn Rd., Sechelt* ☎ *604/980–7749, 888/236–6606* 🌐 *www.rockwoodadventures.com.*

HOCKEY

The Canucks have sold out every game since 2004, though tickets can be purchased at legal resale outlets. Watching NHL hockey in a Canadian city is one of sport's greatest spectacles, so try and catch a game, if possible at BC Place or Rogers Arena. If you can't attend in person, head into any bar on game night, especially Saturday, which is "Hockey Night" in Canada.

Vancouver Canucks. The city's most beloved sports team, the Vancouver Canucks, plays at Rogers Arena. ✉ *800 Griffiths Way, Downtown* ☎ *604/899–7676* 🌐 *canucks.nhl.com.*

JOGGING

Vancouverites jog at any time of day, in almost any weather, and dozens of well-trodden routes go through the leafy streets of the city's west side. The seawall around the downtown peninsula remains the most popular route, though the hilly byways of the North Shore are also popular with serious runners. Visiting runners staying downtown will be drawn to the 10-km (6.2-mile) route around Stanley Park, or the 4-km (2.5-mile) circuit around Lost Lagoon.

Running Room. This Canadian-based business is a good source of advice and downloadable route maps. There are many other branches around the city and throughout British Columbia. A running club leaves from this location at 6 pm on Wednesday and 8:30 am on Sunday. ✉ *679 Denman St., Suite 103, West End* ☎ *604/684–9771* 🌐 *www.runningroom.com* ✉ *1578 W. Broadway, Central Vancouver* ☎ *604/879–9721* 🌐 *www.runningroom.com.*

SKIING AND SNOWBOARDING

While Whistler Resort, a two-hour drive from Vancouver, is the top-ranked ski destination in the region, the North Shore Mountains hold three excellent ski and snowboard areas. All have rentals, lessons, night skiing, and a variety of runs suitable for all skill levels. Grouse Mountain can be reached by TransLink buses. Cypress and Seymour each run shuttle buses from Lonsdale Quay and other North Shore stops.

Although ski areas and trails are generally well marked, once you ski outside the boundaries you're entering rugged wilderness that can be distinctly unfriendly to humans. Pay close attention to maps and signposts. The ski season generally runs from early December through early spring.

DOWNHILL SKIING AND SNOWBOARDING

Cypress Mountain. The newest of three North Shore commercial ski resorts, Cypress Mountain is nonetheless well equipped, and was made even more so with the completion of freestyle skiing and snowboarding venues built for the 2010 Winter Olympics. Facilities include five quad or double chairs, 38 downhill runs, and a vertical drop of 1,750 feet. The resort has a snow-tubing area and snowshoe tours. This is also a major cross-country skiing area. ✉ *Cypress Bowl Rd., West Vancouver* ☎ *604/419–7669* 🌐 *www.cypressmountain.com.*

Grouse Mountain. Reached by gondola from the upper reaches of North Vancouver, much of the Grouse Mountain ski resort inhabits a slope overlooking the city. Although the views are fine on a clear day, at night (the area is known for its night skiing) they're spectacular. Facilities include two quad chairs, 26 skiing and snowboarding runs, and several all level freestyle terrain parks. The vertical drop is 1,210 feet. There's a choice of upscale and casual dining in a handsome stone-and-timber lodge. ✉ *6400 Nancy Greene Way, North Vancouver* ☎ *604/980–9311, 604/986–6262 snow report* 🌐 *www.grousemountain.com.*

Mount Seymour. A full-service winter activity area, the Mount Seymour ski resort sprawls over 200 acres accessed from eastern North Vancouver. With three chairs for varying abilities; a beginner's rope tow, equipment rentals, and lessons; and toboggan and tubing runs, it's a popular destination for families. Snowboarding is particularly popular. The eateries aren't fancy. ✉ *1700 Mt. Seymour Rd., North Vancouver* 🌐 *www.mountseymour.com.*

WATER SPORTS

BOATING AND SAILING

With an almost limitless number and variety of waterways—from Indian Arm near Vancouver, up Howe Sound and the Sunshine Coast, across Georgia Strait to the Gulf Islands, and on to Vancouver Island, southwestern British Columbia is a boater's paradise. And much of this territory has easy access to marine and public services. One caution: this ocean territory is vast and complex; maritime maps are required. Always consult the Environment Canada marine forecasts (🌐 *www.weatheroffice.gc.ca*).

Blue Pacific Yacht Charters. This company rents speedboats and sailboats for cruising between Vancouver Island and Seattle, including the San Juan Islands, Southern Gulf Islands, and the Sunshine Coast. ✉ *1519 Foreshore Walk, Granville Island* ☎ *604/682–2161, 800/237–2392* 🌐 *www.bluepacificcharters.ca.*

Cooper Boating. Chartered sailboats and cabin cruisers, with or without skippers, are available at Cooper Boating. ✉ *1815 Mast Tower Rd., Granville Island* ☎ *604/687–4110, 888/999–6419* 🌐 *www.cooperboating.com.*

CANOEING AND KAYAKING

Kayaking—seagoing and river kayaking—has become something of a lifestyle in Vancouver. While many sea kayakers start out (or remain) in False Creek, others venture into the open ocean and up and down the Pacific Coast. You can white-water kayak or canoe down the Capilano River and several other North Vancouver rivers. And paddling in a traditional, seagoing aboriginal-built canoe is an increasingly popular way to experience the maritime landscape.

Deep Cove Canoe and Kayak Centre. Ocean-kayak rentals, guided excursions, and lessons for everyone in the family are available between June and September at this company's base in North Vancouver. Winter paddling tours are also available. ✉ *2156 Banbury Rd., North Vancouver* ☎ *604/929–2268* 🌐 *www.deepcovekayak.com.*

DID YOU KNOW?

Seeing the scenery from a kayak or canoe is an unforgettable experience. Tours for beginners and advanced boaters can be arranged at the many Vancouver-area kayak and canoe centers.

Ecomarine Ocean Kayak Centre. Lessons and rentals are offered year-round from this well-regarded company's main branch on Granville Island. There are also locations at Jericho Beach and English Bay. ✉ *1668 Duranleau St., Granville Island* ☎ *604/689–7575, 888/425–2925* 🌐 *www.ecomarine.com* ✉ *English Bay Bath House, 668 Duranleau St., English Bay* ☎ *604/689–7575* 🌐 *www.ecomarine.com* ✉ *1300 Discovery St., Jericho Beach* ☎ *604/222–3565.*

★ **Takaya Tours.** A trip with Takaya Tours is a unique experience: you can paddle a 45-foot oceangoing canoe while First Nations guides relay local legends, sing traditional songs, and point out the sites of ancient villages. The two-hour tours leave from Cates Park in North Vancouver or Belcarra Park in Port Moody. There are also trips along the Burrard Inlet and up Indian Arm on motorized kayaks. Reservations are essential. ✉ *700 Apex Ave.* ☎ *604/904–7410* 🌐 *www.takayatours.com.*

RIVER RAFTING

Snowmelt from the coastal mountains, and broad rivers that run through the Pemberton Valley, north of Squamish, provide some of the best white-water rafting in British Columbia.

Canadian Outback Adventure Company. White-water rafting and scenic, family-oriented floats are offered on day trips from Vancouver. Transportation to and from Vancouver is available for an extra charge. ☎ *604/921–7250, 800/565–8735* 🌐 *www.canadianoutback.com.*

WINDSURFING

The winds aren't heavy on English Bay, making it a perfect place for learning to windsurf. If you're looking for more challenging high-wind conditions, you have to travel north to Squamish.

Windsure Windsurfing School. Sailboard rentals and lessons are available between May and September at Jericho Beach. Skim boarding and stand-up paddling lessons are also offered. ✉ *1300 Discovery St., Point Grey* ☎ *604/224–0615* 🌐 *www.windsure.com.*

4

Vancouver Shops and Spas

WORD OF MOUTH

"Main Street is known as Mount Pleasant and is home to a lot of independent boutiques and a smattering of unique gift shops, coffee shops, and restaurants. It's fairly spread out but can easily eat up an afternoon if all you want to do is wander and windowshop."

—BC_Robyn

Join, Ask, Share. www.fodors.com/community/

Updated by Carolyn B. Heller

Art galleries, ethnic markets, gourmet-food shops, and high-fashion outlets abound in Vancouver, and both Asian and First Nations influences in crafts, home furnishings, and foods are quite prevalent.

Vancouver has a community of budding fashion designers whose creative clothes and accessories populate the boutiques in the Gastown and Main Street/Mt. Pleasant neighborhoods. The Portobello West Market is also an exciting showcase for emerging local designers. Of course, Vancouver does have many of the same chain stores that you can find across North America, primarily downtown on Robson Street and in the malls. "Mall" doesn't just mean the Gap and Abercrombie, though, particularly in suburban Richmond, where shopping destinations cater to an upscale Asian community. If you're not headed to Hong Kong, Beijing, or Tokyo, Richmond could be the next best thing.

In the art scene, look for First Nations and other aboriginal art, from souvenir trinkets to stellar contemporary art; many galleries showcasing First Nations artists are in Gastown. Area artisans also create a variety of fine crafts, exhibiting and selling their wares at Granville Island galleries. We've listed a few of our faves, and the "Artists & Artisans of Granville Island" brochure, available at shops around the island, has a complete listing of island galleries and studios.

Food—especially local seafood (available smoked and packed to travel), cheeses from British Columbia and across Canada, and even locally made chocolates, jams, and other goodies—makes tasty souvenirs (or delicious picnic fare along the way). B.C. also has a rapidly maturing wine industry, and local shops give advice about the region's offerings (and tastings, too). Remember the restrictions about taking alcohol back into your home country before you stock up.

Outdoor-oriented Vancouver is a great place to pick up camping and hiking gear. There's a cluster of outdoor-equipment shops on West Broadway between Yukon and Manitoba streets in the Fairview neighborhood, and you'll find several snowboard, skiing, and bicycle outlets on West 4th Avenue, just east of Burrard Street in Kitsilano.

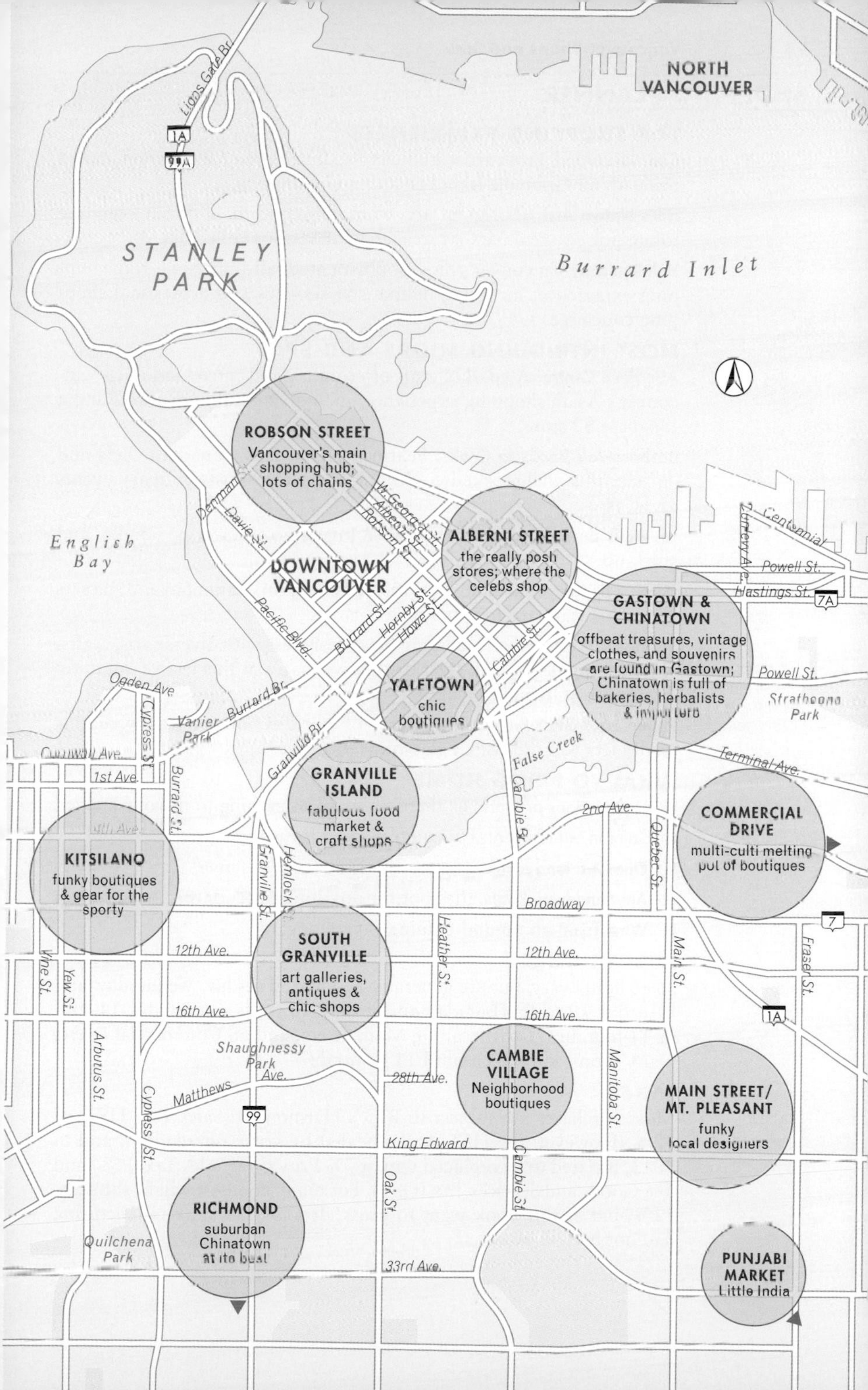

NORTH VANCOUVER
STANLEY PARK
Burrard Inlet
English Bay
DOWNTOWN VANCOUVER
ROBSON STREET
Vancouver's main shopping hub; lots of chains
ALBERNI STREET
the really posh stores; where the celebs shop
GASTOWN & CHINATOWN
offbeat treasures, vintage clothes, and souvenirs are found in Gastown; Chinatown is full of bakeries, herbalists & importers
YALETOWN
chic boutiques
GRANVILLE ISLAND
fabulous food market & craft shops
COMMERCIAL DRIVE
multi-culti melting pot of boutiques
KITSILANO
funky boutiques & gear for the sporty
SOUTH GRANVILLE
art galleries, antiques & chic shops
CAMBIE VILLAGE
Neighborhood boutiques
MAIN STREET/ MT. PLEASANT
funky local designers
RICHMOND
suburban Chinatown at its best
PUNJABI MARKET
Little India
Lions Gate Br.
Denman St.
Davie St.
W. Georgia St.
Alberni St.
Robson St.
Pacific Blvd.
Burrard St.
Hornby St.
Howe St.
Cambie St.
Centennial
Powell St.
Hastings St.
Strathcona Park
False Creek
Terminal Ave.
Ogden Ave.
Cypress St.
Vanier Park
Burrard Br.
Granville Br.
Cornwall Ave.
1st Ave.
4th Ave.
2nd Ave.
Quebec St.
Granville St.
Hemlock St.
Broadway
Heather St.
12th Ave.
16th Ave.
Main St.
Fraser St.
Vine St.
Yew St.
Arbutus St.
Shaughnessy Park
Matthews Ave.
28th Ave.
Manitoba St.
King Edward
Oak St.
Quilchena Park
33rd Ave.
1A
99A
7A
7
99

SHOPPING PLANNER

TOP SHOPPING EXPERIENCES

Granville Island. From artist studios to a jam-packed food market, everything about Granville Island encourages browsing.

Hill's Native Art. Aboriginal art, from chintzy dime-a-dozen keepsake totem poles to real-McCoy treasures for serious collectors.

Holt Renfrew. Vancouver's most sophisticated, all-under-one-roof shopping experience, including deluxe spa services and a personal shopping concierge.

MOST INTRIGUING SHOPS AND SPAS

Aberdeen Centre. A sparkly mall offering a good introduction to Vancouver's Asian shopping experience, including great restaurants and a Japanese $2 store.

Barbara-Jo's Books to Cooks. Featuring local and Canadian chefs and cuisine, this well-stocked cookbook shop also hosts culinary events and classes.

Les Amis du Fromage. Where cheese lovers go to swoon, sample, and stock up.

Miraj. The first of its kind in North America, this hammam and spa sets the exotic standard for luxury steams.

Portobello West Market. Emerging local designers with diverse arts, crafts, and fashion ideas hawk their distinctive wares at this festive quarterly event in the Olympic Village.

Robert Held Glass Studio. The source of world-renowned glassware, this studio lets you can watch glassblowers at work.

WHAT TO BRING HOME

- **First Nations artwork,** as there's always something to fit your budget
- **Salmon,** smoked and vacuum-packed for travel
- **One-of-a-kind fashions** from emerging local designers
- **Anything from Roots,** the spot for anything outdoorsy
- **WIne** from an up-and-coming B.C. vineyard

STORE HOURS

Store hours vary, but are generally Monday, Tuesday, Wednesday, and Saturday 10 to 6; Thursday and Friday 10 to 9; and Sunday 11 to 5 or 11 to 6. In Gastown, along Main Street, and on Commercial Drive, many shops don't open until 11 or noon.

TAXES

Most purchases are subject to B.C.'s Harmonized Sales Tax (HST) of 12%. However, the HST was repealed by voter referendum, and in 2013, is slated to be replaced with a 7% Provincial Sales Tax (PST) and 5% Goods and Services Tax (GST). For many goods, it will be the same 12%, but as this book went to press, details of this tax restructuring had not been announced.

The Lululemon brand of yoga attire was founded in Vancouver in 1998.

CENTRAL VANCOUVER

DOWNTOWN AND THE WEST END

ANTIQUES, AUCTIONS, AND FLEA MARKETS

DoDa Antiques. Concentrating on mid-20th-century jewelry, ceramics, glass, paintings, and prints, this old-timey treasure box is crammed with intriguing finds. It also stocks First Nations art. ✉ *434 Richards St., Downtown* ☎ *604/602–0559* 🌐 *www.dodaantiques.com.*

BOOKS

Chapters. These Canadian shops (most with a Starbucks attached) stock a vast selection of popular books. Check out the display tables for hot sellers, local authors, and bargain books. In addition to the downtown location, there's a convenient South Granville branch at the corner of Broadway and Granville Street. ✉ *788 Robson St., Downtown* ☎ *604/682–4066* 🌐 *www.chapters.indigo.ca.*

MacLeod's Books. One of the city's best antiquarian and used-book stores, this shop is a treasure trove of titles from mainstream to wildly eclectic. ✉ *455 W. Pender St., Downtown* ☎ *604/681–7654.*

CLOTHING: CHILDREN'S

Roots Kids. Synonymous with outdoorsy Canadian style, this Canadian company's signature casual wear is also available in children's sizes. ✉ *1153 Robson St., West End* ☎ *604/684–8801* 🌐 *canada.roots.com.*

DID YOU KNOW?

The Museum of Anthropology at the University of British Columbia has an excellent collection of Northwest Coast First Nations art, and the building and grounds are spectacular. The museum shop sells unusual art and gift items.

CLOTHING: MEN'S AND WOMEN'S

Fodor's Choice ★ **Holt Renfrew.** High on the city's ritzy scale, Holt Renfrew is a swanky showcase for international high fashion and accessories for men and women. Think Prada, Dolce & Gabbana, and other designer labels. ✉ *Pacific Centre, 737 Dunsmuir St., Downtown* ☎ *604/681–3121* 🌐 *www.holtrenfrew.com.*

Leone. Marble alcoves in an elegantly palatial store set the scene for men's and women's fashions by Versace, Alexander McQueen, Moschino, Dior, Miu Miu, and others. On the lower level is L-2 Leone, where you'll find edgier fashions and an Italian café. ✉ *Sinclair Centre, 757 W. Hastings St., Downtown* ☎ *604/683–1133* 🌐 *www.leone.ca.*

★ **Lululemon Athletica.** Everyone from power-yoga devotees to soccer moms covets the fashionable, well constructed workout wear with the stylized "A" insignia from this Vancouver-based company. The stores also provide free drop-in yoga classes. There are several branches around town, including 2113 West 4th Avenue in Kitsilano. ✉ *1148 Robson St., West End* ☎ *604/681–3118* 🌐 *www.lululemon.com.*

Roots. For outdoorsy clothes that double as souvenirs (many sport maple-leaf logos), check out these Canadian-made sweatshirts, leather jackets, and other comfy casuals. In addition to this downtown flagship store, there are branches on South Granville Street in Granville and on West 4th Avenue in Kitsilano. ✉ *1001 Robson St., West End* ☎ *604/683–4305* 🌐 *canada.roots.com.*

DEPARTMENT STORES

The Bay. A Canadian institution (even though it's now owned by Americans), The Bay was founded as part of the fur trade in the 17th century. A whole department sells the signature tri-color blankets and other Canadiana. ✉ *674 Granville St., at Georgia St., Downtown* ☎ *604/681–6211* 🌐 *www.thebay.com.*

Winners. This discount department-store chain is heaven for bargain hunters. Among the regularly changing stock, you might unearth great deals on designer fashions, shoes, and housewares. ✉ *798 Granville St., at Robson St., Downtown* ☎ *604/683–1058* 🌐 *www.winners.ca.*

SHOPPING CENTERS

Pacific Centre. Filling three city blocks in the heart of downtown, this mall is filled with mostly mainstream clothing shops, with some chicer pricier boutiques scattered throughout. There are several street-level entrances as well as access via Holt Renfrew, Sears, and the Vancouver City Centre Station—worth knowing about on rainy days. ✉ *701 W. Georgia St., Downtown* ☎ *604/688–7235* 🌐 *www.pacificcentre.ca.*

Sinclair Centre. Shops in and around this complex cater to sophisticated tastes with outposts such as Leone and Cartier. ✉ *757 W. Hastings St., Downtown* ☎ *604/488–0672* 🌐 *www.sinclaircentre.com.*

FOOD

Purdy's Chocolates. A chocolatier since 1907, Purdy's once made a liqueur-filled line, which was hawked to Americans during Prohibition. These days, Purdy's purple-foiled boxes of chocolate temptations are a popular gift. Outlets are scattered throughout the city. ✉ *Pacific Centre, 700 W. Georgia St., Downtown* ☎ *604/683–3467* 🌐 *www.purdys.com.*

Urban Fare. If you're a fan of Whole Foods, check out Vancouver's most stylish supermarket. The expansive food displays are mouthwatering and come from all corners of the globe. In addition to this downtown store, there are also large branches at 305 Bute Street in Downtown at 177 Davie Street in Yaletown. ✉ *1133 Alberni St., Downtown* ☎ *604/648–2053* 🌐 *www.urbanfare.com.*

Viti Wine and Lager Store. What this diminutive shop lacks in size it makes up for in quality, furnishing a strong selection of wines, beers, and liquors, with an emphasis on regional products. Wine tastings are held Saturday; beer and whiskey tastings are regularly held on Friday. ✉ *Moda Hotel, 900 Seymour St., Downtown* ☎ *604/683–3806* 🌐 *www.vitiwinelagers.com.*

JEWELRY

Birks. Vancouver's link in this Canada-wide chain of high-end jewelers—a national institution since 1879—is in a neoclassical former bank building. An impressive staircase connects the main level to the mezzanine floor—descending, you'll feel like royalty. ✉ *698 W. Hastings St., Downtown* ☎ *604/669–3333* 🌐 *www.birks.com.*

Palladio. This is one of the city's most stylish jewelers. Expect high-fashion pieces in gold and platinum, top-name timepieces, and distinguished accessories. ✉ *855 W. Hastings St., Downtown* ☎ *604/685–3885* 🌐 *www.palladiocanada.com.*

OUTDOOR EQUIPMENT

Atmosphere. At this chain of sporting-goods stores, you can count on finding high-performance (and high-fashion) gear for hiking, camping, or just battling the rain. ✉ *Pacific Centre, 777 Dunsmuir St., Downtown* ☎ *604/687–7668* 🌐 *www.atmosphere.ca.*

GASTOWN AND CHINATOWN

ART AND CRAFTS GALLERIES

★ **Coastal Peoples Fine Arts Gallery.** The gorgeous books and postcards make affordable souvenirs, though you could well be tempted by the impressive collection of First Nations jewelry, ceremonial masks, prints, and carvings. The gallery has a second location at 1024 Mainland Street in Yaletown. ✉ *312 Water St., Gastown* ☎ *604/684–9222* 🌐 *www.coastalpeoples.com.*

Fodor's Choice ★ **Hill's Native Art.** This highly respected store has Vancouver's largest selection of First Nations art. If you think the main level is impressive, go upstairs to where the collector-quality stuff is found. ✉ *165 Water St., Gastown* ☎ *604/685–4249* 🌐 *www.hills.ca.*

Inuit Gallery of Vancouver. In addition to quality Inuit art like the signature carvings in soapstone and antler, there's also an excellent collection of Northwest Coast Native art such as baskets, totems, bentwood boxes, and masks. ✉ *206 Cambie St., Gastown* ☎ *888/615–8399, 604/688–7323* 🌐 *www.inuit.com.*

Spirit Wrestler Gallery. With exhibits that include works of the Pacific Northwest First Nations, the Inuit of the Canadian Arctic, and the New Zealand Māori, this gallery showcases an intriguing comparison of cultural styles. ✉ *47 Water St., Gastown* ☎ *604/669–8813* 🌐 *www.spiritwrestler.com.*

WORD OF MOUTH

"For markets, Granville Island is where you'll want to be from the morning until 7 pm. Granville Island Public Market is the most famous market in the city, with all kinds of food products. Outside of the market in the neighboring buildings are art studios, art galleries, craft shops, unique gift shops, as well as restaurants, waterfront walkways, boat rentals, etc. Really cool place to spend an afternoon."

—Carmanah

CLOTHING: MEN'S AND WOMEN'S

212 Boutique. The folks who run this stylish shop met in New York City (and named their business after that city's area code). These days, this Gastown boutique sells contemporary, moderately priced designer clothing for women. ✉ *454 W. Cordova St., Gastown* ☎ *604/685–2426* 🌐 *www.twoonetwo.net.*

Dream Apparel & Articles for People. Come here to find a variety of wares by up-and-coming local designers. The creative selections target the hip twentysomething crowd. ✉ *311 W. Cordova St., Gastown* ☎ *604/683–7326* 🌐 *www.dreamvancouver.com.*

One of a Few. This clothing from local and international makers may not be one of a kind, but as the name of this funky little shop attests, you won't see the designs at mass-market retailers either. ✉ *354 Water St., Gastown* ☎ *604/605–0685* 🌐 *www.oneofafewblog.blogspot.com.*

Two of a Few. With the same owner as One of a Few, this shop carries both men's and women's lines. ✉ *356 Water St., Gastown* ☎ *604/605–0630* 🌐 *www.oneofafew.com.*

FOOD

T&T Supermarket. Check out this little chain of maxi-size Asian supermarkets for exotic produce, baked goods, and prepared foods. You can assemble an inexpensive lunch-to-go from the extensive hot-food counter. In addition to this Chinatown location, there are branches at 2800 East 1st Avenue on the East Side and at 8181 Cambie Road in Richmond. ✉ *179 Keefer Pl., Chinatown* ☎ *604/899–8836* 🌐 *www.tnt-supermarket.com.*

SHOES AND ACCESSORIES

John Fluevog. You might have seen these shops in New York and Los Angeles, but did you know that these funky shoes were created by a Vancouverite? The Gastown location is worth a look for the store itself, with its striking glass facade and soaring ceilings. There's another branch downtown at 837 Granville Street. ✉ *65 Water St., Gastown* ☎ *604/688–6228* 🌐 *www.fluevog.com.*

ASIAN NIGHT MARKETS

An Asian-style summer night market adds an entertaining dimension to your shopping excursions.

Richmond Night Market. About 80 food vendors, carnival rides, and a children's amuseument area are among the attractions at this night market near River Rock Casino. You can get here on the Canada Line from downtown in about 20 minutes, the market just a short walk from Bridgeport Station. From mid-May to early October, market hours are 7 pm to about midnight on Friday and Saturday, and 6 pm to 11 pm on Sunday. ✉ *8351 River Rd., Richmond* ☎ *604/244–8448.*

Summer Night Market. Much larger than its downtown counterpart, this market features vendors selling everything from socks to mops and food stalls offering noodle bowls, skewered meats, and bubble tea. Concerts, magic shows, and kung fu demonstrations fill out the rotating lineup of special events. Between mid-May and early October, the market runs from 7 pm to about midnight on Friday and Saturday and from 7 pm to 11 pm on Sunday. To get here by public transit, take the Canada Line to Bridgeport Station and change to Bus 407 or 430. ✉ *12631 Vulcan Way, off Bridgeport Rd., Richmond* ☎ *604/278–8000* 🌐 *www.summernightmarket.com.*

Vancouver Chinatown Night Market. Chinatown is at its liveliest in the evening when vendors set up stalls selling food, clothing, and a wide variety of "do I really need this?" bits and bobs. From mid-May to early September, the market is open 6 to 11 pm Friday through Sunday. It's a fun place to wander. ✉ *Keefer St., between Columbia and Main Sts., Chinatown* ☎ *604/682–8998* 🌐 *www.vcma.shawbiz.ca.*

YALETOWN

CLOTHING: MEN'S AND WOMEN'S

Fine Finds Boutique. You're never quite sure what you'll find in this pretty little shop—it's a fun spot to browse for cute women's clothing, jewelry, and accessories. ✉ *1014 Mainland St., Yaletown* ☎ *604/669–8325* 🌐 *www.finefindsboutique.com.*

FOOD

Ganache Patisserie. In true Parisian style, every delicious and decadent item here is a work of art. You can buy whole cakes—perhaps chocolate-banana cake or coconut mango cheesecake—but a slice will perk up your shopping day. ✉ *1262 Homer St., Yaletown* ☎ *604/899–1098* 🌐 *www.ganacheyaletown.com.*

Swirl. To learn more about British Columbia wines, or to pick up a bottle (or a few), visit the knowledgeable staff at this Yaletown store that stocks more than 650 varieties produced within the province. Complimentary tastings let you try before you buy. ✉ *1185 Mainland St., Yaletown* ☎ *604/408–9463* 🌐 *www.swirlwinestore.ca.*

GREATER VANCOUVER

GRANVILLE ISLAND

ART AND CRAFTS GALLERIES

Circle Craft. This artists' co-op sells textiles, wood pieces, jewelry, ceramics, and glass works. ✉ *1–1666 Johnston St., Granville Island* ☎ *604/669–8021* 🌐 *www.circlecraft.net.*

Crafthouse. Run by the Crafts Council of British Columbia, this tiny structure contains a veritable smorgasbord of works by local artisans. ✉ *1386 Cartwright St., Granville Island* ☎ *604/687–7270* 🌐 *www.craftcouncilbc.ca.*

Gallery of B.C. Ceramics. An impressive display of functional and decorative ceramics by local artists is for sale here. ✉ *1359 Cartwright St., Granville Island* ☎ *604/669–3606* 🌐 *www.bcpotters.com.*

PORTOBELLO WEST

Portobello West. Modeled on London's Portobello Road, Portobello West showcases emerging local designers—some are students, others are more established—and their unique, stylish wares. The event is held four weekends each year in March, May, September, and November. The Creekside Community Centre is a 15-minute walk from either the Olympic Village or Main Street SkyTrain station. ✉ *Creekside Community Centre, 1 Athletes Way, False Creek* 🌐 *www.portobellowest.com* 🎫 *$2.*

Lattimer Gallery. Stocking native arts and crafts in all price ranges, this shop is a short stroll from Granville Island. ✉ *1590 W. 2nd Ave., Granville Island* ☎ *604/732–4556* 🌐 *www.lattimergallery.com.*

CLOTHING: MEN'S AND WOMEN'S

Edie Hats. You name the hat and somewhere on the walls, rafters, shelves, or floor you'll find it, whether it's a fedora, cloche, toque, sun hat, rain hat, or straw hat. ✉ *Net Loft, 4–1666 Johnston St., Granville Island* ☎ *604/683–4280, 800/750–2134* 🌐 *www.ediehats.com.*

Little Dream. Under the same ownership as Dream Apparel & Articles for People in Gastown, Little Dream is a smaller version of this fashion-forward shop showcasing local designers. ✉ *Net Loft, 130–1666 Johnston St., Granville Island* ☎ *604/683–6930* 🌐 *www.dreamvancouver.com.*

FOOD

Edible Canada. Opposite the Granville Island Public Market, this shop sells jams, sauces, chocolates, and hundreds of other edible items from around the province. It's a great place to find gifts for foodie friends. ✉ *1596 Johnston St., Granville Island* ☎ *604/682–6675* 🌐 *www.ediblecanada.com.*

Fodor's Choice ★ **Granville Island Public Market.** Locals and visitors alike crowd this indoor market that's part farm stand, part gourmet grocery, and part upscale food court. Stalls are packed with locally made sausages, exotic cheeses, just-caught fish, fresh produce, baked goods, and prepared foods from handmade fudge to frothy cappuccinos. If the sun is out, you can

CLOSE UP

Farmers' Markets

Vancouverites who are passionate about locally grown food flock to the city's weekly farmers' markets, which are also wonderful spots to put together a picnic lunch or track down a gourmet gift. Look for locally made cheeses, honeys, and jams, freshly baked breads, and homegrown raspberries, blueberries, or other seasonal fruits.

- West End Farmers' Market: Saturday 9 am to 2 pm, June to mid-October (Nelson Park, 1100 block Comox Street, West End)
- Main Street Market: Wednesday 3 to 7 pm, June to early October (Thornton Park, in front of the VIA Rail Station, near the Main Street SkyTrain Station)
- Kitsilano Farmers' Market: Sunday 10 am to 2 pm, late May to mid-October (Kitsilano Community Centre, West 10th Avenue and Larch Street, Kitsilano)
- Trout Lake Farmers' Market: Saturday 9 am to 2 pm, mid-May to mid-October (John Hendry Park, between Templeton and Lakewood streets, south of East 13th Avenue, East Side)
- University of British Columbia Farm Market: Saturday 9 am to 1 pm, June to mid-October (6182 South Campus Road, West Side)
- Winter Farmers Market: Saturday 10 am to 2 pm, November to April (Nat Bailey Stadium, East Parking Lot, Ontario Street at East 30th Avenue, Main St./Mt. Pleasant)

dine on your purchases out on the waterfront decks. ✉ *1689 Johnston St., Granville Island* ☎ *604/666–5784* 🌐 *www.granvilleisland.com/public-market.*

Liberty Wine Merchants. The helpful employees at this local chain can assist you in selecting wines from B.C. or around the world. ✉ *1660 Johnston St., Granville Island* ☎ *604/602–1120* 🌐 *www.libertywinemerchants.com.*

SPECIALTY STORES

The Umbrella Shop. This is the place to help you keep obsessively dry. ✉ *1550 Anderson St., Granville Island* ☎ *604/697–0919* 🌐 *www.theumbrellashop.com.*

WEST SIDE AND KITSILANO

ART AND CRAFTS GALLERIES

Museum of Anthropology Gift Shop. This museum store carries an excellent selection of Northwest Coast jewelry, carvings, and prints, as well as books on First Nations history and culture. ✉ *University of British Columbia, 6393 N.W. Marine Dr., Point Grey* ☎ *604/822–3440* 🌐 *www.moa.ubc.ca.*

BOOKS

★ **Barbara-Jo's Books to Cooks.** Local-chef-turned-entrepreneur Barbara-Jo McIntosh spreads the good-food word with scores of cookbooks, including many by Vancouver- and B.C.-based chefs, as well as wine books, memoirs, and magazines. The store also hosts special events, recipe demos, and drop-in classes in its sparkling demonstration kitchen—they're a tasty way to explore local cuisine. ✉ *1740 W. 2nd Ave., Kitsilano* ☎ *604/688–6755* 🌐 *www.bookstocooks.com.*

★ **Kidsbooks.** The helpful staff at this cheery shop is happy to make recommendations about books appropriate for young people ranging from toddlers to teens. Choose from the many titles by Canadian authors—excellent for take-home gifts or on-the-road reading. ✉ *3083 W. Broadway, Kitsilano* ☎ *604/738–5335* 🌐 *www.kidsbooks.ca.*

Wanderlust. Here's where to find thousands of travel books and maps, as well as luggage and accessories. ✉ *1929 W. 4th Ave., Kitsilano* ☎ *604/739–2182* 🌐 *www.wanderlustore.com.*

4

CLOTHING: CHILDREN'S

Please Mum. With its comfortable, brightly colored clothing, this fun Vancouver-based chain is known for its mix-and-match separates for newborns through preteens. There's another branch at 650 West 41st Avenue in South Vancouver. ✉ *2951 W. Broadway, Kitsilano* ☎ *604/732–4574* 🌐 *www.pleasemum.com.*

FOOD

Chocolate Arts. Looking for a present for a chocolate lover? Check out the chocolates in First Nations motifs, specially designed by Robert Davidson, one of Canada's premier artists. This delicious shop is a short walk from Granville Island. ✉ *1620 W. 3rd Ave., Kitsilano* ☎ *604/739–0475, 877/739–0475* 🌐 *www.chocolatearts.com.*

★ **Les Amis du Fromage.** If you love cheese, don't miss the mind boggling array of selections from B.C., the rest of Canada, and elsewhere at this shop of delicacies. The extremely knowledgeable mother-and-daughter owners, Alice and Allison Spurrell, and their staff encourage you to taste before you buy. Yum. The shop is located between Granville Island and Kitsilano Beach—useful to know if you're assembling a seaside picnic. ✉ *1752 W. 2nd Ave., Kitsilano* ☎ *604/732–4218* 🌐 *www.buycheese.com.*

SHOES AND ACCESSORIES

Gravity Pope. Foot fashionistas make tracks to this Kitsilano shop that's jam-packed with trendy choices, including Camper, Puma, Kenneth Cole, and other international brands for men and women. ✉ *2205 W. 4th Ave., Kitsilano* ☎ *604/731–7673* 🌐 *www.gravitypope.com.*

SOUTH GRANVILLE

ART AND CRAFTS GALLERIES

Douglas Reynolds Gallery. In this collection of Northwest Coast First Nations art, particularly strong in woodwork and jewelry, some pieces date back to the 1800s, while others are strikingly contemporary. ✉ *2335 Granville St., South Granville* ☎ *604/731–9292* 🌐 *www.douglasreynoldsgallery.com.*

Marion Scott Gallery. Specializing in fine Inuit art from the Canadian North, exhibits here include sculpture, prints, wall hangings, and

CLOSE UP

A Bit About—and How to Buy—Aboriginal Art

With 198 First Nations peoples in British Columbia alone, it's easy to be mesmerized, even confused, by the range and diversity of the indigenous art you'll see. Different bands have traded materials, skills, and resources for centuries, so today it's often difficult to attribute any particular style to any one group. It's this blending, though, that has created such a rich cultural mosaic. That said, there are still some groups, such as the Haida and Coast Salish, who have strong identifiable traits.

Broadly speaking, First Nations art is a language of symbols, which come together to describe the legends and stories that link one community with another. Contrary to popular belief, although these symbols may share a similar meaning, they are by no means a common language: the Coast Salish, for example, view the hummingbird differently from how the Tsimshian Tribe do.

According to Rikki Kooy, whose Shuswap name is Spirit Elk Woman, there are two heartfelt ways many people purchase First Nations art. "The first is to fall in love with a region of British Columbia, and find the First Nations group that represents that area," she says. "The second is to fall in love with a piece for its calling." Rikki has been involved with retailing aboriginal art for more than 35 years and is a former advisor to Aboriginal Tourism BC.

Once you've found yourself drawn to a particular piece, whether it's jewelry, a mask, or a print, there are three essential questions to consider in judging its integrity and authenticity.

Does the work or design have a title? Because First Nations art is highly symbolic, authentic pieces will be titled. Bear in mind that the title will usually allude to mythical lore, real-life stories, and/or the artist's ancestry.

Is the cultural group identified? Every piece holds a story, against which there is often a broader background of heritage, hierarchy, and geographic origin. For example, a Haida piece will likely have come from the Queen Charlottes, or have been made by a descendant from that region. By knowing the region, the nuances of the piece's symbolic language are more easily identified.

Is the artist identified, or better still, is there a background sheet available? First Nations peoples hold relationships in high esteem, so dealers with integrity will have established a relationship with the artists they represent and should have a background sheet on the artist and his heritage. This adds to the authenticity of the work, as well as giving you some background about the artist and his or her other works.

MADE IN VANCOUVER

Vancouver doesn't just produce overpriced lattes and undersized condos. The city's creative denizens have designed a range of products from shoes to yoga wear.

Happy Planet Juices: Vancouverites have not only embraced this local company's mission to "turn the planet on to 100% organic juices," in 2008 they elected company cofounder Gregor Robertson the city's mayor.

Holey Soles: A competitor of the ubiquitous Crocs, these brightly colored, cloglike, rubber-compound shoes are made in the Vancouver area and sold at outdoor and garden shops around town.

John Fluevog: Yep, those outrageous shoes took their first step in Vancouver.

Lululemon Athletica: The stylized "A" insignia is as recognizable to yoga enthusiasts as the Nike "swoosh" is to sports fans.

Rocky Mountain Bicycles: B.C. invented the "free-riding" or "north shore" (from the North Shore Mountains) style of riding that's taken over the sport, and Rocky Mountain makes the steeds on which the style was pioneered.

4

drawings. ✉ *2423 Granville St., South Granville* ☎ *604/685–1934* 🌐 *marionscottgallery.com.*

★ **Robert Held Art Glass.** At Canada's largest "hot glass" studio, two blocks west of Granville Street, you can watch glassblowers in action, then browse the one-of-a-kind vases, paperweights, bowls, ornaments, and perfume bottles. Held's glass pieces have been exhibited at the Canadian Museum of Civilization in Ottawa and in galleries across North America. ✉ *2130 Pine St., between 5th and 6th Aves., South Granville* ☎ *604/737–0020* 🌐 *www.robertheld.com.*

CLOTHING: MEN'S AND WOMEN'S

Tilley Endurables. Globe-trotters search out this practical, hard-wearing line of Canadian-made travel clothing. The Tilley Hat is an icon of seasoned travelers. ✉ *2401 Granville St., South Granville* ☎ *604/732–4287* 🌐 *www.tilleyvancouver.com.*

CLOTHING: VINTAGE

Turnabout. The quality is so good that "used" is almost a misnomer at this long-established vintage-clothing store, which sells upscale women's wear from labels like Gucci, Missoni, and Prada. A second branch, at 3112 West Broadway in Kitsilano, sells more casual clothing, as well as men's clothes. ✉ *3109 Granville St., South Granville* ☎ *604/734–5313* 🌐 *www.turnaboutclothing.com.*

FOOD

Meinhardt Fine Foods. Pick up fixings for an elegant picnic or find a gift for a foodie friend at this sophisticated neighborhood grocery. ✉ *3002 Granville St., South Granville* ☎ *604/732–4405* 🌐 *www.feedyourcuriosity.com.*

SHOPPING CENTERS

Oakridge Centre. If you're intent on meandering, head to the skylighted atrium of Oakridge Centre. There's a mix of trendy shops, midprice boutiques, and North American chains. It's a quick trip on the Canada Line from downtown to the Oakridge–41st Avenue stop. ✉ *650 W. 41st Ave., at Cambie St., South Vancouver* ☎ *604/261–2511* 🌐 *www.oakridgecentre.com.*

FAIRVIEW

CIGAR SHOPS

City Cigar. Cuban cigars are legal and plentiful (although it's not legal to take them into the United States). Is this why Tommy Lee Jones and Arnold Schwarzenegger stop at this shop when they're in town? ✉ *888 W. 6th Ave., Fairview* ☎ *604/879–0208* 🌐 *www.citycigarcompany.com.*

OUTDOOR EQUIPMENT

★ **Mountain Equipment Co-op.** This warehouse-style outlet stocks a good selection of high-performance clothing and equipment for hiking, cycling, climbing, and kayaking, as well as just hanging around outdoors. You can rent sports gear here, too. A onetime C$5 membership is required for purchases or rentals. ✉ *130 W. Broadway, Fairview* ☎ *604/872–7858* 🌐 *www.mec.ca.*

Taiga. Vancouver-based Taiga sells popular waterproof cycling gear, as well as other outdoor clothing, sleeping bags, and tents. ✉ *301 W. Broadway, Fairview* ☎ *604/875–8388* 🌐 *www.taigaworks.ca.*

Three Vets. This army surplus–style store stocks budget-priced camping equipment, outdoor clothing, and boots. It also has a native art collection worth seeing. ✉ *2200 Yukon St., Fairview* ☎ *604/872–5475.*

MAIN STREET/MT. PLEASANT

CLOTHING: MEN'S AND WOMEN'S

Barefoot Contessa. This cute shop has a creative take on '40s-style glamour. Look for frilly feminine clothing (dresses, dresses, and more dresses), jewelry, and bags—some by local designers—as well as vintage linens and decorative accessories. ✉ *3715 Main St., Main St./Mt. Pleasant* ☎ *604/879–1137* 🌐 *www.thebarefootcontessa.com.*

Hazel & Jools. While many Main Street shops cater to the young and hyper-fashion-conscious, this hip boutique appeals to women of all ages with fashionable labels such as Mexx, Kensie, and its own in-house line. It also carries cool clothes for moms-to-be. ✉ *4280 Main St., Main St./Mt. Pleasant* ☎ *604/730–8689* 🌐 *www.hazelhipmoms.com.*

★ **Twigg & Hottie.** Local and national designers stock this outlet with one-of-a-kind creations ranging from the edgiest of Hollywood glam to chic street-wear funk. Look for the in-house We3 label. ✉ *3671 Main St., Main St./Mt. Pleasant* ☎ *604/879–8595* 🌐 *www.twiggandhottie.com.*

A selection of goodies from Les Amis du Fromage.

CLOTHING: VINTAGE

★ **Front and Company.** Value-conscious fashionistas paw through the consignment and vintage clothing in this smart shop. There's a small section of designer samples and new items, as well as eclectic gifts. ✉ *3772 Main St., Main St./Mt. Pleasant* ☎ *604/879–8431* 🌐 *www.frontandcompany.ca.*

FOOD

Chocolaterie de La Nouvelle France. This petite bonbon of a confectionary shop sells delectable, hand-crafted truffles and caramels, as well as rich, thick "drinking chocolate." Not your mother's hot cocoa, it's the perfect pick-me-up while browsing the nearby boutiques. ✉ *198 E. 21 Ave., Main St./Mt. Pleasant* ☎ *604/566–1065* 🌐 *www.chocolaterienouvellefrance.ca.*

HOUSEWARES

Vancouver Special. This shop offers a stylish selection of household items by local and international designers and stocks an eclectic assortment of books about art, architecture, and design. ✉ *3612 Main St., Main St./Mt. Pleasant* ☎ *604/568–3673* 🌐 *www.vanspecial.com.*

EAST SIDE

ANTIQUES, AUCTIONS, AND FLEA MARKETS

Vancouver Flea Market. Housed in a "big red barn," this weekend market is a five-minute walk from the Main Street SkyTrain station. You'll find all manner of treasures at all sorts of prices. ✉ *703 Terminal Ave., East Side* ☎ *604/685–0666* 🌐 *www.vancouverfleamarket.com.*

Inside the Coastal Peoples Fine Arts Gallery.

ART AND CRAFTS GALLERIES

Doctor Vigari Gallery. In keeping with its offbeat environs on "the Drive," this gallery is home to a wildly eclectic assortment of jewelry, crafts, paintings, and household items, most by B.C. artists. ✉ *1816 Commercial Dr., East Side* ☎ *604/255–9513* 🌐 *www.doctorvigarigallery.com.*

CLOTHING: CHILDREN'S

Dandelion Kids. If you're shopping for style-conscious babies, toddlers, and grade-schoolers, check out this store's new, organic, and "recycled" duds. Fair-trade toys also fill the shelves. ✉ *1206 Commercial Dr., East Side* ☎ *604/676–1862* 🌐 *www.dandelionkids.ca.*

CLOTHING: MEN'S AND WOMEN'S

Roots 73 Outlet. You can pay top dollar downtown or head to this factory outlet, which stocks good quality off-season and closeout items at bargain prices. ✉ *3695 Grandview Hwy., at Boundary Rd., East Side* ☎ *604/433–4337.*

SHOES AND ACCESSORIES

Dayton Boot Company. These biker boots have a cultlike following because they're durable and hip, too. Celebrities like Kurt Russell, Harry Connick Jr., Cindy Crawford, and Sharon Stone are wearers. ✉ *2250 E. Hastings St., East Side* ☎ *604/253–6671* 🌐 *www.daytonboots.com.*

Kalena's. You'll find everything from traditional leather sandals to fanciful purple pumps at this family-run store that's been a fixture on Commercial Drive since the 1960s. Fine Italian shoes are a specialty. ✉ *1526 Commercial Dr., East Side* ☎ *604/255–3727* 🌐 *www.kalenashoes.com.*

SHOPPING CENTERS

Metropolis at Metrotown. With 450 stores—mostly North American chains—this mall is the province's largest shopping destination, easily reached via a 20-minute SkyTrain ride from downtown. Teens and serious shoppers alike flock here. ✉ *4700 Kingsway, Burnaby* ☎ *604/438–4715* 🌐 *www.metropolisatmetrotown.com.*

NORTH SHORE

ART AND CRAFTS GALLERIES

Khot-la-Cha Art Gallery & Gift Shop. On the Capilano First Nations Reserve in North Vancouver, this longhouse-style gallery showcases items crafted by members of the Squamish Indian Band, as well as other aboriginal artists in British Columbia and western Canada. You'll find ceremonial masks, hand-knit sweaters, and jewelry made of silver, gold, porcupine quill, or bone. The store is owned by Nancy Nightingale, the daughter of Chief Simon Baker, whose traditional name, Khot-la-Cha, means "kind heart" in the Squamish language. ✉ *270 Whonoak St., North Vancouver* ☎ *604/987–3339* 🌐 *www.khot-la-cha.com.*

FOOD

Lonsdale Quay Market. At this two-level indoor market—less frenzied than its Granville Island counterpart—vendors sell prepared foods, just-caught seafood, and fresh produce. Also look for arts and crafts, kitchenware, and delicious pastries that can be enjoyed on a terrace with views of the city skyline. The market is a short ride from downtown on the SeaBus. ✉ *123 Carrie Cates Ct., North Vancouver* ☎ *604/985–6261* 🌐 *www.lonsdalequay.com.*

RICHMOND

SHOPPING CENTERS

★ **Aberdeen Centre.** First-rate Asian restaurants, vendors hawking everything from kimchi to cream puffs, clothing stores stocking the latest Hong Kong styles, and Daiso—a Japanese bargain-hunters' paradise where most items sell for $2—make this swank mall a good introduction to Vancouver's Asian shopping experience. Take the Canada Line south to Aberdeen station, about 20 minutes from downtown. ✉ *4151 Hazelbridge Way, Richmond* ☎ *604/270–1234* 🌐 *www.aberdeencentre.com.*

SPAS

Vancouver's spa scene is as diverse as its population and includes everything from exotic steam experiences to over-the-top indulgence. While many services give the nod to ancient wisdoms such as Ayurveda, you'll also find holistic spa and wellness destinations that incorporate elements of traditional Chinese medicine, Japanese Reiki, and New Age energy therapies alongside medical aesthetics like Botox, microdermabrasion, and teeth whitening.

4

A luxurious Wedgewood hotel spa treatment.

As in many cities, hair salons often try to parlay "spa" into their mix to broaden their appeal, which usually means having to battle the noise and chemical smells of hairdressing to get to a backroom for your spa services. Ugh! Skip those in favor of the authentic spa experiences below.

Absolute Spa at the Century. This expansive spa has an A-list of celebrity clients—Jennifer Lopez, Ethan Hawke, Gwyneth Paltrow, and Ben Affleck, to name a few. What makes this 15,000-square-foot spa really stand out, though, are all the extras that turn even a simple manicure into an experience: every treatment comes with a complimentary eucalyptus steam, a swim in the ozonated pool, and a healthful snack (champagne and chocolate-coated strawberries are optional extras). Jet-lagged? The spa's several branches at Vancouver International Airport give antifatigue treatments and quick chair massages. Prefer to stay put? Absolute Mobile will come to you. ✉ *Century Plaza Hotel, 1015 Burrard St., Downtown* ☎ *604/684–2772* 🌐 *www.absolutespa.com/century-plaza-hotel.*

Absolute Spa at the Fairmont Hotel Vancouver. Although women enjoy the aura and services, this spa is really geared to men—with black-leather pedicure thrones, wide-screen TVs, video games, and computers to check on sports scores and stock prices. Robes and slippers are a bit larger, and many treatments emphasize their manliness, such as the "Gentlemen's Facial" or the "Professional Sports" foot-care regimen. ✉ *Fairmont Hotel Vancouver, 900 W. Georgia St., Downtown* ☎ *604/684–2772* 🌐 *www.absolutespa.com/fairmont-hotel-vancouver.*

BLO. Canada's first blow-dry bar specializes in catwalk-quality blowout styles for only C$35 in about 30 minutes. A visit to these funky pink-and-plastic outfitted lounges is a must-do for your do before a fancy dinner, or just because. Guys can get in on the act with the C$21 "Blo Bro" service. There are also shops at 1150 Hamilton Street in Yaletown and 1329 West 11th Avenue in South Granville. ✉ *Four Seasons Hotel, 719 W. Georgia St., Yaletown* ☎ *604/609–5460* 🌐 *www.blomedry.com.*

Miraj. This is just about the most luxuriously authentic steam bath you'll get outside of Turkey. The entire experience feels at the periphery of the *Arabian Nights,* with Middle Eastern–inspired architecture and Jerusalem marble that stays cool to the touch as the temperature rises. A steam includes a light body scrub with black Moroccan soap and the option of a full body massage—highly recommended. Afterward, you get to curl up among the plethora of silk cushions, where you're served Moroccan mint tea and a sweet cake. Snoozing is encouraged. ✉ *1495 W. 6th Ave., South Granville* ☎ *604/733–5151* 🌐 *www.mirajhammam.com.*

Skoah. By specializing in facials, Skoah has created a niche for itself. There's no froufrou here, just top quality skin care that puts the facial on a level all its own. The contemporary design has a New York sassiness, and treatments are for women and men. The staff even does foot and hand "facials." There are branches at 2737 Granville Street in South Granville and 2258 West 4th Avenue in Kitsilano. ✉ *1007 Hamilton St., Yaletown* ☎ *604/642–0200* 🌐 *www.skoah.com.*

Spa Utopia. If you're looking for the ultimate in pampering, it's hard to beat this lavish spa at the Pan Pacific Hotel. Freestanding fountains, floor-to-ceiling windows, and waterfront views add a luxurious touch. There's a wide range of services, but the massages are especially enjoyable; practitioners are trained by the man who wrote the training manual on therapeutic spa massage. For the ultimate treat, book one of the hotel's spa suites and let the treatments come to you. ✉ *Pan Pacific Hotel, 999 Canada Pl., Downtown* ☎ *604/641–1351* 🌐 *www.spautopia.ca.*

Spruce Body Lab. Urban and hip, Spruce could almost be described as a medical spa since treatments such as Botox and acupuncture are on the menu in addition to regular spa services. Geo-Thermal Stone Therapy, one of the lab's signature treatments, involves the placement of warm and cool stones on the body's different energy centers. It also includes a full body massage, making it a much more dynamic experience than the usual stone massage. ✉ *1128 Richards St., Yaletown* ☎ *604/683–3220* 🌐 *www.sprucebodylab.com.*

Vida Wellness Spa. Ayurvedic treatments based on the 5,000-year-old Indian science of holistic wellness are the specialty here, alongside the usual facials and body wraps. All the herbs, spices, and oils used in the Swedana, Shirodhara, and Abhyanga massages (to name a few) are customized to your particular body composition, or "dosha." Services include a complimentary steam. There are also branches at the Sutton Place Hotel and the Westin Bayshore Hotel. ✉ *Sheraton Wall Centre Hotel, 1088 Burrard St., Downtown* ☎ *604/682–8410, 800/401–4018* 🌐 *www.vidaspas.com.*

Wedgewood Hotel Spa. What it lacks in size, the Wedgewood Hotel Spa makes up for in intimacy. With only two treatment rooms (each large enough for couples), this second-story spa has understated elegance and graceful attention to detail. Many services include extras like a foot, hand, or scalp massages, and the complimentary steam room gets hot enough to soak the tension out of you. The spa carries Epicuren, a live-enzyme skin-care line favored by many dermatologists. The hotel also has an in-room spa program for guests. ✉ *Wedgewood Hotel, 845 Hornby St., Downtown* ☎ *604/608–5340* 🌐 *www.wedgewoodhotel.com.*

5

Vancouver Nightlife and the Arts

WORD OF MOUTH

"The secret to Vancouver's nightlife is that different areas offer different experiences. If you just randomly wander around, you might find something, but not necessarily the scene you want. . . . Yaletown is trendy, sleek, sexy lounges and restaurants . . . if you're serious about your drinking, Gastown is the place."

—BC_Robyn

Join, Ask, Share. www.fodors.com/community/

Updated by Paige Donner

With easy access to the sea and mountains, it's no surprise that Vancouver is such an outdoorsy town, but once the sun goes down, the city's dwellers trade in their kayaks, hiking shoes, and North Face windbreakers for something decidedly more chic.

There's plenty to choose from in just about every neighborhood: hipster Gastown has caught up with Yaletown for clusters of late-night establishments and is now the place to go for racy clubs and trendy wine bars, with venues in the newly cool Chinatown giving them some good competition. The West End—that's Denman, Davie (gay-friendly), and Robson streets—is all about bumpin' and grindin' in retro bars and clubs, while a posh crowd of after-work professionals and glitterati flocks to Coal Harbour's chic bars and stylish lounges. Meanwhile, Kitsilano (the Venice Beach of Vancouver) attracts a laid-back bunch that enjoys sipping beer and cocktails on outdoor patios with killer views, especially in the summer. The up-and-coming SoMa neighborhood is where you'll rub shoulders with youthful working folk as you knock back a lager and listen to live jams of emerging Canadian musicians. With its fair share of galleries, film festivals, cutting-edge theater, comedy, opera, and ballet, Vancouver (*aka* Hollywood North) also has all manner of cultural stimuli available for the asking.

NIGHTLIFE AND THE ARTS PLANNER

BEST BETS

Best Bartender: Brad Stanton, Hawksworth Bar and Lounge

Best Classic Cocktails: Market by Jean-Georges, at Shangri-La

Best Hipster Bar: The Keefer Bar

Best Patio: Bridges Restaurant, Granville Island

Best Sake: Tojo's

CULTURAL FESTIVALS

FEB.: The **Vancouver International Mountain Film Festival** (☎ *604/990–1505* 🌐 *www.vimff.org*) is a great intro to the mountain and wilderness culture of Canada.

Vancouver has one of North America's largest **Chinese New Year** (🌐 *www.tourismvancouver.com*) celebrations.

At the **Vancouver Playhouse International Wine Festival** (☎ *604/872–6622* 🌐 *www.playhousewinefest.com*), wines from countries around the world are presented.

APR.: More than 3,000 cherry trees bloom each April, and the **Vancouver Cherry Blossom Festival** (☎ *604/257–8120* 🌐 *www.vcbf.ca*) marks the occasion with a variety of programs and a haiku invitational.

MAY: The **Vancouver International Children's Festival** (☎ *604/708–5655* 🌐 *www.childrensfestival.ca*) is a week of storytelling, puppetry, circus arts, music, and theater.

JUNE–SEPT.: The **Vancouver International Jazz Festival** (☎ *888/438–5200* 🌐 *www.coastaljazz.ca*) **takes place the last week in June every year in more than 20 venues throughout the city.**

The **Bard on the Beach Shakespeare Festival** (☎ *604/739–0559 or 877/739–0559* 🌐 *www.bardonthebeach.org*) is held on the waterfront in Vanier Park.

JULY: Vancouver Pride Week (☎ *604/687–0955* 🌐 *www.vancouverpride.ca*) is a celebration of the gay community with tea dances, cruises, and parties.

The **Vancouver Folk Music Festival** (☎ *604/602–9798* 🌐 *www.thefestival.bc.ca*) welcomes singers and storytellers for three days of performances and children's programs.

Canada Day, on July 1, is celebrated with music and dancing at Canada Place and with interactive games and displays on Granville Island.

AUG.: The **Vancouver Queer Film Festival** (☎ *604/844–1615* 🌐 *www.queerfilmfestival.ca*) is an 11-day showcase of drama, comedy, documentaries, and musicals. There are also plenty of parties.

Musicfest Vancouver (☎ *604/688–1152* 🌐 *www.musicfestvancouver.ca*) is two weeks of orchestral, chamber, choral, world music, opera, and jazz performances around the city.

SEPT.: The **Vancouver International Comedy Festival** (☎ *604/683–0883* 🌐 *www.comedyfest.com*) is a week of wild antics, short films, stand-up, and theater.

The **Vancouver Fringe Festival** (☎ *604/257–0350* 🌐 *www.vancouverfringe.com*) is an eclectic mix of more than 500 theatrical offerings.

SEPT.–OCT.: The **Vancouver International Film Festival** (☎ *604/685–0260* 🌐 *www.viff.org*) draws more than 150,000 people to view films from more than 50 countries.

HOURS

Don't expect New York City hours on a night out in Vancouver. Although the city's bars, pubs, and lounges are usually open seven nights a week, they do close at a respectable 1 or 2 am. Dance clubs get lively at about 10 pm and, depending on the Vancouver Police Department's ever-changing regulations, stay open until 3 or even 4 am on weekends; many are closed on Sunday and Monday.

INFORMATION

For event information, pick up a copy of the free *Georgia Straight* (available at cafés and bookstores and street boxes around town) or look in the entertainment section of the *Vancouver Sun*: Thursday's paper has listings in the "Queue" section. Check the online Scout (🌐 *www.scoutmagazine.ca*) for a cheekier look at the city. Web-surf over to Gay Vancouver (🌐 *www.gayvancouver.net*) for an insider's look at the gay-friendly scene.

PRICES

Painting the town red in Vancouver costs. Perhaps not as much as it would in New York, Paris, or London, but don't leave your credit cards at home. If you're hitting the clubs, expect to pay a cover charge of around C$15 (usually waived for women before 11 pm). To see a name band or DJ perform at a club, you'll need to buy tickets well in advance—and expect to pay anywhere from C$25 to C$60. A beer will set you back around C$5, while a glass of wine or cocktail can cost between C$9 and C$15. Don't forget the 10% liquor tax added to the price of any alcoholic beverage, whether you're ordering at a bar, club, or restaurant. Tuesday and Wednesday are your best bets for a cheap night out: the comedy clubs charge about C$5 and neighborhood bars, featuring live music, often don't charge a cover.

WHAT TO WEAR

During the day, the Vancouver dress code usually falls somewhere between the fleece-pragmatism of Seattle, the cosmopolitan flair of San Francisco, and the lumberjacks of the Canadian Rockies. Especially during the drizzly winter days, people dress for warm comfort first—and you probably should, too—saving the skimpy for the summer months. But when it comes to nightlife, Vancouverites get serious. They love to dress up, so expect to see clubs and lounges filled with women in dresses and heels and lots of smartly dressed men. While many clubs maintain strict dress codes, it's really your partying peers who will look twice should you hit the dance floors in fleece.

WHERE TO GET TICKETS

Ticketmaster. You can buy half-price day-of-the-event tickets and full-price advance tickets to theater, concerts, festivals, and other performing-arts events in Vancouver from Ticketmaster at **Tickets Tonight**, a kiosk located at the Tourism Vancouver Visitor Centre. Tickets for many events around Vancounver can be booked online. ✉ *Tourism Vancouver Visitor Centre, 200 Burrard St.* ☎ *855/985–4357* 🌐 *www.ticketmaster.ca*.

NIGHTLIFE

CENTRAL VANCOUVER

DOWNTOWN, COAL HARBOUR, AND THE WEST END

BARS, PUBS, AND LOUNGES

Bacchus. Always an elegant choice, Bacchus is a gathering place for Vancouver's movers and shakers. There's music most evenings, as well as classic cocktails. ✉ *Wedgewood Hotel, 845 Hornby St., Downtown* ☎ *604/608–5319* 🌐 *www.wedgewoodhotel.com.*

Fountainhead Pub. With one of the largest street-side patios on Davie Street, you can do as the cruisin' locals do here: sit back, down a few beers, and watch the beautiful people pass by. It's also a gay-friendly space, so everyone feels welcome. ✉ *1025 Davie St., West End* ☎ *604/687–2222* 🌐 *www.thefountainheadpub.com.*

Mill Marine Bistro. This waterfront pub and restaurant has one of the best views of Stanley Park and the North Shore Mountains from its expansive patio. ✉ *1199 W. Cordova St., Coal Harbour* ☎ *604/687–6455* 🌐 *www.millbistro.ca.*

Sanafir. Lavish draperies, soaring ceilings, handcrafted urns, and low-slung seating adds to the sensual aura at this restaurant and lounge (the name is Arabic for "meeting place"). The tapas menu features small plates of Asian, Mediterranean, and Indian dishes. You can dine like pashas in the harem-style beds on the upper level—but it doesn't come cheap. DJs and bellydancers liven things up. ✉ *1026 Granville St., Downtown* ☎ *604/678–1049* 🌐 *www.sanafir.ca.*

BARS: HOTEL BARS

Hawksworth Bar and Lounge. Vancouver's reigning hotspot, you'll find quality cocktails here blended with house-made bitters, fresh herbs, and other local ingredients. For being so leather-paneled and clubby, it's surprisingly unstuffy. Head barman Brad Stanton has invented (or revived) a few cocktails worth stopping by for, including the Crimson Punch: vodka, honey, and flavors of black cherry, lime, and allspice. The dark mahogany floors and stark white walls of the Prohibition Lounge, also in the Rosewood Georgia Hotel, offer a completely different vibe. ✉ *Rosewood Hotel Georgia, 801 W. Georgia St., Downtown* ☎ *604/673–7000* 🌐 *www.hawksworthrestaurant.com.*

Xi Shi Lounge. In the Shangri-La Hotel, the Xi Shi Lounge has Asian-inspired cocktails served by waitresses in dresses reminiscent of 1920s Shanghai. Weekends are a good time to enjoy the live music and sip on the bar's original cocktail, the Casablanca (sparkling wine, gin, and hints of lemon and peach). The signature Iron Lotus is also blended with sparkling wine, adding vodka, elderflower, and ginger. ✉ *Shangri-La Hotel, 1128 W. Georgia St., Downtown* ☎ *604/695–1115.*

★ **Yew.** The tree-level bar at the Four Seasons provides a diverse environment of glass, natural wood, and sleek granite to reflect B.C.'s stunning natural environment. Happy hour attracts business executives, and at other times you'll see Canucks fans before or after the game. There are

5

more than 150 wines by the glass and a perpetually changing cocktail list. Stop by on Sunday for half-price bottles of wine. ✉ *Four Seasons Vancouver, 791 W. Georgia St., Downtown* ☎ *604/692–4939* 🌐 *www.yewrestaurant.com.*

BARS: WINE BARS

Tableau Bar Bistro. One of the few places in town you can order Moët & Chandon by the glass, this French bistro's wine bar includes B.C. gems such as Le Vieux Pin's '08 Syrah, which hails from Oliver, Canada's wine capital. Featured drinks change with the seasons at this Coal Harbour venue, and you can ask for the weekly "experimental cocktail." The patio seating views are worth waiting for, weather willing. ✉ *1181 Melville St., Coal Harbour* ☎ *604/639–8692* 🌐 *www.tableaubarbistro.com.*

Wine Room. A new concept in Vancouver, the Wine Room is devoted to nurturing the inner oenophile in all of us by offering wines that you usually can't get by the glass. In other words, at long last there's a place in Vancouver that's taking wine seriously. It's part of Joey Bentall One, but has its own dedicated entrance. Cocktails at the Long Bar aren't too bad, either. Signature martinis include the Hawaiian Hi Five (rum sloshed with fruit juice) and the Thai Lover (lychee-flavored liqueur, pineapple, and passion fruit). ✉ *507 Burrard St., Coal Harbour* ☎ *604/915–5639* 🌐 *www.joeyrestaurants.com/bentall-one.*

GAY NIGHTLIFE

1181. This place is all about stylish interior design—plush sofas, glass coffee tables, wood-paneled ceiling—and standard cocktails (think caipirinhas and mojitos). It gets particularly crowded on Saturdays, when a DJ spins behind the bar. ✉ *1181 Davie St., West End* ☎ *604/787–7130* 🌐 *www.1181.ca.*

Celebrities. A multimillion-dollar face-lift brought the celeb status back to this gay hot spot. It features a scantily clad crowd bumping and grinding to Top 40 hits, hip-hop, and R&B on a huge dance floor equipped with the latest in sound, lighting, and visuals. Men and women are welcome. ✉ *1022 Davie St., West End* ☎ *604/681–6180* 🌐 *www.celebritiesnightclub.com.*

Numbers. This renovated veteran of the Davie Street strip features five levels of furious fun, from live music to karaoke and an amateur strip night on the first Monday of the month. ✉ *1042 Davie St., West End* ☎ *604/685–4077* 🌐 *www.numbers.ca.*

MUSIC: DANCE CLUBS

AuBAR. A fixture of the city's nightlife scene for as long as we can remember, this dimly lit space seems to please a diverse crowd of clubbers. The music ranges from reggae to hip-hop to Top 40. It's open Thursday to Saturday, with the emphasis on the latter. ✉ *674 Seymour St., Downtown* ☎ *604/648–2227* 🌐 *www.aubarnightclub.com.*

Barcelona. There are enough cozy corners in this cavernous club for you to find a spot to sip a cocktail and chill. But mostly it's the electronic music that packs the dance floor. It's a good thing for the neighbors the place is soundproofed. ✉ *1180 Granville St., Downtown* ☎ *604/249–5151* 🌐 *www.barcelonanights.ca.*

Caprice. Wannabe movie stars queue up at this former movie theater that's been transformed into a two-level dance bar and lounge. Tag along with a hipster local or expect to wait in line. The much hyped L.E.D. bar, with backlit ceilings and walls resembling mirror balls, opened in 2012. As hip as it is, the dress is fairly casual, meaning hoodies will likely get past the doormen. ✉ *967 Granville St., Downtown* ☎ *604/685–3288* 🌐 *www.capricenightclub.com.*

Commodore Ballroom. This 1929 dance hall has been restored to its art-deco glory, complete with massive dance floor and state-of-the-art sound system. Indie rock bands and renowned DJs play here most nights. ✉ *868 Granville St., Downtown* ☎ *604/739–7469.*

ginger 62. This '60s-inspired lounge—with plush red carpets, comfy sofas, and black-and-white films projected on the wall—attracts a crowd of beautiful locals and the occasional VIP dressed to the nines. Be prepared to spend at least an hour waiting in line before setting foot in the dark, moody interior. ✉ *1219 Granville St., Downtown* ☎ *604/688–5494* 🌐 *www.ginger62.com.*

5

MUSIC: JAZZ AND BLUES

O'Doul's Restaurant & Bar. Open morning to night, this mahogany-paneled bistro and bar draws a mixed crowd of chic tourists and locals intent on hearing some of the best local jazz musicians play nightly. Jazz ensembles play on weekends. The name, by the way, is a tribute to baseball player Lefty O'Doul. ✉ *Listel Hotel, 1300 Robson St., West End* ☎ *604/661–1400* 🌐 *www.odoulsrestaurant.com.*

MUSIC: ROCK AND BLUES

Railway Club. In the early evening, this spot attracts film and media types to its pub-style rooms; after 8 it becomes a venue for local bands. Technically it's a private social club, but everyone of age is welcome. A dart board offers distraction while you enjoy a cold lager. ✉ *579 Dunsmuir St., Downtown* ☎ *604/681–1625* 🌐 *www.therailwayclub.com.*

Vogue Theatre. A former art-deco movie palace, the Vogue hosts a variety of concerts by local and visiting performers. ✉ *918 Granville St., Downtown* ☎ *604/569–1144* 🌐 *www.voguetheatre.com.*

GASTOWN AND CHINATOWN

BARS, PUBS, AND LOUNGES

★ **Chambar.** This restaurant and lounge has great character. The back dining room has views of False Creek while the bar is all exposed-brick walls, vibrant art, and soft lighting. If you're thirsty, try the Crosstown Southside, made with lavendar syrup and gin. ✉ *562 Beatty St., Crosstown* ☎ *604/879–7119* 🌐 *www.chambar.com.*

Chill Winston. Decked out with black-leather sofas, exposed wood beams, warm lighting, and a view of Gastown's lively Alexander Square, this restaurant and lounge attracts a well-heeled crowd of urban locals. ✉ *3 Alexander St., Gastown* ☎ *604/288–9575* 🌐 *www.chillwinston.com.*

Fodor'sChoice ★ **The Diamond.** At the top of a narrow staircase above Maple Tree Square, the Diamond occupies one of the city's oldest buildings. A bartending school by day, cocktail lounge by night, the venue's official name is the

Diamond Preparatory School For All Things Drinks. Standing at the bar, co-owner Josh Pape is like a conductor at the symphony. You can choose among "boozy," "proper," or "delicate" options on the drinks menu. The Buck Buck Mule is a refreshing mix of gin, sherry, cucumber juice, cilantro, lime juice, and ginger beer; the Tequila Martinez features tequila, vermouth, Lillet, peach bitters, and an orange twist. ⊠ *6 Powell St., at Carrall St., Gastown* ☎ *604/568–8272.*

The Irish Heather. Expect a mixed crowd of local hipsters and out-of-towners enjoying properly poured pints of Guinness, mixed beer drinks (try a shandy, which is beer mixed with lemonade), and live Irish music. There's a restaurant upstairs, and out back in an atmospheric coach house is the **Shebeen,** or whiskey house, where you can try any of about 130 whiskeys. Reserve ahead for Sunday evening's Long Table Series, where you can make 40 or so new friends as you enjoy ales and tasty food. ⊠ *210 Carrall St., Gastown* ☎ *604/688–9779* ⊕ *www.irishheather.com.*

The Keefer Bar. The creative director of cocktails at the Keefer Bar has fully capitalized on the Chinatown connection, using ingredients sourced from local herbalists. Try one of their prescriptions: Lost in Chinatown, a blend of Yellow Chartreuse, Pernod, bourbon, and the exotic-sounding yun xhi syrup. Small plates of Asian dishes make good nibbling. The decor is dark and red, with hanging cylindrical neon lights. There's usually a weekly (and well-attended) burlesque night. ⊠ *135 Keefer St., Chinatown* ☎ *604/688–1961* ⊕ *www.thekeeferbar.com.*

Fodor's Choice ★ **Pourhouse Vancouver.** Familiar with the 1862 bartending bible *How To Mix Drinks* by Jerry Thomas? It includes the golden-era-of-cocktails classics from which the Pourhouse draws its inspiration. Before this very first bartending manual was published, there was only an oral tradition of how to blend a mint julep or a sloe gin fizz. Test the bartender's skill and dedication to the bar's theme by asking for a Pick-Me-Up, a Chain-Lightning, or a Corpse Reviver when you drop by this Gastown hotspot. ⊠ *162 Water St., Gastown* ☎ *604/568–7022* ⊕ *www.pourhousevancouver.com.*

BARS: BREWPUBS

Alibi Room. Instead of pairing wine with food, this place serves the perfect beer with your meal. Kegs of microbrews from around B.C. and beyond are its pride and joy. In additon to boasting the best selection of craft beers in Vancouver, there are also organic wines and a few fun cocktails. ⊠ *157 Alexander St., Gastown* ☎ *604/623–3383.*

Steamworks. A coffee hangout early in the day, this hipster and urban-professional hangout morphs into a pub by early afternoon. Its traditional ales and lagers are brewed in small batches. There's nice patio seating with harbor views, weather permitting. ⊠ *375 Water St., Gastown* ☎ *604/689–2739* ⊕ *www.steamworks.com.*

BARS: WINE BARS

★ **Salt Tasting Room.** This place has communal tables, concrete floors, and a selection of local and international wines, beers, and sherries. They're perfect for pairing with the mix-and-match cured meats and artisanal cheese selections that constantly change. By the way, Blood Alley was once the city's meat-packing district. Legend has it that the ghoulish

Yaletown has hip restaurants and bars (many with patios) for lounging in the evening.

name came from the buckets of blood butchers threw down the cobblestone street. ✉ *45 Blood Alley, Gastown* ☎ *604/633–1912* 🌐 *www.salttastingroom.com.*

MUSIC: DANCE CLUBS

Fortune Sound Club. In the city's hipper-than-grit Chinatown, this sound-system-centric dance club is all modern and fresh on the scene. It manages to incorporate some eco-friendly elements into the design—so Vancouver! ✉ *147 E. Pender St., Chinatown* ☎ *604/569–1758* 🌐 *www.fortunesoundclub.com.*

Guilt & Co. The menu at this Gastown favorite features lagers, ales, pale ales, pilsners, stouts, and ciders, and then there's what's on tap, a wine list, and a cocktail menu. There are also about a dozen different ways to say cheese plate, including "chunk of cheese." Rock bands aren't all the music club hosts—there are also painting nights. ✉ *1 Alexander St., Gastown* ☎ *604/288–1704.*

Post Modern. In a historic building and equipped with top-notch sound and light systems, this club has a look that's ultra-hip, including polished concrete floors, dark smoked glass, countless mirrors, and neon lights. House and guest DJs spin an eclectic mix of funk, rock, soul, and Top 40 hits to a mostly thirtysomething crowd. ✉ *7 Alexander St., Gastown* ☎ *604/647–0121.*

Shine Nightclub. Big-name DJs, good tunes, and a cozy space are the draw here.Trendsetters and college kids come to lounge and listen to the '80s classics, dancehall, rap, and rock-and-roll. A red chill-out room in back is the perfect place to end a sweaty night on the dance floor. ✉ *364 Water St., Gastown* ☎ *604/408–4321* 🌐 *www.shinenightclub.com.*

YALETOWN

BARS, PUBS, AND LOUNGES

AFTERglow. Typically packed by 10 pm, this Yaletown bar and lounge gets its radiance from the fuchsia lighting on the pink-and-white brick walls. It's a great place to lounge on comfy sofas, sip colorful martinis, and practice the art of see-and-be-seen. It's a part of the Glowbal Grill. ✉ *1079 Mainland St., Yaletown* ☎ *604/602–0835* 🌐 *www.glowbalgrill.com.*

Blue Water Café and Raw Bar. The patio at this Yaletown café fills up quickly with an after-work crowd during warm weather, and inside you can count on the cozy bar to take the chill out of winter. You'll find a dozen varieties of B.C. oysters paired expertly with one of the largest selections of local wines in the city. The vast back bar serves more than 100 different malt whiskeys, as well as rare tequilas and cognacs. ✉ *1095 Hamilton St., Yaletown* ☎ *604/688–8078* 🌐 *www.bluewatercafe.net.*

George. One of Vancouver's swankiest cocktail bars, George is dedicated to classic cocktails and the people who drink them, from the local glitterati to executives in Armani suits. The wine cellar includes a choice sampling of Okanagan vintages as well as French, Chilean, and Australian wines by the bottle or by the glass. DJs spin the latest tunes. ✉ *1137 Hamilton St., Yaletown* ☎ *604/628–5555* 🌐 *www.georgelounge.com.*

BARS: BREWPUBS

Yaletown Brewing Company. In a renovated warehouse with a glassed-in brewery turning out several tasty beers, this always-crowded pub and patio has a lively singles' scene. Despite its popularity it still feels like a neighborhood place. ✉ *1111 Mainland St., Yaletown* ☎ *604/681–2739* 🌐 *www.markjamesgroup.com/yaletown.html.*

BARS: HOTEL BARS

Opus Bar. Local hipsters, executives in suits, and film-industry types sip martinis (or perhaps a cocktail made with vodka, passion fruit, and blood oranges) while scoping out the room. The voyeuristic washrooms have video cameras and one-way glass walls. ✉ *Opus Hotel, 350 Davie St., Yaletown* ☎ *604/642–0557* 🌐 *www.opusbar.ca.*

CASINOS

Edgewater Casino. This casino features 500 slot machines, a poker room, 48 table games, and a bistro. It's open around the clock. ✉ *311–750 Pacific Blvd. S, Yaletown* ☎ *604/687–3343* 🌐 *www.edgewatercasino.ca.*

MUSIC: DANCE CLUBS

Bar None. Once you hit Bar None you never really have to leave Yaletown. This is the place to get your groove on after dinner and drinks. They like to call the vibe "NYC," but it's really Yaletown through and through. Celebrated Vancouver deejays spin house and electronica several nights a week, and international stars sometimes take over as well. There's a revived cocktail scene, making this longtime favorite seem new again. ✉ *1222 Hamilton St., Yaletown* ☎ *604/899–3229* 🌐 *www.donnellygroup.ca.*

GREATER VANCOUVER

GRANVILLE ISLAND

BARS, PUBS, AND LOUNGES

Bridges. This local landmark near the Granville Public Market has a cozy nautical-theme pub and the city's biggest marina-side deck. In warm weather you're treated to breathtaking views of the harbor, mountains, and city. ✉ *1696 Duranleau St., Granville Island* ☎ *604/687–4400* 🌐 *www.bridgesrestaurant.com.*

The Sandbar. With a seafood restaurant, a wine bar, and piano Sunday to Thursday nights in the Teredo Lounge, this venue has something for everyone, including televised sports on game days. For dramatic views over False Creek, reserve a table on the rooftop patio in the summer. ✉ *1535 Johnson St., Granville Island* ☎ *604/669–9030* 🌐 *www.vancouverdine.com/sandbar.*

BARS: BREWPUBS

Dockside Restaurant. A 50-foot aquarium, modern fireplaces, and floor-to ceiling windows lend atmosphere to a casual seating area where you can take in picturesque Yaletown and North Shore mountain views. Listen to the soft sounds of boats navigating False Creek from the seaside patio as you enjoy a house-brewed German-style beer. ✉ *Granville Island Hotel, 1253 Johnston St., Granville Island* ☎ *604/685–7070* 🌐 *www.docksidevancouver.com.*

COMEDY CLUBS

Vancouver TheatreSports League. A hilarious improv troupe performs Wednesday to Saturday before an enthusiastic crowd at the Improv Centre on Granville Island. ✉ *1502 Duranleau St., Granville Island* ☎ *604/738–7013* 🌐 *www.vtsl.com.*

MUSIC: ROCK AND BLUES

Backstage Lounge. Local bands of unpredictable talent perform Wednesday through Saturday nights. Hit or miss. ✉ *1585 Johnston St., Granville Island* ☎ *604/687–1354* 🌐 *www.thebackstagelounge.com.*

KITSILANO

BARS, PUBS, AND LOUNGES

Kits Beach Boathouse. A summer visit to Vancouver isn't complete without an afternoon enjoying cocktails on this rooftop patio overlooking the beach volleyball matches at Kits Beach. Views of the vivid sunsets and dramatic winter storms are exceptional, though you may want to retreat behind the floor-to-ceiling windows to sip in comfort. ✉ *1305 Arbutus St., Kitsilano* ☎ *604/738–5487.*

BARS: WINE BARS

Abigail's Party. The wine and cheese menus, curated to complement one another, change weekly at this friendly establishment. It's best to go either before or after the dinner hour, so you can sample inventive cocktails with intoxicating names like the Wicca (elderflower and peach syrups with a dash of sauvignon blanc). ✉ *1685 Yew St., Kitsilano* ☎ *604/739–4677.*

5

DID YOU KNOW?

The Opus Bar, with its handcrafted, top-of-the-line cocktails, is one of Vancouver's hippest and hottest venues. And Yaletown as a whole delivers great cocktails and equally great people-watching.

ALL THAT JAZZ

Vancouver is home to one of the most sophisticated and accessible jazz scenes in Canada, with lots of clubs, bars, and restaurants hosting local and international talent. Two local groups will make sure you're in the know.

Coastal Jazz and Blues Society. Coastal Jazz and Blues Society has a hotline that details upcoming concerts and clubs. The society also runs the Vancouver International Jazz Festival, which lights up 40 venues around town the last week in June. ☎ *888/438-5200* 🌐 *www.coastaljazz.ca.*

Rogue Folk Club. This nonprofit organization presents folk, roots, and traditional Celtic concerts at various venues around town. ☎ *604/736-3022* 🌐 *www.roguefolk.bc.ca.*

5

MUSIC: JAZZ AND BLUES

Cellar. This is the city's top venue for jazz, and the calendar features a who's who of the Canadian music scene. Think New York's Village Vanguard, B.C. style. ✉ *3611 W. Broadway, Kitsilano* ☎ *604/738–1959* 🌐 *www.cellarjazz.com.*

MAIN STREET/MOUNT PLEASANT

COMEDY CLUBS

Yuk Yuk's. This is the place to go Tuesday to Saturday evenings to check out some of Canada's best professional stand-up comedians and up-and-coming amateurs. ✉ *2837 Cambie St., at 12th Ave., Main St./Mt. Pleasant* ☎ *604/696–9857* 🌐 *www.yukyuks.com.*

EAST SIDE/SOMA

BARS, PUBS, AND LOUNGES

Cascade Room. Named after the signature beer that the Vancouver Brewery once produced on this very spot, the Cascade Room is a solid SoMa neighborhood pub. ✉ *2616 Main St., at Broadway, SoMa* ☎ *604/709–8650* 🌐 *www.thecascade.ca.*

Habit Lounge. For C$8 you get a whiskey shot and a 20-ounce beer—now you see why many people find this place habit-forming. This up-and-coming neighborhood is where the young working stiffs hang out. Think vinyl-covered padded booths and neon-lit deer heads and you'll get an idea of the decor. This is a Canadian pub, as the young, hip folks would have it. ✉ *2610 Main St., SoMa* ☎ *604/877–8582.*

The Main. This local favorite draws a crowd that enjoys drinking beer and listening to live music in a huge steel-beamed warehouse. If you're a fan of Canadian crooners, this is the place for you. The Main is inviting and yes, the beer is on tap. ✉ *4210 Main St., SoMa* ☎ *604/709–8555* 🌐 *www.themainonmain.ca.*

Whip Gallery. It's a bit out of the way, but this lofty space with Douglas fir–beamed ceilings and exposed brick attracts a hip, SoMa crowd. There's a bar, atrium, and mezzanine with a DJ, not to mention the featured artist of the moment. Order what's on tap, choose from one of seven "deadly sin" martinis, or indulge in the house-made sangria.

There's also a respectable whiskey list. ✉ *209 E. 6th Ave., at Main St., SoMa* ☎ *604/874–4687* 🌐 *www.thewhiprestaurant.com.*

THE ARTS

From performing arts to theater, classical music, dance, and a thriving gallery scene, there's much for an art lover to choose from in Vancouver.

CLASSICAL MUSIC

With so much going on at different classical music venues around town, you can easily enjoy something different every day you're in town.

CHAMBER MUSIC AND SMALL ENSEMBLES

Early Music Vancouver. Medieval, Renaissance, baroque, and early classical music is performed on period instruments year-round. The society also hosts the Vancouver Early Music Programme and Festival from mid-July to mid-August at the University of British Columbia. ☎ *604/732–1610* 🌐 *www.earlymusic.bc.ca.*

Friends of Chamber Music. A diverse selection of ensembles performs as part of the Friends of Chamber Music. ☎ *604/437–5747* 🌐 *www.friendsofchambermusic.ca.*

Vancouver Recital Society. The society presents both emerging and well-known classical musicians in concert September to May at the Chan Centre for the Performing Arts, the Vancouver Playhouse, and the Orpheum Theatre. In summer, it hosts the Vancouver Chamber Music Festival. ☎ *604/602–0363* 🌐 *www.vanrecital.com.*

OPERA

Vancouver Opera. From October through May, the city's opera company stages four productions a year at the Queen Elizabeth Theatre in downtown Vancouver. ✉ *Queen Elizabeth Theatre, 630 Hamilton St., Downtown* ☎ *604/683–0222* 🌐 *www.vancouveropera.ca.*

ORCHESTRAS

Vancouver Symphony Orchestra. The resident company at the Orpheum Theatre presents classical and popular music. It also has performances at the Chan Centre. ✉ *Smith St. and Seymour St., Downtown* ☎ *604/876–3434* 🌐 *www.vancouversymphony.ca.*

DANCE

A few of the many modern-dance companies in town are DanceArts Vancouver and New Works; besides the Scotia Bank Dance Centre, the Firehall Arts Centre and the "Cultch," Vancouver East Cultural Centre, are among their performance venues.

Ballet British Columbia. Innovative dances and timeless classics by internationally acclaimed choreographers are presented by the Ballet British Columbia. Most performances are at the Queen Elizabeth Theatre. ✉ *677 Davie St., Downtown* ☎ *604/732–5003* 🌐 *www.balletbc.com.*

The Dance Center. The hub of dance in British Columbia, this striking building with an art-deco facade hosts full-scale performances, informal showcases, and other events by national and international artists. ■ **TIP→ It often presents informal noon performances as part of the**

The Centre in Vancouver for Performing Arts showcases a wide variety of international shows.

Discover Dance! series. ✉ *677 Davie St., Scotia Bank Dance Centre, Downtown* ☎ *604/606–6400* 🌐 *www.thedancecentre.ca.*

MOVIES

Locals sometimes refer to Vancouver as Hollywood North, mostly because of the frequent film shoots around town. Movie theaters featuring first- and second-run, underground, experimental, alternative, and classic films make up the urban fabric. Here's a tip from the locals: tickets are half-price on Tuesday at most chain-owned movie theaters.

Fifth Avenue Cinemas. This small multiplex shows foreign and independent films. ✉ *2110 Burrard St., Kitsilano* ☎ *604/734–7469.*

Pacific Cinémathèque. The not-for-profit society is dedicated to all things celluloid, from exhibitions and lectures to independent and international features. ■ **TIP→ Cinema Sundays are especially good for families, as discussions, games, and activities follow the movies.** ✉ *1131 Howe St., Downtown* ☎ *604/688–3456* 🌐 *www.cinematheque.bc.ca.*

Ridge Theatre. A long-established art-house cinema, the Ridge is popular with the artsy crowd. ✉ *3131 Arbutus St., Kitsilano* ☎ *604/738–6311.*

THEATER

Vancouver has a sophisticated theater scene featuring more than 30 local companies.

Arts Club Theatre Company. This well-regarded company stages productions, a few even by local playwrights, on three principal stages: the Stanley Industrial Alliance Stage, the Revue Stage, and the Granville Island Stage. ✉ *Stanley Industrial Alliance Stage, 2750 Granville St., at 12th Ave., Shaughnessy* ☎ *604/687–1644* 🌐 *www.artsclub.com.*

Carousel Theatre for Young People. Children's theater is the focus here, with performances at the Waterfront Theatre and sometimes outdoors at Performance Works. ✉ *Waterfront Theatre, 1412 Cartwright St., Granville Island* ☎ *604/685–6217* 🌐 *www.carouseltheatre.ca.*

Centre in Vancouver for Performing Arts. This large space attracts big international shows, from Broadway musicals to Chinese dance productions. ✉ *777 Homer St., Downtown* ☎ *604/602–0616* 🌐 *www.centreinvancouver.com.*

Chan Centre for the Performing Arts. There's a 1,200-seat concert hall, a theater, and a cinema in this vast arts complex on the campus of the University of British Columbia. ✉ *University of British Columbia, 6265 Crescent Rd., Point Grey* ☎ *604/822–9197* 🌐 *www.chancentre.com.*

The Cultch. The Vancouver East Cultural Centre, now referred to as the Cultch, is a multipurpose performance space hosting music concerts, theater productions, food festivals, and more. ✉ *1895 Venables St., East Vancouver* ☎ *604/251–1363* 🌐 *www.thecultch.com.*

Firehall Arts Centre. Innovative theater and modern dance are showcased at this intimate downtown space on the border of trendy Gastown. ✉ *280 E. Cordova St., Downtown* ☎ *604/689–0926* 🌐 *www.firehallartscentre.ca.*

Queen Elizabeth Theatre. This is a major venue for ballet, opera, and similar large-scale events. Seating 2,781 people, the Queen Elizabeth is one of the largest theaters in Canada. ✉ *630 Hamilton St., Downtown* ☎ *604/665–3050.*

Theatre Under the Stars. In summer, family-friendly musicals like *The Music Man* and *Titanic* are the main draw at Malkin Bowl, an outdoor amphitheater in Stanley Park. You can watch the show from the lawn or from the Rose Garden Tea House as part of a dinner–theater package. ■ **TIP→ Ask about the Family Package Deal when buying tickets.** ✉ *2099 Beach Ave., Stanley Park* ☎ *877/840–0457* 🌐 *www.tuts.ca/tickets.*

Waterfront Theatre. Next door to Granville Island's Kids Market, this theater often hosts children's and youth-oriented performances. ✉ *1412 Cartwright St., Granville Island* ☎ *604/685–1731* 🌐 *www.waterfronttheatre.ca.*

6

Vancouver Where to Eat

WORD OF MOUTH

"Not an expert, but I have never had better sushi anywhere than I had in Vancouver. And the prices are extremely reasonable and some just very cheap. Enjoy. We loved eating in Vancouver, so many places to choose from."

—annetti

Updated by Carolyn B. Heller

From inventive neighborhood bistros to glamorous downtown dining rooms to Asian restaurants that rival those in the capitals of Asia, Vancouver has a diverse array of gastronomic options.

Many cutting-edge establishments are perfecting Modern Canadian fare, which—at this end of the country—incorporates regional seafood (notably salmon, halibut, and spot prawns) and locally grown produce. Vancouver is a hotbed of "localism," with many restaurants emphasizing the provenance of their ingredients and embracing products that hail from within a 100-mile-or-so radius of the city, or at least from within B.C.

With at least a third of the city's population of Asian heritage, it's no surprise that Asian eateries abound in Vancouver. From mom-and-pop noodle shops, curry houses, and corner sushi bars to elegant and upscale dining rooms, cuisine from China, Taiwan, Hong Kong, Japan, and India (and to a lesser extent, from Korea, Thailand, Vietnam, and Malaysia) can be found all over town. Look for restaurants emphasizing Chinese regional cuisine (particularly in the suburb of Richmond), contemporary Indian-influenced fare, and different styles of Japanese cooking, from casual ramen shops to lively *izakayas* (Japanese tapas bars) that serve an eclectic array of small plates. Even restaurants that are not specifically "Asian" have long adopted abundant Asian influences—your grilled salmon may be served with *gai lan* (Chinese broccoli), black rice, or a coconut-milk curry.

British Columbia's wine industry is enjoying great popularity, and many restaurants serve wines from the province's 200-plus wineries. Most B.C. wines come from the Okanagan Valley in the province's interior, but Vancouver Island is another main wine-producing area. Merlot, Pinot Noir, Pinot Gris, and Chardonnay are among the major varieties; also look for ice wine, a dessert wine made from grapes that are picked while they are frozen on the vines.

If you enjoy strolling to scope out your dining options downtown, try Robson Street, Denman and Davie Streets, Yaletown's Hamilton and Mainland Streets, or Kitsilano's West 4th Avenue between Burrard and Balsam Streets.

VANCOUVER DINING PLANNER

DRESS

Dining is informal. Neat casual dress is appropriate everywhere; nice jeans are fine, though you might want something dressier than sneakers in the evening.

HOURS

Most restaurants that serve lunch are open from 11:30 until 2 or 2:30. Downtown spots that serve a business clientele may not open for lunch on weekends. Dinner is usually served from 5:30 until at least 10. Some dining rooms are open later on weekends, but in general, Vancouver isn't a late-night eating city. Some restaurants close on Sunday or Monday.

RESERVATIONS

Except in cafés and casual eateries, reservations are always a good idea, particularly for weekend evenings.

SMOKING

Smoking is prohibited by law in all Vancouver restaurants.

TIPPING AND TAXES

A 15% tip is expected. Restaurant meals are currently subject to a 12% Harmonized Sales Tax (HST). However, in 2013, the HST is slated to be repealed, which means that only a 5% Goods and Services Tax (GST) will be levied on the food portion of restaurant bills and a 10% liquor tax will be charged on wine, beer, and spirits.

WINE

Many restaurants serve excellent B.C. wines. Sometimes the most interesting wines are from small producers, so ask for recommendations.

WHAT IT COSTS

Vancouver's top tables can be as pricey as the best restaurants in major American cities. You can often dine more economically at some of the smaller but just-as-inventive bistros or by sharing small plates at one of the many tapas-style eateries. Some restaurants have reasonably priced prix fixe menus, and at certain times of the year, including the midwinter Dine Out Vancouver promotion, even the top dining rooms offer these fixed-price options. Check the website for Tourism Vancouver (🌐 *www.tourismvancouver.com*) for details. Family-style Asian restaurants and noodle shops are generally a good value year-round, and when the sun is shining, you can always pick up some cheese, bread, and fruit, and picnic at the beach.

Prices in the reviews are the average cost of a main course at dinner or, if dinner is not served, at lunch.

A SIDE TRIP TO CHINA—FOR DINNER

With one of the largest Asian populations of any city outside of Asia, metropolitan Vancouver has a wealth of opportunities for Asian-food lovers.

The area's Chinese food, in particular, ranks among the best in North America. There are still many Chinese restaurants, markets, and bakeries in Vancouver's city-center Chinatown—the "old" Chinatown near downtown—but Richmond, the suburban "new" Chinatown near the airport, is where interesting things are really happening, food-wise.

Richmond is full of shiny shopping malls and upscale Chinese restaurants that cater to the well-to-do Asian community and rival the best of Hong Kong, Shanghai, or Taipei. Also abundant are hole-in-the-wall noodle shops, modest storefront eateries, bakeries selling golden-baked pastries or freshly steamed buns, and grab-and-go food courts. And best of all for visitors, the Canada Line—which links downtown and Richmond in less than 30 minutes—is a direct line to Richmond's Chinese eateries.

EAT REGIONALLY

Richmond's Chinese restaurants often focus on a style of cooking, so although the menu may be wide-ranging, stick with regional specialties—delicate steamed fish in a Cantonese dining room, and a fiery stir-fry or hotpot in a Sichuan eatery. You can also check out Vancouver's annual Chinese Restaurant Awards (🌐 www.chineserestaurantawards.com), which recognize standout dishes at area restaurants.

EATING ALONG THE CANADA LINE

Aberdeen Station: A portrait of Chairman Mao welcomes you to **Bushuair Restaurant** (✉ *4600 No. 3 Rd.* ☎ *604/285-3668*) in a strip mall—very appropriate, as the eatery serves the fiery food of Hunan, Mao's home province. The extensive picture menu (with some endearingly quirky translations) can help you order; try a whole fish buried in chilies, or anything with the smoky Chinese bacon. Casual and fun, **Northern Delicacy** (✉ *Aberdeen Centre, 4151 Hazelbridge Way* ☎ *604/233-7050*) cooks up northern-style small plates for young Asian hipsters. Although the exterior is modest, **Sea Harbour Seafood Restaurant** (✉ *3711 No. 3 Rd.* ☎ *604/232-0816*) north of Aberdeen Station serves first-rate Hong Kong–style seafood to well-heeled locals. Ask for whatever fish is freshest, and try the distinctive pork with chayote squash. Reservations are recommended.

Lansdowne Station: Get off at Lansdowne Station for this branch of Little Sheep Mongolian Hot Pot (✉ *Lansdowne Centre, 5300 No. 3 Rd.* ☎ *604/231-8966*). You choose a variety of meats (lamb is the specialty), vegetables, and noodles to cook at your table in a bubbling cauldron of broth. Look for the "Mongolian hot pot" sign on the east side of Lansdowne Centre Mall.

Richmond-Brighouse Station: Shanghai River Restaurant (✉ *7831 Westminster Hwy.* ☎ *604/233-8885*) specializes in Shanghai-style fare, including handmade dumplings and noodles (you can watch the chefs at work in the open kitchen). Book in advance or prepare to wait. The basic but delicious food stalls on the second floor of **Richmond Public Market** (✉ *8260 Westminster Hwy* ☎ *604/821-1888*) reward adventurous diners with authentic Asian street foods.

DIM SUM

Dim sum (Chinese small plates) is wildly popular in Richmond, particularly for weekend brunch. Most local restaurants eschew the custom of food carts circling the room. Instead, after you order from a (bilingual) menu, dishes are brought hot from the kitchen directly to your table. Many dim sum spots are less crowded before 11 am. For Shanghai-style dim sum, walk south from Lansdowne Station to **Dinesty Restaurant** (✉ *8111 Ackroyd Rd., at No. 3 Rd.,* ☎ *604/303-7772*), where the *xiao long bao* (soup dumplings) are excellent. Make your way to **Fisherman's Terrace** (✉ *Aberdeen Centre, 4151 Hazelbridge Way* ☎ *604/303-9739*) in a shopping mall for traditional Hong Kong-style dim sum. At **Shiang Garden Seafood Restaurant** (✉ *4540 No. 3 Rd.* ☎ *604/273-8858*), south of Aberdeen Station, you can sample both classic and contemporary dim sum dishes. The upscale, multilevel dining area is a respite from the hustle and bustle.

A PASSAGE TO INDIA

From modest curry houses to more upscale dining rooms, Vancouver's Indian restaurants reflect the increasingly varied nature of the city's South Asian community, offering regional specialties from across India.

The Punjabi Market neighborhood, at Main Street and 49th Avenue, is a long-established "Little India" that was populated largely by migrants from northwest India. While many newer Indo-Canadian immigrants have settled outside Vancouver, in Surrey and other suburbs, the Punjabi Market is still worth a visit for its jewelry stores, sari shops, and—naturally—restaurants.

Two long-standing eateries, **Original All India Sweets** (✉ *6507 Main St.* ☏ *604/327–0891*) and **Himalaya Restaurant** (✉ *6587 Main St.* ☏ *604/324–6514*) serve traditional Punjabi dishes and vast, well-priced buffets.

DIWALI

Vancouver in the fall means Diwali (🌐 *www.vandiwali.ca*), the South Asian festival of lights celebrated by Hindus, Sikhs, and Jains around the world. The festival showcases Indian music and dance; vendors sell Indian food; and community centers offer Indian craft workshops in sari wrapping and henna application. Restaurants and snack shops in the Punjabi Market district sell colorful holiday sweets.

AROUND VANCOUVER, AROUND INDIA

To explore the food of Indian regions other than the Punjab, you'll need to venture farther afield. There's no one neighborhood in Vancouver proper that will satisfy all your Indian cravings, but Bus no. 19 between Stanley Park and Metrotown stops near all of the following restaurants.

Chutney Villa. For south Indian fare, with its *dosa* (rice and lentil pancakes), *idli* (steamed rice cakes), and seafood and coconut curries, try this comfortably classy dining room. ✉ *147 E. Broadway, west of Main St., Main St./Mt. Pleasant* ☎ *604/872-2228* 🌐 *www.chutneyvilla.com.*

House of Dosas. If you're a big dosa fan, it's worth the trek to this modest spot where the specialty is massive—and massively tasty—versions of this South Indian classic. ✉ *1391 Kingsway, at Knight St., East Side* ☎ *604/875-1283* 🌐 *www.houseofdosas.ca.*

Some members of Vancouver's Indian community have their roots in Africa, particularly Uganda, and this cultural mix has created additional dining options.

Jambo Grill. At the cheerful Jambo Grill, you can pair the first-rate tandoori chicken or spicy grilled ribs with addictive *mogo* (cassava fries), curries, or masala fish. ✉ *3219 Kingsway, East Side* ☎ *604/433-5060* 🌐 *www.jambogrill.ca.*

FINE DINING, INDIAN-STYLE

When Vikram Vij opened his eponymous restaurant in the mid-1990s, **Vij's** shook up the Vancouver food scene. This contemporary South Asian dining room that paired traditional flavors and techniques with local produce and ingredients was unique in Canada, and indeed in North America. Vij's is still going strong—waits of over an hour for a table at this no-reservations spot are routine—and now Vij and his wife Meeru Dhalwala also run the more casual **Rangoli** next door. Both are reviewed later in this chapter.

WHERE INDIA MEETS CHINA

With Vancouver's large Indian and Chinese communities, perhaps it's no surprise to find food that fuses the fare of these two nations. Two restaurants on Vancouver's East Side serve Indian-style Chinese dishes, where the sweet, sour, and hot tastes of India and China come together. For many South Asians, this hybrid cuisine is comfort food, akin to the chop suey and ginger beef served at old-style Chinese-American or Chinese-Canadian eateries. At **Green Lettuce** (✉ *1949 Kingsway* ☎ *604/876-9883*), you'll find *paneer* (cheese) in ginger sauce, chili chicken, Manchurian cauliflower, and crispy hot-and-spicy tofu. At the popular **Chili Pepper House** (✉ *3003 Kingsway* ☎ *604/431-8633*), the menu ranges from hot-and-sour soup to okra and potato curry to Hakka-style vegetable chow mein.

BEYOND THE SUSHI BAR

Vancouverites joke that they could eat sushi every day for months and never visit the same restaurant twice. And while sushi bars do seem numerous, Japanese food in Vancouver means far more than just *maki* and *nigiri*.

Ramen shops are one popular, moderately priced Japanese option, and if you're thinking packaged instant noodles, think again. The area around the intersection of Denman and Robson Streets in the West End is ramen-central. Ignore the bare-bones setting. The lines out the door at long-standing favorite **Kintaro Ramen** (✉ *788 Denman St.* ☎ *604/682–7568*) attest to the quality of its hearty, comforting noodle soups. At **Motomachi Shokudo** (✉ *740 Denman St.* ☎ *604/609–0310*), the Japanese-style wooden furnishings reveal some flair, and the menu offers choices for patrons who don't eat pork; a specialty here is smoky charcoal ramen (trust us, it tastes better than it sounds). The first Canadian outpost of a Japanese ramen chain, **Santouka Ramen** (✉ *1690 Robson St.* ☎ *604/681–8121*) is known for its *toroniko ramen*, made with fresh pork cheeks.

SIPPING SAKE

Sake (rice wine)—along with beer or green tea—is the drink of choice for Japanese meals, and most Japanese restaurants serve at least one or two varieties of sake; higher-end spots offer an array of sake types. Vancouver even has its own sake brewery. With tastings in the shop **Artisan Sake Maker** (✉ *1339 Railspur Alley* ☎ *604/685–7253*), this is the place to get to know sake.

FOR JAPANESE SMALL PLATES, SAY "IZAKAYA"

Vancouverites have fallen hard for *izakayas* (Japanese tapas bars), which combine the casual West Coast vibe with intriguing, easy-to-share small plates. Most izakaya dishes are in the C$8–C$12 range, so you can afford to experiment. Behind its ornate wooden door, **Kingyo** (✉ *871 Denman St.* ☎ *604/608–1677*) occupies the stylish end of the spectrum, with a carved wood bar, lots of greenery, and sexy mood lighting. The intriguing small plates, from salmon carpaccio to cucumber kimchi to the chicken and cod-roe spring roll, are delicious. The branches of the **Guu** (✉ *838 Thurlow St.* ☎ *604/685–8817* 🌐 *guu-izakaya.com*) local chain of izakayas are just plain fun, serving up tasty bar snacks—like *kabocha karokke* (pumpkin and egg croquette), garlicky barbecue ribs, or spicy calamari—to pair with beer, sake, or funky cocktails. Besides this West End branch, you'll find Guu at 1698 Robson Street in the West End and 375 Water Street in Gastown. Mix and match skewers to make a meal at one of the branches of the laid-back *yakitori* chain **Zakkushi** (✉ *823 Denman St.* ☎ *604/685–1136* 🌐 *www.zakkushi.com*). In addition to this branch in the West End, try 1833 West 4th Avenue in Kitsilano and 4075 Main Street in Main St./Mt. Pleasant.

HOT DOG!

Only in multi-culti Vancouver? Perhaps. But the **Japadog** (✉ *530 Robson St.* ☎ *604/569–1158*) storefront selling Japanese-style hot dogs—a sit-down spin-off of a wildly successful food cart—has a loyal following, topping its bratwurst and wieners with teriyaki sauce, nori, and other Asian condiments. You can still find the carts at two Burrard Street locations—between Robson Street and Smithe Street and at the corner of West Pender Street—and at another near Waterfront Station on West Cordova Street at Granville.

AND SUSHI, TOO . . .

If it is sushi you're craving, Vancouver is happy to oblige. From haute Japanese dining rooms like **Tojo's** *(see full listing for contact info)*, to the cheap-and-cheerful sushi bars on nearly every corner, the city offers plenty of options for raw-fish fans.

Juno Bistro. This tiny storefront eatery is a good choice for classic sushi and sashimi, along with contemporary izakaya-style small plates. ✉ *572 Davie St., Downtown* ☎ *604/568–8805* 🌐 *www.junobistro.ca.*

Miku. In a bright modern space with floor-to-ceiling windows, Miku specializes in *aburi* sushi, which is lightly seared with a blowtorch, rather than served raw. It also prepares *nigiri* and *maki* in both traditional and more innovative combinations. ✉ *2–1055 W. Hastings St., Downtown* ☎ *604/568–3900* 🌐 *www.mikurestaurant.com.*

6

RESTAURANT REVIEWS

Listed alphabetically within neighborhoods.

Use the coordinate at the end of each listing (⊕ B2) to locate a property on the Where to Eat in Vancouver map.

CENTRAL VANCOUVER

DOWNTOWN AND THE WEST END

$$ ECLECTIC

✕ **Bin 941.** Part tapas restaurant, part up-tempo bar, this bustling, often noisy hole-in-the-wall claims to have launched Vancouver's small-plates trend. Among the adventurous snack-size dishes, you might find smoked black cod paired with a cauliflower and goat cheese puree, crab cakes topped with burnt-orange chipotle sauce, or braised lamb shank with a spicy pomegranate-date glaze. Snack on one or two, or order a bunch and have a feast. The Bin is open until 2 am most nights. *Average main: C$16 ✉ 941 Davie St., Downtown ☎ 604/683–1246 www.bin941.com Reservations not accepted No lunch ⊕ D4.*

$$$$ SEAFOOD Fodor's Choice ★

✕ **C Restaurant.** Save your pennies, fish fans—dishes such as seared scallops paired with pork belly, apple beignets, and foie gras in a burnt-apple sauce; trout served with crispy squid and a chorizo-lemon risotto; or lingcod with poached clams, sidestripe prawns, and bok choy have established this spot as Vancouver's most innovative seafood restaurant. Start with shucked oysters from the raw bar, or perhaps the seared scallops with rabbit terrine and carrot *panna cotta,* and finish with an assortment of handmade chocolate truffles and petits fours. The elaborate tasting menus with optional wine pairings highlight regional seafood. Both the ultramodern interior and the waterside patio overlook False Creek, but dine before dark to enjoy the view. *Average main: C$33 ✉ 2–1600 Howe St., Downtown ☎ 604/681–1164 www.crestaurant.com ⊕ C5.*

$$ BELGIAN

✕ **Café Medina.** For casual breakfast and lunch fare, from omelets to *merguez* sausages to a daily curry creation, try this café next door to its sister restaurant, Chambar *(see below)*. Belgian waffles—with toppings like dark chocolate or raspberry caramel—are the specialty. *Average main: C$14 ✉ 556 Beatty St., Downtown ☎ 604/879–3114 www.medinacafe.com No dinner ⊕ G4.*

$$$ BELGIAN

✕ **Chambar.** A smartly dressed crowd hangs out at the bar of this hip Belgian eatery sipping imported beer or funky cocktails like the Blue Fig (gin infused with oven-roasted figs and served with a side of Stilton cheese). But the high-ceiling room is not just a pretty (and prettily populated) space. Classic Belgian dishes are reinvented with flavors from North Africa and beyond. The *moules* are justifiably popular, either steamed in white wine or sauced with exotic smoked chilies, cilantro, and coconut cream. Butternut squash gnocchi might be paired with elk meatballs, while arctic char could be served with sautéed rapini and quinoa tabouleh. Unusual, perhaps, but definitely delicious. *Average main: C$26 ✉ 562 Beatty St., Downtown ☎ 604/879–7119 www.chambar.com No lunch ⊕ G4.*

BEST BETS FOR VANCOUVER DINING

With so many restaurants, how will you decide where to eat? Fodor's writers and editors have chosen their favorites by price, cuisine, and experience:

Fodor's Choice ★

Blue Water Cafe, p. 154
Boneta, p. 153
C Restaurant, p. 142
Go Fish, p. 157
Hawksworth Restaurant, p. 147
L'Abbatoir, p. 153
Maenam, p. 157
Vij's, p. 158
West, p. 158

By Price

$

Go Fish, p. 157
Kintaro Ramen, p. 148
Legendary Noodle, p. 149
Nuba, p. 153

$$

Campagnolo, p. 161
Maenam, p. 157

$$$

Boneta, p. 153
Chambar, p. 142
Cibo Trattoria, p. 146
L'Abbatoir, p. 153
Raincity Grill, p. 151
Vij's, p. 158

$$$$

Bishop's, p. 157
Blue Water Cafe, p. 154
C Restaurant, p. 142
Hawksworth Restaurant, p. 147
Le Crocodile, p. 149
Tojo's, p. 160
West, p. 158

By Cuisine

CHINESE

Bao Bei, p. 151
Sea Harbour Seafood Restaurant, p. 137
Sun Sui Wah Seafood Restaurant, p. 162

FRENCH

Jules, p. 153
Le Crocodile, p. 149
Le Gavroche, p. 149
Mistral French Bistro, p. 157

INDIAN

Chutney Villa, p. 139
Rangoli, p. 158
Vij's, p. 158

ITALIAN

Campagnolo, p. 161
Cibo Trattoria, p. 146
CinCin, p. 146

JAPANESE

Hapa Izakaya, p. 147
Tojo's, p. 160

MODERN CANADIAN

Bishop's, p. 157
Boneta, p. 153
Hawksworth Restaurant, p. 147
L'Abbatoir, p. 153
Raincity Grill, p. 151
West, p. 158

SEAFOOD

Blue Water Cafe, p. 154
C Restaurant, p. 142
Coast Restaurant, p. 146
Sea Harbour Seafood Restaurant, p. 137
Tojo's, p. 160

VEGETARIAN

Foundation Lounge, p. 161
The Naam, p. 158
Nuba, p. 153
Rangoli, p. 158
Vij's, p. 158

By Experience

DISTINCTIVELY VANCOUVER

Bin 941, p. 142
Hapa Izakaya, p. 147
Japadog, p. 141
Maenam, p. 157
Vij's, p. 158

GREAT VIEW

C Restaurant, p. 142
Raincity Grill, p. 151
Salmon House on the Hill, p. 162
The Teahouse in Stanley Park, p. 156

HOT SPOTS

Boneta, p. 153
Chambar, p. 142
Cibo Trattoria, p. 146
Coast Restaurant, p. 146
Hawksworth Restaurant, p. 147

LOTS OF LOCALS

Bob Likes Thai Food, p. 161
Campagnolo, p. 161
The Flying Tiger, p. 157
Rodney's Oyster House, p. 155
Two Chefs and a Table, p. 154

ROMANTIC

Le Crocodile, p. 149
Raincity Grill, p. 151

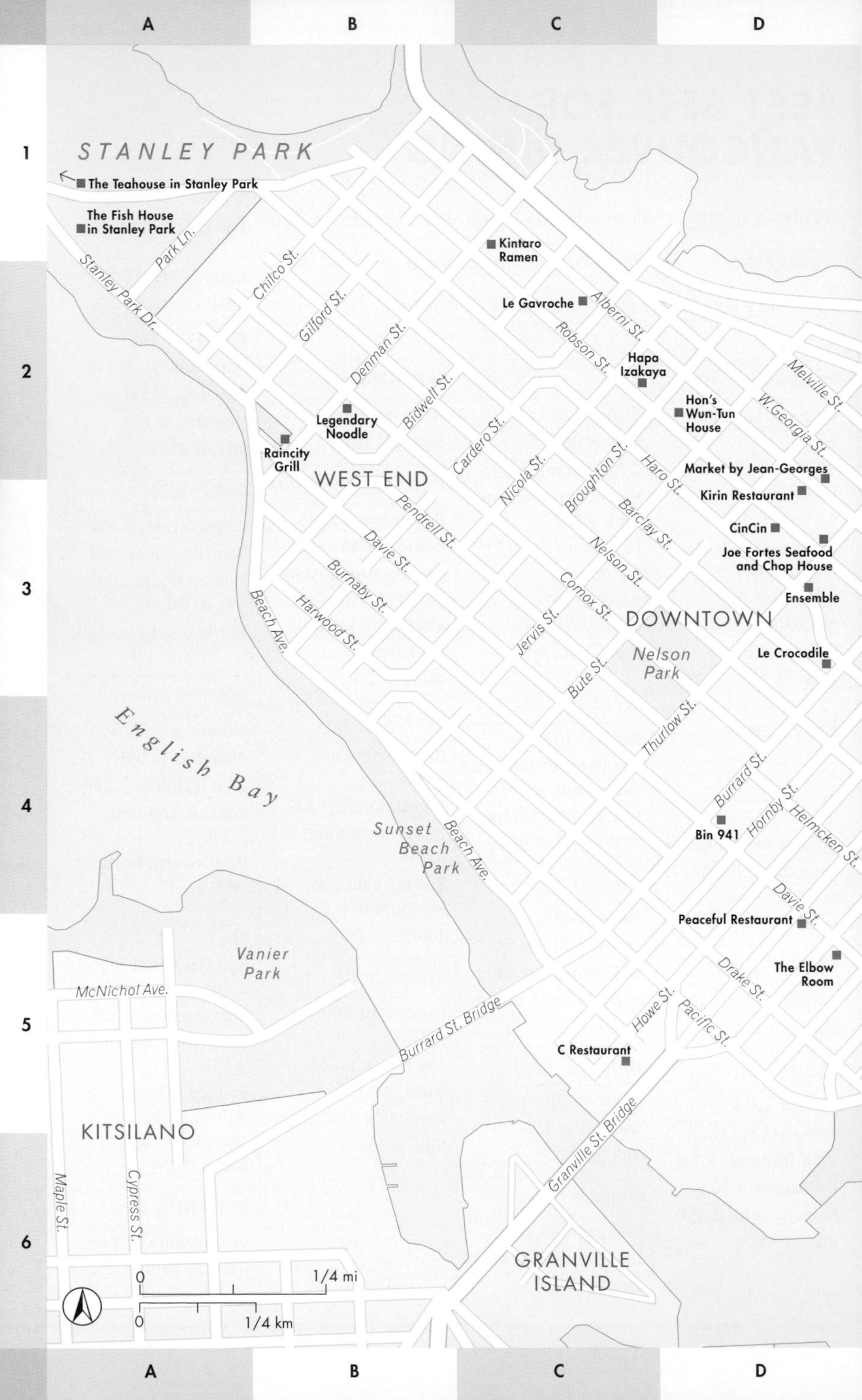

A
B
C
D
1
2
3
4
5
6
STANLEY PARK
The Teahouse in Stanley Park
The Fish House in Stanley Park
Park Ln.
Stanley Park Dr.
Chilco St.
Gilford St.
Denman St.
Bidwell St.
Kintaro Ramen
Le Gavroche
Alberni St.
Robson St.
Hapa Izakaya
Hon's Wun-Tun House
Melville St.
W. Georgia St.
Legendary Noodle
Raincity Grill
WEST END
Cardero St.
Nicola St.
Broughton St.
Haro St.
Market by Jean-Georges
Kirin Restaurant
CinCin
Joe Fortes Seafood and Chop House
Ensemble
Pendrell St.
Davie St.
Burnaby St.
Harwood St.
Beach Ave.
Barclay St.
Nelson St.
Comox St.
Jervis St.
DOWNTOWN
Nelson Park
Le Crocodile
Bute St.
Thurlow St.
English Bay
Burrard St.
Bin 941
Hornby St.
Helmcken St.
Sunset Beach Park
Beach Ave.
Davie St.
Peaceful Restaurant
The Elbow Room
Drake St.
Vanier Park
McNichol Ave.
Burrard St. Bridge
Howe St.
Pacific St.
C Restaurant
KITSILANO
Granville St. Bridge
Maple St.
Cypress St.
GRANVILLE ISLAND
0
1/4 mi
0
1/4 km

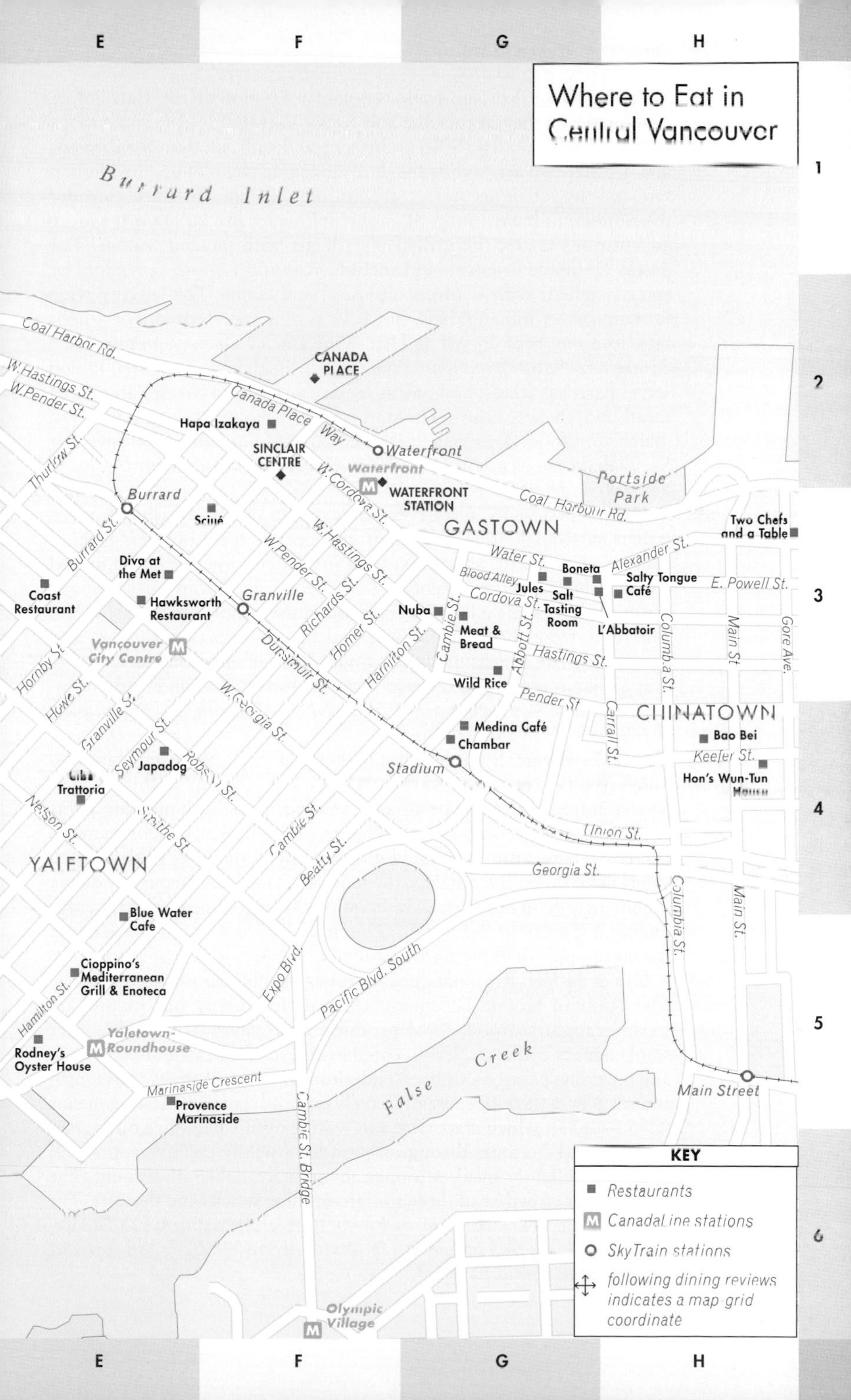

Where to Eat in Central Vancouver
Burrard Inlet
CANADA PLACE
Hapa Izakaya
SINCLAIR CENTRE
Waterfront
WATERFRONT STATION
Burrard
Sciué
GASTOWN
Portside Park
Two Chefs and a Table
Diva at the Met
Coast Restaurant
Hawksworth Restaurant
Granville
Boneta
Jules
Salt Tasting Room
Salty Tongue Café
L'Abbatoir
Nuba
Meat & Bread
Wild Rice
Vancouver City Centre
CHINATOWN
Medina Café
Chambar
Bao Bei
Hon's Wun-Tun House
Japadog
Stadium
Trattoria
YALETOWN
Blue Water Cafe
Cioppino's Mediterranean Grill & Enoteca
Rodney's Oyster House
Yaletown-Roundhouse
Provence Marinaside
False Creek
Main Street
Olympic Village
KEY
Restaurants
Canada Line stations
SkyTrain stations
following dining reviews indicates a map grid coordinate

$$$ ITALIAN ✕ **Cibo Trattoria.** Chef Neil Taylor cooked at London's River Café before running the kitchen at this fine and funky trattoria. It's the space that's funky—a mix of early-1900s architectural details, modern furnishings, and oversize pop art—while the daily changing menu of updated Italian fare and the solicitous service are nothing but fine. To start, consider the *ribollita* (a hearty soup of cannellini beans and kale) or, for more adventurous tastes, the grilled pig's heart with pickled walnut. The pastas are made in-house and include veal and fontina cannelloni or spicy spaghetti with scallops, mussels, and clams. The lengthy wine list emphasizes Italian labels, but B.C. is ably represented. For a light bite, join the local crowd at **Uva Wine Bar** (*$ Average main: C$17 ☎ 604/632–9560 ⊕ www.uvawinebar.ca*) in the Moda Hotel, which serves pastries, salads, and pastas by day and Italian cheeses and cured meats until the wee hours. The staff is always happy to suggest wines to match your food. *$ Average main: C$26 ✉ Moda Hotel, 900 Seymour St., Downtown ☎ 604/602–9570 ⊕ www.cibotrattoria.com ⊗ Closed Sun. No lunch ⊕ E4.*

$$$ ITALIAN ✕ **CinCin.** Gold walls, terra-cotta tiles, and a crowd-pleasing modern Italian menu make this restaurant appropriate for a business meal, a romantic tête-à-tête, or a relaxing dinner after a long day. The heated terrace, shielded with greenery, feels a long way from busy Robson Street. Inside there's a lively scene around the hand-carved marble bar. The food, from the open kitchen and the wood-fire grill, oven, and rotisserie, changes seasonally but might include sablefish marinated in grappa, lamb osso bucco served with saffron risotto, and crispy thin-crust pizza. *$ Average main: C$28 ✉ 1154 Robson St., Downtown ☎ 604/688–7338 ⊕ www.cincin.net ⊗ No lunch Sat.–Sun. ⊕ D3.*

$$$$ SEAFOOD ✕ **Coast Restaurant.** If a fish house makes you think of lobster traps and buoys, you'll be pleasantly surprised when you cruise up to this see-and-be-seen seafood palace. Expect plenty of bling, from the shimmering lights to the sparkle-sporting patrons. What to eat? Why, seafood, of course—from oysters to sushi to fish-and-chips to any of the day's fresh catches. (The kitchen also served steaks, if you must.) The Coast frequently does a swimmingly good business, so reservations are recommended. *$ Average main: C$32 ✉ 1054 Alberni St., Downtown ☎ 604/685–5010 ⊕ www.coastrestaurant.ca ⊗ No lunch weekends ⊕ E3.*

$$$ MODERN CANADIAN ✕ **Diva at the Met.** Regional cuisine shines at this chic restaurant in the Metropolitan Hotel. The menu changes frequently but focuses on freshly caught seafood, local produce, and wines. You might order smoked black cod in a celery-scented broth, steelhead salmon with leeks and fingerling potatoes, or beef tenderloin with hen-of-the-woods mushrooms. Where the kitchen really excels is the adventurous tasting menus (C$55–C$75), which start with innovative tidbits like olive oil marshmallows and continue through a parade of wildly creative courses. If you want a lighter meal, a lounge menu is available all evening. The after-theater crowd heads here for late-evening snacks and desserts. The suits meet up over breakfast or lunch. *$ Average main: C$28 ✉ Metropolitan Hotel, 645 Howe St., Downtown ☎ 604/602–7788 ⊕ www.metropolitan.com/diva ⊕ E3.*

$$ AMERICAN **The Elbow Room.** Known for the good-natured abuse the staff sometimes dishes out, this entertaining diner, its walls decorated with celebrity photos, is a Vancouver institution. Breakfast is served all day—the omelets are fluffy, the bacon is crisp, and the portions are generous—and lunchtime brings burgers and hearty sandwiches. *Average main: C$13 ✉ 560 Davie St., Downtown ☎ 604/685–3628 🌐 www.theelbowroomcafe.com Reservations not accepted ⊙ No dinner ✥ D5.*

$$ MODERN CANADIAN **Ensemble Restaurant.** If you're more about a lively place to kick back than a staid palace of gastronomy, come sip and graze in this dark, lounge-y space run by celebrity chef Dale MacKay. You might go simple with the signature pulled-pork sandwich or the roasted beet, watercress, and mascarpone salad, or take it up a notch with the cornmeal-crusted scallops with a tamarind-date puree or the Thai-style soup swimming with B.C. spot prawns, housemade sausage, and bok choy. Sweets like the homey apple-pie sundae strike the same simple-sophisticated symmetry. For well-prepared bar food, check out Ensemble Tap at 990 Smithe Street in Downtown. *Average main: C$16 ✉ 850 Thurlow St., Downtown ☎ 604/569–1770 🌐 www.ensemblerestaurant.com ⊙ Closed Mon. No lunch ✥ D3.*

$$ JAPANESE **Hapa Izakaya.** Serving small plates designed for sharing, this sleek Japanese tapas bar is known for its mackerel, cooked table-side with a blowtorch. Also worth trying are the *ebi mayo* (tempura shrimp with spicy mayonnaise) and the *ishi-yaki* (a Korean-style stone bowl filled with rice, pork, and vegetables). Sake or Japanese beer are the drinks of choice. If you're looking for Japanese fare elsewhere around town, Hapa has branches at 1193 Hamilton Street in Yaletown and at 1516 Yew Street in Kitsilano, one block from Kits Beach. *Average main: C$14 ✉ 1479 Robson St., West End ☎ 604/689–4272 🌐 www.hapaizakaya.com ⊙ No lunch ✥ C2.*

$$$$ MODERN CANADIAN Fodor's Choice ★ **Hawksworth Restaurant.** With sleek white tables and sparkling chandeliers, chef David Hawksworth's hotly anticipated restaurant is the kind of place where you can toast a new client or celebrate a romance. The food (and the crowd) is suave and swanky, too. A stellar starter is the yellowfin tuna ceviche tossed with avocado and served over toasted amaranth, but don't overlook the charred octopus salad with smoked potato or the quail paired with glazed sweetbreads and preserved lemon. Although the menu changes frequently, mains might include grilled sturgeon with wild rice and bacon, handmade tagliatelle with walnut pesto and ricotta salata, or the popular crispy chicken paired with bitter greens and a sweet-and-sour vinaigrette. Look out, yoga-pants-wearing Vancouver—fine dining is back. *Average main: C$33 ✉ Rosewood Hotel Georgia, 801 W. Georgia St., Downtown ☎ 604/673–7000 🌐 www.hawksworthrestaurant.com ✥ E3.*

$ CHINESE **Hon's Wun-Tun House.** This Vancouver chain has been keeping residents and tourists in Chinese comfort food since the 1970s. You can find better Chinese food elsewhere, but Hon's locations are convenient and the prices are reasonable. The best bets on the 300-item menu are the dumplings and noodle dishes, any of the Chinese vegetables, and anything with barbecued meat. There's a separate kitchen for vegetarians. Another branch is lcoated in the heart of Chinatown at 268

6

CLOSE UP

Snack Attack

The food truck revolution has come to Vancouver. A growing number of mobile kitchens have taken to the streets, selling fresh juices, spicy tacos, downhome barbecue, freshly caught seafood, and more. Needless to say, the assortment is as eclectic as the region's multicultural mix. Most trucks operate downtown during the lunch hours, generally from 11 or 11:30 until 2:30 or 3, although when they sell out, they close up for the day. Some trucks roll into town only on weekdays.

Feastro. This purple "rolling bistro" serves local seafood (salmon or halibut tacos, Fanny Bay oysters, fish-and-chips), sweet-potato fries, soups, and other options. It's usually found at West Cordova Street at Thurlow Street, near the Vancouver Convention Centre in Downtown (🌐 *www.feastro.ca*).

The Juice Truck. Freshly squeezed juices and fruit smoothies are on offer at the corner of Abbott Street and Water Street in Gastown (🌐 *www.thejuicetruck.ca*).

La Brasserie. Run by the Davie Street bistro of the same name, this truck sells tasty rotisserie chicken sandwiches on buttermilk buns. Look for it at West Georgia Street at Granville Street in Downtown (🌐 *www.labrasserievancouver.com*).

Mom's Grilled Cheese Truck. Triple-decker grilled cheese sandwiches (made with love, of course) can be had at Howe Street at West Georgia Street in Downtown (🌐 *www.momsgrilledcheesetruck.com*).

Re-Up BBQ. Pulled pork on a Portuguese bun, beef brisket sandwiches, and sweet iced tea are on the bill of fare at two Downtown locations: 700 Hornby Street at West Georgia Street, and 800 Robson Street between Hornby and Howe (🌐 *www.reupbbq.com*).

Roaming Dragon. A changing menu of Pan-Asian creations, including Korean short-rib tacos, soba-noodle salad, and Chinese pork sliders, is available at the Kitsilano Farmer's Market, Burrard Street at Robson Street (🌐 *www.roamingdragon.com*).

Keefer Street. [$] *Average main: C$11* ✉ *1339 Robson St., West End* ☎ *604/685–0871* 🌐 *www.hons.ca/* ✍ *Reservations not accepted* ✢ *D2.*

$$$$ SEAFOOD ✕ **Joe Fortes Seafood and Chop House.** Named for a much-loved English Bay lifeguard, this lively brasserie has a piano bar, bistro, oyster bar, and a delightful covered rooftop patio. The menu is wide ranging, but steaks, chops, and generous portions of fresh seafood are the main draw. Try the cedar-plank salmon, the *cioppino* (a seafood stew), or the Seafood Tower on Ice—a lavish assortment that's meant to be shared. [$] *Average main: C$35* ✉ *777 Thurlow St., at Robson St., Downtown* ☎ *604/669–1940* 🌐 *www.joefortes.ca* ✢ *D3.*

$ JAPANESE ✕ **Kintaro Ramen.** If your only experience with ramen is instant noodles, get thee to this authentic Japanese soup joint. With thin, fresh egg noodles and homemade broth (it's a meat stock, so vegetarians won't find much on the menu), a bowl of noodle soup here is cheap, filling, and ever so tasty. Expect long lines, but you can use the wait to decide between lean or fatty pork and miso or soy stock. Once you're inside the bare-bones storefront, the harried staff doesn't tolerate any dithering. *Average main: C$10 ✉ 788 Denman St., West End ☎ 604/682–7568 Reservations not accepted No credit cards ⊙ Closed Mon. ✥ C1.*

$$$ CHINESE ✕ **Kirin Restaurant.** A striking silver mural of a *kirin*, a mythical dragonlike creature, presides over this elegant two-tier restaurant. Specialties here are northern Chinese and Szechuan dishes, which tend to be richer and spicier than the Cantonese cuisine served at Kirin's other locations. If you're adventurous, start with the spicy jellyfish, redolent with sesame oil. Then try the Peking duck or the sautéed lobster meat served with a deep-fried lobster claw. Dim sum is served daily. *Average main: C$21 ✉ 1172 Alberni St., Downtown ☎ 604/682–8833 ⊕ www.kirinrestaurants.com ✥ D3.*

$$$$ FRENCH ✕ **Le Crocodile.** Chefs prepare classic Alsatian-inspired food (such as the signature onion tart) at this long-established downtown restaurant. Despite the white-tablecloth sophistication, the breezy curtains, golden yellow walls, and burgundy banquettes keep things cozy. Favorite dishes include lobster with beurre blanc, veal medallions with morel sauce, and sautéed Dover sole. Many lunch options, including a black truffle omelet and a mixed grill of halibut, prawns, and wild salmon, are moderately priced. *Average main: C$34 ✉ 100–909 Burrard St., Downtown ☎ 604/669–4298 ⊕ www.lecrocodilerestaurant.com ⊙ Closed Sun. No lunch Sat. ✥ D3.*

6

$$$$ FRENCH ✕ **Le Gavroche.** Classic French cuisine is paired with contemporary ingredients at this romantic restaurant in a century-old house tucked amid the downtown towers. Seafood entrées range from wild B.C. salmon confit (poached in olive oil and paired with a corn-and-crab cake) to smoked Pacific gray cod served with sweet-pea risotto; meat options might include pork chops roasted with olives, anchovies, and tomatoes or rich beef tenderloin. Vegetarian choices are always available. One of the few places with table-side service of steak tartare and Caesar salad, Le Gavroche also has a 5,000-label wine cellar. *Average main: C$33 ✉ 1616 Alberni St., West End ☎ 604/685–3924 ⊕ www.legavroche.ca ⊙ No lunch weekends ✥ C2.*

$ CHINESE ✕ **Legendary Noodle.** As you'd expect from the name, this compact storefront specializes in noodles, and they're made by hand in the open kitchen. The choices are simple—noodles in soup or in simple stir-fries—but you might also order a plate of garlicky pea shoots or a steamer of dumplings. The eatery is just a short stroll from English Bay. *Average main: C$10 ✉ 1074 Denman St., West End ☎ 604/669–8551 ⊕ www.legendarynoodle.ca Reservations not accepted ✥ B2.*

$$$$ MODERN CANADIAN ✕ **Market by Jean-Georges.** Although globetrotting celebrity chef Jean-Georges Vongerichten is rarely spotted at this contemporary dining room, his signature Asian influences abound, as in the rice cracker–crusted tuna with a citrus and chili emulsion, the crunchy roasted sablefish with glazed mushrooms, or the soy-glazed short ribs. If you don't fancy a full meal, you can dine lightly (and less expensively) on stylish salads or creative appetizers. Either way, you'll want to dress up a bit to match the sleek space. *Average main: C$30 ✉ Shangri-La Hotel, 1115 Alberni St., 3rd floor, Downtown ☎ 604/695–1115 ⊕ www.marketbyjgvancouver.com ✥ D2.*

DID YOU KNOW?

The Chinatown night market, on Keefer Street between Columbia and Main streets, is filled with stalls selling food, T-shirts, and all sorts of odds and ends.

$ CHINESE ✕ **Peaceful Restaurant.** Northern Chinese dishes are the specialty at this modest and, yes, relatively peaceful, storefront eatery. Particularly good are the hand-pulled noodles that the cooks knead and stretch in the open kitchen, and other good choices include the mustard-seed vegetable salad (crisp, shredded vegetables fired up with hot mustard), Szechuan green beans, and cumin-scented lamb. Vegetarians have plenty of options, including many of the dumplings. They'll make beef with broccoli or kung pao chicken if those are your thing, but the helpful staff is happy to guide you to more authentic Mandarin fare. *Average main: C$11 ✉ 630 Davie St., Downtown ☎ 604/488–0399 🌐 www.peacefulrestaurant.com ▭ No credit cards ✥ D5.*

$$$ MODERN CANADIAN ✕ **Raincity Grill.** One of the best places to try British Columbian food and wine is this lovely candlelit bistro overlooking English Bay. The menu changes regularly and relies almost completely on local and regional products, from salmon and shellfish to game and fresh organic vegetables. Vegetarian selections are always available, and the exclusively Pacific Northwest and Californian wine list has at least 40 choices by the glass. Popular alternatives include the 100 Mile Tasting Menu (all ingredients are sourced from within 100 miles of the restaurant) and the vegetarian regional tasting menu. The prix-fixe early dinner, served from 5 to 6 pm, is a steal at C$30. Reservations are required for these prix-fixe dinners. *Average main: C$27 ✉ 1193 Denman St., West End ☎ 604/685–7337 🌐 www.raincitygrill.com ✥ B2.*

$ CAFÉ ✕ **Sciué.** Inspired by the street foods of Rome, this cafeteria-style bakery–café (pronounced "Shoe-eh") starts the day serving espresso and pastries, then moves to panini, soups, and pastas. One specialty is the *pane romano*, essentially a thick-crust pizza, sold by weight. There can be lines out the door at lunch, so try to visit early or late. (Not *too* late, as it's open until 6:30 pm on weekdays and 6 pm on Saturday.) If you're in Yaletown, look for the second location at 126 Davie Street. *Average main: C$10 ✉ 110–800 W. Pender St., Downtown ☎ 604/602–7263 🌐 www.sciue.ca Reservations not accepted ⏲ Closed Sun. No dinner ✥ F3.*

GASTOWN AND CHINATOWN

$$ CHINESE ✕ **Bao Bei.** Start with an eclectic Chinatown storefront, stir in funky Asian-flavored cocktails, then add a creative take on traditional Chinese dishes, and you've got the recipe for this hip hangout. Grab a drink while you wait—perhaps a Guizhou Donkey (lemongrass-infused *shochu,* almond syrup, lime, and ginger beer) or a Dan Dan Flip (Sichuan-spiced rum, vanilla, lime, and whole egg). Afterward you can load your table with nibbles like Chinese pickles and truffled pork dumplings or tapas-size dishes like *shao bing* (sesame flatbread with cumin-scented lamb, pickled red onion, cilantro, and chilies), *mantou* (steamed buns stuffed with pork belly and preserved turnip), or a salad of wok-charred octopus, crispy potatoes, and cucumber kimchi. *Average main: C$15 ✉ 163 Keefer St., Chinatown ☎ 604/688–0876 🌐 www.bao-bei.ca Reservations not accepted ⏲ Closed Sun. No lunch ✥ H4.*

6

CLOSE UP

Fueled by Caffeine

"Fuelled by Caffeine" is the slogan of a Vancouver-based minichain of coffeehouses, and it's also an apt description of the city. Although the Starbucks invasion is extensive, there are plenty of more colorful places—from sleek and modern to comfortably bohemian. You'll find the same variety of coffee drinks that you can get across North America, though some places refer to an "americano" (an espresso made with extra hot water) as a "canadiano." Many—but not all—provide free Wi-Fi, too.

Bean Around the World. This local minichain, of the "Fuelled by Caffeine" slogan, runs a number of comfortable coffeehouses around town. There are also locations at 2528 Main Street and 3598 Main Street in Main Street/ Mt. Pleasant, 1002 Mainland Street in Yaletown, and 2977 Granville Street in South Granville. ✉ *1945 Cornwall Ave., Kitsilano* ☎ *604/739–1069* 🌐 *www.fuelledbycaffeine.com.*

Blue Parrot Coffee. Granville Island has several coffee places, but only the Blue Parrot provides sweeping views of False Creek. ✉ *Granville Island Public Market, 1689 Johnston St., Granville Island* ☎ *604/688–5127* 🌐 *www.blueparrotcoffee.com.*

Caffè Artigiano. Some of Vancouver's best coffee is served at the several locales of Caffè Artigiano, where the baristas have won prizes for their "Latte Art," making patterns in the froth. There are other locations at 740 West Hastings Street and 763 Hornby Street in Downtown, 1745 Commercial Drive in the East Side, and 3036 West Broadway in Kitsilano. ✉ *1101 W. Pender, Downtown* ☎ *604/685–5333* 🌐 *www.caffeartigiano.com.*

Delany's Coffee House. This friendly, frequently crowded coffee bar sits near English Bay. ✉ *1105 Denman St., West End* ☎ *604/662–3344* 🌐 *www.delanyscoffeehouse.com.*

Serious coffee drinkers head for Commercial Drive on the East Side. It's a bohemian 'hood full of spots to fuel a caffeine habit.

Caffe Calabria. With its marble-top tables and espresso drinks, Caffe Calabria is one of many traditional Italian cafés along "The Drive." ✉ *1745 Commercial Dr., East Side* ☎ *604/253–7017* 💳 *No credit cards.*

Continental Coffee. This place has a boho vibe and weekend lines that attest to its first-rate coffee. The americano is particularly good. ✉ *1806 Commercial Dr., East Side* ☎ *604/255–0712* 💳 *No credit cards.*

Prado Café. With an industrial-chic decor, Prado Café has gunmetal-gray chairs and blond-wood tables. ✉ *1938 Commercial Dr., East Side* ☎ *604/255–5537* 🌐 *www.pradocafe.com.*

Vancouverites don't live by coffee alone:

O-Cha Tea Bar. Tiny O-Cha Tea Bar serves 60 of its own blends, including rich, milky "Lat-Teas." ✉ *1116 Homer St., Yaletown* ☎ *604/633–3929.*

$$$ MODERN CANADIAN Fodor's Choice ★ ✕ **Boneta.** Some of the city's most innovative dishes—and drinks—grace the tables of this Gastown restaurant, named after co-owner Mark Brand's mother. The tucked-away location in Gaoler's Mews makes the room feel like a secluded speakeasy, as do the almost-too-cool-for-school cocktails, including the Trade Routes (tequila, Benedictine, smoked tea syrup, and lemon oil) and the Roman Holiday (Campari, Cointreau, and citrus). The deep-fried octopus chips, halibut paired with baby artichokes and fava beans, and lamb sirloin with ramps are creations that would make any foodie mother proud. Nobody could say no to the chocolate mascarpone cheesecake with raspberry sorbet and thyme sable cookies. *Average main: C$25 ✉ 12 Water St., Gastown ☎ 604/684–1844 www.boneta.ca No lunch ✣ G3.*

$$$ FRENCH ✕ **Jules.** From garlicky escargots and steak frites to duck confit and crème caramel, traditional French bistro fare is alive and well at this buzzing Gastown spot. You won't find funky fusion creations or east-meets-west innovations—just the classic dishes you might find at a neighborhood bistro in Paris. It's cozy (some might say cramped), but that's part of the charm. Need a mid-afternoon pick-me up? Light meals are served from 2:30 to 5:30. *Average main: C$22 ✉ 216 Abbott St., Gastown ☎ 604/669–0033 www.julesbistro.ca Closed Sun. ✣ G3.*

6

$$$ MODERN CANADIAN Fodor's Choice ★ ✕ **L'Abbatoir.** Located on the site of Vancouver's first jail, this two-level restaurant with exposed brick walls and classic black-and-white floor tiles has a bold collection of cocktails and an adventurous modern menu. In the glass, choices range from classics like the Hanky Panky (gin, sweet vermouth, and Fernet Branca) to more contemporary concoctions like the Meat Hook (Sazerac rye, Italian vermouth, and 10-year-old whiskey). From the restaurant's name—French for "slaughterhouse" (the surrounding neighborhood was once a meat-packing district)—you'd expect a meat-focused menu, and although you'll find veal sweetbreads on toast or milk-poached pork with salsa verde, seafood shines in dishes like potato gnocchi with scallops and chestnuts or pan-fried cod paired with an endive tart. Before plotting your escape into the night, share a dark-chocolate pudding for two. *Average main: C$27 ✉ 217 Carrall St., Gastown ☎ 604/568–1701 www.labattoir.ca No lunch ✣ G3.*

$ DELI ✕ **Meat & Bread.** Like the name, the concept at this trendy sandwich shop is simple. You wait in line and choose from the short daily menu of sandwiches. The rich and crispy housemade porcetta with *salsa verde* on a freshly baked *ciabatta* is a must-try. Add a cup of soup, if you want, and a drink, then find a spot at the counter or the long communal table. Who knew simplicity could taste so good? *Average main: C$8 ✉ 370 Cambie St., Gastown ☎ 604/566–9003 Reservations not accepted Closed Sun. No dinner ✣ G3.*

$ MIDDLE EASTERN ✕ **Nuba.** You could make a meal of *meze*—appetizers like falafel, tabbouleh, or crispy cauliflower served with tahini—at this subterranean Lebanese restaurant. If you're looking for something heartier, try a plate of *mjadra,* a spicy mix of lentils and rice. The kitchen serves roast chicken glazed with honey and red pepper, lamb kebabs, and other meat dishes, but much of the menu is vegetarian friendly. In the evening, the vibe turns more loungelike with occasional live music. There are several other locations around town—1206 Seymour Street in Downtown,

3116 West Broadway in Kitsilano, 146 East 3rd Avenue in Main St./Mt. Pleasant, and 1489 East Hastings Street on the East Side—that offer a smaller, quick-serve menu. *Average main: C$11 207B W. Hastings St., Gastown 604/668–1655 www.nuba.ca Reservations not accepted No lunch Sun. G3.*

$$ ECLECTIC **Salt Tasting Room.** If your idea of a perfect lunch or light supper revolves around fine cured meats, artisanal cheeses, and a glass of wine from a wide-ranging list, find your way to this sleek space in a decidedly unsleek Gastown location. The restaurant has no kitchen and simply assembles its first-quality provisions, perhaps meaty *bunderfleisch* (cured beef), smoked pork chops, or B.C.–made Camembert, with accompanying condiments, into artfully composed grazers' delights—more like an upscale picnic than a full meal. There's no sign out front, so look for the salt-shaker flag in Blood Alley, off Abbott Street. *Average main: C$15 45 Blood Alley, Gastown 604/633–1912 www.salttastingroom.com G3.*

$ CAFÉ **Salty Tongue Café.** Tongues are always wagging at this deli-café's long communal table—a cheerful spot for a quick bite in Gastown. In the morning, you can pop in for coffee, muffins, or a full Irish breakfast, while at midday you can build your own sandwich or choose bangers-and-mash, quiche, or a potpie. *Average main: C$10 212 Carrall St., Gastown 604/688–9779 www.saltytongue.ca Reservations not accepted No dinner H3.*

$$$ MODERN CANADIAN **Two Chefs and a Table.** Sometimes you have to go the extra mile for an excellent meal. To reach this storefront bistro, which glows like a beacon in the emerging Railtown neighborhood, you have to go the extra kilometer—it's about a half-mile east of the Gastown Steam Clock. There are fewer than 30 seats, including eight at the communal eponymous table (and yes, there are two chefs in the open kitchen). The menu is small, too, but the frequently changing selections, which might range from classic steak frites to a grilled boar chop with handmade gnocchi to pan-seared tuna with white bean and bacon ragout, are all well executed. At lunch, the place keeps busy serving up pastas, burgers, and rice bowls. *Average main: C$24 305 Alexander St., Gastown 778/233–1303 www.twochefsandatable.com No dinner Sun.–Mon. H3.*

$$ MODERN ASIAN **Wild Rice.** The look is decadent postmodern, with couches and a glowing aquamarine bar; the food, served in portions meant for sharing, borrows from China and across Asia but has a contemporary spin and an emphasis on local ingredients. You might find Chinese ravioli stuffed with local fish and sauced with green curry, truffle-salted tofu paired with pureed cauliflower, or locally raised *char siu* (barbecued pork). An assortment of cocktails plays on the menu's Asian flavors, including the Lotus (lychee-infused vodka, lime, and ginger ale) and the Pink Pearl (gin, pink grapefruit juice, tonic, and cassis). *Average main: C$16 117 W. Pender St., Chinatown 604/642–2882 www.wildricevancouver.com No lunch G3.*

YALETOWN

$$$$ SEAFOOD Fodor's Choice ★ **Blue Water Cafe.** Executive chef Frank Pabst features both popular and lesser-known local seafood (including frequently overlooked varieties like mackerel and herring) at this fashionable fish restaurant. You might start with Gulf Island scallops baked with tomatoes, olives, and

capers; Dungeness crab and white asparagus *panna cotta*; or a selection of raw oysters. Main dishes are seafood-centric, too—perhaps white sturgeon with beets, or arctic char with trout caviar and pearl couscous. Ask the staff to recommend wine pairings from the B.C.–focused list. You can dine in the warmly lit interior or outside on the former loading dock that's now a lovely terrace. ■ **TIP→ The sushi chef turns out both classic and new creations—they're pricey but rank among the city's best.** $ *Average main: C$34* ✉ *1095 Hamilton St., Yaletown* ☎ *604/688–8078* 🌐 *www.bluewatercafe.net* ⏲ *No lunch* ✣ *E5.*

CHINATOWN NIGHT MARKET

For interesting eats, check out the stalls at the Chinatown night market, open from mid-May to early September, 6:30 pm to 11 pm, Friday through Sunday. The market is on Keefer Street, between Columbia and Main streets.

$$$$ MEDITERRANEAN ✕ **Cioppino's Mediterranean Grill & Enoteca.** A fragrant seafood stew, cioppino is the signature dish at this lofty candlelit room. Chef Pino Posteraro impresses with homemade pastas and such Italian-Mediterranean dishes as Dover sole with fresh tomatoes and basil, and spit-roasted duck breast in a chocolate-espresso sauce. More rustic Italian fare, such as veal scallopini and braised beef short ribs, is also on offer. In good weather, you can dine on the street-side patio. $ *Average main: C$35* ✉ *1133 Hamilton St., Yaletown* ☎ *604/688–7466* 🌐 *www.cioppinosyaletown.com* ⏲ *Closed Sun. No lunch* ✣ *E5.*

6

$$$ MEDITERRANEAN ✕ **Provence Marinaside.** This airy, modern, Mediterranean-style eatery on Yaletown's waterfront presents French and Italian takes on seafood, including a delicious bouillabaisse and lush, garlicky wild prawns. The rack of lamb and an extensive antipasti selection are also popular. The marina-view patio makes a sunny breakfast or lunch spot, and the take-out counter is a great place to put together a picnic. $ *Average main: C$29* ✉ *1177 Marinaside Crescent, at Davie St., Yaletown* ☎ *604/681–4144* 🌐 *www.provencevancouver.com* ✣ *E5.*

$$ SEAFOOD ✕ **Rodney's Oyster House.** This faux fishing shack in Yaletown has one of the city's widest selections of oysters (up to 18 varieties), from locally harvested bivalves to exotic Japanese kumamotos. You can pick your oysters individually—they're laid out on ice behind the bar—or try the clams, scallops, mussels, and other mollusks from the steamer kettles. If you're fishing for an afternoon snack, swim in between 3 and 6 (except Sunday) when a light menu of raw oysters, steamed clams, garlic prawns, and a few additional seafood nibbles is served. $ *Average main: C$18* ✉ *1228 Hamilton St., Yaletown* ☎ *604/609–0080* 🌐 *www.rodneysoysterhouse.com* ⏲ *No lunch Sun.* ✣ *E5.*

STANLEY PARK

$$$$ SEAFOOD ✕ **The Fish House in Stanley Park.** Surrounded by gardens, this 1930s former sports pavilion with a fireplace and two verandas is tucked between Stanley Park's tennis courts and putting green. Chef Karen Barnaby's food, including fresh oysters, grilled ahi tuna with a green-peppercorn sauce, and cornflake-crusted salmon with bacon mashed potatoes, is flavorful and unpretentious. Check the board for the current day's catch. Traditional English afternoon tea is

Izakaya are Japanese small plates, similar to Spanish tapas.

served daily between 2 and 4. $ *Average main: C$31* ✉ *8901 Stanley Park Dr., Stanley Park* ☎ *604/681–7275, 877/681–7275* 🌐 *www.fishhousestanleypark.com* ✥ *A1.*

$$$ MODERN CANADIAN **The Teahouse in Stanley Park.** The former officers' mess in Stanley Park is perfectly poised for watching sunsets over the water. The Pacific Northwest menu is not especially innovative, but it includes such specialties as Caesar salad with Parmesan crostini, mushrooms stuffed with cream cheese and crab, and seasonally changing treatments of B.C. salmon, halibut, and steak. In summer you can dine on the patio. $ *Average main: C$25* ✉ *7501 Stanley Park Dr., Stanley Park* ☎ *604/669–3281* 🌐 *www.vancouverdine.com* ✥ *A1.*

GREATER VANCOUVER

GRANVILLE ISLAND

$$$ MODERN CANADIAN **Edible Canada Bistro.** Looking for a sit-down meal while exploring Granville Island? At this contemporary bistro with a people-watching patio, you can sample foods from B.C. and across Canada. Smaller appetites might gravitate toward the salad with locally raised beets, arugula, and goat cheese, or the coconut-based seafood soup swimming with mussels, clams, and seasonal fish. Hungrier travelers can sup on Alberta elk stew, pappardelle with braised Peace Country lamb, or steelhead salmon from B.C.'s Lois Lake served with a Dungeness crab croquette. If you'd like to wrap up your meal with a foodie souvenir of your Canadian sojourn, pop into the adjacent retail store for regional jams, chocolates, and other treats. $ *Average main: C$22* ✉ *1596 Johnston St., Granville Island* ☎ *604/682–6681* ✥ *A3.*

KITSILANO

$$$$ MODERN CANADIAN

Bishop's. Before "local" and "seasonal" were all the rage, this highly regarded room was serving West Coast cuisine with an emphasis on organic regional produce. The menu changes regularly, but highlights include such starters as elk carpaccio with mountain huckleberries and horseradish crème fraiche. Wild pacific salmon with herb parsnip latkes and locally raised beef tenderloin are among the tasty main dishes. All are expertly presented and impeccably served with suggestions from Bishop's extensive local wine list. The split-level room displays elaborate flower arrangements and selections from owner John Bishop's art collection. *Average main: C$38* *2183 W. 4th Ave., Kitsilano* *604/738–2025* *www.bishopsonline.com* *Closed Mon. No lunch* *A2.*

$$ ASIAN

The Flying Tiger. Inspired by the street foods of Asia, this laid-back lounge has a menu that roams from the Philippines to Thailand to Singapore. Start with a creative cocktail, perhaps the Bengal Breeze (rum, mint, coconut syrup, and fresh lime juice) or a glass of B.C. wine, then sample a range of small plates, including green papaya salad, petite pancakes heaped with duck confit and fresh herbs, or steamed clams in a coconut-lemongrass broth. This is a fun place to come with a group. *Average main: C$16* *2958 W. 4th Ave., Kitsilano* *604/737–7529* *www.theflyingtiger.ca* *No lunch weekdays* *A1.*

6

$ SEAFOOD Fodor's Choice ★

Go Fish. If the weather's fine, head for this seafood stand on the docks near Granville Island. The menu is short—highlights include fish-and-chips, grilled salmon or tuna sandwiches, and fish tacos—but the quality is first-rate. It's hugely popular, and on sunny summer days the waits can be maddening, so try to avoid the busiest times: noon to 2 pm and 5 pm to closing (which is at dusk). Since there are just a few outdoor tables, be prepared to take your food to go. Though you won't have the waterfront setting, you might find fewer crowds at the indoor location at 1521 West Broadway in South Granville, which is also open later into the evening. *Average main: C$10* *Fisherman's Wharf, 1505 W. 1st Ave., Kitsilano* *604/730–5039* *www.bin941.com* *Closed Mon. No dinner* *A3, B3.*

$$ THAI Fodor's Choice ★

Maenam. This moderately priced Thai menu brings this Asian cuisine to a new level. Although some of chef Angus An's dishes may sound familiar—green papaya salad, pad thai, curries—they're amped up with local ingredients, fresh herbs, and vibrant seasonings. Look for delicious innovations, too: perhaps crispy B.C. oysters, a banana blossom salad with a tamarind and palm-sugar dressing, or "eight-spice fish" that balances sweet, salty, and sour flavors. The bar sends out equally exotic cocktails, such as the Siam Sun Ray (vodka, lime, chili, ginger, coconut water, and soda). The sleek Kitsilano dining room is stylish enough that you could dress up a bit, but you wouldn't be out of place in jeans. *Average main: C$16* *1938 W. 4th Ave., Kitsilano* *604/730–5579* *www.maenam.ca* *No lunch Sun. and Mon.* *A2.*

$$$ FRENCH

Mistral French Bistro. Even on a dreary winter day, this sunny bistro is a bright spot in Vancouver's culinary landscape. Chef-owner Jean-Yves Benoît is in the kitchen, while his wife Minna welcomes guests, offers wine, and ensures that the dining room runs smoothly. The menu emphasizes Provençal classics, including pasta topped with *pistou* (basil, garlic, and Parmesan cheese), *cassoulet* (a hearty casserole of duck confit, sausages, bacon, and beans), and seafood *bourride* (a garlicky stew of fresh fish, prawns, and scallops). The lunch menu includes soups and salads along with more substantial fare. $ *Average main: C$24* ✉ *2585 W. Broadway, Kitsilano* ☎ *604/733–0046* 🌐 *www.mistralbistro.ca* ⏲ *Closed Sun. and Mon.* ✥ *B1.*

$ VEGETARIAN ✕ **The Naam.** Vancouverites have a love-hate relationship with the city's oldest natural-foods eatery. Some go gaga for the famous baked fries with miso gravy and pack the wooden tables for the Thai noodle dishes, burritos, enchiladas, fresh-squeezed juices, and wicked chocolate desserts, while others grumble that this aging hippie is past its prime. Still, live blues, folk, and jazz most evenings keep things homey, and if you need to satisfy a late-night craving for a veggie burger, rest easy—the place is open 24 hours. Reservations are accepted only for groups of six or more and only between Monday and Thursday. $ *Average main: C$11* ✉ *2724 W. 4th Ave., Kitsilano* ☎ *604/738–7151* 🌐 *www.thenaam.com* ✥ *A1.*

SOUTH GRANVILLE

$$ INDIAN ✕ **Rangoli.** This storefront bistro serves innovative Indian fare in a relaxed environment. Nab a table on the sidewalk or in the small but modern interior and sample grilled chicken marinated in tamarind and yogurt, pulled pork with sautéed greens, or a curry of portobello mushrooms and red peppers paired with a beet salad. Wash it all down with ginger lemonade or the Bollywood 411, a cocktail of Prosecco, pomegranate, and mango juice. $ *Average main: C$14* ✉ *1488 W. 11th Ave., South Granville* ☎ *604/736–5711* 🌐 *www.vijsrangoli.ca* ✍ *Reservations not accepted* ✥ *B3.*

$$$ INDIAN Fodor's Choice ★ ✕ **Vij's.** At Vancouver's most innovative Indian restaurant, genial proprietor Vikram Vij and his wife Meeru Dhalwala use local ingredients to create exciting takes on South Asian cuisine. Dishes such as lamb "popsicles" in a creamy curry, spot prawns served with a wheatberry pilaf, or roasted eggplant and butternut squash with black chickpeas are far from traditional but are beautifully executed. Mr. Vij circulates through the room, greeting guests and suggesting dishes or cocktail pairings. Expect to cool your heels at the bar sipping a cold beer while you wait up to an hour for a table, but if you like creative Indian fare, it's worth it. $ *Average main: C$27* ✉ *1480 W. 11th Ave., South Granville* ☎ *604/736–6664* 🌐 *www.vijs.ca* ✍ *Reservations not accepted* ⏲ *No lunch* ✥ *B3.*

$$$$ MODERN CANADIAN Fodor's Choice ★ ✕ **West.** Contemporary regional cuisine is the theme at this chic restaurant, one of the city's most innovative dining rooms. Among executive chef Quang Dang's creations are grilled quail with chanterelle mushroom tortellini, milk-poached sablefish with späetzle, and herb-crusted lamb served with crispy sweetbreads, beets, and pickled ramps. The decadent desserts might include pears sautéed in maple syrup and paired with a blue-cheese biscuit, or a surprisingly delectable tofu "cheesecake" wrapped in a crepe and served with roasted pineapple. If you can't decide, order from the tapas-style "Elements" menu (C$8–C$15) or opt for one of the elaborate multicourse tasting menus (C$58–C$78), which include vegetarian, seafood, and meat options. Marble floors,

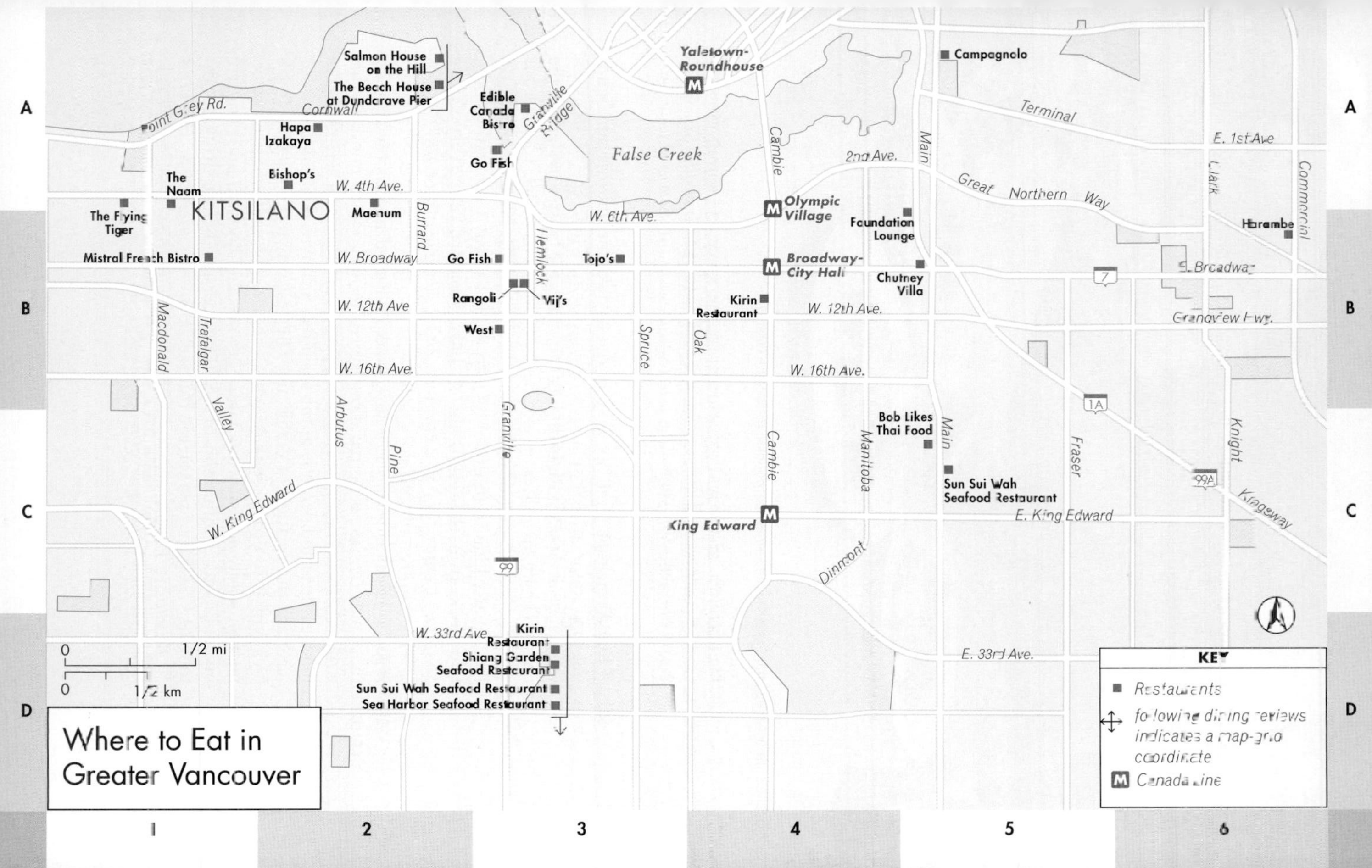

Where to Eat in Greater Vancouver
KEY
Restaurants
following dining reviews indicates a map-grid coordinate
Canada Line
0 1/2 mi
0 1/2 km
A
B
C
D
1
2
3
4
5
6
KITSILANO
False Creek
Salmon House on the Hill
The Beach House at Dundarave Pier
Hapa Izakaya
Bishop's
The Naam
The Flying Tiger
Maenum
Mistral French Bistro
Edible Canada Bistro
Go Fish
Go Fish
Rangoli
Vij's
West
Tojo's
Yaletown-Roundhouse
Olympic Village
Broadway-City Hall
King Edward
Kirin Restaurant
Campagnolo
Foundation Lounge
Chutney Villa
Harambe
Bob Likes Thai Food
Sun Sui Wah Seafood Restaurant
Kirin Restaurant
Shiang Garden Seafood Restaurant
Sun Sui Wah Seafood Restaurant
Sea Harbor Seafood Restaurant
Point Grey Rd.
Cornwall
Granville Bridge
W. 4th Ave.
W. 6th Ave.
W. Broadway
W. 12th Ave
W. 12th Ave.
W. 16th Ave.
W. 16th Ave.
W. King Edward
W. 33rd Ave.
E. 33rd Ave.
E. King Edward
Macdonald
Trafalgar
Valley
Arbutus
Pine
Burrard
Hemlock
Granville
Spruce
Oak
Cambie
Cambie
Manitoba
Main
Main
Fraser
Knight
Kingsway
Dinmont
Terminal
E. 1st Ave
2nd Ave.
Great Northern Way
Clark
Commercial
E. Broadway
Grandview Hwy.
7
1A
99A
99

Chefs prepare regional Canadian cuisine at the popular restaurant West.

high ceilings, and a wall of wine make the space feel simultaneously energetic and cozy. *Average main: C$40 ✉ 2881 Granville St., South Granville ☎ 604/738–8938 🌐 www.westrestaurant.com ⊕ B3.*

FAIRVIEW

$$$ CHINESE ✕ **Kirin Restaurant.** You can take in the city skyline and the surrounding mountains at this spacious dining room, where the focus is on Cantonese-style seafood, including fish, crab, and lobster fresh from the tanks. The kitchen does an excellent job with vegetables, too; ask for whatever's fresh that day. Dim sum is served daily. It's an easy ride on the Canada Line from downtown to the Broadway/City Hall station, two blocks from the restaurant. *Average main: C$21 ✉ City Square Shopping Centre, 555 W. 12th Ave., 2nd fl., Fairview ☎ 604/879–8038 🌐 www.kirinrestaurants.com ⊕ B4.*

$$$$ JAPANESE ✕ **Tojo's.** Hidekazu Tojo is a sushi-making legend in Vancouver, with thousands of special preparations stored in his creative mind. In this strikingly modern, high-ceilinged space, complete with a separate sake lounge, the prime perch is at the sushi bar, a convivial ringside seat for watching the creation of edible art. The best way to experience Tojo's creativity is to order *omakase* (chef's choice); the chef will keep offering you wildly adventurous fare, both raw and cooked, until you cry uncle. Budget a minimum of C$80 per person (before drinks); tabs topping C$120 per person are routine. *Average main: C$32 ✉ 1133 W. Broadway, Fairview ☎ 604/872–8050 🌐 www.tojos.com Reservations essential ⏲ Closed Sun. No lunch ⊕ B3.*

KEBAB QUEST

Among the many ethnic groups that have settled in greater Vancouver is a large Persian community, centered on the North Shore. Wander along North Vancouver's Lonsdale Avenue between 13th and 19th streets, and you can catch glimpses of Persian culture—and sample Persian tastes.

Yaas Bazaar. Part grocery store and part cafeteria, the good-value Yaas Bazaar lets you can pick up olives, feta cheese, and chewy sesame-topped breads for a picnic. You can also lunch on savory kebabs, stews, or one of the daily specials. ✉ *1860 Lonsdale Ave., North Vancouver* ☎ *604/990–9006* 🌐 *www.yaas.ca.*

Golestan. Looking for sweets? Head to this bakery, where the Persian pastries include rosewater-scented baklava. ✉ *1554 Lonsdale Ave., North Vancouver* ☎ *604/990–7767.*

Ayoub's Dried Fruits and Nuts. At Ayoub's Dried Fruits and Nuts, the freshly roasted pistachios, almonds, and watermelon seeds make excellent snacks. ✉ *1332 Lonsdale Ave., North Vancouver* ☎ *604/982–9682* 🌐 *www.ayoubsdriedfruitsandnuts.com.*

6

MAIN STREET/MT. PLEASANT

$ THAI ✕ **Bob Likes Thai Food.** Who's Bob? The staff at this no-frills storefront explains that he's just an average guy, and if he likes the authentically prepared Thai fare, then so will you. The menu includes all the classics, from green payaya salad to *laab* (minced pork with roasted rice, mint, fish sauce, and lime) to *pad si ew* (fried rice noodles with pork and vegetables). There's an assortment of curries, including fish with a creamy yellow curry. Some dishes are on the small side, so if you're hungry ask your server to recommend the right number of plates to share. $ *Average main: C$12* ✉ *3755 Main St., Main St./Mt. Pleasant* ☎ *604/568–8538* 🌐 *www.boblikesthaifood.com* ✣ *C5.*

$$ ITALIAN ✕ **Campagnolo.** On a dark block near the Main St./Science World Sky-Train station, this relaxed trattoria lights up the neighborhood with its welcoming vibe and casually contemporary Italian fare. The kitchen cures its own *salumi*, including soppressata, capicola, and various sausages—these make good starters, as do the addictive *ceci* (chick peas). House-made pastas and a small selection of mains take their inspiration from the Emiglia-Romagna and Piemonte regions, updated with B.C. ingredients. Reservations are accepted only for groups of eight or more, but you can unwind with a glass of wine in the lounge if you have to wait. $ *Average main: C$18* ✉ *1020 Main St., Main St./Mt. Pleasant* ☎ *604/484–6018* 🌐 *www.campagnolorestaurant.ca* ✣ *A5.*

$ VEGETARIAN ✕ **Foundation Lounge.** The interior at this East Side vegetarian joint—mismatched Formica tables, 1950s-style vinyl chairs, a cinder-block bar—may not win design prizes, and the service can be rather laid-back, but the bohemian vibe is friendly and the meat-free fare is tasty. Try the satay salad—mixed greens, tofu, and broccoli topped with a warm, tangy peanut sauce—or opt for the hearty veggie burger or the tofu-and-mango scramble. This storefront restaurant is hopping from midday until 1 am. $ *Average main: C$8* ✉ *2301 Main St., Main St./Mt. Pleasant* ☎ *604/708–0881* ✣ *B5.*

$$ CHINESE ✕ **Sun Sui Wah Seafood Restaurant.** This bustling Cantonese restaurant is best known for its excellent dim sum (served 10–3 daily), which ranges from traditional handmade dumplings to some highly adventurous fare. Dinner specialties include roasted squab marinated in the restaurant's secret spice blend and king crab plucked live from the tanks, then steamed with garlic. Bring a group so you can sample more dishes. *Average main: C$18 ✉ 3888 Main St., Main St./Mt. Pleasant ☎ 604/872–8822, 866/872–8822 ⊕ www.sunsuiwah.com ✣ C5.*

EAST SIDE

$$ ETHIOPIAN ✕ **Harambe.** The name means "working together" in Swahili, and the family that owns this welcoming restaurant does just that as it introduces guests to traditional Ethiopian fare. Savory stews are served atop platter-size pancakes of *injera,* a tangy, almost spongy flatbread used to scoop up every drop. Order a combination platter to sample a range of flavors; the vegetarian version, which includes spinach, lentils, peas, assorted vegetables, and salad, is especially tasty. *Average main: C$14 ✉ 2149 Commercial Dr., East Side ☎ 604/216–1060 ⊕ www.harambeerestaurant.com ⊙ No lunch Tues. ✣ B6.*

WEST VANCOUVER

$$$ MODERN CANADIAN ✕ **The Beach House at Dundarave Pier.** It's worth the drive over the Lions Gate Bridge to West Vancouver for a lunch or dinner at this 1912 seaside house. Whether inside the terraced dining room or on the heated beachside patio, most every table has views over Burrard Inlet and Stanley Park. The Pacific Northwest menu changes seasonally but includes accessible takes on meat, poultry, and seafood, including halibut or wild B.C. salmon. After your meal, take a stroll along the pier or the seaside walkway. *Average main: C$27 ✉ 150 25th St., off Marine Dr., West Vancouver ☎ 604/922–1414 ⊕ www.thebeachhouserestaurant.ca ✣ A2.*

$$$$ SEAFOOD ✕ **Salmon House on the Hill.** Perched halfway up a mountain, this restaurant has stunning water and city views by day and expansive vistas of city lights by night. It's best known for its alder-grilled salmon, though the smoked sablefish is also tempting; you can opt for companion pairings of B.C. wines. The "Folkestone Feast Bowl"—halibut, salmon, sablefish, a Dungeness crab leg, clams, mussels, and prawns in a lemongrass tomato broth, is served with grilled bannock, a traditional First Nations bread. The Northwest Coast interior is tastefully done, though it can hardly compete with what's outside the windows. The Salmon House is about 30 minutes from Vancouver by car. Head over the Lions Gate Bridge, follow Highway 1 west, then take the Folkestone Way exit. *Average main: C$32 ✉ 2229 Folkestone Way, West Vancouver ☎ 604/926–3212 ⊕ www.salmonhouse.com ⊙ No lunch weekdays ✣ A2.*

Vancouver Where to Stay

WORD OF MOUTH

"I would recommend staying in downtown Vancouver . . . you can walk along the harbor, take a water taxi, take the shuttle and drop right into the center. Stay out of East Vancouver, east of Gastown; stay in Yaletown, downtown, Kitsilano, Shaughnessy out towards the University of British Columbia."

—julia_mei

Updated by Paige Donner

Although Vancouver is a pretty compact city, each area has a distinct character and accommodation options. From hip boutique hotels to historic bed-and-breakfasts to sharp-angled glass-and-mirror towers, there are lodging choices for every style and neighborhood, whether it's the center of shopping on Robson Street, gracious tree-lined boulevards near Stanley Park, or the pulsing heart of the city's core.

The 2010 Winter Olympics changed the face of Vancouver in just a handful of years, but the city managed to retain, and make the most of, some of its defining characteristics. For example, Vancouver is an extremely outdoorsy community, so hotel amenities can sometimes include free bicycles and free ski storage, and many concierges can put you in contact with hiking and running groups that welcome visitors.

The city is extremely pet-friendly, especially when it comes to pooches. Not only can you bring your dog with you to many Vancouver properties, some even let you borrow *their* dog for a walk (check out the Fairmont Hotel Vancouver, for instance). You'll also find dog delis (we're talking all-natural dog cookies) and doggie beaches (Ambleside in West Vancouver being the top one). If it's a dog-sitting or kennel service you're looking for, check out the directory at Raincity Dogs (🌐 *www.raincitydogs.com*).

The local penchant for healthy living has given rise to some top-quality spas, many of which reflect the cultural mosaic of the city. Services run the gamut from Ayurvedic body treatments to therapies incorporating traditional Chinese medicine. Local ingredients are often featured, so you can even indulge in a Canadian maple pedicure.

Hotels with a water view are coveted and book up well in advance, as do some of the historic B&Bs you'll find in the more fashionable neighborhoods like the West End and near Stanley Park.

PLANNING

APARTMENT RENTALS

The trend toward self-catered apartments for families or business executives has only increased in recent years. Vancouver has a number of hotels that offer lower rates or separate wings for longer-term residents. Options often include housekeeping, parking, satellite TV, or Wi-Fi access. Make Yourself at Home (☎ *604/874–7817* 🌐 *www.makeyourselfathome.com*) provides a terrific range of private homes and apartments for short-term rentals; this site is especially good for last-minute bookings. On the higher end of the spectrum, Dream Rentals (🌐 *www.vancouverdreamrentals.com*) lists many luxury condominiums and executive homes.

COMPLIMENTARY TRANSPORTATION

Some properties have complimentary bicycles, others extend free limo services to the theater or pickups when you've shopped yourself silly. That can be extremely handy, depending on your priorities and your location.

EXTRA COSTS

Most hotels let children under 18 stay free in their parents' room, though you may be charged extra for more than two adults. Parking runs about C$25 to C$40 per day at downtown hotels, and can be free outside the downtown core. Watch out for phone and Internet charges, which can add up. You'll also be charged a 10% accommodations tax and a 5% Goods and Services Tax (GST).

Prices in the reviews are the lowest cost of a standard double room in high season.

7

HOTEL REVIEWS

Hotels are isted alphabetically within neighborhoods. Use the coordinate at the end of each listing (✣ B2) to locate a property on the Where to Stay in Vancouver map.

For expanded hotel reviews, visit Fodors.com.

DOWNTOWN

$$ HOTEL **The Burrard.** Freebies abound at the fun and funky Burrard: water in recyclable bottles, biodegradable bath products, iPod docks, and movie channels on the huge flat-screen TVs for starters. **Pros:** doesn't take it self too seriously; laid-back atmosphere; complimentary bicycles and umbrellas. **Cons:** overreaches a bit in achieving its "cool" vibe. *Rooms from: C$189* ✉ *1100 Burrard St., Downtown* ☎ *604/681–2331* 🌐 *www.theburrard.com* *72 rooms* *No meals* ✣ *D4.*

$$$ HOTEL **Century Plaza Hotel & Spa.** Full kitchens and an indoor pool make this 30-story downtown high-rise a good family choice. **Pros:** pampering spa; on site entertainment; large rooms. **Cons:** an average-quality hotel trying to be a bit grand. *Rooms from: C$235* ✉ *1015 Burrard St., Downtown* ☎ *604/687–0575* 🌐 *www.century-plaza.com* *240 rooms* *No meals* ✣ *D4.*

BEST BETS FOR VANCOUVER LODGING

Fodor's offers a selective listing of quality lodging experiences in every price range, from the city's best budget beds to its most sophisticated luxury hotels. Here, we've compiled our top recommendations by price and experience. The very best properties—in other words, those that provide a particularly remarkable experience in their price range—are designated in the listings with the Fodor's Choice logo.

Fodor's Choice★

L'Hermitage Hotel, p. 170

Opus Vancouver Hotel, p. 176

Sylvia Hotel, p. 175

Wedgewood Hotel & Spa, p. 173

By Price

$$

Barclay House, p. 173

Sylvia Hotel, p. 175

Victorian Hotel, p. 173

$$$

L'Hermitage Hotel, p. 170

Opus Vancouver Hotel, p. 176

$$$$

Fairmont Pacific Rim, p. 167

Pan Pacific Vancouver, p. 171

Shangri-La Hotel, p. 172

Wedgewood Hotel & Spa, p. 173

By Experience

FOR FAMILIES

Century Plaza Hotel & Spa, p. 165

Lord Stanley Suites on the Park, p. 175

Renaissance Vancouver Harbourside Hotel, p. 172

MOST CENTRAL

Fairmont Hotel Vancouver, p. 167

Four Seasons Hotel Vancouver, p. 170

Wedgewood Hotel & Spa, p. 173

BEST HISTORIC CONVERSION

St. Regis Hotel, p. 172

MOST DOG-FRIENDLY

Fairmont Hotel Vancouver, p. 167

Fairmont Waterfront, p. 170

Sheraton Vancouver Wall Centre, p. 172

MOST ROMANTIC

Barclay House, p. 173

L'Hermitage Hotel, p. 170

Wedgewood Hotel & Spa, p. 173

BEST SPA

Century Plaza Hotel & Spa (Spa at the Century), p. 165

Pan Pacific Vancouver (Spa Utopia), p. 171

Shangri-La Hotel (Chi Spa), p. 172

Sheraton Vancouver Wall Centre (Vida Spa), p. 172

BEST B&B

Granville House B&B, p. 176

WHERE SHOULD I STAY?

	Vibe	Pros	Cons
Downtown (Robson to the Waterfront)	Central commercial/financial district hotels are mostly mid- to high-end, catering to tourists and business travelers. Low to moderately priced hotels are on Granville Street, south of Robson.	Within walking distance of nearly all downtown sights and handy to the Canada Place cruise-ship terminal.	A little dull come evening as few people live in the area, but Granville Street, south of Robson, is lined with bars, clubs, and movie theaters.
West End/ Stanley Park	A lovely tree-filled, gay-friendly residential neighborhood close to downtown. Hotels in all price ranges are on the main arteries; historic hotels and B&Bs are on the side streets.	A pleasant alternative to the central business district. The beach at English Bay is the West End's hot spot for people-watching and casual dining.	Could be too quiet for some folks.
West Side	A combination of neighborhoods from tony Kerrisdale to old-money Shaughnessy to gentrified (partially hippie) Kitsilano, as well as Granville Island and posh Point Grey.	Handy to beaches, the University of British Columbia campus, parks and gardens, and close to great shopping and local eats along West 4th Avenue and South Granville.	You may feel "out of the action" since these are residential areas. Although bus transit is excellent, having a car makes navigation easier.
Yaletown	Also on the downtown peninsula, this is where urban chic translates into New York–style loft apartments, beneath which lie trendy restaurants and boutique shops.	Lots of hip shopping, bars, and restaurants nearby, and a short ferry ride to Granville Island.	Sidewalks can be noisy; this is one of the most densely populated, high-rise areas of the city.

$$$ HOTEL **Delta Vancouver Suites.** Exuding a New York vibe, this business hotel welcomes you with a striking marble-and-cherrywood lobby that soars three stories high. **Pros:** central location; great restaurant; windows that actually open. **Cons:** one-way roads make getting here a bit of a headache. *Rooms from: C$249 ✉ 550 W. Hastings St., Downtown ☎ 604/689–8188 www.deltavancouversuites.ca 225 suites No meals F3.*

$$$$ HOTEL **Fairmont Hotel Vancouver.** The copper roof of this 1939 château-style hotel dominates Vancouver's skyline, and the elegantly restored hotel is considered the city's gracious grande dame. **Pros:** full-service spa; great location for shopping; stunning architecture. **Cons:** "standard" room sizes vary greatly. *Rooms from: C$359 ✉ 900 W. Georgia St., Downtown ☎ 604/684–3131 www.fairmont.com/hotelvancouver 556 rooms, 37 suites No meals E3.*

$$$$ HOTEL **Fairmont Pacific Rim.** Overlooking the downtown waterfront, this 47-story tower represents the chain's first foray into the condominium-hotel format. **Pros:** prime location; the usual high quality of Fairmont

7

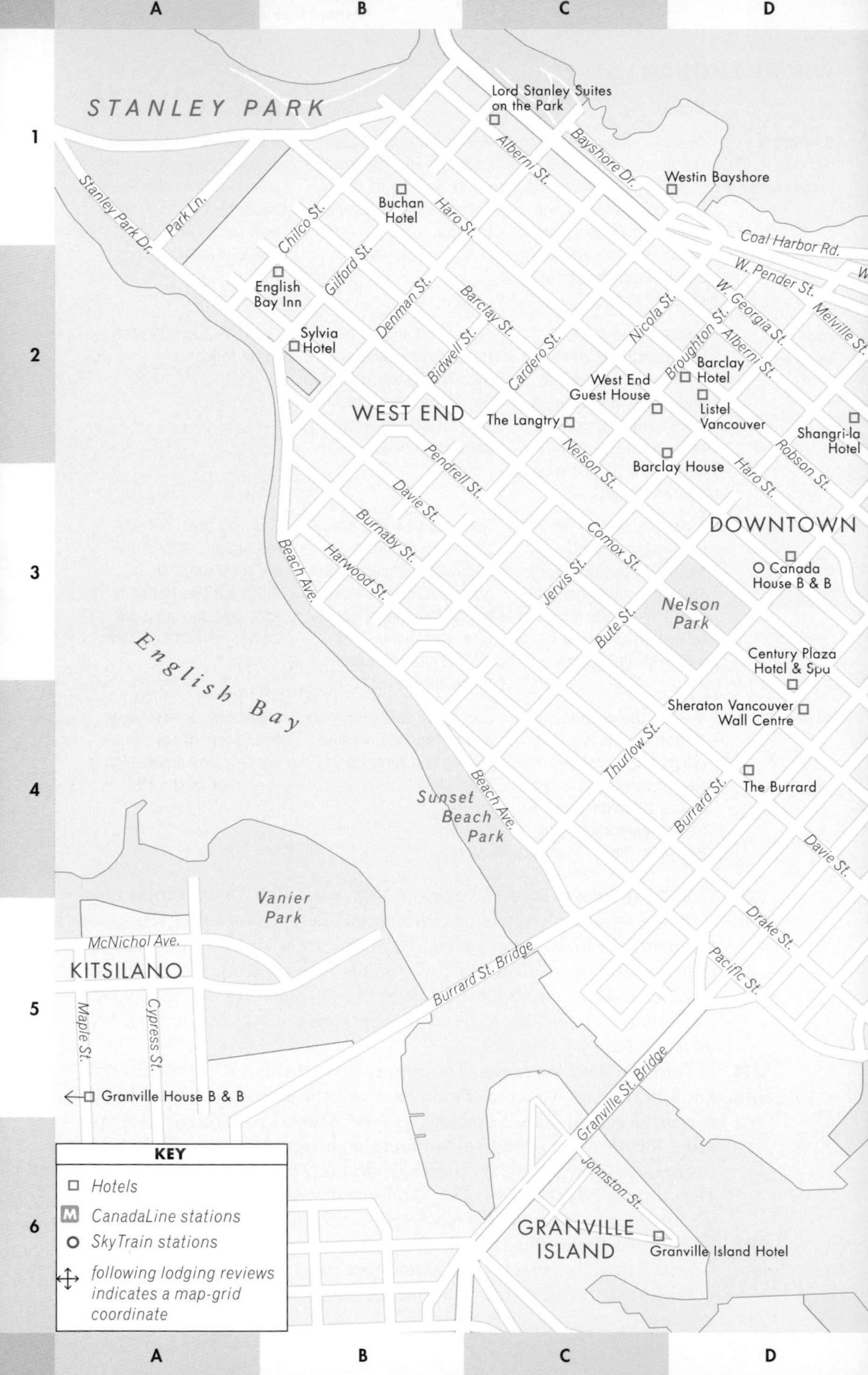
A
B
C
D
1
2
3
4
5
6
STANLEY PARK
Lord Stanley Suites on the Park
Westin Bayshore
Buchan Hotel
English Bay Inn
Sylvia Hotel
WEST END
The Langtry
West End Guest House
Barclay Hotel
Listel Vancouver
Shangri-la Hotel
Barclay House
DOWNTOWN
O Canada House B & B
Nelson Park
Century Plaza Hotel & Spa
Sheraton Vancouver Wall Centre
The Burrard
English Bay
Sunset Beach Park
Vanier Park
KITSILANO
Granville House B & B
GRANVILLE ISLAND
Granville Island Hotel
Stanley Park Dr.
Park Ln.
Chilco St.
Gilford St.
Denman St.
Bidwell St.
Barclay St.
Cardero St.
Alberni St.
Bayshore Dr.
Haro St.
Coal Harbor Rd.
W. Pender St.
W. Georgia St.
Melville St.
Nicola St.
Broughton St.
Robson St.
Nelson St.
Pendrell St.
Davie St.
Burnaby St.
Harwood St.
Beach Ave.
Comox St.
Jervis St.
Bute St.
Thurlow St.
Burrard St.
Drake St.
Pacific St.
Burrard St. Bridge
Granville St. Bridge
Johnston St.
McNichol Ave.
Maple St.
Cypress St.
KEY
Hotels
CanadaLine stations
SkyTrain stations
following lodging reviews indicates a map-grid coordinate

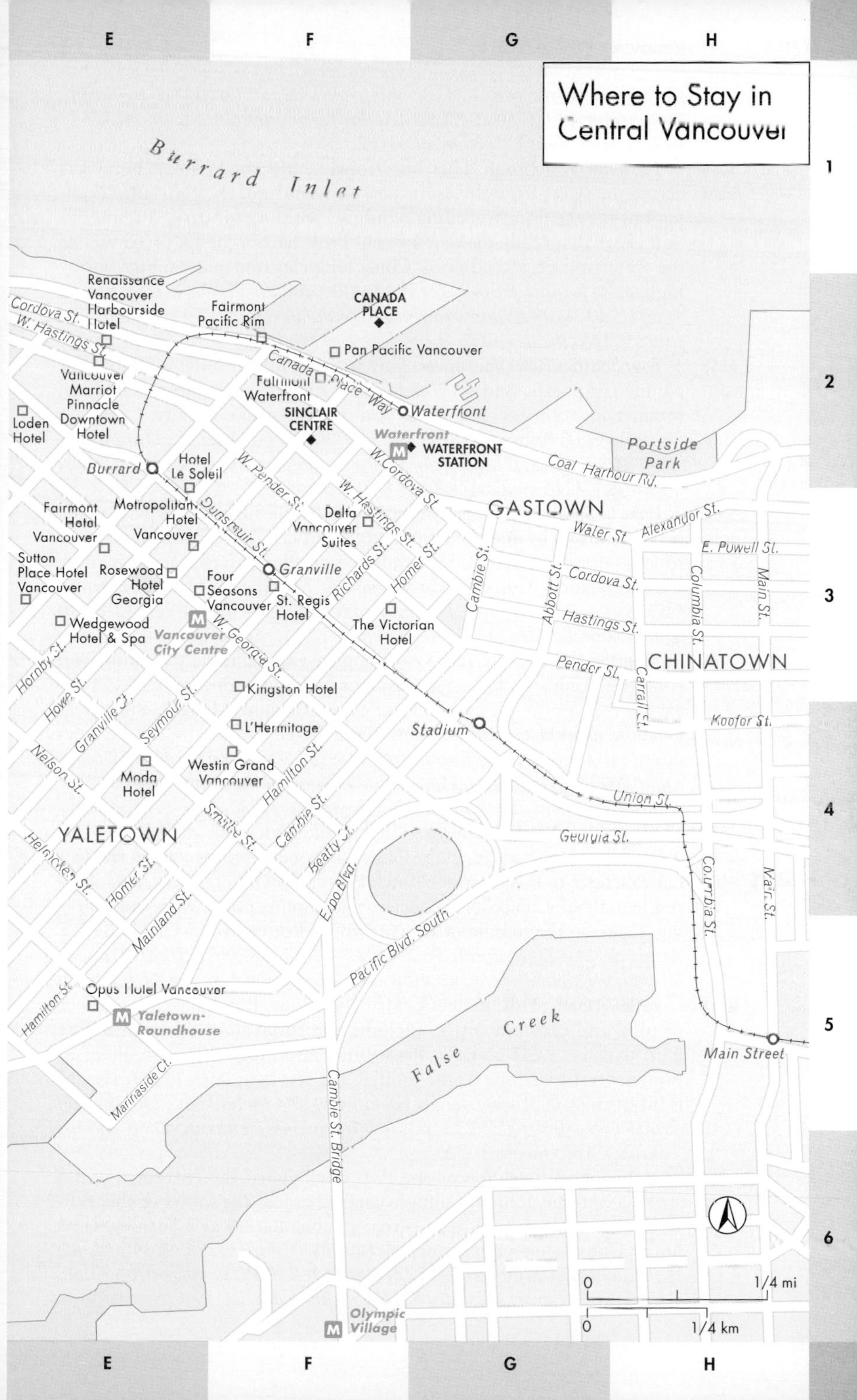

Where to Stay in Central Vancouver
E
F
G
H
1
2
3
4
5
6
Burrard Inlet
Renaissance Vancouver Harbourside Hotel
Fairmont Pacific Rim
CANADA PLACE
Pan Pacific Vancouver
Vancouver Marriot Pinnacle Downtown Hotel
Fairmont Waterfront
Loden Hotel
SINCLAIR CENTRE
Waterfront
WATERFRONT STATION
Portside Park
Coal Harbour Rd.
Burrard
Hotel Le Soleil
Fairmont Hotel Vancouver
Metropolitan Hotel Vancouver
Delta Vancouver Suites
GASTOWN
Sutton Place Hotel Vancouver
Rosewood Hotel Georgia
Four Seasons Vancouver
Granville
St. Regis Hotel
The Victorian Hotel
Wedgewood Hotel & Spa
Vancouver City Centre
CHINATOWN
Kingston Hotel
L'Hermitage
Stadium
Westin Grand Vancouver
Moda Hotel
YALETOWN
Opus Hotel Vancouver
Yaletown-Roundhouse
False Creek
Main Street
Olympic Village
Cordova St.
W. Hastings St.
Canada Place Way
W. Pender St.
W. Cordova St.
W. Hastings St.
Dunsmuir St.
Richards St.
Homer St.
Cambie St.
Abbott St.
Cordova St.
Hastings St.
Pender St.
Water St.
Alexander St.
E. Powell St.
Columbia St.
Main St.
W. Georgia St.
Hornby St.
Howe St.
Granville St.
Seymour St.
Nelson St.
Hamilton St.
Cambie St.
Smithe St.
Beatty St.
Carrall St.
Keefer St.
Union St.
Georgia St.
Helmcken St.
Homer St.
Mainland St.
Expo Blvd.
Pacific Blvd. South
Hamilton St.
Marinaside Ct.
Cambie St. Bridge
Columbia St.
Main St.
0
1/4 mi
0
1/4 km

properties. **Cons:** pricey. *Rooms from: C$559 ✉ 1038 Canada Pl., Downtown ☎ 877/900–5350 www.fairmont.com/pacificrim 37 suites, 340 rooms No meals ⊕ F2.*

$$$$ HOTEL **Fairmont Waterfront.** This luxuriously modern 23-story hotel sits across the street from the cruise-ship terminal and the convention center, but it's the floor-to-ceiling windows with ocean, park, and mountain views that really make it special. **Pros:** harbor views; proximity to the waterfront; terraced pool. **Cons:** long elevator queues; busy lobby lounge. *Rooms from: C$459 ✉ 900 Canada Pl. Way, Downtown ☎ 604/540–4509 www.fairmont.com/waterfront 489 rooms, 29 suites No meals ⊕ F2.*

$$$$ HOTEL **Four Seasons Hotel Vancouver.** This 30-story luxury hotel is famous for pampering guests, and as you'd expect the service is top-notch. **Pros:** premier location for shopping; you're treated like royalty. **Cons:** no on-site spa. *Rooms from: C$425 ✉ 791 W. Georgia St., Downtown ☎ 604/689–9333 www.fourseasons.com/vancouver 306 rooms, 66 suites No meals ⊕ E3.*

$$$$ HOTEL **Hotel Le Soleil.** At this classy boutique hotel, the intimate fireplace in the neoclassical lobby and the vibrant gold-and-crimson fabrics in the guest rooms—most are small suites—radiate warmth. **Pros:** chic and romantic; central location. **Cons:** no on-site spa or health club. *Rooms from: C$325 ✉ 567 Hornby St., Downtown ☎ 604/632–3000, 877/632–3030 www.hotellesoleil.com 109 suites, 10 rooms ⊕ F2.*

$$ B&B/INN **Kingston Hotel.** Convenient to shopping and nightlife, the family-run Kingston occupies a four-story elevator building dating back to 1910—exactly the type of establishment you'd expect to find in Europe. **Pros:** great location; breakfast included. **Cons:** some shared bathrooms; limited amenities; early checkout. *Rooms from: C$155 ✉ 757 Richards St., Downtown ☎ 604/684–9024, 604/684–9024 www.kingstonhotelvancouver.com 52 rooms, 13 with bath Breakfast ⊕ F3.*

$$$ HOTEL Fodor's Choice ★ **L'Hermitage Hotel.** Get beyond the marble floors, silk and velvet walls, and gold-cushion benches in the lobby and you'll discover a warm residential character to this boutique hotel. **Pros:** uptown hotel has refreshingly residential vibe; excellent concierge; complimentary valet car parking. **Cons:** in the middle of downtown. *Rooms from: C$240 ✉ 788 Richards St., Downtown ☎ 778/327–4100, 888/855–1050 www.lhermitagevancouver.com 40 rooms, 20 suites No meals ⊕ F4.*

$$$$ HOTEL **Loden Hotel.** This gadget-centric boutique hotel has all manner of plug-and-play amenities, including in-room iPod docks and TVs with oversize LCD screens. **Pros:** intimate lounge inspires conversation; central location. **Cons:** limited spa services; dark lobby; service is hit-or-miss. *Rooms from: C$415 ✉ 1177 Melville St., Downtown ☎ 604/669–5060, 877/225–6336 www.theloden.com 70 rooms, 7 suites No meals ⊕ E2.*

$$$ HOTEL **Metropolitan Hotel Vancouver.** Two lions guard the entrance, and a striking antique gold-leaf temple carving graces the lobby of this full-service business-district hotel. **Pros:** genuine luxury at a business-class hotel. **Cons:** a bit pretentious. *Rooms from: C$295 ✉ 645 Howe St., Downtown ☎ 604/687–1122, 800/667–2300 www.metropolitan.com 104 rooms, 18 suites No meals ⊕ E3.*

CLOSE UP

The Ten Hippest Hotel Lounges

900 West Lounge at Fairmont Hotel Vancouver: The wine bar, soaring ceilings, and piano stylings set the stage for a romantic rendezvous.

Bacchus Piano Lounge at the Wedgewood: Its decadent opulence makes any occasion special.

Beyond at the Century Plaza: High style on a budget, including hand-crafted cocktails.

Diva at the Met: Small, elegant, and as much a Mecca for foodies as the restaurant itself.

Gerard Lounge at Sutton Place: The clubby scene and exceptional martinis have made it the city's top spot for Hollywood stars.

Herons at Fairmont Waterfront: Upmarket cosmopolitan comfort for international travelers hanging around the Canada Place complex.

O'Doul's Bar at the Listel Hotel: Hot jazz and cool cocktails in a New York-chic atmosphere.

Opus Bar at Opus Hotel: Mingle with gorgeous people over innovative cocktails and a tapas-style menu.

Reflections Outdoors Lounge at Hotel Georgia: Sip B.C. wines while reclining on the oversize couches and in the private cabanas of this fourth-floor courtyard lounge.

Sylvia's at Sylvia Hotel: A longtime favorite of locals and writers who scribe away in dark corners.

Terrace Bar at Four Seasons: Snazzy and indulgent with its fair share of Armani-clad business travelers.

$$ HOTEL **Moda Hotel.** Across from the opulent Orpheum Theatre, it would be easy to bypass this century-old boutique hotel—which would be a shame, because renovations have restored some of its original architectural features, including recessed ceilings, gold-painted sconces, and the lobby's 1920s-style black-and-white tile floor. **Pros:** good value for location; nicely renovated; discounted parking. **Cons:** noisy location; limited services. *Rooms from: C$193* ✉ *900 Seymour St., Downtown* ☎ *604/683–4251* *www.modahotel.ca* *67 rooms* *No meals* ✣ *E4.*

$$$$ HOTEL **Pan Pacific Vancouver.** In the waterfront Canada Place, the luxurious Pan Pacific has easy access to the city's convention center and the main cruise-ship terminal. **Pros:** lovely harbor views; staff has a "go the extra mile" attitude. **Cons:** atrium is open to the convention center, so it's often full of business executives talking shop. *Rooms from: C$349* ✉ *999 Canada Pl., Downtown* ☎ *604/662–8111, 800/663–1515 in*

Canada, 800/937–1515 in U.S. www.panpacific.com 465 rooms, 39 suites F2.

$$$ HOTEL **Renaissance Vancouver Harbourside Hotel.** With a lobby of glass walls and strategically arranged rooms, this hotel takes full advantage of its view-filled waterfront location. **Pros:** on the outer edge of the financial district; waterfront views. **Cons:** a five-block walk to shopping. *Rooms from: C$269 1133 W. Hastings St., Downtown 604/689–9211, 888/236–2427 www.renaissancevancouver.com 434 rooms, 8 suites No meals E2.*

$$$$ HOTEL **Rosewood Hotel Georgia.** One of Vancouver's newest hotels, the Rosewood is also one of its most historic.This 1927 Georgian Revival building once welcomed such prestigious guests as Elvis Presley and Katharine Hepburn. **Pros:** at the center of the city's action; soothing spa; great restaurant. **Cons:** expensive valet parking. *Rooms from: C$379 801 W. Georgia St., Downtown 604/682–5566 www.rosewoodhotels.com/en/hotelgeorgia 156 rooms No meals E3.*

$$$$ HOTEL **Shangri-La Hotel.** On the first 15 floors of the tallest building in Vancouver—a 61-story tower of angled glass studded with gold squares that glint in the sunshine—is this upscale Asian chain's first hotel in North America. **Pros:** first-rate concierge service; stellar spa. **Cons:** public areas could be more inviting; on the city's busiest thoroughfare. *Rooms from: C$375 1128 W. Georgia St., Downtown 604/689–1120 www.shangri-la.com 81 rooms, 38 suites No meals D2.*

$$$ HOTEL **Sheraton Vancouver Wall Centre.** This stunning pair of ultramodern glass high-rises and their landscaped courtyard take up an entire city block. **Pros:** amazing views from higher floors; intriguing spa; dog-friendly packages with beds and treats. **Cons:** "cool" actually feels a bit cold; in a no-man's land between downtown and Yaletown. *Rooms from: C$255 1088 Burrard St., Downtown 604/331–1000, 800/663–9255 www.sheratonwallcentre.com 669 rooms, 64 suites No meals D4.*

$$$ HOTEL **St. Regis Hotel.** While its renovations are clearly inspired by New York, this 1916 boutique hotel retains a distinctly Canadian feel. **Pros:** hot location; in-room wine delivery service; full breakfast and other perks. **Cons:** no views; slow elevator sometimes make the stairs a faster option (you can view original artwork at every turn in the stairwell). *Rooms from: C$239 602 Dunsmuir St., Downtown 604/681–1135, 800/770–7929 www.stregishotel.com 50 rooms, 15 suites Breakfast E3.*

$$$ HOTEL **Sutton Place Hotel Vancouver.** More like an exclusive European guest-house, this refined hotel has rooms furnished in a Parisian style with soft neutrals and lush fabrics; the service is gracious and attentive. **Pros:** terrific lounge bar for romantic trysts; wonderful spa. **Cons:** nondescript corridor joining restaurant and lounge couldn't be further from the hotel's discreet style. *Rooms from: C$289 845 Burrard St., Downtown 604/682–5511, 800/961–7555 www.suttonplace.com 350 rooms, 46 suites, 164 apartments No meals E3.*

$$$ HOTEL **Vancouver Marriott Pinnacle Downtown Hotel.** A soaring atrium lobby makes a striking entrance to this 38-story hotel, located a few blocks from the cruise-ship terminal and central business district. **Pros:** modern

vibe; in the financial district between shopping and Stanley Park. **Cons:** rooms sometimes not available until 4 pm; generic decor; pricey parking. *Rooms from: C$299 ✉ 1128 W. Hastings St., Downtown ☎ 604/684–1128, 800/207–4150 🌐 www.vancouvermarriottpinnacle.com 🛏 432 rooms, 6 suites 🍴 No meals ✥ F2.*

$$ B&B/INN **Victorian Hotel** Budget hotels can be handsome, as in the gleaming hardwood floors, high ceilings, and chandeliers at this prettily restored 1898 European-style pension. **Pros:** Gastown location; complimentary breakfast; Wi-Fi access. **Cons:** the neighborhood is relatively safe, but you'll probably want to take a cab after midnight. *Rooms from: C$159 ✉ 514 Homer St., Downtown ☎ 604/681–6369, 877/681–6369 🌐 www.victorianhotel.ca 🛏 39 rooms, 18 with bath 🍴 Breakfast ✥ F3.*

$$$$ HOTEL Fodor's Choice ★ **Wedgewood Hotel & Spa.** A member of the exclusive Relais & Châteaux Group, the lavish Wedgewood is owned by a woman who cares fervently about her guests. **Pros:** personalized service; great location close to shops. **Cons:** small size means it books up quickly. *Rooms from: C$402 ✉ 845 Hornby St., Downtown ☎ 604/689–7777, 800/663–0666 🌐 www.wedgewoodhotel.com 🛏 41 rooms, 43 suites ✥ F3.*

WEST END

$ HOTEL **Barclay Hotel.** A location steps from great shopping and affordable rates make this three-story building one of the city's best-value pension-style hotels. **Pros:** primo address; spacious rooms. **Cons:** can be noisy; rooms book up fast. *Rooms from: C$95 ✉ 1348 Robson St., West End ☎ 604/688–8850 🌐 www.barclayhotel.com 🛏 76 rooms, 10 suites 🍴 No meals ✥ D2.*

$$ B&B/INN **Barclay House.** Stained glass, fine antiques, and art-nouveau fixtures decorate this comfortable 1904 house a few blocks from Stanley Park; a fireplace, leather couch, and extensive DVD library make it a cozy rainy-day hangout. **Pros:** snazzy historic building; residential neighborhood; helpful staff. **Cons:** there are a number of steps to climb. *Rooms from: C$180 ✉ 1351 Barclay St., West End ☎ 604/605–1351, 800/971–1351 🌐 www.barclayhouse.com 🛏 6 rooms 🍴 Breakfast ✥ D2.*

$$ HOTEL **Buchan Hotel.** On a tree-lined residential street a block from Stanley Park, this 1926 pension-style hotel is one of Vancouver's best values. **Pros:** quiet neighborhood; close to the beach; airport shuttle a five-minute walk away. **Cons:** parking is expensive; some rooms share a bath; not wheelchair accessible. *Rooms from: C$139 ✉ 1906 Haro St., West End ☎ 604/685–5354, 800/668–6654 🌐 www.buchanhotel.com 🛏 60 rooms, 34 with bath 🍴 No meals ✥ B1.*

$$ B&B/INN **English Bay Inn.** European antiques, stained-glass windows, and touches of Asian art furnish this 1930s Tudor-style house near Stanley Park. **Pros:** elegant atmosphere; knowledgeable and effective concierge. **Cons:** one too many gilt-edged mirrors; leaded-glass windows make rooms a bit dark. *Rooms from: C$195 ✉ 1968 Comox St., West End ☎ 604/683–8002, 866/683–8002 🌐 www.englishbayinn.com 🛏 4 rooms, 2 suites 🍴 Breakfast ✥ B2.*

$$$ RENTAL **The Langtry.** Staying at this inconspicuous 1930 former apartment building near Robson Street and Stanley Park is about as near as you can get to feeling like a West End resident. **Pros:** feel like a Vancouver

Fodor's Choice ★

L'Hermitage Hotel

Opus Vancouver Hotel

Sylvia Hotel

Wedgewood Hotel & Spa

resident; reasonable parking. **Cons:** in a quiet neighborhood, but nearby fire station might disturb your sleep. *$ Rooms from: C$235 ✉ 968 Nicola St., West End ☎ 604/687–7892 🌐 www.thelangtry.com 6 suites ✣ C2.*

$$$$ HOTEL **Listel Hotel Vancouver.** Art and accommodations come together in this hotel on the city's most vibrant shopping street. **Pros:** eclectic decor; green attitude. **Cons:** a longish walk from designer-label shops. *$ Rooms from: C$309 ✉ 1300 Robson St., West End ☎ 800/663–5491, 800/663–5491 🌐 www.listel-vancouver.com 119 rooms, 10 suites No meals ✣ D2.*

$$$ HOTEL **Lord Stanley Suites on the Park.** These small, enticing, and fully equipped suites are in a modern high-rise building right at the edge of Stanley Park. **Pros:** residential neighborhood; fabulous views; great longer-stay option. **Cons:** few facilities; not many common areas; furnishings are a bit plain. *$ Rooms from: C$249 ✉ 1889 Alberni St., Stanley Park ☎ 604/688–9299, 888/767–7829 🌐 www.lordstanley.com 100 suites Breakfast ✣ C1.*

$$$ B&B/INN **O Canada House B&B.** This beautifully restored 1897 Victorian is where the first version of "O Canada," the country's national anthem, was penned in 1909. **Pros:** gracious service; fantastic breakfast; within walking distance of downtown. **Cons:** many rooms on the small side; not wheelchair accessible. *$ Rooms from: C$240 ✉ 1114 Barclay St., West End ☎ 604/688–0555, 877/688–1114 🌐 www.ocanadahouse.com 7 rooms Breakfast ✣ D3.*

$$ HOTEL Fodor's Choice ★ **Sylvia Hotel.** This Virginia-creeper-covered 1912 building is popular because of its affordable rates and its near-perfect location a stone's throw from the beach on scenic English Bay. **Pros:** beachfront location; close to restaurants; a good place to mingle with the locals. **Cons:** older building; parking can be difficult; walk to downtown is slightly uphill. *$ Rooms from: C$179 ✉ 1154 Gilford St., West End ☎ 604/681–9321 🌐 www.sylviahotel.com 97 rooms, 22 suites No meals ✣ B2.*

$$$ B&B/INN **West End Guest House.** Built in 1906, this Victorian B&B is painted the deep pink of the "Painted Lady" variety; it's just as adorable inside, with a gracious front parlor, cozy fireplace, and period-appropriate furniture. **Pros:** historic interior; quiet residential location; free use of mountain bikes. **Cons:** furnishings a bit precious. *$ Rooms from: C$205 ✉ 1362 Haro St., West End ☎ 604/681–2889, 888/546–3327 🌐 www.westendguesthouse.com 8 rooms Breakfast ✣ C2.*

$$$$ RESORT **Westin Bayshore.** Beside Stanley Park, the Westin Bayshore has the marina on its doorstep, as well as impressive harbor and mountain views. **Pros:** resort amenities within minutes of downtown; fabulous water views; great waterside walkways. **Cons:** away from downtown; conference center draws many business travelers; tower rooms are a long walk from registration. *$ Rooms from: C$359 ✉ 1601 Bayshore Dr., off Cardero St., West End ☎ 604/682–3377 🌐 www.westinbayshore.com 482 rooms, 28 suites No meals ✣ D1.*

7

YALETOWN

$$$ HOTEL Fodor's Choice ★ **Opus Vancouver Hotel.** The design team had a ball with this boutique hotel, creating fictitious characters and decorating rooms for each. **Pros:** great Yaletown location, right by rapid transit; funky and hip vibe; the lobby bar is a fashionable meeting spot. **Cons:** surrounding neighborhood is mostly high-rises; trendy nightspots nearby can be noisy at night. *Rooms from: C$259* ✉ *322 Davie St., Yaletown* ☎ *604/642–6787, 866/642–6787* 🌐 *www.opushotel.com* *85 rooms, 11 suites* *No meals* ✣ *E5.*

$$$$ HOTEL **Westin Grand Vancouver.** With its dramatic modern design and all-suites layout, the Westin Grand is one of Vancouver's most stylish hotels. **Pros:** you can walk to major theater and stadium events. **Cons:** escalator access to reception; smallish rooms. *Rooms from: C$329* ✉ *433 Robson St., Yaletown* ☎ *604/602–1999, 604/602–1999* 🌐 *www.westingrandvancouver.com* *23 rooms, 184 suites* *No meals* ✣ *F4.*

GRANVILLE ISLAND

$$$$ HOTEL **Granville Island Hotel.** Granville Island is one of Vancouver's more entertaining neighborhoods, but unless you've moored up in a houseboat, the only overnight option is the Granville Island Hotel. **Pros:** unique island location; creek views. **Cons:** island gets busy on weekends; '80s-style furnishings seem dated. *Rooms from: C$300* ✉ *1253 Johnston St., Granville Island* ☎ *604/683–7373, 800/663–1840* 🌐 *www.granvilleislandhotel.com* *74 rooms, 8 suites* ✣ *C6.*

WEST SIDE

$$$ B&B/INN **Granville House B&B.** At the edge of posh Shaughnessy, this Tudor-revival house is Vancouver's only five-star B&B, and it exudes a peaceful elegance that belies its address on one of Vancouver's busiest thoroughfares. **Pros:** top-notch service; hot breakfasts. **Cons:** on the neighborhood's main drag; everything is so pristine that you might feel hesitant to muss the linens. *Rooms from: C$245* ✉ *5050 Granville St., Shaughnessy* ☎ *866/739–9002* 🌐 *www.granvillebb.com* *4 rooms* *Breakfast* ✣ *A5.*

8

Victoria and Vancouver Island Side Trips

WORD OF MOUTH

"The [Butchart Gardens] were beautiful. It was raining but our bus driver was great and gave a wonderful commentary on Victoria. The gardens supplied clear umbrellas so everything was doable . . . Back at The Fairmont Empress we had a royal tea . . . and the service was wonderful."

—milliebest

VICTORIA AND VANCOUVER ISLAND SIDE TRIPS

TOP REASONS TO GO

★ **The journey here:** Yup, getting here is one of the best things about Victoria. Whether by ferry meandering past the Gulf or San Juan islands, by floatplane (try to travel at least one leg this way), or on a whale-watching boat, getting to Victoria is a memorable experience.

★ **Spend an afternoon at the Butchart Gardens:** Nearly a million annual visitors can't be wrong—these lavish gardens north of town truly live up to the hype.

★ **Tour the Royal British Columbia Museum:** One of Canada's best regional museums warrants repeat visits just to take in the myriad displays and exhibits.

★ **Embark on a whale-watching cruise:** It's an amazing way to view these magnificent animals in the wild.

★ **Traverse the Inner Harbour via a ferry boat:** The tiny foot-passenger ferries zipping across the Inner Harbour afford passengers a new perspective of the city center.

1 Downtown. Most of Victoria's shopping and sightseeing are in and around the Inner Harbour and a few blocks north, along Government Street up to Chinatown. The lovely residential area of James Bay is within walking distance of the downtown core. Vic West, with its rapidly rising condo developments, is just across the Johnson Street Bridge.

2 Oak Bay, Rockland, and Fairfield. The winding tree-lined streets of Victoria's oldest residential districts are home to gardens, mansions, and the extremely British-feeling Oak Bay Village. All of these areas take in expansive and stunning ocean and mountain views.

3 Sidney and the Saanich Peninsula. The B.C. and Washington State ferry terminals and the airport lie along this bucolic peninsula north of town, which is also home to Butchart Gardens, an emerging wine region, several beaches, and the pleasant town of Sidney, with its many bookshops.

4 The West Shore and the Malahat. Wilderness parks, viewpoints, and historic sites—including Hatley Castle and Fort Rodd Hill—encourage exploration of these western Victoria suburbs.

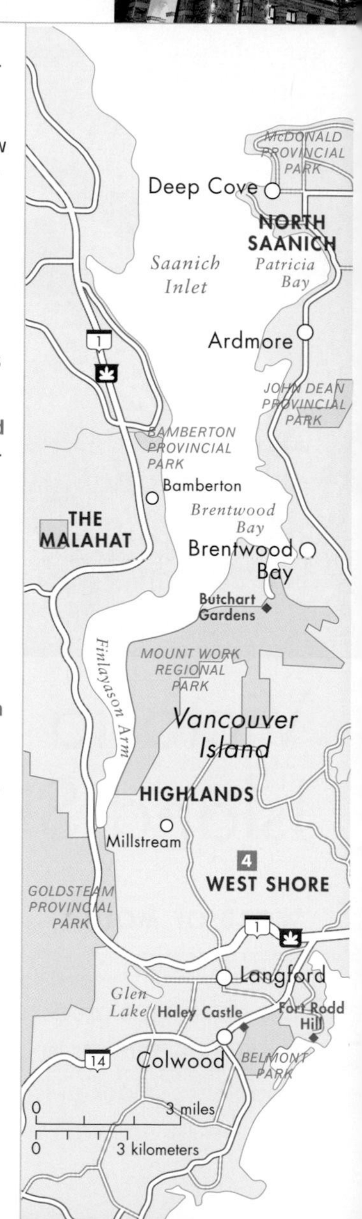

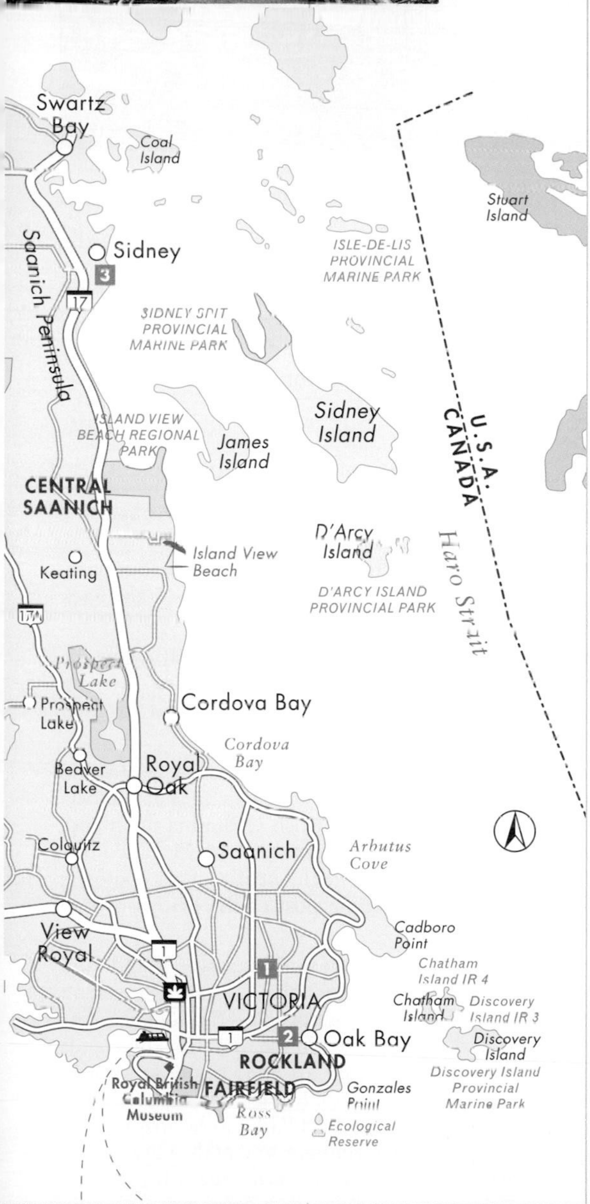

GETTING ORIENTED

Victoria's iconic buildings are clustered around the Inner Harbour. To the south, Beacon Hill Park and James Bay extend to Dallas Road, which runs along the shore of Juan de Fuca Strait. A short walk north along the shop-lined Government Street leads to historic Bastion Square, Market Square, and Chinatown—which are sometimes collectively called Old Town. The Johnson Street Bridge, which separates the Inner Harbour from the Upper Harbour, leads to the waterfront walkways of Vic West. About a mile east of downtown are the gardens and mansions of Rockland, Fairfield, and Oak Bay, the city's older residential districts. Running parallel to Government Street are Blanshard Street, which becomes Highway 17 and leads to the Saanich Peninsula, and Douglas Street, which leads to Highway 1 and the rest of Vancouver Island.

Updated by Carolyn B. Heller

Victoria, the capital of a province whose license plates brazenly label it "The Best Place on Earth," is a walkable, livable seaside city of fragrant gardens, waterfront paths, engaging museums, and beautifully restored 19th-century architecture. In summer, the Inner Harbour—Victoria's social and cultural center—buzzes with visiting yachts, horse-and-carriage rides, street entertainers, and excursion boats heading out to visit pods of friendly local whales.

Yes, it might be a bit touristy, but Victoria's good looks, gracious pace, and manageable size are instantly beguiling, especially if you stand back to admire the mountains and ocean beyond.

At the southern tip of Vancouver Island, Victoria dips slightly below the 49th parallel. That puts it farther south than most of Canada, giving it the mildest climate in the country, with virtually no snow and less than half the rain of Vancouver.

The city's geography, or at least its place names, can cause confusion. Just to clarify: the city of Victoria is on Vancouver Island (not Victoria Island). The city of Vancouver is on the British Columbia mainland, not on Vancouver Island. At any rate, that upstart city of Vancouver didn't even exist in 1843 when Victoria, then called Fort Victoria, was founded as the westernmost trading post of the British-owned Hudson's Bay Company.

Victoria was the first European settlement on Vancouver Island, and in 1868 it became the capital of British Columbia. The British weren't here alone, of course. The local First Nations people—the Songhees, the Saanich, and the Sooke—had already lived in the areas for thousands of years before anyone else arrived. Their art and culture are visible throughout southern Vancouver Island. You can see this in private and public galleries, in the totems at Thunderbird Park, in the striking collections at the Royal British Columbia Museum, and at the Quw'utsun' Cultural and Conference Centre in nearby Duncan. Spanish explorers were the first foreigners to explore the area, although they left little more than place names (Galiano Island and Cordova Bay, for example). The thousands of Chinese immigrants drawn by the gold rushes of the late 19th century had a much greater impact, founding Canada's oldest Chinatown and adding an Asian influence that's still quite pronounced in Victoria's multicultural mix.

Despite its role as the provincial capital, Victoria was largely eclipsed, economically, by Vancouver throughout the 20th century. This, as it turns out, was all to the good, helping to preserve Victoria's historic downtown and keeping the city largely free of skyscrapers and highways. For much of the 20th century, Victoria was marketed to tourists as "The Most British City in Canada," and it still has more than its share of Anglo-themed pubs, tea shops, and double-decker buses. These days, however, Victorians prefer to celebrate their combined indigenous, Asian, and European heritage, and the city's stunning wilderness backdrop. Locals do often venture out for afternoon tea, but they're just as likely to nosh on dim sum or tapas. Decades-old shops sell imported linens and tweeds, but newer upstarts offer local designs in hemp and organic cotton. And let's not forget that fabric prevalent among locals: Gore-Tex. The outdoors is ever present here. You can hike, bike, kayak, sail, or whale-watch straight from the city center, and forests, beaches, offshore islands, and wilderness parklands lie just minutes away. A little farther afield, there's surfing near Sooke, wine touring in the Cowichan Valley, and kayaking among the Gulf Islands.

PLANNING

WHEN TO GO

Victoria has the warmest, mildest climate in Canada: snow is rare and flowers bloom in February. Summers are mild, too, rarely topping 75°F. If you're here for dining, shopping, and museums, winter is a perfectly nice time for a visit: it's gray and wet, and some minor attractions are closed, but hotel deals abound. If your focus is the outdoors—biking, hiking, gardens, and whale-watching—you need to come with everyone else, between May and October. That's when the streets come to life with crafts stalls, street entertainers, blooming gardens, and the inevitable tour buses. It's fun and busy but Victoria never gets unbearably crowded.

MAKING THE MOST OF YOUR TIME

You can see most of the sights in Downtown Victoria's compact core in a day, although there's enough to see at the main museums to easily fill two days. Many key sights, including the Royal BC Museum and the Parliament Buildings, are open on some summer evenings as well. You can save time by prebooking tea at the Empress Hotel and buying tickets online for the Royal British Columbia Museum.

You should also save at least half a day or a full evening to visit Butchart Gardens. The least busy times are first thing in the morning, or on weekdays in the late afternoon and early evening; the busiest but most entertaining time is during the Saturday-evening fireworks shows. If you have a car, you can make a day of it visiting the nearby town of Sidney and some of the Saanich Peninsula wineries.

An extra day allows for some time on the water, either on a whale-watching trip—it's fairly easy to spot orca in the area during summer—or on a Harbour Ferries tour, with stops for tea at Point Ellice House, a microbrew at Spinnakers' Brewpub, or fish-and-chips at Fisherman's Wharf. You can also explore the shoreline on foot, following all, or part, of the 7-mile waterfront walkway.

With more time, you can explore some of the outlying neighborhoods; visit the Art Gallery of Greater Victoria, Craigdarroch Castle, or the delightful Abkhazi Gardens in the Oak Bay and Rockland areas; or head east to see Hatley Park and Fort Rodd Hill.

It rains often in Victoria, so if you get a fine day, set it aside for garden touring, whale-watching, kayaking, or cycling. Car-free bike paths run north to Sidney and east to Sooke.

If you're here for a while and have a car (or really enjoy cycling), the wineries of the Cowichan Valley and the beaches past Sooke warrant a full day each—although it is possible to see both the Southwest Coast and the Cowichan Valley in a one-day circle tour from Victoria. Salt Spring Island can be done as a day trip (market Saturdays are a highlight), though ferry schedules mean that the other islands usually require an overnight. Be warned, though: many people have planned day trips to the islands and ended up staying for years.

FESTIVALS

Victoria's top festivals take place in summer, when you're apt to encounter the best weather. For 10 nights in late June, international musicians perform during JazzFest International. July brings the week long International Buskers Festival, and in early August, during Symphony Splash, the Victoria Symphony plays a free outdoor concert from a barge moored in the middle of Victoria's Inner Harbour. August and September is the time for the Victoria Fringe Theatre Festival, when you can feast from a vast menu of offbeat, original, and intriguing performances around town.

GETTING HERE AND AROUND

It's easy to visit Victoria without a car. Most sights, restaurants, and hotels are in the compact walkable core, with bikes, ferries, horse-drawn carriages, double-decker buses, step-on tour buses, taxis, and pedicabs on hand to fill the gaps. For sights outside the core—Butchart Gardens, Hatley Castle, Scenic Marine Drive—tour buses are your best bet if you don't have your own vehicle.

Bike paths lace downtown and run along much of Victoria's waterfront, and long-haul car-free paths run to the ferry terminals and as far west as Sooke. Most buses and ferries carry bikes.

AIR TRAVEL

Victoria International Airport is 15 miles north of downtown Victoria. The flight from Vancouver to Victoria takes about 25 minutes. To make the 30-minute drive from the airport to downtown, take Highway 17 south. A taxi is about C$55. The Airporter bus service drops off passengers at most major hotels. The one-way fare is C$21. By public transit, take BC Transit Bus 83, 86, or 88 to the McTavish Exchange, where you transfer to Bus 70, which will take you to downtown Victoria. The one-way fare is C$2.50.

There is floatplane service to Victoria's Inner Harbour in downtown Victoria with West Coast Air and Harbour Air. West Coast Air also flies from Whistler to downtown Victoria, May–October. Kenmore Air has daily floatplane service from Seattle to Victoria's Inner Harbour. Helijet has helicopter service from downtown Vancouver and Vancouver International Airport to downtown Victoria.

For the Gulf Islands, Harbour Air Seaplanes has regular service from downtown Vancouver to Salt Spring and Pender islands. Seair Seaplanes fly from Vancouver Airport to the Southern Gulf Islands. Saltspring Air flies from downtown Vancouver and Vancouver International Airport to the Southern Gulf Islands and to Maple Bay, near Duncan, in the Cowichan Valley. Kenmore Air has summer floatplane service from Seattle to the Gulf Islands. There is no scheduled floatplane service between Victoria and the Gulf Islands.

Contacts and Local Airlines Airporter ☎ *250/386–2525, 877/386–2525* 🌐 *www.victoriaairporter.com.* **Harbour Air Seaplanes** ☎ *604/274–1277, 800/665–0212* 🌐 *www.harbour-air.com.* **Helijet** ☎ *604/273–4688, 800/665–4354* 🌐 *www.helijet.com.* **Kenmore Air** ☎ *425/486–1257, 866/435–9524* 🌐 *www.kenmoreair.com.* **Seair Seaplanes** ☎ *604/273–8900, 800/447–3247* 🌐 *www.seairseaplanes.com.* **Saltspring Air** ☎ *250/537–9880, 877/537–9880* 🌐 *www.saltspringair.com.* **West Coast Air** ☎ *604/274–1277, 800/665–0212* 🌐 *www.westcoastair.com.*

BOAT AND FERRY TRAVEL

FROM THE B.C. MAINLAND

BC Ferries has daily service between Tsawwassen, about an hour south of Vancouver, and Swartz Bay, at the end of Highway 17 (the Patricia Bay Highway), about 30 minutes north of Victoria. Sailing time is about 1½ hours. Fares are C$14.85 per adult passenger and C$49.25 per vehicle each way. Vehicle reservations on Vancouver–Victoria and Nanaimo routes are optional and cost an additional C$15 to C$17.50. Foot passengers and cyclists don't need reservations.

To reach the Tsawwassen ferry terminal from downtown Vancouver, take the Canada Line south to Bridgeport Station and change to Bus 620. In Swartz Bay, BC Transit buses 70 (express) and 72 (local) meet the ferries. However, if you're traveling without a car, it's easier to just take a Pacific Coach Lines bus between downtown Vancouver and downtown Victoria; the bus travels on the ferry.

BC Ferries also sail from Horseshoe Bay, north of Vancouver, to Nanaimo, about two hours north of Victoria—convenient if you're traveling by car from Whistler or Vancouver's north shore to Vancouver Island.

An excellent option is combining four hours of whale-watching with travel between Vancouver and Victoria, offered by the Prince of Whales. The 74-passenger boat leaves the Westin Bayshore Hotel in downtown Vancouver daily at 9 am (June–early Sept., one-way C$190), arriving in Victoria at 1 pm; there are also departures from Victoria's Inner Harbour at 1:45 pm (one-way C$145).

WITHIN VICTORIA

The Victoria Harbour Ferry serves the Inner Harbour; stops include the Fairmont Empress, Chinatown, Point Ellice House, the Delta Victoria Ocean Pointe Resort, and Fisherman's Wharf. Fares start at C$5;

multiple-trip and two-day passes are available. Boats make the rounds every 15 to 20 minutes, daily, March–October. The 45-minute harbor tours cost $22, and gorge cruises cost $26. At 10:45 am on summer Sundays, the little ferries perform a water ballet set to classical music in the Inner Harbour.

Boat and Ferry Info BC Ferries ☎ *250/386–3431, 888/223–3779* 🌐 *www.bcferries.com.* **Prince of Whales** ☎ *250/383–4884, 888/383–4884* 🌐 *www.princeofwhales.com.* **Victoria Harbour Ferry** ☎ *250/708–0201* 🌐 *www.victoriaharbourferry.com.*

BUS TRAVEL

Pacific Coach Lines has daily service between Vancouver and Victoria; the bus travels on the ferry. BC Transit serves Victoria and around, including the Swartz Bay ferry terminal, Victoria International Airport, the Butchart Gardens, Sidney, and Sooke. One-way fare is C$2.50 (exact change); an all-day pass is C$7.75.

Mid-June–August, Gray Line's Butchart Gardens Express shuttle runs every 45 to 90 minutes from the bus depot behind the Fairmont Empress. Round-trip fare is C$48, including admission to the gardens.

CVS Cruise Victoria operates the summertime Peninsula Attractions Connector, a shuttle service that takes passengers between the Swartz Bay ferry terminal, Butchart Gardens, Victoria Butterfly Gardens, Shaw Ocean Discovery, Sea Cider Farm and Cider Works, and Brentwood Bay Lodge; prices start at C$29.95. It runs a separate shuttle to Butchart Gardens, with departures from the Fairmont Empress and from several other downtown hotels; the C$50 round-trip fare includes entrance to the gardens.

Bus Info BC Transit ☎ *250/382–6161* 🌐 *www.bctransit.com.* **CVS Cruise Victoria** ☎ *250/386–8652, 877/578–5552* 🌐 *www.cvscruisevictoria.com.* **Gray Line** ☎ *800/472–9546* 🌐 *www.grayline.com/Victoria.* **Pacific Coach Lines** ☎ *604/662–7575, 800/661–1725* 🌐 *www.pacificcoach.com.*

TAXI TRAVEL

In Victoria, call Bluebird, Victoria Taxi, or Yellow Cab. Salt Spring and Pender also have cab companies.

Contacts Bluebird Taxi ☎ *250/382–2222* 🌐 *www.taxicab.com.*
Pender Island Cab Company ☎ *250/629–2222* 🌐 *www.penderislandcab.com.*
Salt Spring Silver Shadow Taxi ☎ *250/537–3030* 🌐 *www.silvershadow.ca.*
Victoria Taxi ☎ *250/383–7111* 🌐 *www.victoriataxi.com.*
Yellow Cab ☎ *250/381–2222* 🌐 *www.yellowcabofvictoria.com.*

TOUR OPTIONS

AIR TOURS

Harbour Air Seaplanes has 20-minute flightseeing tours of Victoria and beyond, starting at C$99.

BOAT TOURS

The best way to see the sights of the Inner and Upper Harbour, and beyond, is by Victoria Harbour Ferry; 45- and 50-minute tours cost C$22 to C$26.

BUS TOURS

Gray Line's double-decker buses tour downtown, Chinatown, and the Inner Harbour; a Butchart Gardens Express shuttle is also available. Big Bus has narrated tours on open-top and trolley-style buses, April–October; you can get on and off at any of the 22 stops. You can buy a two-day ticket on board for C$37, but buy online and you get a third day free.

CARRIAGE TOURS

Tally-Ho Carriage Tours and Victoria Carriage Tours both operate horse-drawn tours.

FOOD AND WINE TOURS

On the second and fourth Saturdays of the month (June–September), Travel with Taste leads culinary tours of Victoria with a tea tasting, a wine tasting, and a chance to try artisanal delicacies. The company also runs day trips to the Cowichan Valley and Saanich Peninsula, and multiday trips to Sooke and Salt Spring Island. Vancouver Island Wine Tours will take you to the Cowichan Valley or the Saanich Peninsula.

WALKING TOURS

The Architectural Institute of B.C. conducts walking tours of Victoria's historic neighborhoods for C$10 in July and August. Discover the Past Tours offers Ghostly Walks and Chinatown Tours. Victorian Garden Tours takes you to private and public gardens.

Info Architectural Institute of British Columbia. ☎ *800/683-8588* 🌐 *www.aibc.ca.* **Big Bus Victoria** ☎ *250/389-2229, 888/434-2229* 🌐 *www.bigbusvictoria.ca.* **Discover the Past Tours** ☎ *250/384-6698* 🌐 *www.discoverthepast.com.* **Gray Line** ☎ *800/472-9546* 🌐 *www.grayline.com/victoria.* **Harbour Air Seaplanes** ☎ *250/385-9131, 800/665-0212* 🌐 *www.harbour-air.com.* **Tally-Ho Carriage Tours** ☎ *250/514-9257, 866/383-5067* 🌐 *www.tallyhotours.com.* **Travel With Taste** ☎ *250/385-1527* 🌐 *www.travelwithtaste.com.* **Vancouver Island Wine Tours** ☎ *250/661-0044* 🌐 *www.vancouverislandwinetours.com.* **Victoria Carriage Tours** ☎ *250/383-2207, 877/663-2207* 🌐 *www.victoriacarriage.com.* **Victoria Harbour Ferry** ☎ *250/708-0201* 🌐 *www.victoriaharbourferry.com.* **Victorian Garden Tours** ☎ *250/380-2797* 🌐 *www.victoriangardentours.com.*

VISITOR INFORMATION

Tourist Information Galiano Island Travel InfoCentre ☎ *250/539-2233* 🌐 *www.galianoisland.com.* **Salt Spring Island Visitor Information Centre** ☎ *250/537-5252, 866/216-2936* 🌐 *www.saltspringtourism.com.* **Sooke Region Museum and Visitor Centre** ☎ *250/642-6351, 866/888-4748* 🌐 *www.sookeregionmuseum.com.* **Tourism British Columbia** ☎ *800/435-5622* 🌐 *www.hellobc.com.* **Tourism Cowichan** ☎ *800/665-3955* 🌐 *www.cvrd.bc.ca.* **Tourism Vancouver Island** ☎ *250/754-3500, 888/655-3483* 🌐 *www.vancouverisland.travel.* **Tourism Victoria Visitor Centre** ✉ *812 Wharf St.* ☎ *250/953-2033, 800/663-3883* 🌐 *www.tourismvictoria.com.*

RESTAURANTS

Wild salmon, locally made cheeses, Pacific oysters, organic vegetables, local microbrews, and wines from the island's farm-gate wineries (really small wineries are allowed to sell their wines "at the farm gate") are tastes to watch for. Vegetarians and vegans are well catered to in this health-conscious town, and seafood choices go well beyond traditional fish-and-chips. You may notice an Ocean Wise symbol on a growing number of menus: this indicates that the restaurant is committed to serving only sustainably harvested fish and seafood.

Some of the city's best casual (and sometimes not-so-casual) fare is served in pubs—particularly in brewpubs; most have an all-ages restaurant as well as an adults-only bar area.

Afternoon tea is a Victoria tradition, as is good coffee—despite the Starbucks invasion, there are plenty of fun and funky local caffeine purveyors around town.

SHOPPING

In Victoria, as in the rest of B.C., the most popular souvenirs are First Nations arts and crafts, which you can pick up at shops, galleries, street markets, and—in some cases—directly from artists' studios. Look for silver jewelry and cedar boxes carved with traditional images and, especially around Duncan, the thick hand-knit sweaters made by the Cowichan people. B.C. wines, from shops in Victoria or directly from the wineries, make good souvenirs, as most are unavailable outside the province.

VICTORIA

Exploring Victoria is easy. A walk around downtown, starting with the museums and architectural sights of the Inner Harbour, followed by a stroll up Government Street to the historic areas of Chinatown and Old Town, covers most of the key attractions, though seeing every little interesting thing along the way could easily take two days. Passenger ferries dart across the Inner and Upper harbors to Point Ellice House and Fisherman's Wharf, while more attractions, including Craigdarroch Castle and the Art Gallery of Greater Victoria, lie about a mile east of downtown in the residential areas of Rockland and Oak Bay. Most visitors also make time for the Butchart Gardens, a stunning exhibition garden a 20-minute drive north on the Saanich Peninsula. Free time is also well spent strolling or biking through Beacon Hill Park and along the Dallas Road waterfront, heading out to such less-visited sights as Hatley Castle and Fort Rodd Hill, or checking out any of the area's beaches, wilderness parks, or wineries.

DOWNTOWN VICTORIA

TOP ATTRACTIONS

★ **Chinatown.** Chinese immigrants built much of the Canadian Pacific Railway in the 19th century, and their influence still marks the region. Victoria's Chinatown, founded in 1858, is the oldest such district in Canada. If you enter from Government Street, you'll pass under the elaborate **Gate of Harmonious Interest,** made of Taiwanese ceramic tiles and decorative panels. Along Fisgard Street, merchants display paper lanterns and exotic produce. Mah-jongg, fan-tan, and dominoes were games of chance played on **Fan Tan Alley,** said to be the narrowest street in Canada. Once the gambling and opium center of Chinatown,

The grand Fairmont Empress Hotel has a commanding position on Victoria's Inner Harbor.

it's now lined with offbeat shops, few of which sell authentic Chinese goods. Look for the alley on the south side of Fisgard Street between Nos. 545½ and 549½. At just two square blocks, Victoria's Chinatown is much smaller than Vancouver's. It's still pleasant to stroll through, particularly as hip boutiques and eateries have moved into the district. ✉ *Fisgard St., between Government and Store Sts., Chinatown.*

★ **Fairmont Empress.** Opened in 1908 by the Canadian Pacific Railway, the Empress is one of the grand château-style railroad hotels that grace many Canadian cities. Designed by Francis Rattenbury, who also designed the Parliament Buildings across the way, the solid Edwardian grandeur of the Empress has made it a symbol of the city. The elements that made the hotel an attraction for travelers in the past—old-world architecture, ornate decor, and a commanding view of the Inner Harbour—are still here. Nonguests can reserve ahead for afternoon tea (the dress code is smart casual), meet for a curry under the tiger skin in the Bengal Room, enjoy a treatment at the hotel's Willow Stream spa, or sample the superb Pacific Northwest cuisine in the Empress Room. In summer, lunch, snacks, and cocktails are served on the Terrace Verandah overlooking the Inner Harbour. ✉ *721 Government St., Downtown* ☎ *250/384–8111, 250/389–2727 tea reservations* 🌐 *www.fairmont.com/empress.*

★ **Parliament Buildings.** Officially the British Columbia Provincial Legislative Assembly Buildings, these massive stone structures are more popularly referred to as the Parliament Buildings. Designed by Francis Rattenbury (who also designed the Fairmont Empress Hotel) when he was just 25 years old, and completed in 1897, they dominate the Inner

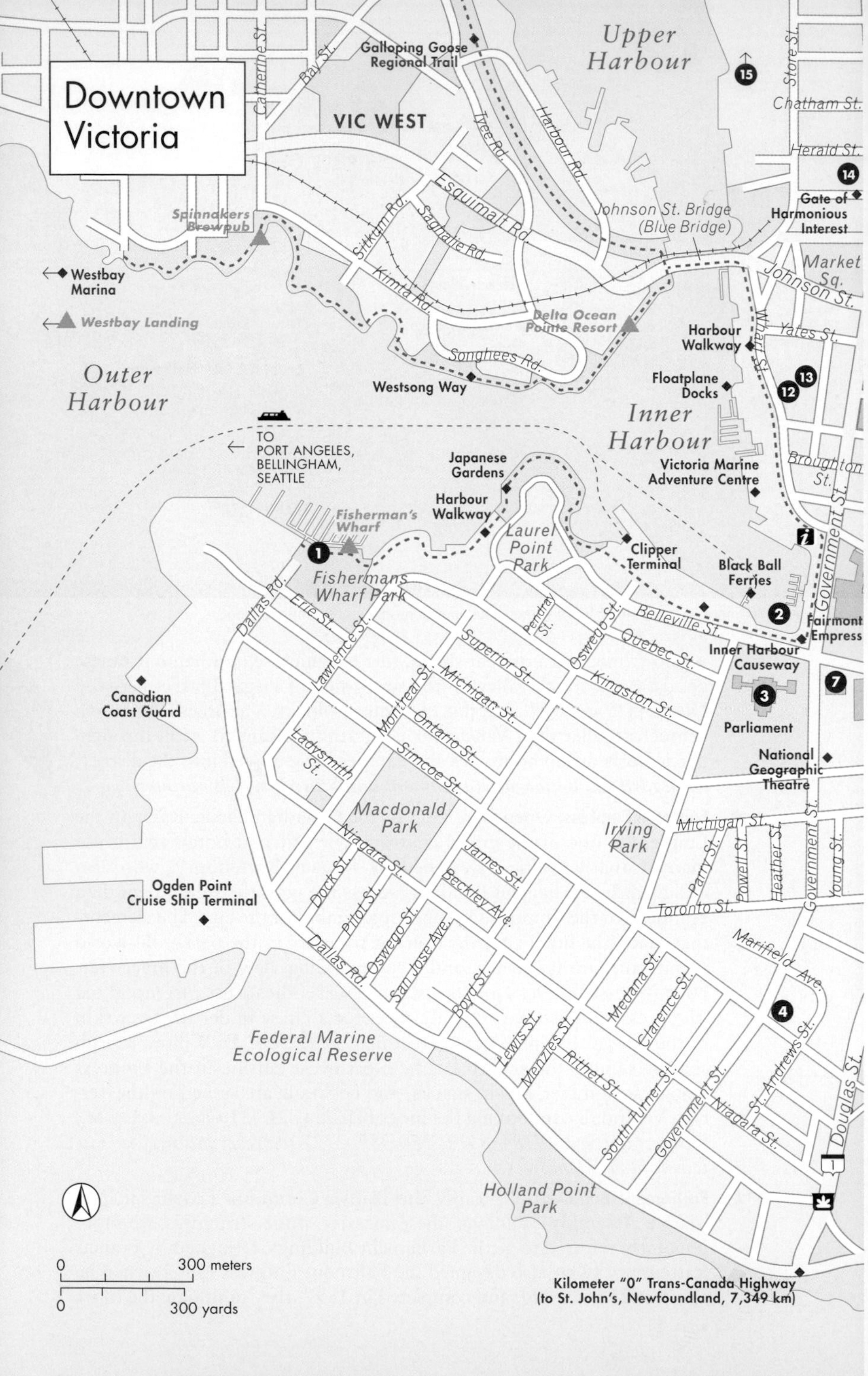

Downtown Victoria
VIC WEST
Upper Harbour
Galloping Goose Regional Trail
Bay St.
Catherine St.
Tyee Rd.
Harbour Rd.
Store St.
Chatham St.
Herald St.
Gate of Harmonious Interest
Esquimalt Rd.
Johnson St. Bridge (Blue Bridge)
Spinnakers Brewpub
Sitkum Rd.
Saghalie Rd.
Market Sq.
Johnson St.
Westbay Marina
Kimta Rd.
Westbay Landing
Delta Ocean Pointe Resort
Wharf St.
Harbour Walkway
Yates St.
Songhees Rd.
Outer Harbour
Westsong Way
Floatplane Docks
Inner Harbour
TO PORT ANGELES, BELLINGHAM, SEATTLE
Japanese Gardens
Victoria Marine Adventure Centre
Broughton St.
Harbour Walkway
Fisherman's Wharf
Laurel Point Park
Clipper Terminal
Black Ball Ferries
Government St.
Fishermans Wharf Park
Dallas Rd.
Erie St.
Lawrence St.
Pendray St.
Oswego St.
Belleville St.
Fairmont Empress
Superior St.
Quebec St.
Inner Harbour Causeway
Canadian Coast Guard
Montreal St.
Michigan St.
Kingston St.
Parliament
Ontario St.
Ladysmith St.
Simcoe St.
National Geographic Theatre
Macdonald Park
Irving Park
Michigan St.
Niagara St.
James St.
Parry St.
Powell St.
Heather St.
Government St.
Young St.
Ogden Point Cruise Ship Terminal
Dock St.
Beckley Ave.
Pilot St.
Toronto St.
Oswego St.
San Jose Ave.
Marifield Ave.
Dallas Rd.
Boyd St.
Medana St.
Clarence St.
Federal Marine Ecological Reserve
Lewis St.
Menzies St.
Rithet St.
St. Andrews St.
Douglas St.
South Turner St.
Government St.
Niagara St.
1
Holland Point Park
0 300 meters
0 300 yards
Kilometer "0" Trans-Canada Highway (to St. John's, Newfoundland, 7,349 km)

Central Park
Pembroke St.
Discovery St.
Royal Athletic Park
Green St.
Caledonia Ave.
Herald St.
North St.
Park St.
McPherson Playhouse
Fisgard St.
Balmoral St.
Centennial Square
Cormorant St.
City Hall
Mason St.
Pandora Ave.
Broad St.
Douglas St.
Rudlin St.
Johnson St.
Yates St.
View St.
Blanshard St.
Quadra St.
Bay Centre
Fort St.
Cook St.
Gordon St.
Broughton St.
Pioneer Square
Meares St.
Courtney St.
Rockland Ave.
Burdett Ave.
Humboldt St.
McClure St.
Vancouver St.
Fairfield Rd.
Richardson St.
Helmcken House
Cridge Park
Collinson
Elliot St.
Academy St.
St. Ann's Schoolhouse
Southgate St.
Pakington St.
Arbutus Way
Heywood Ave.
Pendergast St.
Sutlej St.
Linden Ave.
Beacon Hill Park
Oliphant St.
Park Blvd.
Circle Dr.
May St.
Children's Farm
TO ROSS BAY AND STRAIT OF JUAN DE FUCA

KEY

Visitor Information Centre
Trans-Canada Hwy.
Ferry
Pedestrian trail
Harbour Ferries

Bastion Square **12**
Beacon Hill Park **5**
Chinatown **14**
Emily Carr House **4**
Fairmont Empress **8**
Fisherman's Wharf **1**
Legacy Art Gallery **11**
Maritime Museum of British Columbia **13**
Miniature World **9**
Pacific Undersea Gardens **2**
Parliament Buildings **3**
Point Ellice House **15**
Royal British Columbia Museum **7**
St. Ann's Academy National Historic Site **6**
Victoria Bug Zoo **10**

DID YOU KNOW?

More than 3,300 lights outline Victoria's Parliament Buildings; like the Fairmont Empress hotel, the buildings have a prominent position in the Inner Harbor, and were designed by the same architect: Francis Rattenbury.

CLOSE UP

Victoria Waterfront on Foot

You can walk most of the way around Victoria's waterfront from Westbay Marina on the Outer Harbour's north shore, to Ross Bay on the Strait of Juan de Fuca. The entire 7-mile route takes several hours, but it passes many of the city's sights and great scenery. Waterfront pubs and cafés supply sustenance; ferries and buses offer transport as needed.

Begin with a ride on Harbour Ferries to Westbay Marina, the start of Westsong Way. This 2-mile pedestrian path (no cyclists permitted) follows the waterfront past Vic West to the Johnson Street Bridge. The views across the harbor are rewarding, as is a stop at the waterfront Spinnakers Brewpub. Harbour Ferries stop at Spinnakers and at the Delta Ocean Pointe Resort, so you can choose to start from either point.

Once across the Johnson Street Bridge you can detour to Chinatown and Market Square or, to continue the walk, turn right to Yates Street, then right again down to the water (a Downtown Walk/Harbour Walkway sign shows the way). The route runs past floatplane docks and whale-watching outfitters (where a fish-tacos snack at Red Fish, Blue Fish—a waterfront take-out spot—may be in order) to the Inner Harbour Causeway. Starting from the Visitor Information Centre, this waterfront walkway—busy all summer with street entertainers and crafts and snack vendors—curves around the Inner Harbour. It's only about a quarter mile around, but could take a while if you stop to watch all the torch jugglers and caricature artists. The Fairmont Empress, the Royal BC Museum, and the Parliament Buildings are all here—just across the road from the water.

Detour along Belleville Street past the ferry terminals and pick the path up where it enters Laurel Point Park just past the Clipper terminal. From here, the route leads through the pretty waterfront park and past a marina to Fisherman's Wharf, where you can stop for fish-and-chips on the dock, or grab a ferry back downtown. To keep going, follow Dallas Road to the Ogden Point Cruise Ship terminal, where you can walk out on the breakwater for a view of the ships or grab a snack on the ocean-view deck of the Ogden Point Café.

You're now on the shore of Juan de Fuca Strait, where a footpath runs another 4 miles along cliff tops past Beacon Hill Park to the historic cemetery at Ross Bay. Dog walkers, joggers, and kite flyers are usually out in force on the grassy cliff top; stairways lead down to pebbly beaches. A hike north through Beacon Hill Park will get you back downtown.

Harbour. Atop the central dome is a gilded statue of Captain George Vancouver (1757–98), the first European to sail around Vancouver Island. A statue of Queen Victoria (1819–1901) reigns over the front of the complex. More than 3,300 lights outline the buildings at night. The interior is lavishly done with stained-glass windows, gilt moldings, and historic photographs, and in summer actors play historic figures from B.C.'s past. When the legislature is in session, you can sit in the public gallery and watch British Columbia's democracy at work (custom has the opposing parties sitting 2½ sword lengths apart). Free,

The wooly mammoth at the Royal British Columbia Museum.

informative, 30- to 45-minute tours run every 20 to 30 minutes in summer and several times a day in the off-season (less frequently if school groups or private tours are coming through). Tours are obligatory on summer weekends (mid-May until Labor Day) and optional the rest of the time. ✉ *501 Belleville St., Downtown* ☎ *250/387–3046* 🌐 *www.leg.bc.ca* 💵 *Free* 🕓 *Mid-May–early Sept., daily 9–5; early Sept.–mid-May, weekdays 9–5.*

8

Fodor's Choice ★ **Royal British Columbia Museum.** This excellent museum, one of Victoria's leading attractions, traces several thousand years of British Columbian history. Especially strong is its First Peoples Gallery, home to a genuine Kwakwaka'wakw big house and a dramatically displayed collection of masks and other artifacts. The Environmental History Gallery traces B.C.'s natural heritage, from prehistory to modern-day climate change, in realistic dioramas. An Ocean Station exhibit gets kids involved in running a Jules Verne–style submarine. In the Modern History Gallery, a replica of Captain Vancouver's HMS *Discovery* creaks convincingly, and a re-created frontier town comes to life with cobbled streets, silent movies, and the rumble of an arriving train. An IMAX theater presents films on a six-story-tall screen.

Optional one-hour tours, included in the admission price, run roughly twice a day in summer and less frequently in winter. Most focus on a particular gallery, though the 90-minute Highlights Tour touches on all galleries. Special exhibits, usually held between April and October, attract crowds despite the higher admission prices. Skip ticket lines by booking online.

The museum complex has several more interesting sights, beyond the expected gift shop and café. In front of the museum, at Government and Belleville streets, is the **Netherlands Centennial Carillon.** With 62 bells, it's the largest bell tower in Canada; the Westminster chimes ring out every hour, and free recitals are played most Sunday afternoons. Behind the main building, bordering Douglas Street, are the grassy lawns of **Thunderbird Park,** home to 10 totem poles (replicas of originals that are preserved in the museum). One of the oldest houses in B.C., **Helmcken House** (✉ *10 Elliot St.* ☎ *250/356–7226* 🌐 *www.royalbcmuseum.bc.ca* ⏲ *Late May–early Sept., daily noon–4*) was built in 1852 for pioneer doctor and statesman John Sebastian Helmcken. Inside are displays of the family's belongings, including the doctor's medical tools. Behind it is **St. Ann's School House,** built in 1858. One of British Columbia's oldest schools, it is thought to be Victoria's oldest building still standing. Both buildings are part of the Royal British Columbia Museum. ✉ *675 Belleville St., Downtown* ☎ *250/356–7226, 888/447–7977, 877/480–4887 theater show times* 🌐 *www.royalbcmuseum.bc.ca* 🎟 *C$15, IMAX theater C$11, combination ticket C$23* ⏲ *Daily 9–5.*

WORTH NOTING

Bastion Square. James Douglas, the former colonial governor for whom Douglas Street was named, chose this spot for the original Fort Victoria and Hudson's Bay Company trading post in 1843. In summer the square comes alive with street performers, crafts vendors, and a weekly farmers' market. The former courthouse houses the Maritime Museum of British Columbia. ✉ *Off Wharf St., at View St., Downtown* ☎ *250/885–1387* 🌐 *www.bastionsquare.ca.*

QUICK BITES

You might be tempted to dismiss Paradiso di Stelle (✉ *10 Bastion Sq.* ☎ *250/920-7266*), with its busy patio and prime Bastion Square location, as a bit of a tourist trap. True, it's popular, but the service is quick and friendly, and the authentic Italian coffee, house-made gelato, panini, and pastas are excellent. A water-view and people-watching table right in the action of Bastion Square is irresistible on a summer day.

★ **Beacon Hill Park.** The southern lawns and waterfront path of this 154-acre park afford great views of the Olympic Mountains and the Strait of Juan de Fuca. There are ponds, jogging and walking paths, flowers and gardens, a cricket pitch, and a petting zoo (open daily 10–5). There's live music in the bandshell on summer evenings, and on Saturday nights in August the Victoria Film Festival screens free movies. ✉ *Bordered by Douglas St., Southgate St., and Cook St., Downtown* ☎ *250/361–0600* 🌐 *www.victoria.ca* 🎟 *Free.*

Emily Carr House. One of Canada's most celebrated artists and a respected writer, Emily Carr (1871–1945) lived in this extremely proper, wooden Victorian house before she abandoned her middle-class life to live in the wilds of British Columbia. Carr's own descriptions, from her autobiography *Book of Small,* were used to restore the house. Art on display includes reproductions of Carr's work—visit the Art Gallery of Greater Victoria or the Vancouver Art Gallery to see the originals.

✉ *207 Government St., James Bay* ☎ *250/383–5843* 🌐 *www.emilycarr.com* 🎫 *C$6.75* 🕑 *May–Sept., Tues.–Sat. 11–4.*

Fisherman's Wharf. Victoria Harbour Ferries has its terminal at this fun nautical spot, just west of the Inner Harbour. You can watch fishers unload their catches and admire the various vessels, or picnic in the shoreside park. Among the candy-color houseboats bobbing along the dock are several floating shacks where you can buy ice cream, fish-and-chips, live crabs, kayak tours, and tickets for whale-watching tours. Other booths sell fish to feed the harbor seals who often visit the quay. The busiest vendor is Barb's, an esteemed fish-and-chips spot. ✉ *Corner of Superior and St. Lawrence Sts., Downtown.*

Legacy Art Gallery. Rotating exhibits from the University of Victoria's vast art collection, as well as contemporary installations, are displayed in this airy downtown space. Shows in the 3,000-square-foot space include mostly Canadian works, including many by First Nations artists, but international painters are represented, too. ✉ *630 Yates St., Downtown* ☎ *250/381–7645* 🌐 *www.legacygallery.ca* 🎫 *Free* 🕑 *Wed.–Sat. 10–5.*

Maritime Museum of British Columbia. In Victoria's original courthouse, these two floors of model ships, weaponry, ships' wheels, and photographs chronicle the province's seafaring history, from its early explorers to whale hunters to pirates. Among the hand-built boats on display is the *Tilikum,* a dugout canoe that sailed from Victoria to England between 1901 and 1904. On the third floor, the original 1888 vice-admiralty courtroom looks ready for a court-martial. ✉ *28 Bastion Sq., Downtown* ☎ *250/385–4222* 🌐 *www.mmbc.bc.ca* 🎫 *C$12* 🕑 *Daily 10–5.*

Miniature World. At this charmingly retro attraction, more than 85 miniature dioramas—including space, castle, fairy-tale scenes, and one of the world's largest model railways—are housed in kid-height glass cases with recorded narration. The level of detail is impressive in the models, some of which date to the site's 1969 opening. Some of the models are animated and you can start and stop trains and turn dollhouse lights on and off with push buttons. Most people walk through in 30 minutes, but dollhouse collectors, model-train builders, and preschoolers can be absorbed for hours. ✉ *Fairmont Empress Hotel, 649 Humboldt St., Downtown* ☎ *250/385–9731* 🌐 *www.miniatureworld.com* 🎫 *C$12* 🕑 *Mid-May–mid-Sept., daily 9–9; mid-Sept.–mid-May, daily 9–5.*

Pacific Undersea Gardens. If you want an up-close look at a wolf eel or an octopus, check out this underwater sea-life display, housed inside and under a barge floating in the Inner Harbour. If you're at all claustrophobic, though, be warned: a dark staircase leads to a dark narrow tunnel 15 feet below water where you can see marine creatures darting about behind high windows. The more worthwhile experience is in the underwater theater where a 20-minute narrated dive show, run roughly every hour in summer (less frequently in winter), gives everyone a chance to view the more interesting of the 5,000 or so creatures in the tanks. The biggest room of all is the above-water gift shop. The site isn't wheelchair or stroller accessible, the windows are too high for small children (unless you pick them up), and the tunnel can get uncomfortably crowded. Tickets are good all day, though, so you can return later if need be. ✉ *490 Belleville St., Downtown* ☎ *250/382–5717* 🌐 *www.pacificunderseagardens.com* 🎟 *C$11.95* ⏲ *July and Aug., daily 9–8; Sept.–Apr., weekdays 10–4, weekends 10–5; May and June, daily 10–5.*

Point Ellice House. The O'Reilly family home, an 1861 Italianate cottage overlooking the Selkirk Waterway, has been restored to its original splendor, with the largest collection of Victorian furnishings in western Canada. Tea and fresh-baked goodies are served under an awning on the lawn daily from 11 to 2:30. You can take a half-hour audio tour of the house (presented from a servant's point of view), stroll in the English country garden, or try your hand at croquet. Point Ellice House is only a few minutes' drive north of downtown, but it's in an industrial area, so it's more fun to come by sea. Victoria Harbour Ferries leave from a dock in front of the Fairmont Empress; the sailing lasts about 15 minutes and takes in the sights of the harbor. ✉ *2616 Pleasant St., Downtown* ☎ *250/380–6506* 🌐 *www.pointellicehouse.ca* 🎟 *C$6* ⏲ *Early May–early Sept., daily 11–4.*

St. Ann's Academy National Historic Site. This former convent and school, founded in 1858, played a central role in British Columbia's pioneer life. The academy's little chapel—the first Roman Catholic cathedral in Victoria—has been restored to look just as it did in the 1920s. The 6-acre grounds, with their fruit trees and herb and flower gardens, have also been restored as historic landscapes. ✉ *835 Humboldt St., Downtown* ☎ *250/953–8829* 🌐 *www.stannsacademy.com* 🎟 *By donation* ⏲ *Mid-May–early Sept., daily 10–4; early Sept.–mid-May, Thurs.–Sun. 1–4.*

Victoria Bug Zoo. Local kids clamor to visit this offbeat minizoo, home to the largest live tropical insect collection in North America. You can even hold many of the 70 or so varieties, which include walking sticks, scorpions, millipedes, and a pharnacia—at 22 inches, the world's longest insect. The staff members know their bug lore and are happy to dispense scientific information. ✉ *631 Courtney St., Downtown* ☎ *250/384–2847* 🌐 *www.bugzoo.bc.ca* 🎟 *C$10* ⏲ *Mid-June–early Sept., daily 10–6; early Sept.–mid-June, Mon.–Sat. 10–5:30, Sun. 11–5.*

OAK BAY, ROCKLAND, AND FAIRFIELD

The winding shady streets of Victoria's older residential areas—roughly bordered by Cook Street, Fort Street, and the seaside—are lined with beautifully preserved Victorian and Edwardian homes. These include many stunning old mansions now operating as bed-and-breakfasts, and Victoria's most elaborate folly: Craigdarroch Castle. With mansions come gardens, and several of the city's best are found here. Clusters of high-end shops include the extraordinarily British Oak Bay Village, described as a place "behind the tweed Curtain" for its adherence to Tudor facades and tea shops. Among the lavish waterfront homes are plenty of public parks and beaches offering views across Juan de Fuca Strait to the Olympic Mountains of Washington State.

GETTING AROUND

A car or a bike is handy, but not essential, for exploring this area. No wheels? Big Bus, Gray Line, and other tour companies offer Oak Bay and Marine Drive tours.

By public transit, take Bus 11 or 14 from the corner of Fort and Douglas streets to Moss Street (for the Art Gallery of Greater Victoria), or to Joan Crescent (for Craigdarroch Castle). Government House is a few blocks south. The walk, about a mile past the antiques shops of Fort Street, is also interesting. To get to Oak Bay Village, take Bus 2 (or Bus 2A, which continues to Willows Beach) from Johnson and Douglas streets downtown. If you're visiting the castle and gallery first, continue on Bus 11 and change to Bus 2 at Oak Bay and Fort Street. Another useful route is Bus 7: from Johnson and Douglas streets, it travels to Ross Bay Cemetery, Abkhazi Garden, and Oak Bay Village.

TOP ATTRACTIONS

★ **Abkhazi Garden.** Called "the garden that love built," this once-private garden is as fascinating for its history as for its innovative design. The seeds were planted, figuratively, in Paris in the 1920s, when Englishwoman Peggy Pemberton-Carter met exiled Georgian Prince Nicholas Abkhazi. World War II internment camps (his in Germany, hers near Shanghai) interrupted their romance, but they reunited and married in Victoria in 1946. They spent the next 40 years together cultivating their garden. Rescued from developers and now operated by the Land Conservancy of British Columbia, the one-acre site is recognized as a leading example of West Coast horticultural design, resplendent with native Garry Oak trees, Japanese maples, and mature rhododendrons. The tearoom, in the sitting parlor of the modest, modernist home, serves lunch and afternoon desserts, as well as breakfast on weekends. Watch for evening concerts in the garden. ✉ *1964 Fairfield Rd., Fairfield* ☎ *250/598–8096* 🌐 *www.conservancy.bc.ca* 🎫 *Mar.–Oct. C$10; Nov.–Feb. by donation* 🕒 *Daily 11–5.*

★ **Art Gallery of Greater Victoria.** Attached to an 1889 mansion, this modern building houses one of Canada's largest collections of Asian art. The Japanese garden between the buildings is home to the only authentic Shinto shrine in North America. The gallery, a few blocks west of Craigdarroch Castle, displays a permanent exhibition of works by well-known Canadian artist Emily Carr and regularly changing exhibits of Asian and Western art. ✉ *1040 Moss St., at Fort St., Rockland* ☎ *250/384–4171* 🌐 *www.aggv.ca* 🎫 *C$13* 🕒 *May–Sept., Mon.–Wed. and Fri.–Sat. 10–5, Thurs. 10–9, Sun. noon–5; Oct.–Apr., Tues.–Wed. and Fri.–Sat. 10–5, Thurs. 10–9, Sun. noon–5.*

★ **Craigdarroch Castle.** This resplendent mansion complete with turrets and Gothic rooflines was built as the home of one of British Columbia's wealthiest men, coal baron Robert Dunsmuir, who died in 1889, just a few months before the castle's completion. Now a museum depicting life in the late 1800s, the castle's 39 rooms have ornate Victorian furnishings, stained-glass windows, carved woodwork, and a beautifully restored painted ceiling in the drawing room. A winding staircase climbs four floors to a tower overlooking Victoria. Castles run in the family: son James went on to build the more lavish Hatley Castle west of Victoria. The castle is not wheelchair accessible and has no elevators. ✉ *1050 Joan Crescent, Rockland* ☎ *250/592–5323* 🌐 *www.thecastle.ca* 🎫 *C$13.75* ⏲ *Mid-June–early Sept., daily 9–7; early Sept.–mid-June, daily 10–4:30.*

WORTH NOTING

Government House Gardens. Take a stroll through the walled grounds and formal rose garden of Government House, residence of British Columbia's lieutenant governor, the Queen's representative in B.C. The stately modern house isn't open to the public, though the 35 acres of gardens are. ✉ *1401 Rockland Ave., Rockland* 🎫 *Free* ⏲ *Daily dawn–dusk.*

Oak Bay Village. Described as the land "behind the tweed curtain," this historically British area (with its own municipal hall) is home to the Penny Farthing Pub, as well as sweet shops, bookstores, galleries, and antiques stores, most behind mock-Tudor facades. A few more contemporary boutiques and eateries have moved in, too. ✉ *Oak Bay Ave., between Foul Bay Rd. and Monterey Ave.* 🌐 *www.oakbayvillage.ca.*

Willows Beach Park. This neighborhood park has a nice sandy beach, a grassy park with a playground, and, this being Oak Bay, a teahouse. ✉ *Esplanade, at Dalhousie St., Oak Bay.*

SIDNEY AND THE SAANICH PENINSULA

30 km (18 miles) north of Victoria on Hwy. 17.

Home to the B.C. and Washington State ferry terminals as well as the Victoria International Airport, the Saanich Peninsula, with its rolling green hills and small family farms, is the first part of Vancouver Island that most visitors see. Although it's tempting to head straight for downtown Victoria, 25 minutes to the south, there are many reasons to linger here, including Butchart Gardens, one of the province's leading attractions. Sidney's parklike waterfront, which houses a modern aquarium and marine ecology center as well as cafés, restaurants, and a wheelchair-accessible waterfront path, is a launching point for kayakers, whale-watchers, and eco-tour boats heading out to explore the Gulf Islands National Park Reserve offshore.

GETTING HERE AND AROUND

To reach the area by car from downtown Victoria, follow the signs for the ferries straight up Highway 17, or take the Scenic Marine Drive starting at Dallas Road and following the coast north. It joins Highway 17 at Elk Lake (but take a map—even locals get lost). Victoria transit buses serve the area, though not frequently. Bus tours to Butchart Gardens run several times a day and many tours take in other sights in the area; several companies also offer winery tours. Gray Line and CVS Cruise Victoria also run shuttles to Butchart Gardens. Cyclists can take the Lochside Trail, which runs from Victoria to Sidney, detouring, perhaps, to some wineries along the way.

British Columbia Aviation Museum. Volunteers passionate about the history of flight have lovingly restored several dozen historic military and civilian airplanes, and even re-created a 19th-century flying machine at this museum near Victoria's International Airport. Precomputer flight simulators, flight attendant uniforms, and a World War II–era aviation radio set are displayed in the museum's hangar and on the tarmac outside. Tours take about an hour. ✉ *1910 Norseman Rd., Sidney* ☎ *250/655–3300* 🌐 *www.bcam.net* 🎟 *C$8* ⏲ *May–Sept., daily 10–4; Oct.–Apr., daily 11–3.*

WORD OF MOUTH

"Butchart Gardens—beautiful place!! We took the Evening Illuminations tour with Gray Line and got to see the Gardens right before sunset and on into the late night.... Seeing the Gardens lit up at night was unique."

—globetrotterxyz

Fodor's Choice ★

Butchart Gardens. This stunning 55-acre garden and National Historic Site has been drawing visitors since it was planted in a limestone quarry in 1904. Seven hundred varieties of flowers grow in the site's Japanese, Italian, rose, and sunken gardens. Highlights include the view over the ivy-draped and flower-filled former quarry, the dramatic 70 foot-high Ross Fountain, and the formal and intricate Italian garden, complete with a gelato stand.

From mid-June to mid-September the gardens are illuminated at night with hundreds of hidden lights. In July and August, kids' entertainers perform Sunday through Friday afternoons; jazz, blues, and classical musicians play at an outdoor stage each evening; and fireworks draw crowds every Saturday night. The wheelchair- and stroller-accessible site is also home to a seed-and-gift shop, a plant identification center, two restaurants (one offering traditional afternoon tea), and a coffee shop; you can even call ahead for a picnic basket on fireworks nights. To avoid crowds, try to come at opening time, in the late afternoon or evening (except Saturday evenings, which also draw many visitors), or between September and June, when the gardens are still stunning. The grounds are especially magical at Christmas, with themed lighting and an ice rink.

The gardens are a 20-minute drive north of downtown; parking is free but fills up on fireworks Saturdays. You can get here by city bus 75 from Douglas Street in downtown Victoria, but service is slow and infrequent. Both Gray Line and CVS Cruise Victoria run shuttles from downtown Victoria, and CVS Cruise Victoria also operates a shuttle from the Swartz Bay ferry terminal. ✉ *800 Benvenuto Ave., Brentwood Bay* ☎ *250/652–5256, 866/652–4422* 🌐 *www.butchartgardens.com* 🎟 *C$29.60* ⏲ *Mid-June–Aug., daily 9 am–10 pm; Sept.–mid-June, daily 9 am–dusk.*

Centre of the Universe. You can enjoy great views of Victoria and the night sky through a 1.8-meter telescope, join astronomers and stargazers for summer-evening star parties, or catch a planetarium show at Dominion Astrophysical Observatory. The hilltop site also offers great views over the surrounding countryside. ✉ *5071 W. Saanich Rd., Saanich* ☎ *250/363–8262* 🌐 *www.nrc-cnrc.gc.ca* 🎟 *C$10.25 before 6 pm, C$13.50 after 6 pm* ⏲ *May–Sept., hours vary.*

8

Mount Douglas Regional Park. A footpath and a road lead to the 213-meter (758-foot) summit of Mt. Douglas, offering a 360-degree view of Victoria and the Saanich Peninsula. On a clear day, you can even see the Gulf and San Juan islands and the mountains of Washington. The park, known locally as Mt. Doug, is also home to a long sandy beach, evergreen forests, hiking trails, and wildflower meadows. ✉ *Off Cedar Hill Rd., Saanich* ☎ *250/475–5522* 🌐 *www.saanich.ca* 🎫 *Free.*

★ **Shaw Ocean Discovery Centre.** A simulated ride underwater in a deep-sea elevator is just the beginning of a visit to this fun and educational marine interpretive center. Devoted entirely to the aquatic life and conservation needs of the Salish Sea—the waters south and east of Vancouver Island—the small but modern center displays local sea life, including luminous jellyfish, bright purple starfish, wolf eels, rockfish, and octopi. Hands-on activities and touch tanks delight kids, who also love the high-tech effects, including a floor projection that ripples when stepped on and a pop-up tank you can poke your head into. ✉ *9811 Seaport Pl., Sidney* ☎ *250/665–7511* 🌐 *www.oceandiscovery.ca* 🎫 *$14* ⏲ *July–Aug., daily 10–5; Sept.–June daily 10–4.*

Sidney Spit. In summer, a passenger ferry costing C$19 makes the half-hour run to this long stretch of beach on Sidney Island, part of the Gulf Islands National Park Reserve. Hiking trails and picnic sites make for a pleasant day on the island. The ferry leaves several times a day from Beacon Wharf at the end of Beacon Avenue in Sidney. ☎ *250/474–5145 ferry information, 250/654–4000 park information* 🌐 *www.pc.gc.ca/gulf* 🎫 *Free* ⏲ *Mid-May–June, weekends; July–early Sept., daily.*

★ **Victoria Butterfly Gardens.** Hundreds of butterflies—of 50 different species—flutter freely in an indoor tropical garden that's also home to orchids and carnivorous plants, koi, cockatoos, flamingos, tortoises, geckos, and poison dart frogs. The 20-minute guided tours depart several times a day. The site is a popular stop en route to the Butchart Gardens, and children—and many adults—are entranced. The butterflies, which are bred for the center and not captured in the wild, are most active on sunny days. ✉ *1461 Benvenuto Ave., corner of West Saanich Rd. and Keating Cross Rd., Brentwood Bay* ☎ *250/652–3822, 877/722–0272* 🌐 *www.butterflygardens.com* 🎫 *C$15* ⏲ *Jan.–Apr. and early Sept.–Nov., daily 10–5; May–early Sept., daily 9–7; Dec., daily 10–7.*

THE WEST SHORE AND THE MALAHAT

West of downtown Victoria, along highways 1 and 14, are the rapidly growing communities of View Royal, Colwood, the Highlands, Langford, and Metchosin, collectively known as the West Shore Communities. Although its rural nature is quickly giving way to suburban development, the area is worth a visit for its wilderness parks and national historic sites. Heading north, Highway 1 cuts through deep forests and over the 1,155-foot Malahat Summit on its way to the Cowichan Valley wine country. A viewpoint at the top, accessible only from the northbound lane, offers sweeping views over Finlayson Arm and the surrounding forested slopes.

Fort Rodd Hill and Fisgard Lighthouse National Historic Sites of Canada. The world's best preserved coastal artillery fort (it dates to 1895) and Canada's oldest West Coast lighthouse occupy a parklike backdrop 8 miles west of Victoria. You can walk through most of the buildings, including the lighthouse keeper's house, married quarters, guard houses, and the delightfully named fortress-plotting room. Interactive exhibits let you navigate a 19th-century schooner. Wandering deer, forest trails, and historic military hardware share the rolling seaside site, and the views from the gun emplacements over the entrance to Esquimalt Harbour are fabulous. To get here, take Highway 1A west to Ocean Boulevard. *603 Fort Rodd Hill Rd., off Ocean Blvd., West Shore 250/478–5849 www.pc.gc.ca C$4 Mid-Feb.–Oct., daily 10–5:30; Nov.–mid-Feb., daily 9–4:30.*

Goldstream Provincial Park. Eagles, bears, and three species of salmon thrive in this 477-hectare (1,180-acre) wilderness park 10 miles north of downtown Victoria. Picnic areas, easy riverside walks, and challenging hikes draw visitors in summer. In winter, viewing stations are set up to watch thousands of bald eagles gather to feed on salmon. Naturalists provide guidance at the Nature House, a visitor center that's a 10-minute walk from the parking lot. *Hwy. 1, at Finlayson Arm Rd., West Shore 250/478–9414 www.env.gov.bc.ca/bcparks Donations accepted Nature House daily 9–4:30.*

OFF THE BEATEN PATH

Hatley Park National Historic Site. Envisioned by James Dunsmuir, a former premier of British Columbia and son of the man who built Craigdarroch Castle, this ivy-draped 40-room manor and its 565 acres of oceanfront grounds make up one of the finest intact Edwardian estates in Canada. Started in 1908 and built in just 18 months, the manor mixes Norman and Renaissance styles, which are meant to suggest a house that had stood for centuries. It's now part of Royal Roads University, and the interior of the castle can be seen only by guided tour. The tours are informative, although almost none of the original furnishings—except a billiard table that was too big to remove—remain. You don't need to join a tour to see the beautifully preserved Italian, Japanese, and English rose gardens. To get here, take Highway 1A west from Victoria. Royal Roads University is on your left about half a mile past the turn-off to Fort Rodd Hill. *2005 Sooke Rd., Colwood 250/391–2666, 866/241–0674 www.hatleypark.ca Gardens C$9.50, house tours C$18 Gardens mid-Apr.–mid-Sept., daily 10–7; mid-Sept.–mid-Apr., hrs vary. House tours mid-Apr.–mid-Sept., daily at 10:30, 11:45, 1:30, and 2:45; mid-Sept.–mid-Apr., hrs vary.*

8

Hatley Park's 40-room castle is one of Canada's finest intact Edwardian estates; the gardens are quite spectacular, too.

WHERE TO EAT

Victoria has a tremendous number and variety of restaurants for such a small city; this fact, and the glorious pantry that is Vancouver Island—think wild salmon and Pacific oysters, locally made cheese, and organic fruits and veggies—keeps prices down (at least compared to Vancouver) and standards up. Restaurants in the region are generally casual. Smoking is banned in all public places, including restaurant patios, in Greater Victoria and on the Southern Gulf Islands. Victorians tend to dine early—restaurants get busy at 6, and many kitchens close by 9. Pubs, lounges, and the few open-late places mentioned here are your best options for an after-hours nosh.

Prices in the reviews are the average cost of a main course at dinner or, if dinner is not served, at lunch.

DOWNTOWN

Use the coordinate (⊕ B2) at the end of each listing to locate a site on the corresponding map.

$$$ MODERN CANADIAN Fodor's Choice ★

✕ **Aura.** Creative Pacific Rim cuisine and the city's best waterfront patio make this chic eatery on the Inner Harbour's south shore a winner. Always using local ingredients, the seasonally changing fare reveals Asian leanings such as poached B.C. salmon paired with barbecued eel and a Japanese rice-cabbage roll; buffalo short ribs braised with fennel and star anise and served with wild mushroom bread pudding; or free-range chicken with a wasabi pea crust. The wine cellar is full of hard-to-find Vancouver Island wines and Okanagan labels. Sleek lines, warm colors, and water-view windows create a room that's both stylish and cozy. *Average main: C$25* *Inn at Laurel Point, 680 Montreal St., James Bay* *250/414–6739* *www.aurarestaurant.ca* *C1.*

$$ SEAFOOD **Barb's Fish & Chips.** Funky Barb's, a tin-roof take-out shack, floats on the quay at Fisherman's Wharf, west of the Inner Harbour off St. Lawrence Street. Halibut, salmon, oysters, mussels, crab, burgers, and chowder are all prepared fresh. The picnic tables on the wharf provide a front-row view of the brightly colored houseboats moored here, or you can carry your food to the grassy park nearby. Ferries sail to Fisherman's Wharf from the Inner Harbour, or you can work up an appetite with a leisurely stroll along the waterfront. *Average main: C$13* *Fisherman's Wharf, St. Lawrence St., Downtown* *250/384–6515* *www.barbsplace.ca* *Closed Nov.–early Mar.* *B5.*

$ BURGER **Bin 4 Burger Lounge.** This hip little burger joint elevates the humble patty with local ingredients and naturally raised meats, serving up intriguing burger combos like beef with chipotle-bourbon barbecue sauce, B.C.–raised bison with aged cheddar and fried onions, or chicken with bacon, Brie, and balsamic red-onion jam. Vegetarians can substitute crispy tofu on any sandwich or opt for the "Mr. Bean," a chickpea, black bean, and goat cheese burger. Sandwiches come with excellent fries or salad; ask for half and half, and make sure to sample one of the housemade dips, perhaps roasted garlic aioli or lime-and-tomatillo hot sauce. Kids are welcome, but this fun, lounge-y room, where drink choices include creative cocktails, beer from island microbrewies, and house-made berry ice tea, serves up happy meals for grown-ups. *Average main: C$13* *911 Yates St., Downtown* *250/590–4154* *www.bin4burgerlounge.com* *H3.*

8

$$ FRENCH **Bon Rouge.** Craving a *croque madame* or a prawn crepe? Bouillabaisse, salade niçoise, or maybe just a really classy bacon-and-Gruyère cheeseburger? This casual bistro just off the Inner Harbour serves West Coast takes on French classics and has one of the city's nicest covered patios. Two inside rooms are done in high-energy red, white, and black; outside is a big shady space warmed by fireplaces, framed in greenery, and cooled with a wall fountain. There are sidewalk tables, too. The chef sources fare from nearby farms for the crepe-and-egg brunches, casual lunches, and romantic dinners. You can even buy fresh baguettes for a picnic to go. *Average main: C$20* *611 Courtney St., Downtown* *250/220–8008* *www.bonrouge.ca* *F4.*

$$$ FRENCH Fodor's Choice ★ **Brasserie L'ecole.** French-country cooking shines at this informal Chinatown bistro, and the historic room—once a schoolhouse for the Chinese community—evokes a timeless brasserie, from the white linens and patina-rich fir floors to the chalkboards above the slate bar listing the day's oyster, mussel, and steak options. Sean Brennan, one of the city's better-known chefs, works with local farmers and fishers to source the best seasonal, local, and organic ingredients. The menu changes daily but lists such contemporary spins on classic bistro fare as duck breast with chick-pea fries and asparagus, or tuna with chervil aioli. Be prepared for lines, as this petite spot does not take reservations. *Average main: C$24* *1715 Government St., Downtown* *250/475–6260* *www.lecole.ca* *Reservations not accepted* *Closed Sun. and Mon. No lunch* *F2.*

$$$$ MODERN CANADIAN Fodor's Choice ★ ✕ **Cafe Brio.** In this bustling Italian villa–style room, long one of Victoria's favorites, the frequently changing menu adds Mediterranean influences to the regional, mostly organic fare. You might find local rockfish pan-roasted and paired with chick-pea polenta, grilled albacore tuna with an olive vinaigrette, red wine–braised duck legs, rigatoni with spicy sausage, or house-made charcuterie. Most dishes come in full or half sizes, the better to sample more items or cater to smaller appetites. Virtually everything, including the bread, pasta, and desserts, is made in-house. The 400-label wine list has a top selection of B.C. choices. *Average main: C$27* ✉ *944 Fort St., Downtown* ☎ *250/383–0009, 866/270–5461* 🌐 *www.cafe-brio.com* ⊗ *No lunch* ✥ *H4.*

$$$ MODERN CANADIAN ★ ✕ **Camille's.** Working closely with independent farmers, the chef at this long-established favorite concentrates on such locally sourced products as lamb, duck, and seafood; quail and venison often make an appearance, too. The menu is based on what's fresh, but might include spot-prawn bisque with lemon and ginger; wild salmon with beet papardelle; or organic beef tenderloin. The wine cellar–like backdrop, on the lower floor of a historic building on Bastion Square, is candlelit and romantic, with exposed brick, soft jazz and blues, and lots of intimate nooks and crannies hung with local art. The wine list is well selected. *Average main: C$28* ✉ *45 Bastion Sq., Downtown* ☎ *250/381–3433* 🌐 *www.camillesrestaurant.com* ⊗ *Closed Sun. and Mon. No lunch* ✥ *E3.*

$$ CANADIAN ✕ **Canoe Brewpub.** The lofty windows of this power station–turned–brewpub open onto one of Victoria's best waterfront patios, overlooking the kayaking and ferry action on the gorge. The casual, locally sourced menu runs from such high-end pub snacks as tuna tacos and steamed edamame to pappardelle with shrimp and scallops, flatbread pizzas, and good old fish-and-chips. Choose from the adults-only brewpub or the all-ages restaurant—both have water-view patios. And try the beer—the Beaver Brown Ale, River Rock Bitter, and other signature creations are brewed the old-fashioned way. You can even see the vats from the pub. *Average main: C$19* ✉ *450 Swift St., Downtown* ☎ *250/361–1940* 🌐 *www.canoebrewpub.com* ✥ *E2.*

$$ MODERN CANADIAN ✕ **Devour.** Expect to devour plenty of local, seasonal ingredients at this order-at-the-counter bistro with a daily changing menu. The bill of fare typically includes homemade soup, salads, and innovative sandwiches—perhaps "smashed chick peas" with roasted peppers and olives, or lamb merguez sausage with mint cashew pesto—as well as more substantial fare, like seafood with Thai green curry and yams or a trout salad with bacon, green beans, and a tomato vinaigrette. You can pop in for a muffin and coffee in the morning, or take a break with a chocolate-oatmeal cookie or a raspberry-coconut bar later in the day. There are just a few tables, so expect to wait or take your meal to go. *Average main: C$13* ✉ *762 Broughton St., Downtown* ☎ *250/590–3231* 🌐 *www.devour.ca* ⊗ *Closed Sat.–Sun. No dinner Mon.–Wed.* ✥ *G4.*

$$$$ CANADIAN ★ ✕ **Empress Room.** Candlelight dances beneath a carved mahogany ceiling at the Fairmont Empress Hotel's flagship restaurant, where one of the two gracious rooms has expansive harbor views. The classically influenced Pacific Northwest menu changes seasonally, but might feature

Cafe Brio is one of Victoria's premier dining destinations due to the top-notch regional food, an extensive wine list, and the casual and friendly ambience.

such appetizers as seared local scallops or a confit of venison tart; mains include wild salmon with Dungeness crab, mustard-crusted rack of lamb, or a "farm to fork" vegetarian dish. The service is discreet and attentive, and there are more than 800 labels on the wine list. If the weather is fine, the summer-only Veranda serves lunch, cocktails, and early-evening snacks. *[$] Average main: C$35 ✉ Fairmont Empress, 721 Government St., Downtown ☎ 250/389–2727 🌐 www.fairmont.com/empress/ ⊙ No lunch in the Empress Room ✣ E5.*

$$$ ITALIAN ★ ✕ **Il Terrazzo.** A cute redbrick terrace edged with potted greenery and warmed by fireplaces and overhead heaters makes Il Terrazzo—tucked away off Waddington Alley near Market Square and not visible from the street—the locals' choice for romantic alfresco dining. Starters might include a *fritto misto* of halibut and baby squid, or steamed mussels with sun-dried tomatoes and spicy banana peppers, while mains range from such traditional Northern Italian favorites as breaded scallopini of pork tenderloin to a more local-leaning halibut with blackberries. Thin-crust pizzas come piping hot from the restaurant's open-flame stone oven. *[$] Average main: C$24 ✉ 555 Johnson St., off Waddington Alley, Downtown ☎ 250/361–0028 🌐 www.ilterrazzo.com ⊙ No lunch Sun. No lunch Sat. Oct.–May ✣ E3.*

$$ CHINESE ✕ **J & J Wonton Noodle House.** Lunchtime queues attest to the popularity of the fresh house-made noodles and wontons at this long-standing Chinese spot. The lines move fast, though, thanks to the efficient service. Szechuan and Shanghai specialties, from shrimp noodle soup to beef with hot-chili bean sauce, dominate the long menu, but Singapore-style noodles and Indonesian chow mein appear, too. The diner-style eatery is low on character, but the crowds of locals and an open kitchen keep

things buzzing. Reservations are accepted only for groups of four or more. *Average main: C$14 1012 Fort St., Downtown 250/383–0680 www.jjnoodlehouse.com Closed Sun. and Mon. H4.*

$$$ MODERN CANADIAN **Lure.** Walls of windows embrace Inner Harbour views at the Delta Victoria Ocean Pointe Resort's flagship restaurant. Seafood lovers book window-side tables at sunset to watch the lights come on across the water: the large, comfortable room with upholstered chairs and beige walls doesn't even try to compete with the view. The food puts on a good show, though, whether you go casual with burgers and fried calamari or more upscale with regionally sourced fare like wild salmon with sea asparagus or smoked sablefish from the Queen Charlotte Islands. *Average main: C$23 Delta Victoria Ocean Pointe Resort, 45 Songhees Rd., Vic West 250/360–5873 www.lurevictoria.com D3.*

$$$ FRENCH ★ **Matisse.** The gracious owner greets each guest personally at this tiny gem of a traditional French restaurant where white linens, fresh flowers, and candlelight on the dozen or so tables set the stage for meals of such seasonally changing, well-executed bistro classics as crepes, rack of lamb, or a sauté of lobster, prawns, and scallops. The primarily French wine list has plenty of affordable options, and the bread pudding, crème brûlée, and house-made sorbets are much-loved finales. Piaf *chansons* on the speakers and Matisse originals on the wall add to the pleasing character. *Average main: C$29 512 Yates St., Downtown 250/480–0883 www.restaurantmatisse.com Closed Mon.–Tues. No lunch E3.*

$$ CANADIAN ★ **Mo:Lé.** A good choice for vegans, this brick-lined Chinatown café has plenty of wholesome, organic, local fare for meat eaters, too. At breakfast, large helpings of free-range eggs, locally made sausages, and organic spelt griddle cakes fuel a post-party, pre-yoga crowd. At lunch, locals might pop in for an avocado, seaweed, and sprout sandwich, a yam wrap, or an organic beef burger. The place is tiny, so expect to wait. *Average main: C$13 554 Pandora St., Downtown 250/385–6653 www.molerestaurant.ca Reservations not accepted No dinner F2.*

$ ASIAN **The Noodle Box.** Noodles, whether Indonesian style with peanut sauce, thick Japanese udon in teriyaki, or Thai-style chow mein, are scooped straight from the open kitchen's steaming woks into bowls or cardboard take-out boxes. Malaysian-, Singapore-, and Cambodian-style curries tempt those who like it hot. The brick, rose, and lime walls keep things modern and high energy at the Douglas Street location near the Inner Harbour. The branch at 626 Fisgard Street is a tiny hole-in-the-wall near Chinatown. *Average main: C$12 818 Douglas St., Downtown 250/384–1314 www.thenoodlebox.net Reservations not accepted F4.*

$$$ ITALIAN **Pagliacci's.** Expect long lines at this lively New York–meets-Victoria trattoria where the tables are tightly packed to accommodate the crowds. Opened by Brooklyn's Siegel brothers in 1979, Pagliacci's is all showbiz, from the signed photos of the owners' movie-star friends plastering the walls to the live jazz playing several nights a week. The menu runs from the "Mae West" (veal with artichoke hearts) to the

CLOSE UP

Afternoon Tea in Victoria

Maybe it's the city's British heritage, but afternoon tea—a snack of tea, cakes, and sandwiches taken mid-afternoon, not to be confused with "high tea," a hot meal eaten at dinnertime—lives on in Victoria. The most authentic places are near the Inner Harbour and in the very British Oak Bay district, often described as being "behind the tweed curtain."

Fairmont Empress Hotel. Victoria's most elaborate and most expensive afternoon tea is served, as it has been since 1908, in the ornate lobby of the Fairmont Empress Hotel. The tea is the hotel's own blend, and the cakes, scones, and crustless sandwiches are prepared by some of Victoria's finest pastry chefs. As you face the bill of C$60 per person in high season, remember that tea here is more than a snack; it was, historically, a way to keep civilization alive in this farthest outpost of the empire. Seatings start daily at noon. ■ **TIP→ The price drops to C$48 per person October to April.** ✉ *721 Government St., Downtown* ☎ *250/389–2727* 🌐 *www.fairmont.com/empress.*

Pacific Restaurant. For a Pacific Rim twist on the tea tradition, try this window-lined restaurant in the Hotel Grand Pacific. You can choose from an assortment of Asian-style teas, like the nutty Japanese Hoji-Cha or the delicate Imperial White Mandarin, while you nibble on spot-prawn brochettes, bannock with clotted cream and lemon curd, green tea–cured salmon, and mini chocolate *pots de crème*. Tea is served 2 to 4:30 daily, for C$38 per person. ✉ *Hotel Grand Pacific, 463 Belleville St., Downtown* ☎ *250/380–4458.*

White Heather Tea Room. Everything, including the jam, is homemade for the Scottish-style teas served in the White Heather Tea Room, a lovely place with big windows. Tuesday to Saturday, lunch and afternoon tea are served 11:15 to 5. ✉ *1885 Oak Bay Ave., Oak Bay* ☎ *250/595–8020* 🌐 *www.whiteheather-tearoom.com.*

Several of Victoria's gardens and historic homes make atmospheric settings for tea.

Abkhazi Garden. Although they don't serve a full traditional afternoon tea, the sun-drenched living room of the Abkhazi Garden is lovely for lunch and mid-afternoon pastries. They also serve breakfast on Saturdays and Sundays. ✉ *1964 Fairfield Rd., Fairfield* ☎ *250/598–8096* ⏲ *Mar.–Oct., weekdays 11:30–3:30, weekends 8–11 am and noon–3:30.*

Butchart Gardens. The dining room at the Butchart Gardens serves traditional English afternoon tea daily noon to 3 year-round (except for the first three weeks in November) for $29 per person. ✉ *800 Benvenuto Ave., Brentwood Bay* ☎ *250/652–8222* 🌐 *www.butchartgardens.com.*

Point Ellice House. Wicker armchairs under an awning on the lawn of the Victorian Point Ellice House are a lovely setting for afternoon tea with home-baked goodies. Harbour Ferries from the Inner Harbour deliver you directly to the garden. From early May to early September, tea is served daily 11 to 2:30. The C$25 cost includes admission to the house. ✉ *2616 Pleasant St., Downtown* ☎ *250/380–6506* 🌐 *www.pointellicehouse.ca.*

"Prawns Al Capone" (shell-on butterfly shrimp sauteed in butter and white wine). Pag's is crowded, frenetic, and buckets of fun. *Average main: C$24 1001 Broad St., Downtown 250/386–1662 www.pagliaccis.ca Reservations not accepted F4.*

$ BARBECUE **Pig BBQ Joint.** The food's as no-nonsense as the name at this funky little downtown barbecue corner that dispenses with such niceties as table service and plates. No matter—the overflowing pulled pork, brisket, or smoked chicken sandwiches served on butcher paper are hearty and delicious. Add a side of beans or cole slaw, or for a heart-stopping mashup of Southern 'cue and Canadian homestyle cuisine, there's also pulled pork *poutine*. Beer, iced tea, or bourbon wash it all down. **TIP→ If you're headed to the West Shore, stop at their mobile Pigmobile, located at 1913 Sooke Road, in the Colwood Corners Plaza parking lot.** *Average main: C$10 1325 Blanshard St., Downtown 250/590–5193 Reservations not accepted G3.*

$$ VEGETARIAN **ReBar Modern Food.** Bright and casual, with lime-green walls and a splashy Bollywood poster, this kid-friendly café in Bastion Square is *the* place for vegetarians in Victoria—but don't worry, the almond burgers, decadent baked goodies, and big breakfasts keep omnivores happy, too. Try the yam and pumpkin-seed quesadillas or the vegan Monk's Curry. An extensive selection of teas, fresh juices, and wheat-grass concoctions shares space on the drinks list with espresso, microbrews, and B.C. wines. *Average main: C$14 50 Bastion Sq., Downtown 250/361–9223 www.rebarmodernfood.com No dinner Sun. E3.*

$ SEAFOOD **Red Fish Blue Fish.** If you like your fish both yummy *and* ecologically friendly, look no further than this former shipping container on the pier at the foot of Broughton Street. From the soil-topped roof and biodegradable packaging to the sustainably harvested local seafood, this waterfront take-out shop minimizes its ecological footprint. The chef offers a choice of local wild salmon, tuna, oysters, and scallops from the barbecue. Portuguese buns are baked daily for the seafood sandwiches, fish tacos come in grilled tortilla cones, and even plain old fish-and-chips is taken up a notch with a choice of wild salmon, halibut, or cod in tempura batter with hand-cut fries. Be prepared for queues on sunny days. *Average main: C$12 1006 Wharf St., Downtown 250/298–6877 www.redfish-bluefish.com Reservations not accepted No dinner E4.*

$$ CANADIAN ★ **Spinnakers Gastro Brewpub.** Victoria's longest list of handcrafted beers is just one reason to trek over the Johnson Street Bridge or hop a Harbour Ferry to this Vic West waterfront pub. Canada's oldest licensed brewpub, Spinnakers relies almost exclusively on locally sourced ingredients for its top-notch casual fare. Opt for the pubby adults-only taproom, with its covered waterfront deck, double-sided fireplace, and wood-beamed ceilings, or dine in the all-ages waterfront restaurant. Either way you can enjoy such high-end pub grub as mussels steamed in ale, shiitake mushroom and roasted garlic fettuccine, or fish-and-chips with thick-cut fries. You can also sample the house-made fare in the take-away deli and bakery. *Average main: C$20 308 Catherine St., Vic West 250/386–2739, 877/838–2739 www.spinnakers.com A2.*

$$$ MODERN CANADIAN ✕ **Ulla Restaurant.** Victoria's foodies are buzzing about this Chinatown restaurant that's serving up some of the city's most innovative fare. From the frequently changing, locally sourced menu, you could choose starters like garlic and celery root ravioli in a basil emulsion or the albacore tuna carpaccio, then continue your meal with chicken (a poached breast and crispy leg paired with tortellini and a trio of carrots and peas), short-rib steak (with Swiss-style potatoes, spring onions, and oyster mushrooms), or halibut (with a lemon and black olive dressing). Vegetarians might opt for a plate of kale shoots, fiddlehead ferns, asparagus, and other delectable plant matter. The high arched windows, solid fir tables, and art-filled walls make the room feel both airy and relaxed. *Average main: C$27 ✉ 509 Fisgard St., Downtown ☎ 250/590–8795 🌐 www.ulla.ca ⏲ Closed Sun.–Mon. No lunch ⊕ E2.*

$ CAFÉ ✕ **Willie's Bakery & Café.** Housed in a handsome Victorian building near Market Square, this eatery goes organic, free-range, and local in its omelets, brioches, French toast, and homemade granola breakfasts and its lunches of homemade soups, thick sandwiches, and tasty baked treats. A brick patio with an outdoor fireplace is partially glassed in so you can lunch alfresco even on chilly days. Willie's claims to be the oldest bakery in British Columbia, and bread is still baked in the back room, just as it has been since 1887. *Average main: C$11 ✉ 537 Johnson St., Downtown ☎ 250/381–8414 🌐 www.williesbakery.com Reservations not accepted ⏲ No dinner ⊕ E3.*

$$$ ITALIAN ★ ✕ **Zambri's.** This lively trattoria, in a glam space with floor-to-ceiling windows and eclectic chandeliers, has a setting to match the top-notch Italian food. The kitchen uses local and organic ingredients to turn out contemporary versions of traditional dishes. During the always-busy lunch service, choose from pizzas, pastas, and hot sandwiches, while in the evening you might opt for tagliatelle with duck and olive ragù, grilled tuna with a balsamic vinegar sauce, or crispy pork shoulder served on a bed of greens, potatoes, and grapes. The mostly Italian wine list includes lesser-known labels, with many available by the glass. *Average main: C$22 ✉ 820 Yates St., Downtown ☎ 250/360–1171 🌐 www.zambris.ca ⊕ G3.*

8

OAK BAY AND ROCKLAND

$$$ SEAFOOD ✕ **Marina Restaurant.** This circular room with art-deco rosewood booths and a 180-degree view over the sailboats of Oak Bay Marina has a chef with a flair for seafood. Grills and pastas are on the menu, but it's the daily specials—with such local catches as lingcod, trout, and wild salmon served lightly sauced and teamed with local organic vegetables—where things get interesting. Starters, such as smoked salmon chowder or Salt Spring Island mussels, a lunch menu of salads, burgers, and fish, and an evening-only sushi bar also favor local ingredients. An attached marina-side coffee bar makes a handy stop on a seaside drive or cycle tour. *Average main: C$26 ✉ 1327 Beach Dr., Oak Bay ☎ 250/598–8555 🌐 www.marinarestaurant.com.*

$$$ MODERN CANADIAN ✕ **Paprika Bistro.** Local farmers, fishers, and winemakers provide most of the ingredients at this intimate neighborhood bistro, where the French- and Italian-inspired seasonal menus might include such starters

as Cortes Island mussels and house-made charcuterie, followed by just-caught local fish. Three small rooms with brocade booths and local art on the walls are warm, romantic, and informal. The cozy 80-seat restaurant is a local favorite. *Average main: C$25* ✉ *2524 Estevan Ave., Oak Bay* ☎ *250/592–7424* 🌐 *www.paprika-bistro.com* ⏲ *Closed Sun. No lunch.*

$$ MODERN CANADIAN ✕ **Vis à Vis Wine and Charcuterie Bar.** If you think that Oak Bay is all British tweeds and shepherd's pies, pull up a stool at the long, polished-wood bar in this thoroughly modern storefront bistro. The imaginative small-plates menu emphasizes local ingredients and regional purveyors in dishes like grilled octopus with an herbaceous salsa verde served over squid ink fettucini, seared Qualicum Bay scallops with a salted licorice glaze, or chicken confit tostados. You can also graze on hot smoked trout, pork hock terrine, or other charcuterie made on the premises. Most of the wines on the lengthy list—from B.C. and farther afield—come in one-, five-, or eight-ounce pours, making it easy to pair different wines with the various tapas. You might top off your meal with a milk chocolate and foie gras truffle or the churros with maple-bacon sugar, since what's a thoroughly modern bistro without a pork-infused sweet? *Average main: C$18* ✉ *2232 Oak Bay Ave., Oak Bay* ☎ *250/590–7424* 🌐 *www.visavisoakbay.com.*

SIDNEY AND THE SAANICH PENINSULA

$$$ CANADIAN ✕ **Seagrille Seafood & Sushi.** Local seafood paired with wines from neighboring vineyards shine at this lofty ocean-view restaurant in the Brentwood Bay Resort. Start with a salad of greens and smoked fish, Dungeness crab cakes, or something from the sushi bar, then opt for pistachio-crusted halibut, roasted lingcod, or wild Pacific salmon. Beef, lamb, and poultry dishes appear as well: duck brined in juniper berries, for example, or filet mignon. Wood-burning fireplaces, two-story-high windows, and a wonderful array of Canadian art warm the interior; outside, a heated patio takes in views of Saanich Inlet. A more casual marina-view pub offers burgers, pizzas, and craft beers at lunch and dinner. *Average main: C$27* ✉ *849 Verdier Ave., Brentwood Bay* ☎ *250/544–5100* ⏲ *No lunch.*

THE WEST SHORE AND THE MALAHAT

$$$ CANADIAN ✕ **Malahat Mountain Inn.** This roadhouse near the Malahat Summit, about 30 minutes north of Victoria, doesn't look like much from the highway, but inside, the view over Finlayson Arm and the Gulf Islands is magnificent. The scenery is especially striking from the large outdoor deck, perched 600 feet over Saanich Inlet. The lunch menu lists such casual fare as burgers, flatbread pizzas, and pastas; dinner brings more contemporary meat and seafood dishes. If you can't tear yourself away from the scenery, consider a room at the 10-room inn next door, run by the same folks. *Average main: C$25* ✉ *265 Trans-Canada Hwy., Malahat* ☎ *250/478–1979, 800/913–1944* 🌐 *www.malahatmountaininn.ca* ⏲ *Closed Mon. Oct.–May.*

WHERE TO STAY

Victoria has a vast range of accommodation, with what seems like whole neighborhoods dedicated to hotels. Options range from city resorts and full-service business hotels to midpriced tour-group haunts and family-friendly motels, but the city is especially known for its lavish B&Bs in beautifully restored Victorian and Edwardian mansions. Outlying areas, such as Sooke and Saanich, pride themselves on destination spa resorts and luxurious country inns, though affordable accommodation can be found there, too.

British Columbia law prohibits smoking inside any public building or within 20 feet of an entrance. As a result, all Victoria hotels are completely smoke-free, including on patios and balconies, and in public areas. Only the larger modern hotels have air-conditioning, but it rarely gets hot enough to need it. Advance reservations are always a good idea, especially in July and August. Watch for discounts of up to 50% in the off-season (roughly November to February); though even then you'll need to book, as many rooms fill with retirees escaping prairie winters. Most downtown hotels also charge at least C$15 per day for parking. Ask about phone and Internet charges (these can range from free to excessive) and have a look at the hotel breakfast menu; nearby cafés are almost always cheaper.

Downtown hotels are clustered in three main areas. James Bay, on the south side of the Inner Harbour near the Parliament Buildings, is basically a residential and hotel neighborhood. Bordered by the waterfront and Beacon Hill Park, the area is quiet at night and handy for sightseeing by day. It is, however, thin on restaurants and a bit of a hike to the main shopping areas. Hotels in the downtown core, particularly along Government and Douglas streets, are right in the thick of shopping, dining, and nightlife, but get more traffic noise. If you're willing to walk a few blocks east of the harbor, several quieter hotels and small inns are clustered amid the condominium towers. Vic West, across the Johnson Street Bridge on the harbor's north shore, is another quiet option, but it's a 15-minute walk or ferry ride to the bulk of shopping, dining, and sightseeing. Even so, you won't need a car to stay in any of these areas, and, given parking charges, you may be better off without one.

Outside of downtown, Rockland and Oak Bay are lush, peaceful, tree-lined residential districts; the mile or so walk into town is pleasant, but you won't want to do it every day. The resorts and inns that we've listed farther afield, in Saanich, the West Shore, and Sooke are, for the most part, self-contained resorts with restaurants and spas. Each is about 30 minutes from downtown Victoria, and you'll need a car if you want to make day trips into town.

Prices in the reviews are the lowest cost of a standard double room in high season. For expanded hotel reviews, visit Fodors.com.

Use the coordinate (⊕ B2) at the end of each listing to locate a site on the corresponding map.

8

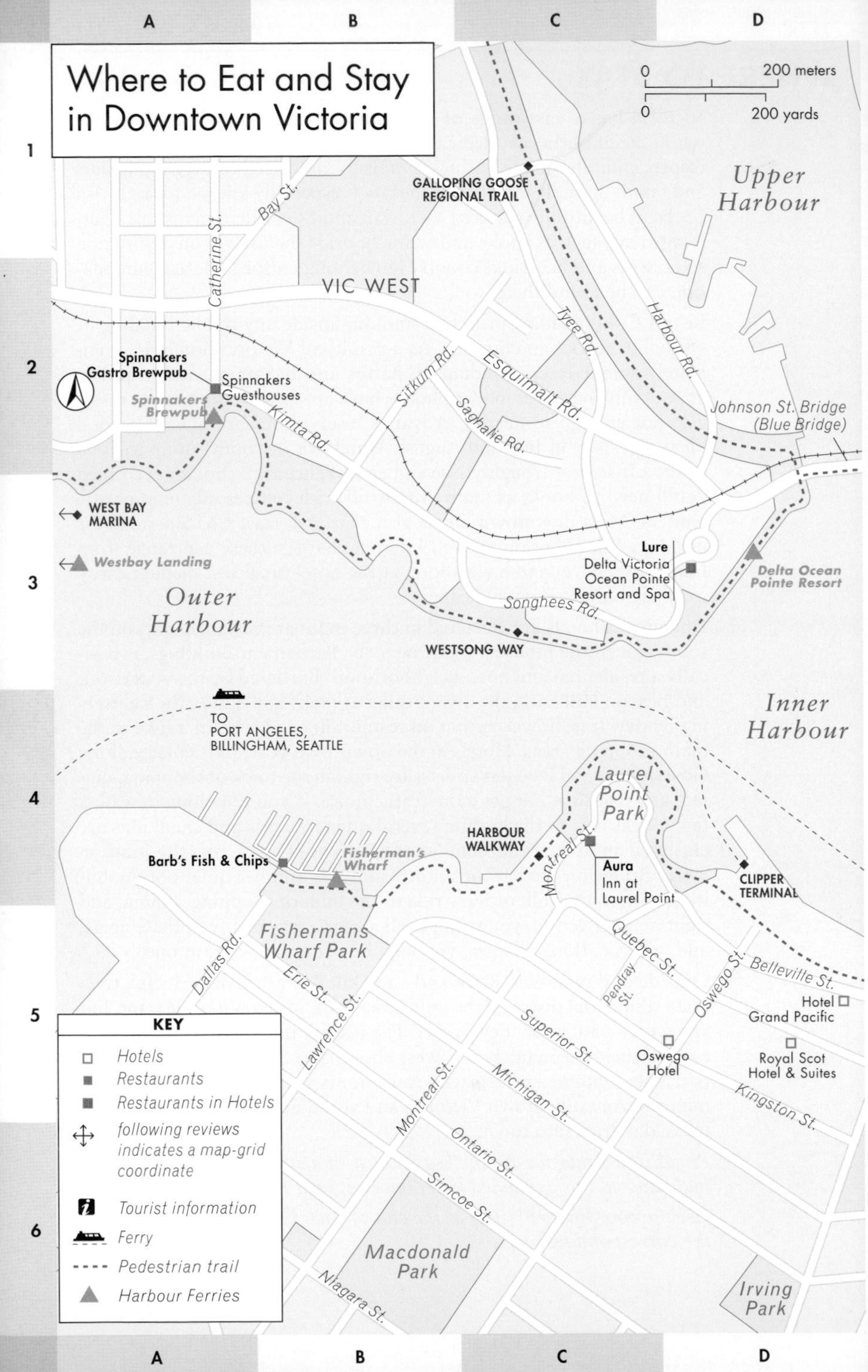
Where to Eat and Stay in Downtown Victoria
A
B
C
D
1
2
3
4
5
6
0
200 meters
0
200 yards
Upper Harbour
GALLOPING GOOSE REGIONAL TRAIL
Bay St.
Catherine St.
VIC WEST
Tyee Rd.
Harbour Rd.
Spinnakers Gastro Brewpub
Spinnakers Guesthouses
Spinnakers Brewpub
Kimta Rd.
Sitkum Rd.
Esquimalt Rd.
Saghalie Rd.
Johnson St. Bridge (Blue Bridge)
WEST BAY MARINA
Westbay Landing
Lure
Delta Victoria Ocean Pointe Resort and Spa
Delta Ocean Pointe Resort
Outer Harbour
Songhees Rd.
WESTSONG WAY
Inner Harbour
TO PORT ANGELES, BILLINGHAM, SEATTLE
Laurel Point Park
HARBOUR WALKWAY
Montreal St.
Aura
Inn at Laurel Point
CLIPPER TERMINAL
Barb's Fish & Chips
Fisherman's Wharf
Fishermans Wharf Park
Dallas Rd.
Erie St.
Lawrence St.
Quebec St.
Pendray St.
Oswego St.
Belleville St.
Hotel Grand Pacific
Superior St.
Oswego Hotel
Royal Scot Hotel & Suites
Michigan St.
Kingston St.
Montreal St.
Ontario St.
Simcoe St.
Macdonald Park
Niagara St.
Irving Park
KEY
Hotels
Restaurants
Restaurants in Hotels
following reviews indicates a map-grid coordinate
Tourist information
Ferry
Pedestrian trail
Harbour Ferries

E
F
G
H
1
2
3
4
5
6
Central Park
Pembroke St.
Discovery St.
Store St.
Chatham St.
Caledonia Ave.
Green St.
Herald St.
North St.
Park St.
Swift St.
Brasserie L'ecole
Ulla Restaurant
Canoe Brewpub
CENTENNIAL SQUARE
Fisgard St.
Balmoral St.
Mo:Lé
Swans Suite Hotel
Pandora Ave.
Cormorant St.
CITY HALL
Mason St.
Johnson St.
Market Sq.
Willie's Bakery & Café
Waddington Alley
Wharf St.
HARBOUR WALKWAY
Il Terrazzo
Matisse
Rudlin St.
Broad St.
Pig BBQ Joint
Re-Bar Modern Food
BASTION SQUARE
Camille's
Government St.
Douglas St.
Zambri's
Yates St.
View St.
BAY CENTRE
Blanshard St.
Quadra St.
Bin 4 Burger Lounge
FLOATPLANE DOCKS
Fort St.
Paglicacci's
Broughton St.
Café Brio
Red Fish Blue Fish
Gordon St.
Devour
J&J Won Ton Noodle House
Courtney St.
Bon Rouge
Magnolia Hotel & Spa
Pioneer Square
Humboldt St.
The Noodle Box
Rockland Ave.
Chateau Victoria Hotel & Suites
Burdett Ave.
Empress Room
The Fairmont Empress
BLACK BALL FERRIES
The Victoria Marriott Inner Harbor
Fairfield Rd.
Vancouver St.
McClure St.
Belleville St.
Parkside Victoria Resort & Spa
Abigail's Hotel
ROYAL B.C. MUSEUM
Richardson St.
Collinson
PARLIAMENT BUILDINGS
Elliot St.
Academy St.
Southgate St.
Beaconsfield Inn
Michigan St.
Pakington St.
TO ROSS BAY AND STRAIT OF JUAN DE FUCA

DOWNTOWN

$$$$ B&B/INN **Abigail's Hotel.** A Tudor-style inn built in 1930, Abigail's is four blocks from the Inner Harbour. **Pros:** luxurious feel; atmospheric. **Cons:** no pool or gym. *Rooms from: C$250 ✉ 906 McClure St., Downtown ☎ 250/388–5363, 800/561–6565 🌐 www.abigailshotel.com 23 rooms 🍽 Breakfast ✥ H5.*

$$$ B&B/INN ★ **Beaconsfield Inn.** This 1905 building four blocks from the Inner Harbour is one of Victoria's most faithfully restored, antique-filled mansions. **Pros:** luxurious; opportunities to mingle over breakfast or sherry. **Cons:** romantic ambience is not suited for kids; several blocks from shopping and dining. *Rooms from: C$199 ✉ 998 Humboldt St., Downtown ☎ 250/384–4044, 888/884–4044 🌐 www.beaconsfieldinn.com 5 rooms, 4 suites 🍽 Breakfast ✥ H6.*

$$ HOTEL **Chateau Victoria Hotel & Suites.** Far-reaching views from the upper-floor suites are a plus at this good-value, centrally located, independent hotel. **Pros:** free parking; free Internet; free local calls; great rates and location. **Cons:** standard rooms lack views. *Rooms from: C$159 ✉ 740 Burdett Ave., Downtown ☎ 250/382–4221, 800/663–5891 🌐 www.chateauvictoria.com 59 rooms, 118 suites 🍽 No meals ✥ F5.*

$$$ HOTEL **Delta Victoria Ocean Pointe Resort and Spa.** Across the Johnson Street Bridge from downtown Victoria, this waterfront resort has all sorts of amenities, from tennis and squash courts to a popular spa, an around-the-clock gym, and a waterfront walking path. **Pros:** water views; free Internet; downtown shuttle and harbor ferry service. **Cons:** not right downtown; gets busy with conferences. *Rooms from: C$229 ✉ 45 Songhees Rd., Vic West ☎ 250/360–2999, 800/667–4677 🌐 www.deltavictoria.com 233 rooms, 6 suites ✥ D3.*

$$$$ HOTEL **Fairmont Empress.** Opened in 1908, this ivy-draped harborside château and city landmark has aged gracefully, with top-notch service and sympathetically restored Edwardian furnishings. **Pros:** central location; professional service; great spa and restaurant. **Cons:** small to average-size rooms and bathrooms; tourists in the public areas; pricey. *Rooms from: C$349 ✉ 721 Government St., Downtown ☎ 250/384–8111, 866/540–4429 🌐 www.fairmont.com/empress 436 rooms, 41 suites ✥ E5.*

$$$ HOTEL ★ **Hotel Grand Pacific.** The city's best health club (with yoga classes, squash courts, and state-of-the-art equipment) and a prime Inner Harbour location appeal to savvy regulars, including Seattleites stepping off the ferry across the street. **Pros:** great health club; staffed business center; complimentary Wi-Fi. **Cons:** standard hotel decor. *Rooms from: C$199 ✉ 463 Belleville St., Downtown ☎ 250/386–0450, 800/663–7550 🌐 www.hotelgrandpacific.com 258 rooms, 46 suites 🍽 No meals ✥ D5.*

$$$$ HOTEL Fodor's Choice ★ **Inn at Laurel Point.** A seaside Japanese garden, a museum-quality art collection, and harbor views from every room make this Asian-inspired independent hotel on the Inner Harbour's quiet south shore a favorite among Victoria regulars. **Pros:** views; quiet, parklike setting. **Cons:** 10-minute walk from downtown. *Rooms from: C$254 ✉ 680 Montreal St., Downtown ☎ 250/386–8721, 800/663–7667 🌐 www.laurelpoint.com 135 rooms, 65 suites 🍽 No meals ✥ C4.*

Fodor's Choice ★

Inn at Laurel Point

Brentwood Bay Resort & Spa

$$$ HOTEL **Magnolia Hotel & Spa.** From the on-site spa to the soaker tubs, sauna, and herb tea, the Magnolia, without actually saying so, caters beautifully to the female traveler—though the attention to detail, hop-to-it staff, and central location won't be lost on men either. **Pros:** great location; friendly and helpful service; welcoming lobby with fireplace, tea, and coffee. **Cons:** no room service at breakfast; small fitness room; no on-site pool or hot tub. *Rooms from: C$219 ✉ 623 Courtney St., Downtown ☎ 250/381–0999, 877/624–6654 ⊕ www.magnoliahotel.com ⇨ 64 rooms ‖ Breakfast ✣ F4.*

$$$ HOTEL ★ **Oswego Hotel.** In quiet-but-handy James Bay, this chic all-suites boutique property has 80 sleek studio, one-, and two-bedroom units. **Pros:** stylish design; friendly staff; free local calls and Internet. **Cons:** Murphy beds in the studios; 10-minute walk to town center; no pool. *Rooms from: C$199 ✉ 500 Oswego St., Downtown ☎ 250/294–7500, 877/767–9346 ⊕ www.oswegovictoria.com ⇨ 21 studios, 44 one-bedroom suites, 15 two-bedroom suites ‖ No meals ✣ C5.*

$$$$ HOTEL **Parkside Victoria Resort and Spa.** From the three-story glass atrium with babbling fountains to the rooftop terrace with summer yoga classes, this downtown condo-hotel feels like an escape from the city. **Pros:** spacious accommodations; family-friendly vibe; close to downtown attractions. **Cons:** modern but not luxurious; no doors on en-suite bathrooms. *Rooms from: C$249 ✉ 810 Humboldt St., Downtown ☎ 250/940–1200, 866/941–4175 ⊕ www.parksidevictoria.com ⇨ 126 suites ✣ G5.*

$$ HOTEL **Royal Scot Hotel & Suites.** Large suites, great rates, a handy location, and a friendly staff keep couples, families, and bus tours coming back to this well-run James Bay hotel—the games room, pool table, indoor pool, hot tub, laundry room, and small grocery store make this an especially good choice. **Pros:** great for kids; quiet neighborhood; free Internet and local calls. **Cons:** kids and tour groups. *Rooms from: C$165 ✉ 425 Quebec St., Downtown ☎ 250/388–5463, 800/663–7515 ⊕ www.royalscot.com ⇨ 30 rooms, 146 suites ‖ No meals ✣ D5.*

$$$ B&B/INN **Spinnakers Guesthouses.** Three houses make up the accommodations at this B&B, run by the owner of the popular Spinnakers Gastro Brewpub. **Pros:** suites are beautiful; breakfast is delivered; free parking. **Cons:** 15-minute walk to downtown; little else in the neighborhood. *Rooms from: C$179 ✉ 308 Catherine St., Vic West ☎ 250/386–2739, 877/838–2739 ⊕ www.spinnakers.com ⇨ 5 rooms, 4 suites, 1 cottage ‖ Breakfast ✣ A2.*

$$$ B&B/INN **Swans Suite Hotel.** This 1913 former warehouse in Victoria's old town is one of the city's most enticing small inns. **Pros:** handsome suites with kitchens; great for families; handy to shopping and restaurants. **Cons:** tiny lobby; pub noise on the lower floors; parking is off-site. *Rooms from: C$185 ✉ 506 Pandora Ave., Downtown ☎ 250/361–3310, 800/668–7926 ⊕ www.swanshotel.com ⇨ 30 suites ‖ No meals ✣ E2.*

$$$ HOTEL **Victoria Marriott Inner Harbour.** Film people, business travelers, and tourists like this full-service hotel located two blocks east of the Inner Harbour. **Pros:** great service; work-friendly rooms; indoor pool. **Cons:** local calls cost C$1 each. *Rooms from: C$199 ✉ 728 Humboldt St., Downtown ☎ 250/480–3800, 877/333–8338 ⊕ www.marriottvictoria.com ⇨ 228 rooms, 8 suites ‖ No meals ✣ G5.*

OAK BAY AND ROCKLAND

$$$ B&B/INN ★ **Abbeymoore Manor.** This 1912 mansion has the wide verandas, dark wainscoting, and high ceilings of its era, but the attitude is informal and welcoming, from the super-helpful hosts to the free snacks to the coffee on tap all day. **Pros:** good value; friendly hosts; excellent service. **Cons:** a mile from the Inner Harbour; often booked in advance. *Rooms from: C$199 ✉ 1470 Rockland Ave., Rockland ☎ 250/370–1470, 888/801–1811 www.abbeymoore.com 5 rooms, 2 suites Breakfast.*

$ B&B/INN **Craigmyle Bed & Breakfast.** Affordable and historic, this four-story manor near Craigdarroch Castle has been a guesthouse since 1913. **Pros:** affordable; atmospheric; family- and single-friendly rooms. **Cons:** a bit removed from downtown; no elevator; street parking only. *Rooms from: C$100 ✉ 1037 Craigdarroch Rd., Rockland ☎ 250/595–5411, 888/595–5411 www.bandbvictoria.com 16 rooms, 1 suite Breakfast.*

$$ B&B/INN ★ **Fairholme Manor.** Original art, Viennese antiques, and dramatic furnishings shine in this lavish, 1885 Italianate mansion. **Pros:** peaceful setting; stunning decor; welcoming hostess. **Cons:** a mile from downtown; no elevator. *Rooms from: C$155 ✉ 638 Rockland Pl., off Rockland Ave., Rockland ☎ 250/598–3240, 877/511–3322 www.fairholmemanor.com 1 room, 5 suites Breakfast.*

$$$ B&B/INN ★ **Villa Marco Polo Inn.** A classical European garden with a stone terrace, reflecting pool, and fountains are all part of the Tuscan-hideaway feel at this 1923 Italian Renaissance–style manor. **Pros:** lots of comfy common areas; gracious hosts; full concierge services. **Cons:** a mile from downtown; no elevator. *Rooms from: C$215 ✉ 1524 Shasta Place, Rockland ☎ 250/370–1524, 877/601–1524 www.villamarcopolo.com 4 rooms Breakfast.*

8

SIDNEY AND THE SAANICH PENINSULA

$$$$ RESORT Fodor's Choice ★ **Brentwood Bay Resort & Spa.** Every room has a private ocean-view patio or balcony at this adult-oriented boutique resort in a tiny seaside village. **Pros:** magnificent setting; great food; free Wi-Fi. **Cons:** pricey rates; 30-minute drive from downtown. *Rooms from: C$369 ✉ 849 Verdier Ave., Brentwood Bay ☎ 250/544–2079, 888/544–2079 www.brentwoodbayresort.com 30 rooms, 3 suites No meals.*

$$$ HOTEL ★ **Sidney Pier Hotel & Spa.** Stylish and ecologically friendly, this glass-and-stone boutique hotel on the parklike waterfront has helped introduce Sidney to more travelers. **Pros:** lovely views; eco-friendly vibe; close to ferries and airport. **Cons:** 30 minutes from downtown; no pool. *Rooms from: C$179 ✉ 9805 Seaport Pl., Sidney ☎ 250/655–9445, 866/659–9445 www.sidneypier.com 46 rooms, 9 suites No meals.*

THE WEST SHORE AND THE MALAHAT

$$$ RESORT **Westin Bear Mountain Golf Resort & Spa.** Two Nicklaus Design golf courses are the draw at this resort community about 30 minutes northwest of the city center. **Pros:** challenging golf; great spa and health club; children's programs in summer. **Cons:** a car is essential. *Rooms*

from: C$199 ✉ *1999 Country Club Way, West Shore* ☎ *250/391–7160, 888/533–2327* 🌐 *www.bearmountain.ca* *78 rooms, 78 suites* 🍴 *No meals.*

NIGHTLIFE AND THE ARTS

Monday Magazine. For entertainment listings, pick up a free copy of this artsy magazine every Thursday. You can also check out listings online. 🌐 *www.mondaymag.com.*

Victoria Visitor Information Centre. Tourism Victoria also has event listings, and you can buy tickets for many events at the Victoria Visitor Information Centre. ✉ *812 Wharf St.* ☎ *250/953–2033, 800/663–3883* 🌐 *www.tourismvictoria.com.*

NIGHTLIFE

Victoria's nightlife is low-key and casual, with many wonderful pubs, but a limited choice of nightclubs. Pubs offer a casual vibe for lunch, dinner, or an afternoon pint, often with a view and an excellent selection of beer. The pubs listed here all serve food and many brew their own beer. Patrons must be 19 or older to enter a bar or pub in British Columbia, but many pubs have a separate restaurant section open to all ages. The city is enjoying a resurgence of cocktail culture, with several of Victoria's trendier restaurants doubling as lounges, offering cocktails and small plates well into the night. Dance clubs attract a young crowd and most close by 2 am. A dress code (no jeans or sneakers) may be enforced, but otherwise, attire is casual. Smoking is not allowed in Victoria's pubs, bars, and nightclubs—this applies both indoors and on the patio.

BARS AND LOUNGES

Bengal Lounge. Deep leather sofas and a tiger skin help to re-create the days of the British Raj at this iconic lounge in the Fairmont Empress Hotel. Martinis and a curry buffet are the draws through the week. On Friday and Saturday nights a jazz combo takes the stage. ✉ *Fairmont Empress Hotel, 721 Government St., Downtown* ☎ *250/384–8111* 🌐 *www.fairmont.com/empress.*

Clive's Classic Lounge. Leading Victoria's cocktail renaissance, the bartenders at this classic lounge in the Chateau Victoria Hotel make their own syrups and bitters and use fresh juices in their traditional and contemporary drinks. ✉ *Chateau Victoria Hotel, 740 Burdett Ave., Downtown* ☎ *250/361–5684* 🌐 *www.clivesclassiclounge.com.*

The Superior. Live acoustic blues and jazz and a small-plates menu of local organic fare attract a hip grown-up crowd to this café and nightspot near Fisherman's Wharf. ✉ *106 Superior St., James Bay* ☎ *250/380–9515* 🌐 *www.thesuperior.ca.*

Vista 18. You can take in lofty views of the city at this lounge on the 18th floor of the Chateau Victoria Hotel. There's live music Thursday, Friday, and Saturday night. ✉ *Chateau Victoria Hotel, 740 Burdett Ave., Downtown* ☎ *250/382–9258* 🌐 *www.vista18.com.*

DANCE CLUBS

Club 9ONE9. This nightclub often hosts live bands, guest DJs, and other special events. Also in the building are a restaurant, a pub, and several bars, including a sports bar and a hillbilly-theme bar—not to mention beach volleyball played on the roof in summer. ✉ *Strathcona Hotel, 919 Douglas St., Downtown* ☎ *250/383–7137* 🌐 *www.strathconahotel.com.*

Hermann's Jazz Club. Dinner, dancing, and live jazz are on the menu at this venerable downtown restaurant and jazz club. ✉ *753 View St., Downtown* ☎ *250/388–9166* 🌐 *www.hermannsjazz.com.*

Lucky Bar. DJs, live bands, and a friendly crowd of locals make the most of Lucky's great sound system and dance floor. ✉ *517 Yates St., Downtown* ☎ *250/382–5825* 🌐 *www.luckybar.ca.*

Paparazzi. Victoria's longest-running gay club draws a mixed crowd with fun drag, karaoke, and club nights. ✉ *642 Johnson St., Downtown* ☎ *250/388–0505* 🌐 *www.paparazzinightclub.com.*

PUBS

The Bard and Banker Pub. This sumptuously decorated British pub, which occupies a historic bank building on Victoria's main shopping street, has live music several nights a week. ✉ *1022 Government St., Downtown* ☎ *250/953–9993* 🌐 *www.bardandbanker.com.*

Canoe Brewpub. One of Victoria's biggest and best pub patios overlooks the Gorge, the waterway just north of the Inner Harbour. The interior of the former power station has been stylishly redone with high ceilings, exposed bricks, and wood beams. There's a wide range of in-house brews, top-notch bar snacks, and an all-ages restaurant. ✉ *450 Swift St., Downtown* ☎ *250/361–1940* 🌐 *www.canoebrewpub.com.*

Irish Times Pub. Stout on tap, live Celtic music nightly, and a menu of traditional and modern pub fare draw tourists and locals to this former bank building on Victoria's main shopping strip. ✉ *1200 Government St., Downtown* ☎ *250/383–7775* 🌐 *www.irishtimespub.ca.*

Spinnakers Gastro Brewpub. You can hop on an Inner Harbour Ferry to this local favorite on the Inner Harbour's north shore. Canada's first modern-day brewpub, it also has the city's longest menu of traditionally made in-house brews. A covered waterfront deck, a double-sided fireplace, excellent pub grub, and an all-ages in-house restaurant make this a popular hangout. ✉ *308 Catherine St., Vic West* ☎ *250/386–2739* 🌐 *www.spinnakers.com.*

Swans Brewpub. A stunning array of First Nations masks and other artworks hangs from the open rafters in this popular downtown brewpub, where jazz, blues, and swing bands play nightly. ✉ *506 Pandora Ave., Downtown* ☎ *250/361–3310* 🌐 *www.swanshotel.com.*

THE ARTS

MUSIC

Summer in the Square. Free jazz, classical, and folk concerts; cultural events; and more run all summer at Centennial Square, next to City Hall. Events start daily at noon. ✉ *Centennial Square, Pandora Ave. and Douglas St.* ☎ *250/361–0388* 🌐 *www.victoria.ca.*

Victoria Jazz Society. Watch for music events hosted by this group, which also organizes the annual JazzFest International in late June. ☎ *250/388–4423* 🌐 *www.jazzvictoria.ca.*

Victoria Symphony. With everything from solo performances to chamber music concerts to full-scale orchestral works, the Victoria Symphony has something for everyone. Watch for Symphony Splash on the first Sunday in August, when the orchestra plays a free concert from a barge in the Inner Harbour. ☎ *250/385–6515* 🌐 *www.victoriasymphony.ca.*

THEATER

Belfry Theatre. Housed in a former church, the Belfry Theatre has a resident company that specializes in contemporary Canadian dramas. ✉ *1291 Gladstone Ave., Fernwood* ☎ *250/385–6815* 🌐 *www.belfry.bc.ca.*

Phoenix Theatre. University of Victoria theater students stage productions at this on-campus venue. ✉ *University of Victoria, 3800 Finnerty Rd.* ☎ *250/721–8000* 🌐 *www.phoenixtheatres.ca.*

Theatre Inconnu. Victoria's oldest alternative theater company, housed in a venue across the street from the Belfry Theatre, Theatre Inconnu offers a range of performances at affordable ticket prices. ✉ *1923 Fernwood Rd., Fernwood* ☎ *250/360–0234* 🌐 *www.theatreinconnu.com.*

Theatre SKAM. This alternative troupe stages summer shows at such offbeat venues as the Galloping Goose Bike Path (the audience pedals from one performance to the next) and the back of a pickup truck in city parks. ☎ *250/386–7526* 🌐 *www.skam.ca.*

Victoria Fringe Festival. Each August and September, a vast menu of original and intriguing performances takes place at several venues around town. It's part of a circuit of fringe-theater events attracting performers—and fans—from around the world. ☎ *250/383–2663* 🌐 *www.victoriafringe.com.*

Victoria Theatre Guild. One of Canada's oldest community theater groups, the Victoria Theatre Guild stages works by internationally known playwrights at the Langham Court Theatre from September through June. ✉ *Langham Court Theatre, 805 Langham Ct., Rockland* ☎ *250/384–2142* 🌐 *www.langhamtheatre.ca.*

SPORTS AND THE OUTDOORS

BEACHES

Cadboro-Gyro Park. A sandy beach backed by a grassy park with a play area draws families to this sheltered bay, accessible via the Scenic Marine Drive. ✉ *Cadboro Bay Rd., Saanich* ☎ *250/475–1775.*

Cordova Bay. A long stretch of sand is the draw at this beach, north of Mount Douglas Park. ✉ *Cordova Bay Rd., Saanich.*

Willows Beach. Close to downtown, this sandy family beach has a tea-room and a grassy, shaded play area. ✉ *Esplanade, at Dalhousie St., Oak Bay.*

Witty's Lagoon Regional Park. About 30 minutes west of downtown Victoria, this park has a sandy beach, forest trails, marshlands, and a large lagoon—and it's home to 160 species of birds. There's also a nature house that presents interpretive programs. ✉ *4115 Metchosin Rd., West Shore* ☎ *250/478–3344* 🌐 *www.crd.bc.ca/parks/wittys.*

BIKING

Victoria is a bike-friendly town with more bicycle commuters than any other city in Canada. Bike racks on city buses, bike lanes on downtown streets, and tolerant drivers all help, as do the city's three long-distance cycling routes, which mix car-free paths and low-traffic scenic routes.

BC Ferries will transport bikes for a nominal fee (just C$2 from Vancouver). You can also rent bikes, bike trailers, and tandem bikes at several Victoria outlets for a few hours, a day, or a week. Helmets are required by law and are supplied with bike rentals.

BIKE ROUTES

Cowichan Valley Trail. This 29-mile path, part of the Trans-Canada trail, runs from Shawnigan Lake to Cowichan Lake in the Cowichan Valley. A rails-to-trails conversion, the route crosses eight historic bridges, including the 614-foot-long Kinsol Trestle, which is reportedly the highest of its kind in Canada. 🌐 *www.cvrd.bc.ca.*

★ **Galloping Goose Regional Trail.** Following an old rail bed, this 33-mile route officially starts at the Johnson Street Bridge in Victoria. The multi-use trail runs across old rail trestles and through forests west to the town of Sooke, finishing at the abandoned gold-mining town of Leechtown. Just north of downtown it links with the Lochside Regional Trail to Sidney, creating a nearly continuous 62-mile car-free route. ☎ *250/478–3344* 🌐 *www.crd.bc.ca/parks.*

Lochside Regional Trail. This fairly level, mostly car-free route follows an old rail bed for 18 miles past farmland, wineries, and beaches from the ferry terminals at Swartz Bay and Sidney to downtown Victoria. It joins the Seaside Touring Route at Cordova Bay and meets the Galloping Goose Trail just north of downtown Victoria. ☎ *250/478–3344* 🌐 *www.crd.bc.ca/parks.*

8

CLOSE UP

Victoria: Whale-watching

The thrill of seeing whales in the wild is, for many, one of the most enduring memories of a trip to Victoria. In summer (roughly April to October), about 85 orca, or killer whales (they're actually large dolphins, but that makes them no less exciting to see), reside in the Strait of Georgia between Vancouver and Victoria. They live in pods, and because their movements are fairly predictable, chances are high that you will see a pod on any given trip. Some operators claim sighting rates of 90 percent; others offer guaranteed sightings, meaning that you can repeat the tour free of charge until you spot a whale.

It's not unheard of to see whales from a BC Ferry en route to Victoria—but the ferries don't alter their routes to take advantage of whale-watching, so your best bet is to take a dedicated tour. A number of companies leave from Victoria's Inner Harbour, a few are based in Richmond (near Vancouver), and others leave from Sidney and Sooke, outside of Victoria.

Not all tours are alike, and the kind of boat you choose determines the kind of experience you're likely to have—though most companies have naturalists on board as guides, as well as hydrophones that, if you get close enough, allow you to listen to the whales singing and vocalizing.

Motor launches, which carry from 30 to more than 80 passengers, are comfortable, with washrooms, protection from the elements, and even snack-and-drink concessions. Seasickness isn't usually a problem in the sheltered waters near Victoria, but if you're not a good sailor, it's wise to wear a seasickness band or take antinausea medication. Ginger candy often works, too.

Zodiacs are open inflatable boats that carry about 12 passengers. They are smaller and more agile than cruisers and offer both an exciting ride bouncing over the waves and an eye-level view of the whales. Passengers are supplied with warm, waterproof survival suits. Zodiac tours are not recommended for people with back or neck problems, pregnant women, or small children.

Note that the kind of boat you choose does not affect how close you can get to the whales. For the safety of whales and humans, government and industry regulations require boats to stay at least 100 meters (328 feet) from the pods, though closer encounters are possible if whales approach a boat when its engine is off.

And, although the focus is on whales, you also have a good chance of spotting marine birds, Dall's porpoises, dolphins, seals, sea lions, and minke, gray, and humpback whales as well as other marine life. And, naturally, there's the scenery of forested islands and distant mountains.

There are dozens of whale-watching operators in the area. We've listed some of the more established: **Great Pacific Adventures.** This company offers year-round tours with both Zodiacs and covered vessels. Boats are equipped with hydrophones and all guides are marine biologists. In summer a three-hour tour starts at C$99. ✉ *1000 Wharf St.* ☎ *250/386–2277, 877/733–6722* 🌐 *www.greatpacificadventures.com.*

Ocean Explorations. With qualified naturalists as guides, Ocean Explorations conducts three-hour whale-watching trips in summer and two-hour marine tours in winter—all on hydrophone-equipped Zodiacs. Summer trips start at C$99. ✉ *602 Broughton St.* ☎ *250/383–6722, 888/442–6722* 🌐 *www.oceanexplorations.com.*

Prince of Whales. Victoria's biggest whale-watching company offers three-hour tours from Victoria staffed by naturalists. Rates for open-air Zodiacs start at C$100. Another option, and one worth planning a trip around, is an *Ocean Magic* cruise that combines four hours of whale-watching with a visit to Butchart Gardens. Staffed with naturalists, the 74-passenger cruiser leaves downtown Vancouver daily at 9 am between June and early September, arriving in Victoria's Inner Harbour in time for lunch; it heads back to Vancouver at 5:30. Fares for this day long excursion are C$275. ☎ *888/383–4884* 🌐 *www.princeofwhales.com.*

Springtide Whale Tours & Charters. Using marine biologists as guides, this company runs tours on Zodiacs and on 61-foot motor yachts. Summer tours are three hours long, and the boats are equipped with hydrophones. Rates are C$99. ✉ *1119 Wharf St.* ☎ *250/384–4444, 800/470–3474* 🌐 *www.springtidecharters.com.*

Vancouver Island has two other whale-watching hot spots. Johnstone Strait, off Telegraph Cove on the island's northeast coast, has one of the world's largest populations of orca in summer and is an important center for whale research. Tofino and Ucluelet, on the island's west coast, draw whale-watchers every March and April when an estimated 20,000 Pacific gray whales cruise by on their annual migration.

Rotary Route. For an ambitious tour of southern Vancouver Island's back roads and bike trails, follow this 68-mile signed route from Swartz Bay up to Nanaimo. 🌐 *www.rotaryroute.org.*

Seaside Touring Route. Starting at the corner of Government and Belleville streets on the Inner Harbour, this 18-mile route, marked with bright yellow signs, leads past Fisherman's Wharf and along the Dallas Road waterfront to Beacon Hill Park. It then follows the seashore to Cordova Bay, where it connects with Victoria's other two long-distance routes: the Lochside and Galloping Goose regional trails.

The Gulf Islands are also popular with cyclists. The scenery is wonderful, but the steep narrow roads and lack of dedicated bike paths can be frustrating.

BIKE RENTALS AND TOURS

Cycle BC Rentals. This centrally located shop rents bikes for adults and children, as well as bike trailers, motorcycles, and scooters. ✉ *685 Humboldt St., Downtown* ☎ *250/380–2453* 🌐 *www.cyclebc.ca.*

CycleTreks. Besides renting bikes, this company runs bike tours of Victoria, the Gulf Islands, and various parts of Vancouver Island, as well as a vineyard tour of the Cowichan Valley. The staff can give you a ride to the start of Galloping Goose Trail or to Butchart Gardens so that you can pedal back. ✉ *1000 Wharf St., Downtown* ☎ *250/386–2277, 877/733–6722* 🌐 *www.cycletreks.com.*

GOLF

You can golf year-round in Victoria and southern Vancouver Island, and you almost have to just to try all the courses. Victoria alone has several public golf courses, ranging from rolling sea-view fairways to challenging mountaintop sites. Southern Vancouver Island is home to the Vancouver Island Golf Trail, where you'll find 10 championship courses.

Arbutus Ridge Golf Club. Mountain and ocean views from the course and the clubhouse are the draws at this challenging par-71 course, 40 minutes north of Victoria in the Cowichan Valley. ✉ *3515 Telegraph Rd., Cobble Hill* ☎ *250/743–5000* 🌐 *www.arbutusridgegolf.com* 🏌 *18 holes. 6,193 yds. Par 71. Greesn Fee: C$54/C$59.*

★ **Bear Mountain Golf & Country Club.** Built near the top of a 1,100-foot mountain about 20 minutes north of Victoria, this is widely regarded as the island's most exciting course. Designed by Jack Nicklaus and his son Steve, the Mountain Course has an extra 19th hole built on a cliff ledge with striking views across the city. A second Nicklaus-designed layout, called the Valley Course, is at a slightly lower elevation. ✉ *1999 Country Club Way, off Millstream Rd. and Bear Mountain Pkwy., West Shore* ☎ *250/744–2327, 888/533–2327* 🌐 *www.bearmountain.ca* 🏌 *Mountain Course: 18 holes. 7,212 yds. Par 72. Greens Fee: C$129. Valley Course: 18 holes. 7,000 yds. Par 71. Greens Fee: C$129.*

Golf Vancouver Island. This organization has details about the island's courses. ✉ *675 Jones Terrace* ☎ *888/465–3239* 🌐 *www.golfvancouverisland.ca.*

Olympic View Golf Club. The distant peaks of the Olympic Mountains are the backdrop to this bucolic par-72 course, home to two waterfalls and 12 lakes. The first B.C. course played by Tiger Woods, it's about 30 minutes' drive west of downtown Victoria. ✉ *643 Latoria Rd., off Veterans' Memorial Parkway, West Shore* ☎ *250/474–3673, 800/446–5322* 🌐 *www.olympicviewgolf.com* 🏌 *18 holes, 6534 yds. Par 72. Green Fee: C$54/C$59.*

HIKING AND WALKING

Victoria is one of the most pedestrian-friendly cities in North America. Waterfront pathways make it possible to stroll virtually all around Victoria's waterfront. For some interesting self-guided walks around the city's historic areas, check out 🌐 *www.victoria.ca/tours* or pick up a free walking-tour map at the city's visitor information center. Though popular with cyclists, the area's long-distance paths are also great for long walks. For views and elevation, check out the trail networks in the area's many provincial and regional parks.

Goldstream Provincial Park. This wilderness park, just 10 miles north of town, has a vast network of trails, from wheelchair-accessible paths through ancient Douglas fir and cedar forests to challenging hikes to the view-blessed peak of Mt. Finlayson. Trails also lead to the 157-foot Niagara Falls. ✉ *Hwy. 1, at Finlayson Arm Rd., West Shore* ☎ *250/478–9414* 🌐 *www.env.gov.bc.ca/bcparks.*

Mount Douglas Regional Park. Trails through the forest to the 758-foot summit of Mt. Douglas reward hikers with a 360-degree view of Victoria, the Saanich Peninsula, and the mountains of Washington State. ✉ *Off Cedar Hill Rd., Saanich* ☎ *250/475–5522* 🌐 *www.saanich.ca.*

Swan Lake Christmas Hill Nature Sanctuary. This sanctuary, with its 23-acre lake set in 150 acres of fields and wetlands, is just a few minutes from downtown Victoria. From the 1½-mile Lake Loop Trail and floating boardwalk, birders can spot a variety of waterfowl and nesting birds year-round. For great views of Victoria, take the 1½-mile round-trip hike to the top of Christmas Hill. The sanctuary's Nature House is open weekdays 8:30–4 and weekends noon–4. ✉ *3873 Swan Lake Rd., Saanich* ☎ *250/479–0211* 🌐 *www.swanlake.bc.ca* 🎫 *Free* ⏲ *Daily dawn–dusk.*

KAYAKING

The Upper Harbour and the Gorge, the waterways just north of the Inner Harbour, are popular boating spots.

Island Boat Rentals. You can rent a kayak, canoe, motorboat, or rowboat at this outlet at the Canoe Marina on the Upper Harbour. ✉ *Canoe Marina, 450 Swift St.* ☎ *250/995–1661* 🌐 *www.greatpacificadventures.com.*

Victoria Kayak. Setting out from the Inner Harbour, this company runs 2½-hour tours to see seals and other marine life around Seal Island. It's a good tour for beginners. The company rents kayaks, too. ✉ *950 Wharf St.* ☎ *250/216–5646* 🌐 *www.victoriakayak.com.*

SCUBA DIVING

The waters off Vancouver Island have some of the best scuba diving in the world, with clear waters and rich marine life; visibility is best in winter. The Ogden Point Breakwater and Race Rocks Underwater Marine Park are popular spots close to town. In Brentwood Bay on the Saanich Peninsula are the Glass Sponge Gardens, a sea mountain covered with sponges that were thought to be extinct. Off Thetis Island, near Chemainus, divers can explore a sunken 737 jetliner. Dive BC (🌐 *www.dive.bc.ca*) has details.

Ogden Point Dive Centre. Guided dives, weekend charters, and a water-view café are all available at this PADI-certified dive center at the Ogden Point Breakwater near downtown Victoria. ✉ *199 Dallas Rd., Downtown* ☎ *250/380–9119, 888/701–1177* 🌐 *www.divevictoria.com.*

Rockfish Divers. Based on the Saanich Peninsula, this internationally accredited PADI dive outfitter offers charters, courses, and equipment rentals. ✉ *Brentwood Bay Resort & Spa, 849 Verdier Ave., Brentwood Bay* ☎ *250/889–7282, 888/544–2079* 🌐 *www.rockfishdivers.com.*

ZIP-TREKKING

A fast-growing sport, zip-trekking involves whizzing through the forest while attached to a cable or zip line.

Adrena Line Zipline Adventure Tours. About 40 minutes west of Victoria (behind the 17 Mile Pub on the road to Sooke), this adventure center has two suspension bridges and eight zip-line routes ranging in length from 150 feet to 1,000 feet. Open daily March to October, it also offers night zipping. A shuttle bus runs twice daily from the Inner Harbour. ✉ *5128C Sooke Rd., Sooke* ☎ *250/642–1933, 877/947–9145* 🌐 *www.adrenalinezip.com.*

SHOPPING AND SPAS

Shopping in Victoria is easy: virtually everything is in the downtown area on or near Government Street stretching north from the Fairmont Empress Hotel.

SHOPPING DISTRICTS AND MALLS

Antique Row. Fort Street between Blanshard and Cook streets is home to antiques, curio, and collectibles shops.

Bay Centre. Downtown Victoria's main shopping mall has about 100 boutiques and restaurants. ✉ *1150 Douglas St., Downtown* ☎ *250/952–5680* 🌐 *www.thebaycentre.ca.*

Chinatown. Exotic fruits and vegetables, children's toys, wicker fans, fabric slippers, and other Chinese imports fill the shops along Fisgard Street. Fan Tan Alley, a narrow lane off Fisgard Street, has more nouveau-hippie goods, with an art gallery and yoga studio tucked in among its tiny storefronts.

Fan Tan Alley, in Victoria's Chinatown, is said to be the narrowest street in Canada.

Design District. The area where Wharf Street runs into Store Street contains a cluster of Victoria's home decor shops. 🌐 *www.victoriadesigndistrict.com.*

Fodors Choice ★ **Lower Johnson Street.** This row of candy-color Victorian shopfronts is Victoria's hub for independent fashion boutiques. Storefronts—some closet size—are filled with local designers' wares, funky boutiques, and no fewer than three shops selling ecologically friendly clothes of hemp and organic cotton. ✉ *Johnson St., between Government and Store Sts., Downtown.*

Market Square. During the late 19th century, this three-level square provided everything a sailor, miner, or lumberjack could want. Restored to its original architectural character, it's now a pedestrian-only hangout lined with cafés and boutiques. Shops sell toys, jewelry, and local art. ✉ *560 Johnson St., Downtown* ☎ *250/386–2441* 🌐 *www.marketsquare.ca.*

Trounce Alley. European designer boutiques and other high-end fashion outlets line this pedestrian-only lane north of View Street between Broad and Government streets.

SPECIALTY STORES

Artina's. Canadian-made jewelry—all handmade, one-of-a-kind pieces—fills the display cases at this unique jewelry shop. ✉ *1002 Government St., Downtown* ☎ *250/386–7000* 🌐 *www.artinas.com.*

Artisan Wine Shop. This offshoot of Mission Hill Family Estate replicates a visit to the winery with a video show and tasting area. The focus is

Okanagan wine, but the staff is also knowledgeable about Vancouver Island vineyards. ✉ *1007 Government St., Downtown* ☎ *250/384–9994* 🌐 *www.artisanwineshop.ca.*

Cook Culture. A hive of foodie activity, this upscale kitchenware store in the Atrium Building is also a cooking school, offering workshops on topics like how to make cheese, pasta fundamentals, and sustainable seafood. ✉ *1317 Blanshard St., Downtown* ☎ *250/590–8161* 🌐 *www.cookculture.com.*

Cowichan Trading. First Nations jewelry, art, moccasins, and Cowichan sweaters are the focus at this long-established outlet. ✉ *1328 Government St., Downtown* ☎ *250/383–0321* 🌐 *www.cowichantrading.com.*

Hill's Native Art. The stock at this shop ranges from affordable souvenirs to original West Coast First Nations art. ✉ *1008 Government St., Downtown* ☎ *250/385–3911* 🌐 *www.hills.ca.*

Irish Linen Stores. In business since 1917, this tiny shop has kept Victorians in fine linen, lace, and hand-embroidered items for generations. ✉ *1019 Government St., Downtown* ☎ *250/383–6812* 🌐 *www.irishlinenvictoria.com.*

★ **Munro's Books.** This beautifully restored 1909 building houses one of Canada's best-stocked independent bookstores. ✉ *1108 Government St., Downtown* ☎ *250/382–2464* 🌐 *www.munrobooks.com.*

★ **Rogers' Chocolates.** The staff at Rogers' has been making chocolates since 1885, and they're getting pretty good at it. Victoria creams are a local favorite, and any of the goodies can be packed for travel. The current shop dates to 1903. ✉ *913 Government St., Downtown* ☎ *250/881–8771* 🌐 *www.rogerschocolates.com.*

Fodor's Choice ★ **Silk Road.** For exotic teas (which you can sample at the tasting bar), aromatherapy remedies, and spa treatments (think green-tea facials), stop at this chic tea shop. ✉ *1624 Government St., Downtown* ☎ *250/704–2688* 🌐 *www.silkroadtea.com.*

STREET MARKETS

Victorians seem to relish any excuse to head outdoors, which may explain the boom in outdoor crafts, farmers', and other open-air markets around town.

Bastion Square Public Market. Crafts vendors and entertainers congregate in this historic square Thursdays, Fridays, and Saturdays from May to September. On Sunday, area farmers join the mix, selling local produce, homemade baked goods, cheeses, jams, and other goodies. ✉ *Bastion Square, off Government St., Downtown* ☎ *250/885–1387* 🌐 *www.bastionsquare.ca.*

James Bay Community Market. Organic food, local produce, creative crafts, and live music draw shoppers to this summer Saturday market south of the Inner Harbour. Look for it behind the Parliament Buildings. ✉ *Superior and Menzies Sts., Downtown* ☎ *250/381–5323* 🌐 *www.jamesbaymarket.com.*

Moss Street Market. "Make it, bake it, or grow it" is the rule for vendors at this street market, held 10 to 2 on Saturdays from May through October. ✉ *Fairfield Rd. at Moss St., Fairfield* ☎ *250/361–1747* 🌐 *www.mossstreetmarket.com.*

Ship Point Night Market. Music and local crafts are spotlighted at this night market, held Friday and Saturday evenings in summer on the Inner Harbour. ✉ *Ship Point Pier, Downtown* ☎ *250/413–6828* 🌐 *www.victoriaharbour.org.*

Sidney Thursday Night Market. More than 150 vendors of food, arts, crafts, and more take over the main street of this town, a 30-minute drive north of Victoria, each Thursday evening in summer. ✉ *Beacon Ave., Sidney* ☎ *250/655–6433* 🌐 *www.sidneybusiness.com.*

SPAS

Since health, nature, and relaxing seem to be the major preoccupations in Victoria, it's not surprising that the city has enjoyed a boom in spas. Aesthetics are important, but natural healing, ancient practices, and the use of such local products as wine and seaweed are more the focus here. Local specialties include vinotherapy (applying the antioxidant properties of wine grapes externally, rather than internally).

Aveda Institute. Vancouver Island's booming spa industry has to be staffed somehow, and this is where the technicians train. Supervised by pros, they offer budget-savvy clients everything from makeup touch-ups to hot-stone massages. Supervised student services top out at around C$65, or you can choose to have your treatment done by a professional. ✉ *1402 Douglas St., Downtown* ☎ *250/386–7993* 🌐 *www.avedainstitutevictoria.ca.*

8

Haven Spa. Natural products and sea-themed treatments are highlights at this full-service spa on the Saanich Peninsula. A pre-treatment steam room and post-treatment lounge add to the pampering. ✉ *Sidney Pier Hotel & Spa, 9805 Seaport Pl., Sidney* ☎ *250/655–9797* 🌐 *www.sidneypier.com.*

Le Spa Sereine. A custom-built pedicure room with fully reclining chairs and sunken basins is a draw at this independent downtown spa. Set in an atmospheric old building, it's also known for salt glows, hydrotherapy, reflexology, and Indian head massages. ✉ *1411 Government St., Downtown* ☎ *250/388–4419, 866/388–4419* 🌐 *www.lespasereine.ca.*

Silk Road Spa. Essential oils and organic skin and body products are the draw at this serene Chinatown spa, located inside the Silk Road tea shop. The green-tea facial is especially popular. ✉ *1624 Government St., Downtown* ☎ *250/704–2688* 🌐 *www.silkroadtea.com.*

Spa at Delta Victoria Ocean Pointe Resort. Organic skin-care products and harbor-view treatment rooms are among the draws at this popular hotel spa. Patrons have access to the hotel's gym and pool. ✉ *Delta Victoria Ocean Pointe Resort, 45 Songhees Rd., Downtown* ☎ *250/360–5938, 800/575–8882* 🌐 *www.thespadeltavictoria.com.*

Spa at the Grand. Traditional Thai, Swedish, and deep-tissue massage as well as facials and beauty treatments, are among the offerings at th intimate Asian-inspired spa. ✉ *Hotel Grand Pacific, 463 Belleville St., Downtown* ☎ *250/380–7862* 🌐 *www.hotelgrandpacific.com.*

Spa Magnolia. All-natural products and a hydrotherapy tub are the hallmark of this Aveda spa. ✉ *Magnolia Hotel, 625 Courtney St., Downtown* ☎ *250/920–7721* 🌐 *www.spamagnolia.com.*

Willow Stream Spa at the Fairmont Empress Hotel. Victoria's most luxurious spa is actually a pretty good value, especially if you arrive, as suggested, an hour before your appointment to soak in the Hungarian mineral bath, sauna, and steam room. ✉ *Fairmont Empress Hotel, 633 Humboldt St., Downtown* ☎ *250/995–4650, 866/854–7444* 🌐 *www.willowstream.com.*

SIDE TRIPS FROM VICTORIA

A few more days in the area gives you time to explore farther afield. Sooke and the Southwest Coast, the Cowichan Valley, or one of the Gulf Islands can make an easy day trip from Victoria, though any of them can warrant a weekend or longer for more serious exploration. These three regions around Victoria can be connected, so you don't have to retrace your steps.

How to choose? For wilderness beaches and forested hiking trails, take Highway 14 or cycle the Galloping Goose Trail to Sooke and the southwest coast. For food, wine, and First Nations culture, head north over the stunning Malahat drive to the Cowichan Valley. A great road trip? Take the Pacific Marine Circle Route around the two regions. Arts, crafts, kayaking, white-shell beaches, and a touch of neo-hippie island culture await those who visit Salt Spring Island, especially on market Saturdays (Salt Spring is also the only side trip easily manageable by public transport). You can truly get away from it all on the islands of Galiano, Mayne, or Pender. For families, the Cowichan Valley, with its interesting nature centers, has the most obvious kid appeal, though all three destinations have beaches, forests, and cute farm animals. Be warned though: the long, winding Highway 14 past Sooke can be challenging for those prone to motion sickness.

GETTING HERE AND AROUND

The *Mill Bay Ferry,* a car ferry operated by BC Ferries, sails several times a day between Brentwood Bay on the Saanich Peninsula and Mill Bay in the Cowichan Valley. BC Ferries also sail several times a day from Swartz Bay, about 30 minutes north of downtown Victoria, to Salt Spring, Pender, Mayne, Galiano, and Saturna islands. Sailings to Salt Spring take 30 minutes. Sailings to the other islands take from 25 minutes to two hours, depending on the destination and number of stops. Reservations are not accepted on these routes. Salt Spring Island can also be reached from Crofton, about 20 minutes north of Duncan, in the Cowichan Valley. The 20-minute sailings leave about once an hour. BC Ferries also sail to the Southern Gulf Islands (Galiano, Mayne, Pender, Saturna, and Salt Spring) from Tsawwassen, about 45 minutes south of Vancouver. Vehicle reservations, at no extra charge, are recommended and are required on some sailings on these routes.

Gulf Islands Water Taxi runs passengers and bicycles between Salt Spring, Mayne, and Galiano islands on Saturdays in July and August. Between September and June, the taxis operate as school boats but will take other passengers when space permits. They run school days only (call for exact days) between Salt Spring, Mayne, Galiano, Saturna, and Pender. Fares are $C20 one-way or $30 round-trip. On Salt Spring Island the *Queen of de Nile* runs from Salt Spring Marina to Ganges town center at C$2 per trip.

Cowichan Valley Regional Transit, a separate BC Transit network, serves Duncan and the Cowichan Valley. Salt Spring Island has a small transit system serving the ferry terminals and the village of Ganges, but it doesn't meet every ferry. The other Gulf Islands don't have transit services.

ESSENTIALS

Bus Information BC Transit ☎ *250/746–9899 Cowichan Valley Regional Transit, 250/538–4282 Salt Spring Transit* 🌐 *www.bctransit.com.*

Ferry Information BC Ferries ☎ *250/386–3431, 888/223–3779* 🌐 *www.bcferries.com.* **Gulf Islands Water Taxi** ☎ *250/537–2510* 🌐 *www.saltspring.com/watertaxi.* **Queen of de Nile** ☎ *250/537–5810 Salt Spring Marina.*

SOOKE AND THE SOUTHWEST COAST

28 km (17 mi) west of Victoria on Hwy. 14.

The village of Sooke, on the shore of Juan de Fuca Strait, about a 45-minute drive west of Victoria, has two claims to fame: it's home to Sooke Harbour House, one of Canada's best-known country inns, and it's the last stop for gas and supplies before heading out to the beaches and hiking trails of the island's wild and scenic southwest coast.

From Sooke, the narrow and winding Highway 14 runs 48 miles through birch and fir woods, with occasional sea views, to the fishing village of Port Renfrew. En route it passes Juan de Fuca Provincial Park, where trailheads lead to a series of forest-backed, driftwood-strewn beaches. The area around Sooke is home to some excellent restaurants and high-end B&Bs, but as you head west, other services are few.

To avoid retracing your steps to Victoria, you can follow the signs for the Pacific Marine Circle Route. This self-guided road trip follows Highway 14 from Victoria to Port Renfrew, where it takes a well-maintained back road through the forest to the village of Lake Cowichan. From here, Highway 18 leads to Highway 1 and back through the Cowichan Valley to Victoria. Driving time is about three hours, but watch your fuel gauge, as there are no gas stations between Sooke and Lake Cowichan and no services at all on the 30 miles between Port Renfrew and Lake Cowichan.

Watch for the red-and-white lighthouse lamp at the first traffic light as you enter Sooke on Highway 14. It sits in front of the Sooke Visitor Information Centre, which also houses a small museum displaying local First Nations artifacts.

GETTING HERE AND AROUND

Sooke is a 45-minute drive, mostly via Highway 14, west from Victoria, or a pleasant 3- to 4-hour cycle along the car-free Galloping Goose Trail. BC Transit also runs buses from downtown Victoria as far as the town of Sooke.

Sooke Regional Tourism Association ✉ *2070 Phillips Rd., off Hwy. 14* ☎ *250/642–6351, 866/888–4748* 🌐 *www.sooke-portrenfrew.com.*

TOP ATTRACTIONS

★ **Juan de Fuca Provincial Park.** Extending from the Jordan River to near Port Renfrew, Juan de Fuca Provincial Park takes in several beaches, including China Beach, with soft, sandy beaches dotted with driftwood; Sombrio Beach, a popular surfing spot; and Botanical Beach, with its amazing tidal pools. The **Juan de Fuca Marine Trail** is a tough 30-mile hike running along the shore from China Beach, west of the Jordan River, to Port Renfrew. Several trailheads along the way—at Sombrio Beach, Parkinson Creek, and Botanical Beach—allow day hikers to walk small stretches of it. ✉ *Hwy. 14, between Jordan River and Port Renfrew* ☎ *250/474–1336* 🌐 *www.env.gov.bc.ca/bcparks.*

WORTH NOTING

Carmanah Walbran Provincial Park. Logging roads west of Port Renfrew lead to this vast wilderness park, home to some of the world's largest spruce trees, some more than 800 years old, and ancient cedars more than 1,000 years old. Be prepared with supplies, because this is an extremely remote region with no services. Watch for logging trucks en route and bears once you're inside the park. ✉ *Off Highway 14, Port Renfrew* 🌐 *www.env.gov.bc.ca/bcparks.*

East Sooke Regional Park. Beautiful beaches, hiking trails, and wildflower-dotted meadows draw visitors to this more than 3,500-acre park 4 miles east of Sooke on the south side of Sooke Harbour. ✉ *East Sooke Rd.* 🌐 *www.crd.bc.ca/parks/eastsooke.*

French Beach Provincial Park. This provincial park, 13 miles west of Sooke, comprises a sand-and-pebble beach, a campground, and seaside trails. Whales like to feed in the area, and sometimes can be seen from shore. ✉ *Hwy. 14, Shirley* ☎ *250/474–1336* 🌐 *www.env.gov.bc.ca/bcparks.*

Port Renfrew. About 67 miles from Victoria, this tiny fishing village has national and regional parks in all directions. At the end of Highway 14 you'll find the grueling West Coast Trail and the more accessible but still daunting Juan de Fuca Marine Trail. Salmon fishing is also a big reason for visiting the area. Resources include a general store, a pub, restaurants, a motel, B&Bs, and a range of rustic cabins. There's no garage in town, but gas is usually available at the marina (it's best to play it safe and fill up your tank before leaving Sooke). From Port Renfrew, a 30-mile paved back road leads inland to Lake Cowichan in the Cowichan Valley. ☎ *250/647–0175* 🌐 *www.portrenfrewcommunity.com.*

Sooke Potholes Provincial Park. Locals and visitors come to cool off at Sooke Potholes Provincial Park, home to a series of natural swimming holes carved out of sandstone by the Sooke River. ✉ *Sooke River Rd., off Hwy. 14* 🌐 *www.crd.bc.ca/parks/sookepotholes.*

Whiffen Spit. West of the village of Sooke, you'll reach this mile-long natural breakwater that makes a scenic walk with great bird-watching. ✉ *Whiffen Spit Rd., off Highway 14.*

WHERE TO EAT AND STAY

$$ MODERN CANADIAN **✕ EdGe Restaurant.** Chef-owner Edward Tuson, who cooked at the Sooke Harbour House for more than a decade, has opened his own place in a homey strip-mall space. His food here is far less formal but no less fine, with starters like crispy squid with spicy cole slaw or a salad of pickled beets and beans with house-cured beef tenderloin. Mains might include grilled pork chops with a creamy cumin corn sauce, or roasted steelhead trout with salsa verde and Israeli couscous. If you're feeling adventurous, let the chef create a cutomized five-course prix-fixe dinner (C$50). At lunchtime, you'll find a simpler selection of salads, sandwiches, and pastas. Ⓢ *Average main: C$20* ✉ *6686 Sooke Rd.* ☎ *778/425–3343* 🌐 *www.edgerestaurant.ca* ✍ *Reservations not accepted* ⏲ *Closed Sun.–Mon.*

$$$ MODERN CANADIAN ★ **✕ Markus' Wharfside Restaurant.** Two art-filled rooms, one with a fireplace, and a small patio overlook Sooke Harbour from this former fisherman's cottage. The European-trained chef-owner makes the most of the local wild seafood and organic produce, much of it from the restaurant's own garden, with such made-from-scratch dishes as seared scallops with olive and preserved lemon tapenade, grilled lamb sirloin with peppered balsamic glaze, and the signature Tuscan-style seafood soup. Ⓢ *Average main: C$30* ✉ *1831 Maple Ave. S* ☎ *250/642–3596* 🌐 *www.markuswharfsiderestaurant.com* ⏲ *Closed Sun. and Mon. No lunch.*

$$$$ MODERN CANADIAN Fodor's Choice ★ **✕ Sooke Harbour House.** The relaxed, ocean-view dining room at this art-filled lodge is the stage for some of the country's most innovative meals. The nightly three- or four-course menus rely almost entirely on local provisions, including seafood from nearby waters, traditional First Nations foods, and about 200 varieties of herbs, vegetables, and edible flowers from the inn's own organic garden. You can also book a Gastronomic Adventure, which includes a visit with the chef and a multicourse tasting menu. The wine cellar is exceptional—cellar tours run nightly at 5 pm. **■ TIP→ Don't want a multicourse meal? On Sunday afternoons a less formal à la carte lunch is served.** Ⓢ *Prix-fixe: C$75* ✉ *1528 Whiffen Spit Rd.* ☎ *250/642–3421, 800/889–9688* 🌐 *www.sookeharbourhouse.com* ⏲ *Closed Tues.–Wed. No lunch Mon.–Sat.*

$$$ HOTEL **Point No Point Resort.** About 15 miles west of Sooke, this cabin compound overlooks a long stretch of private beach, Juan de Fuca Strait, and the Olympic Mountains; no wonder the 24 rooms are often booked well ahead by repeat visitors. **Pros:** remote and scenic; self-contained cottages assure privacy; good restaurant. **Cons:** remote; no phones or TVs. Ⓢ *Rooms from: C$175* ✉ *10829 West Coast Rd., Shirley* ☎ *250/646–2020* 🌐 *www.pointnopoint.com* *24 cabins, 1 4-bedroom house* ⏲ *Restaurant closed for dinner Mon. and Tues., and on weekdays in Jan.* *No meals.*

$$$$ B&B/INN Fodor's Choice ★ **Sooke Harbour House.** Art, food, and gardens work together seamlessly at one of Canada's best-loved country inns. **Pros:** splendid and luxurious. **Cons:** expensive; no pool. Ⓢ *Rooms from: C$299* ✉ *1528 Whiffen Spit Rd.* ☎ *250/642–3421, 800/889–9688* 🌐 *www.sookeharbourhouse.com* *28 rooms* ⏲ *Closed Jan.* *Breakfast.*

8

CLOSE UP

Vancouver's Grape Escape

Thanks to a Mediterranean climate, rich soil, and loads of sunshine—not to mention dedicated winemakers and appreciative consumers—southern Vancouver Island is blossoming into one of North America's fastest-growing, if least known, wine regions. Cool-climate varietals—such as Pinot Noir, Ortega, and Pinot Gris—do well here, at a latitude equivalent to northern France, but it's not all about grapes: English-style craft cider, berry wines, and traditionally made balsamic vinegar are also among the local specialties.

The region centers around the Cowichan Valley, a bucolic area about a 45-minute drive north of Victoria. Dubbed "The New Provence" for its proliferation of organic farms, wineries, restaurants, and specialist food producers, the valley is home to more than a dozen wineries. More are on the Saanich Peninsula, about 20 minutes north of Victoria and, increasingly, dotted across the offshore Gulf Islands.

Touring is easy and wonderfully low-key: burgundy-and-white Wine Route signs, as well as maps available in local tourist offices, show the way. BC Ferries' Mill Bay Ferry links the Cowichan Valley to the Saanich Peninsula.

Most of Vancouver Island's wineries are small, family-run, labor-of-love operations. Finding the wineries, hidden down winding country lanes, tucked between farm stands and artist studios, is part of the fun. Not all the wineries have enough staff to offer tours, but most offer tastings—it's always a good idea to call ahead. Some of the area's best lunches are served on winery patios.

COWICHAN VALLEY WINERIES

Cherry Point Estate Wines. An outdoor bistro on a shady patio, serving lunch May to September, is a draw at this Cowichan Valley winery that produces Pinot Noir, Pinot Blanc, Pinot Gris, Ortega, and a popular blackberry dessert wine. Free tours and tastings run daily in summer (call for hours in winter). ✉ *840 Cherry Point Rd., Cobble Hill* ☎ *250/743–1272* 🌐 *www.cherrypointvineyards.com.*

Merridale Ciderworks. Cider is made in the traditional English way at this cidery and distillery; in addition to several varieties of cider and fortified wines, it also makes spirits, like a fizzy fruity vodka and an apple *eau de vie.* Visitors can tour the cidery, taste the wares, and linger over lunches of local fare served on the orchard-view patio. There's also a shop selling ciders, juices, baked goods, and jams, as well as a day spa with massages and pedicures given in an orchard-view yurt or a meadow-view gazebo. ✉ *1230 Merridale Rd., Cobble Hill* ☎ *250/743–4293, 800/998–9908* 🌐 *www.merridalecider.com.*

Unsworth Vineyards. A relative newcomer among Cowichan Valley wineries, this small producer makes a Pinot Gris, a Merlot and Cabernet-Libre blend, and a port-style dessert wine. In addition to a tasting room, the property is home to Amusé at the Vineyard, a contemporary bistro set in a restored 1907 farmhouse. ✉ *2915 Cameron-Taggart Rd., Mill Bay* ☎ *250/929–2292* 🌐 *www.unsworthvineyards.com* 🕐 *Fri.–Sun. 11–5.*

Zanatta Winery. A local favorite is Zanatta Winery, which produces lovely Ortega, Pinot Grigio, and Damasco entirely from grapes grown on its own 30 acres. If you can, time a visit for an Italian-style lunch on the veranda of the winery's 1903 farmhouse. ✉ *5039 Marshall Rd., Duncan* ☎ *250/748-2338* 🌐 *www.zanatta.ca* ⏲ *Fri.-Sun. noon-4.*

SAANICH PENINSULA WINERIES

Muse Winery. At the northern tip of the Saanich Peninsula, Muse Winery specializes in estate-grown Ortega and Pinot Gris varieties; a patio bistro serves lunch on summer weekends. ✉ *11195 Chalet Rd., North Saanich* ☎ *250/656-2552* 🌐 *www.musewinery.ca* ⏲ *Thurs.-Sun. noon-5.*

Sea Cider Farm & Ciderhouse. Traditional ciders, made with apples grown nearby, are paired with local cheeses, preserves and other delectables at this Saanich Peninsula ciderhouse. It's open year-round for tours and tastings. ✉ *2487 Mt. Saint Michael Rd., off Central Saanich Rd., Saanichton* ☎ *250/544-4824* 🌐 *www.seacider.ca* ⏲ *June-Sept., daily 11-4; Oct.-May, Wed.-Sun. 11-4.*

Victoria Spirits. Canada's first premium gin is made in a wood-fired still at this Saanich Peninsula distillery, which also makes hemp vodka and bitters. You can tour the distillery and sample the wares on weekends from spring through fall. ✉ *6170 Old West Saanich Rd., Victoria* ☎ *250/544-8217* 🌐 *www.victoriaspirits.com* ⏲ *Apr.-Oct., weekends 10-5.*

FOOD AND WINE FESTIVALS

Festivals are a great way to explore the region's food and wine scene.

Art of the Cocktail Festival. It's not only wine drinkers who can enjoy festival fun. Victoria's annual cocktail party includes tastings, workshops, and other sipping and supping events every October. ✉ *Victoria* ☎ *250/389-0444* 🌐 *www.artofthecocktail.ca.*

Cowichan Wine and Culinary Festival. Cowichan Valley wineries and restaurants celebrate the region's bounty with a week of wine and culinary events every September. 🌐 *wines.cowichan.net.*

Taste: Victoria's Festival of Food and Wine. Victoria's annual food and wine fest brings a wealth of local food and wine producers, tastings, and events to town every July. ✉ *Victoria* 🌐 *www.victoriataste.com.*

Vancouver Island Feast of Fields. This lavish celebration of local food is held on an area farm, generally in September. 🌐 *www.ffcfprojects.ca/feast.*

THE COWICHAN VALLEY

60 km (37 miles) north of Victoria on Trans-Canada Hwy., or Hwy. 1.

The Cowichan people were onto something when they called this fertile valley north of Victoria "the Warm Land." The region, roughly from Mill Bay to Ladysmith, is said to be blessed with the warmest year-round temperatures and more hours of sunshine each year than anywhere else in Canada. Home to a quarter of Vancouver Island's productive farmland, and among the most artists per capita anywhere else in the country, the Cowichan Valley has earned another moniker, "The New Provence," thanks to its wealth of wineries, small organic farms, and burgeoning local-food culture.

Highway 1 from Victoria cuts north–south through the valley, while winding side roads lead to studios, wineries, and roadside farm stands. Duncan, the valley's main town, is home to the Quw'utsun' Cultural and Conference Centre, one of B.C.'s leading First Nations cultural centers. A 30-minute drive north is Chemainus, a cute if touristy little town decorated with outdoor murals. Ladysmith, at the valley's north end, has a historic town center and a sandy ocean beach. About 10 minutes south of Duncan are Cowichan Bay, a tiny fishing village with houses built on stilts over the water, and Cobble Hill, home to a cluster of wineries. Lake Cowichan and Shawnigan Lake draw campers, boaters, and summer cottagers. The Cowichan Valley Rail Trail, a long-distance foot-and-bike path, connects the two lakes.

GETTING HERE AND AROUND

There are three ways to get here from Victoria: make the hour's drive north on Highway 1 over the scenic Malahat Summit; take the Mill Bay Ferry from Brentwood Bay on the Saanich Peninsula; or travel via a back road from Port Renfrew, west of Sooke, following the Pacific Marine Circle Route.

COWICHAN BAY

Often called Cow Bay, this funky little town about 10 minutes south of Duncan (take Cowichan Bay Road off Highway 1) is made up largely of houseboats and houses built on pilings over the water. Seafood restaurants, nautical shops, boat builders, kayaking outfitters, and B&Bs line the waterfront.

EXPLORING

Cowichan Bay Maritime Centre. The interesting Cowichan Bay Maritime Centre has maritime paraphernalia, including historic dive suits and model boats, displayed along a pier, which is also a great place to take in views of the village and boats at harbor. You may also be able to watch boat builders and First Nations artists at work in the attached studio. ✉ *1761 Cowichan Bay Rd., Cowichan Bay* ☎ *250/746–4955* 🌐 *www.classicboats.org* 🎫 *Free* ⏲ *Daily 9 am–dusk.*

SHOPPING

Arthur Vickers Gallery at the Shipyard. This well-regarded gallery displays the well-known artist's work, with West Coast and First Nations themes, in a historic shipyard space. ✉ *1719 Cowichan Bay Rd., Cowichan Bay* ☎ *250/748–7650* 🌐 *www.arthurvickers.com/gallery.*

Hilary's Artisan Cheese. This shop draws foodies with its artisanal cheeses. Next door, True Grain Bread offers organic baked goods. ✉ *1737 Cowichan Bay Rd., Cowichan Bay* ☎ *250/748–5992* 🌐 *www.hilarycheese.com.*

DUNCAN

Duncan, the largest town in the valley, is nicknamed the City of Totems for the more than 40 totem poles that dot the small community. Between May and September, free walking tours of the totems leave hourly from the south end of the train station building on Canada Avenue (contact the Duncan Business Improvement Area Society, at ☎ *250/715–1700,* for more information). On Saturdays from March to November the city square at the end of Craig Street hosts an outdoor market, where you can browse for local produce, crafts, and specialty foods. Duncan is also home to the world's largest hockey stick—look for it on the outside wall of the Duncan arena on the west side of Highway 1 as you drive through town.

EXPLORING

British Columbia Forest Discovery Centre. Kids adore riding the rails at the British Columbia Forest Discovery Centre, a 100-acre outdoor museum just north of Duncan. Pulled by a 1910 steam locomotive, a three-carriage train toots through the woods and over a trestle bridge across a lake, stopping at a picnic site and playground on the way. Forestry-related exhibits around the site include a 1930s-era logging camp, historic logging equipment, and indoor exhibits about the modern science of forestry. Interpretive trails through the forest lead to ancient trees, one dating back more than 500 years. During July and August, the steam train runs daily every half hour. In May, June, and September, the train may be replaced with a gas locomotive. ✉ *2892 Drinkwater Rd.* ☎ *250/715–1113, 866/715–1113* 🌐 *www.discoveryforest.com* *C$15* *June–early Sept., daily 10–4:30; early Sept.–mid Oct. and mid-Apr.–May, Thurs.–Mon. 10–4.*

Cowichan Valley Museum & Archives. This small museum, in a 1912 train station, has exhibits and artifacts about the region's First Nations culture and pioneer history. ✉ *130 Canada Ave.* ☎ *250/746–6612* 🌐 *www.cowichanvalleymuseum.bc.ca* *Donations accepted* *June–Sept., Mon.–Sat. 10–4; Oct.–May, Wed.–Fri. 11–4, Sat. 1–4.*

Pacific Northwest Raptors. At Pacific Northwest Raptors, a conservation center about 10 minutes northeast of Duncan, you can see owls, hawks, falcons, and eagles in natural settings. Free-flying bird demonstrations are held daily; you can also join a trainer on a brief falconry or ecology course. ✉ *1877 Herd Rd.* ☎ *250/746–0372* 🌐 *www.pnwraptors.com* *C$14* *Mar.–Oct., daily 11–4:30.*

★ **Quw'utsun' Cultural and Conference Centre.** This village of cedar longhouses, occupying 6 acres of shady riverbank, is one of Canada's leading First Nations cultural and educational facilities. A 20-minute video in a longhouse-style theater introduces the history of the Cowichan people, B.C.'s largest aboriginal group, and a 30-minute walking tour reveals the legends behind the site's dozen totem poles. Crafts demonstrations and dance performances are occasionally offered during summer, and

8

The town of Duncan, in the Cowichan Valley, is nicknamed the City of Totems because there are more than 40 totem poles dotting the community.

the many indigenous plants on-site are labeled with information about their traditional uses. The gift shop stocks, among other things, the hand-knit Cowichan sweaters that the area is known for, and the Riverwalk Café offers a rare opportunity to sample First Nations fare. ✉ *200 Cowichan Way* ☎ *250/746–8119, 877/746–8119* 🌐 *www.quwutsun.ca* 🎫 *C$13* 🕒 *Late May–mid-Sept., Tues.–Sat. 10–4.*

Teafarm. Can tea grow in Canada? The proprietors of this small organic farm just north of Duncan hope so. While their crop is still maturing, they've opened a tea shop and gallery (in the former milking room of a barn), blending and selling teas, offering tastings, and showcasing the ceramics work of co-owner Margit Nellemann and other area artists. ✉ *8350 Richards Trail, North Cowichan* ☎ *250/748–3811, 855/748–3811* 🌐 *www.teafarm.com* 🕒 *Wed.–Sun. 10–5.*

CHEMAINUS

Chemainus, 16 miles north of Duncan, is known for the bold epic murals that decorate its townscape, as well as for its beautifully restored Victorian homes. Once dependent on the lumber industry, the small community began to revitalize itself in the early 1980s when its mill closed down. Since then the town has brought in international artists to paint a total of 40 murals depicting local historical events around town. Footprints on the sidewalk lead you on a self-guided tour of the murals. Tours by horse and carriage, replica-train rides, free outdoor concerts, a weekly night market, and plenty of B&Bs, cafés, and crafts shops all help pass the time here.

PERFORMING ARTS

Chemainus Theatre. The Chemainus Theatre presents family oriented performances. ✉ *9737 Chemainus Rd.* ☎ *250/246–9820, 800/565–7738* 🌐 *www.chemainustheatrefestival.ca.*

WHERE TO EAT AND STAY

For expanded hotel reviews, visit Fodors.com.

$$ MODERN CANADIAN **✕ La Pommeraie.** Neighboring farms supply much of the fare at this bistro, tucked down a country lane at Merridale Ciderworks. The bistro, part of the gambrel-roofed cider house, showcases local art on whitewashed walls within, and orchard and forest views from the wide, covered veranda. You can match house-made ciders to your meal of, say, a local lamb-and-rosemary burger or a simple salad of fennel, toasted pumpkin seeds, and organic greens tossed in an apple-cider dressing. On Sundays, locals flock here for brick-oven pizza and live jazz. $ *Average main: C$14* ✉ *1230 Merridale Rd., Cobble Hill* ☎ *250/743–4293, 800/998–9908* 🌐 *www.merridalecider.com* ⏲ *No dinner Mon.–Thurs. Closed Jan.*

$$$ MODERN CANADIAN **✕ The Masthead.** You know a chef cares about local food when his menu lists how far each ingredient has traveled to reach your plate. At this historic seaside roadhouse in Cowichan Bay, the mussels and clams come from within 5 miles of the restaurant, and the poached Dungeness crab is from the bay outside the door. Many other ingredients—bison, wild salmon, duck breast—are sourced from within 200 miles. The 1863 wood-paneled room offers sea views throughout, but waterside deck tables are favored by the loyal clientele. The long wine list has a good selection of Cowichan Valley labels. $ *Average main: C$28* ✉ *1705 Cowichan Bay Rd., Cowichan Bay* ☎ *250/748–3714* 🌐 *www.themastheadrestaurant.com* ⏲ *No lunch.*

8

$$ CANADIAN **✕ Riverwalk Café.** This little riverside café, part of Duncan's Quw'utsun' Cultural and Conference Centre, offers a rare opportunity to try traditional B.C. First Nations fare. All meals start with warm fried bread with blackberry jam and salmon spread. From there, the menu offers both the familiar (salads, burgers, and fish-and-chips made with salmon) and the more unusual: elk escalope on baby spinach greens, pulled buffalo in barbecue sauce, or a stew of salmon, cod, prawns, and sea asparagus. For a treat, try the Me'Hwulp, a Salish afternoon tea for two with candied salmon, crab cakes, blackberry tarts, and more—all served on a cedar platter. A kids' menu and river-view patio in a parklike environment make this a pleasant family spot. $ *Average main: C$14* ✉ *200 Cowichan Way, Duncan* ☎ *250/746–4370* ⏲ *No dinner. Closed Sun. and Mon. and mid-Sept.–May.*

$$$$ MODERN CANADIAN ★ **✕ Stone Soup Inn.** Chef-owner Brock Windsor grows his own vegetables, forages for mushrooms and herbs, raises pigs to cure his own bacon, and sources most other provisions from farmers, fishers, and growers in the nearby Cowichan Valley. Thursday to Saturday nights he prepares a five-course "chef's choice" dinner in his homey, candlelit farmhouse dining room. His years of experience are revealed in dishes like miso-marinated black cod served with a gingery squash puree, or braised rabbit paired with wild mushrooms, purple carrots, and polenta. Dishes are matched with Vancouver Island wines. Reservations

are recommended; vegetarians and those with food allergies can be accommodated with advance arrangements. The inn is set in the forest about 20 minutes west of Duncan. ■ **TIP→ If you don't want to drive back to civilization after your meal, you can spend the night in one of the two simple B&B rooms upstairs.** *Prix-fixe: C$65 ✉ 6755 Cowichan Lake Rd., Lake Cowichan ☎ 250/749–3848 ⊕ www.stonesoupinn.ca ⊗ Closed Sun.–Wed. No lunch.*

$$ B&B/INN **Damali.** A convenient base for touring the Cowichan Valley wineries, this casual and friendly B&B has three rooms in a contemporary farmhouse set amid lavender fields. **Pros:** pastoral setting; genial owners share tips about the region. **Cons:** no phones. *Rooms from: C$169 ✉ 3500 Telegraph Rd., Cobble Hill ☎ 250/743–4100, 877/743–5170 ⊕ www.damali.ca 3 rooms Breakfast.*

$$ B&B/INN **Fairburn Farmstay and Guesthouse.** This 1896 homestead on 130 pastoral acres is the centerpiece of a historic farm, Canada's first water-buffalo dairy; kids, in particular, enjoy watching the milking. **Pros:** peaceful rural surroundings; family-friendly atmosphere. **Cons:** old-fashioned rooms; at the end of a country road some distance from town. *Rooms from: C$129 ✉ 3310 Jackson Rd., Duncan ☎ 250/746–4637 ⊕ www.fairburnfarm.bc.ca 6 rooms, 1 cottage ⊗ Closed Nov.–Mar. Breakfast.*

THE GULF ISLANDS

Of the hundreds of islands sprinkled across Georgia Strait between Vancouver Island and the mainland, the most popular and accessible are Galiano, Mayne, Pender, Saturna, and Salt Spring. A temperate climate, white-shell beaches, rolling pastures, and forests are common to all, but each island has a unique flavor. Though rustic, they're not undiscovered. Writers, artists, and craftspeople as well as weekend cottagers and retirees from Vancouver and Victoria take full advantage of them. Hotel reservations are a good idea in summer. Only Salt Spring has a town, but food and accommodation are available on all of the islands.

GETTING HERE AND AROUND

BC Ferries sail from Sidney, on the Saanich Peninsula, just north of Victoria, to all five of the islands, several times a day; these routes don't take reservations, so arrive early if you're taking a car—45 minutes to an hour early is a good rule of thumb in summer, half an hour in winter. Sailings range from half an hour to more than an hour, depending on stops. Bikes, pets, and foot passengers are welcome. Ferries from the B.C. mainland leave from Tsawwassen, just south of Vancouver. On these routes to and from the mainland, car reservations are highly recommended; for busier sailings, they're required. The ferry journey from Tsawwassen to Salt Spring takes 90 minutes to three hours (depending on the number of intermediate stops), less for the other islands.

Travel between the islands on BC Ferries is possible but generally requires an overnight stay at one of the islands. A fun, low-cost way to cruise the islands is to take one of BC Ferries' Gulf Islands Day Trips—traveling as foot passenger from Swartz Bay, around the islands and back, without disembarking. It's also possible to visit Mayne and Galiano from Salt Spring via water taxi, which doubles as the island school boat.

Salt Spring Island has the most frequent ferry service, and three terminals: ferries from Swartz Bay, near Victoria, arrive at Fulford Harbour, on the southern tip of the island, 20 miles from Ganges, the main town. Ferries from the B.C. mainland arrive at Long Harbour, on the island's east coast, closer to Ganges. Salt Spring also has BC Ferry service from the Cowichan Valley, with sailings every hour or so from Crofton, 20 minutes north of Duncan, to Vesuvius Bay on Salt Spring. A BC Transit minibus runs from all three ferry terminals to the town of Ganges, but it doesn't meet every ferry; check online schedules first. For a taxi on Salt Spring, call Silver Shadow Taxi.

Transport on the other islands is limited: Pender has the Pender Island Cab Company. Most island accommodations collect guests from the ferry terminal if asked. Cycling is popular on the islands, despite the hilly terrain.

ESSENTIALS

Bus Information BC Transit ☎ *250/538–4282* ⊕ *www.bctransit.com.*

Taxi Information Pender Island Cab Company ☎ *250/629–2222* ⊕ *www.penderislandcab.com.* **Silver Shadow Taxi** ☎ *250/537–3030* ⊕ *www.silvershadow.ca.*

SALT SPRING ISLAND

28 nautical miles from Swartz Bay, 22 nautical miles from Tsawwassen.

With its wealth of studios, galleries, restaurants, and B&Bs, Salt Spring is the most developed, and most visited, of the Southern Gulf Islands. It's home to the only town in the archipelago (Ganges) and, although it can get busy on summer weekends, has not yet lost its relaxed rural feel. Outside of Ganges, the rolling landscape is home to small organic farms, wineries, forested hills, quiet white-shell beaches, and several swimming lakes.

What really sets Salt Spring apart is its status as a "little arts town." Island residents include hundreds of artists, writers, craftspeople, and musicians, many of whom open their studios to visitors. To visit more than 35 local artists in their studios, pick up a free map from the tourist information center in Ganges.

The ferries to Salt Spring arrive at three different docks, in or near the island's three villages. Boats from the mainland and from the southern Gulf Islands dock at Long Harbour, just east of Ganges. Salt Spring's main commercial center is the seaside village of **Ganges**, about 9 miles north of the Fulford Ferry Terminal. It has about a dozen art galleries, as well as the essentials: restaurants, banks, gas stations, grocery stores, and a liquor store. At the south end of Salt Spring Island, the ferries from Victoria dock at the tiny village of **Fulford**, which has a restaurant, a café, and several offbeat boutiques. Ferries from Crofton, on Vancouver Island, arrive on the west side of Salt Spring Island at the small coastal community of **Vesuvius**, with a restaurant, a tiny grocery store-cum-café, and crafts studios.

8

EXPLORING

Burgoyne Bay Provincial Park. Easy hikes and a pretty pebble beach are the draws at this provincial park, at the end of a dirt road toward the southern end of the island. ✉ *Burgoyne Bay Rd., at Fulford-Ganges Rd.* ☎ *250/539–2115* 🌐 *www.env.gov.bc.ca/bcparks.*

Mount Maxwell Provincial Park. Near the center of Salt Spring Island, Baynes Peak in Mount Maxwell Provincial Park has spectacular views of south Salt Spring, Vancouver Island, and other Gulf Islands. The last portion of the drive is steep, winding, and unpaved. ✉ *Mt. Maxwell Rd., off Fulford–Ganges Rd.* ☎ *250/539–2115* 🌐 *www.env.gov.bc.ca/bcparks.*

★ **Ruckle Provincial Park.** This provincial park is the site of an 1872 homestead and extensive fields that are still being farmed. Several small sandy beaches and 5 miles of trails winding through forests and along the coast make this one of the islands' most appealing parks. ✉ *Beaver Point Rd.* ☎ *250/539–2115, 877/559–2115* 🌐 *www.env.gov.bc.ca/bcparks.*

Sculpture Trail. At Hastings House Country House Hotel near Ganges, a Sculpture Trail—with intriguing art installations in the woods—is open to the public. ✉ *Hastings House Country House Hotel, 160 Upper Ganges Rd., Ganges.*

WHERE TO EAT AND STAY

$$ ITALIAN ✕ **Auntie Pesto's Café.** Fresh local ingredients, house-made bread, and Mediterranean flavors keep regulars well fed at this family-run village center spot. Breakfast omelets, enjoyed with fruit salad and good coffee, lunches of homemade soup and grilled sandwiches (the Johnny B—a hearty, open-faced meatball concoction—will feed a hungry teen), and Mediterranean-themed dinners of, say, sablefish, duck, or big plates of pasta make the bustling interior and marina-view deck busy all day. $ *Average main: C$20* ✉ *2104–115 Fulford Ganges Rd., Ganges* ☎ *250/537–4181* 🌐 *www.auntiepestos.com* ⊙ *Closed Sun.*

$$ MODERN CANADIAN ✕ **Bruce's Kitchen.** At this homey bistro with sunny yellow walls and rustic wood tables, it almost feels like you're in Chef Bruce Wood's kitchen. The menus change weekly to keep pace with the seasons. Lunches are simple—soups, salads, and sandwiches—while in the evenings you might find freshly caught seafood, cider-brined Cowichan Valley chicken with smashed new potatoes and braised kale, or pasta tossed with chickpeas and smoked tofu. $ *Average main: C$18* ✉ *3106–115 Fulford Ganges Rd., Ganges* ☎ *250/931–3399* 🌐 *www.bruceskitchen.ca* ⊙ *No dinner Mon. No lunch Sun.*

$$$ SEAFOOD ✕ **Calvin's Bistro.** Seafood—whether in the form of a wild salmon fillet, baby-shrimp linguine, or good old halibut-and-chips—tops the menu at this comfortable marina-view bistro in Ganges. Locals also flock here for such Thai dishes as coconut prawns and spring rolls. A long list of lunchtime sandwiches and burgers includes local lamb, wild salmon, and even Wiener schnitzel. Inside booths are cozy, while the big patio has great harbor views. Friendly Swiss owners account for the homemade European desserts and welcoming service. $ *Average main: C$21* ✉ *133 Lower Ganges Rd., Ganges* ☎ *250/538–5551* 🌐 *www.calvinsbistro.ca* ⊙ *Closed Sun. and Mon.*

$$$ SCANDINAVIAN ★ **House Piccolo.** Piccolo Lyytikainen, the Finnish-born chef-owner of this tiny restaurant in a quaint village house—serves beautifully prepared and presented European cuisine. Creations include Scandinavian-influenced dishes such as B.C. venison with a juniper and-lingonberry demi-glace and charbroiled fillet of beef with Gorgonzola sauce. For dessert the chocolate terrine Finlandia and vodka-moistened lingonberry crepes are hard to resist. The 250-item wine list includes many hard-to-find vintages. The indoor tables are cozy and candlelighted; the outdoor patio is a pleasant summer dining spot. *Average main: C$27 108 Hereford Ave., Ganges 250/537–1844 www.housepiccolo.com No lunch; call ahead for winter hrs.*

$$ ECLECTIC **Rock Salt Restaurant & Cafe.** You can watch the ferry coming across the harbor from the sea-view windows of this Fulford Harbour eatery. Wholesome, organic, and local goodies run the gamut from slow-baked ribs to seafood curries to much-loved yam quesadillas. Vegans are well cared for here, with yummy bean stews and lentil burgers, and the made-from-scratch breakfasts are worth getting up early for. The take-out counter offers provisions for your onward journey. *Average main: C$18 2921 Fulford Ganges Rd., Fulford 250/653–4833 www.rocksaltrestaurant.com.*

$$ RENTAL **Foxglove Farm.** If you'd like to see how the locals live, this 120-acre organic farm on the road to Mount Maxwell rents three basic but comfy family-friendly accommodations. **Pros:** secluded rural setting; good for kids. **Cons:** far from town; cell-phone service may be unreliable. *Rooms from: C$175 1200 Mount Maxwell Rd. 250/537–1989 www.foxglovefarmbc.ca 3 cabins.*

$$$$ HOTEL Fodor's Choice ★ **Hastings House Country House Hotel.** The centerpiece of this 22-acre seaside estate—with its gardens, meadows, and harbor views—is a 1939 country house, built in the style of an 11th-century Sussex manor. **Pros:** wonderful food; top-notch service; historic character. **Cons:** no pool; some rooms overlook a nearby pub; rates are high. *Rooms from: C$395 160 Upper Ganges Rd., Ganges 250/537–2362, 800/661–9255 www.hastingshouse.com 3 rooms, 14 suites, 1 guesthouse Restaurant closed Nov.–Feb. Breakfast.*

SHOPPING

Garry Oaks Winery. This small winery produces Pinot Gris, Pinot Noir, and a popular Bordeaux blend called Fetish. It's open for tastings daily in July and August, less often in spring and fall (call ahead). Tours are offered by appointment. *1880 Fulford-Ganges Rd. 250/653–4687 www.garryoakswinery.com July–early Sept., daily noon–5; call for off-season hrs.*

Mistaken Identity Vineyards. This organic vineyard and winery, just north of Ganges, produces Pinot Gris, Pinot Rosé, and Gewürztraminer. The offbeat name was inspired by tasters who guessed the wine was from Europe, Australia, or anywhere but western Canada. *164 Norton Rd. 250/538–9463, 877/918–2783 www.mistakenidentityvineyards.com Late June–early Sept., Thurs.–Sun. 11–5; rest of year by appointment.*

Salt Spring Island Cheese Company. You can watch the cheesemakers at work at this farm and cheese shop north of Fulford Harbour, where

8

tasting is encouraged. Kids can walk through the farmyard to see the animals that provide the milk for the goat's and sheep's milk cheeses. ✉ *285 Reynolds Rd., off Beaver Point Rd.* ☎ *250/653–2300* 🌐 *www.saltspringcheese.com* ⏲ *May–Sept., daily 11–5; Oct.–Apr., daily 11–4.*

★ **Salt Spring Island Saturday Market.** Locals and visitors flock to Ganges on summer Saturdays for this weekly market, held in Centennial Park April through October. Everything sold at this colorful outdoor bazaar is made or grown on the island; the array and quality of crafts, food, and produce is dazzling. ✉ *Centennial Park, Fulford-Ganges Rd., Ganges* ☎ *250/537–4448* 🌐 *www.saltspringmarket.com.*

Salt Spring Vineyards. Salt Spring Vineyards produces Pinot Gris, Pinot Noir, and blackberry port, almost entirely from island-grown fruit. Wine by the glass, as well as local bread and cheese, is available for summer picnics on the vineyard-view patio. If you don't want to leave, there's a two-room B&B. ✉ *151 Lee Rd., off Fulford-Ganges Rd.* ☎ *250/653–9463* 🌐 *www.saltspringvineyards.com* ⏲ *Mar.–Apr., weekends noon–4; May–mid-June, Fri.–Sun. noon–5; mid-June–Aug., daily 11–5; Sept., daily noon–5; Oct., Fri.–Sun. noon–5; rest of year by appointment.*

GALIANO ISLAND

With its 16-mile-long eastern shore and cove-dotted western coast, Galiano is arguably the prettiest of these islands. It's certainly the best for hiking and mountain biking, with miles of trails through the Douglas fir and Garry Oak forest. Mt. Galiano and Bodega Ridge are classic walks, with far-reaching views to the mainland. Most shops and services—including cash machines, gas pumps, galleries, and a bookstore—are clustered near the Sturdies Bay ferry terminal. A visitor information booth is to your right as you leave the ferry.

EXPLORING

Montague Harbour Marina. You can rent a kayak, boat, or moped at Montague Harbour Marina. ✉ *Montague Rd.* ☎ *250/539–5733.*

QUICK BITES

The Max & Moritz Spicy Island Food House (✉ *Sturdies Bay Ferry Terminal* ☎ *520/539–5888*) catering van at the Sturdies Bay Ferry Terminal offers German and Indonesian takeout. Stop into the cheerful **Sturdies Bay Bakery & Cafe** (✉ *2540 Sturdies Bay Rd.* ☎ *250/539–2004*), a local favorite near the ferry terminal, for freshly made pastries and sandwiches.

★ **Montague Harbour Provincial Marine Park.** This provincial park on the island's southwest shore has a long shell beach famed for its sunset views. ✉ *Montague Park Rd., off Montague Rd.* ☎ *250/539–2115* 🌐 *www.env.gov.bc.ca/bcparks.*

WHERE TO EAT AND STAY

$ CANADIAN ✕ **Harbour Grill Restaurant.** At the Montague Harbour Marina, this casual eatery serves breakfast, lunch, and dinner on its heated ocean-view deck. Keep an eye out for the local wildlife, including herons, eagles, and even river otters. [$] *Average main: C$10* ✉ *Montague Harbour Marina, Off Montague Park Rd., VHF 66A* ☎ *250/539–5733* ⏲ *Closed Oct.–Apr.*

Fresh crab is a delicacy around the Gulf Islands, especially in Ganges Harbour, on Salt Spring Island.

$$$$ RESORT Fodor's Choice ★ **Galiano Oceanfront Inn & Spa.** A yoga suite overlooking a meditation garden, seaside massages, and a mineral flotation bath are among the serenity-inducing highlights at this waterfront retreat on Sturdies Bay. **Pros:** the staff picks you up at the ferry; well-equipped suites encourage long stays; quiet and lovely environment. **Cons:** no pool; no morning room service. *Rooms from: C$249* ✉ *134 Madrona Dr.* ☎ *250/539–3388, 877/530–3939* 🌐 *www.galianoinn.com* *10 rooms, 10 suites* *No meals.*

NIGHTLIFE

Hummingbird Pub. A friendly local hangout, this spot has live music on summer weekends. Also in summer, the pub runs a free shuttle bus to the Montague Harbour Marina. ✉ *47 Sturdies Bay Rd.* ☎ *250/539–5472* 🌐 *www.hummingbirdpub.com.*

MAYNE ISLAND

The smallest of the Southern Gulf Islands, Mayne also has the most visible history. The buildings of Miners Bay, the island's tiny commercial center, date to the 1850s, when Mayne was a stopover for prospectors en route to the gold fields.

GETTING HERE AND AROUND

As the quietest and least hilly of the islands, Mayne is a good choice for cycle touring. It's also a popular spot for kayaking.

EXPLORING

Active Pass Lighthouse. The Active Pass Lighthouse stands on the shore at Georgina Point, part of the Gulf Islands National Park Reserve. Built in 1885, it still signals ships into the busy waterway. The grassy grounds are great for picnicking. ✉ *Georgina Point Rd.*

★ **Bennett Bay.** Part of the Gulf Islands National Park Reserve, this waterfront area has walking trails and one of the island's most scenic beaches. *www.pc.gc.ca.*

Bennett Bay Kayaking. This outfitter rents kayaks and leads kayak day tours from mid-April through mid-October. *250/539–0864 www.bennettbaykayaking.com.*

Farmer's Market. On Saturdays between mid-May and mid-October, check out the Farmer's Market outside the Miners Bay Agricultural Hall. Open 10 to 1, it sells produce and crafts while local musicians entertain shoppers. *430 Fernhill Rd., Miners Bay.*

Japanese Garden. Built entirely by volunteers, this 1-acre garden at Dinner Bay Park honors the island's early Japanese settlers. It's about ½ mile south of the Village Bay ferry terminal. Admission is free. *Dinner Point Rd., Dinner Bay.*

Mt. Parke. A 45-minute hike up this 835-foot peak leads to the island's highest point and a stunning view of the mainland and other Gulf Islands. *Montrose Rd., off Fernhill Rd. www.crd.bc.ca/parks.*

Plumper Pass Lockup. Built in 1896, this former jail is now the minuscule Mayne Museum chronicling the island's history. *433 Fernhill Rd., Miners Bay 250/539–5286 Free July–Labor Day, Fri.–Mon. 10–2.*

Springwater Lodge. You can stop for a meal or a drink on the deck at this lodge, one of the province's oldest hotels. It's been operating since 1892. *400 Fernhill Rd., Miners Bay 250/539–5521 www.springwaterlodge.com.*

WHERE TO STAY

$$ HOTEL ★ **Mayne Island Resort & Spa.** Overlooking Bennett Bay and just steps from Mayne Island's best-loved beach, this chic modern resort enjoys a prime waterfront location. **Pros:** waterfront location; stylish decor; private cottages. **Cons:** steep drop to the water makes it unsuitable for small children. *Rooms from: C$129 494 Arbutus Dr., Mayne Island 250/539–3122, 866/539–5399 www.mayneislandresort.com 18 cottages, 8 rooms No meals.*

PENDER ISLAND

Just a few miles north of the U.S. border, Pender is actually two islands: North Pender and South Pender, divided by a canal and linked by a one-lane bridge. Most of the population of about 2,000 cluster on North Pender, whereas South Pender is largely forested and undeveloped. The Penders are blessed with beaches, boasting more than 30 public beach-access points.

There's no town on either island, but you can find groceries, a bakery, gas, a bank, pharmacy, and liquor store at North Pender's Driftwood Centre. A farmers' market runs on summer Saturdays at Pender Island Community Hall and crafts shops, studios, and galleries are open throughout the islands.

EXPLORING

Gowlland Point Park. The small pebble beach at Gowlland Point Park, at the end of Gowlland Point Road on South Pender, is one of the prettiest on the islands, with views across to Washington State. ✉ *Gowlland Point Rd.*

★ **Gulf Islands National Park Reserve.** Both North Pender and South Pender host sections of the Gulf Islands National Park Reserve. On South Pender a steep trail leads to the 800-foot summit of **Mt. Norman**, with its expansive ocean and island views. Trails start at Ainslie Road, Canal Road, and the Beaumont section of the park. For an easy walk in the woods, visit the delightfully named Enchanted Forest Park. ✉ *Spalding Rd.* ☎ *250/654–4000* 🌐 *www.pc.gc.ca/pn-np/bc/gulf/index.aspx.*

QUICK BITES

You can refuel before catching the ferry at The Stand (✉ *Otter Bay Ferry Terminal, Otter Bay Rd.* ☎ *250/629–3292*), a rustic take-out shack at the Otter Bay ferry terminal. The burgers—whether beef, venison, oyster, or veggie—are enormous, messy, and delicious.

Hope Bay. A waterview café, an artisans' co-op, and views to Saturna and Mayne islands are the draws at Hope Bay, a lovely cove on North Pender's eastern shore. ✉ *4301 Bedwell Harbour Rd., North Pender Island* ☎ *250/629–3166* 🌐 *www.hopebayrising.com.*

Morning Bay Vineyard & Estate Winery. You can sample a glass of Pinot Noir or Rosé on the terrace at Morning Bay Vineyard & Estate Winery, Pender's only winery. In early September, the winery hosts the one-day Winestock Music & Wine Festival. ✉ *6621 Harbour Hill Dr., North Pender Island* ☎ *250/629–8351* 🌐 *www.morningbay.ca* ⏲ *May–early Sept., Wed.–Sun. 10–5; early Sept.–Apr., Fri.–Sun. noon–5.*

Mortimer Spit. The sandy beach at Mortimer Spit is a sheltered spot for swimming and kayaking; it's near the bridge linking the two islands. ✉ *Mortimer Spit Rd., off Canal Rd., South Pender Island.*

Pender Islands Museum. This historic cottage resort on North Pender is now part of the Gulf Islands National Park Reserve. An easy 15-minute walk leads out to a tiny islet, and a 1908 farmhouse on the site houses the Pender Islands Museum. ✉ *2408 South Otter Bay Rd., North Pender Island* ☎ *250/629–6935* 🌐 *www.penderislandmuseum.org* 🎟 *Donations requested* ⏲ *July–Aug., weekends 10–4; Easter–June and Sept.–mid-Oct., weekends 1–4.*

WHERE TO STAY

$$$$ RESORT Fodor's Choice ★ **Poets Cove Resort & Spa.** One of the Gulf Islands' most well-appointed developments fills a secluded cove on South Pender. **Pros:** great views; family-friendly vibe; summer evening children's programs. **Cons:** 20-minute drive from the ferry. $ *Rooms from: C$309* ✉ *9801 Spalding Rd., South Pender Island* ☎ *250/629–2100, 888/512–7638* 🌐 *www.poetscove.com* 22 *rooms, 15 cottages, 9 villas* 🍽 *No meals.*

8

SATURNA ISLAND

With just 300 residents, remote Saturna Island is taken up largely by a section of the Gulf Islands National Park Reserve and is a prime spot for hiking, kayaking, and beachcombing. Said to be the only island whose population is campaigning for less ferry service, Saturna usually takes two ferries to reach. It has no bank or pharmacy but does have an ATM machine, pub, a general store, and a winery.

EXPLORING

Saturna Island Family Estate Winery. When you're visiting Saturna Island, make sure to stop at Saturna Island Family Estate Winery, where between May and October you can lunch on a terrace overlooking the vineyards and the sea. ✉ *8 Quarry Trail, Saturna Island* ☎ *250/539–3521, 877/918–3388.*

Whistler, the Okanagan, and Tofino and the Pacific Rim

WORD OF MOUTH

"In Whistler, taking the gondola to the top contrasts greatly from the . . . village below because of its lack of development and the feel of being in the alpine. In mid-July you might even get some alpine flowers blooming (the purple lupines and yellow daisies are pretty incredible)."

—BC_Robyn

WELCOME TO WHISTLER, THE OKANAGAN, AND TOFINO AND THE PACIFIC RIM

TOP REASONS TO GO

★ **Ski Whistler and Blackcomb:** With more than 8,000 acres of skiing terrain, combined with four seasons of adventure and a cosmopolitan village full of amenities, this is one of North America's premier mountain resorts.

★ **Getting to Whistler:** The Sea-to-Sky Highway, one of North America's most scenic highways, gets you from Vancouver to Whistler in about two hours.

★ **Sample Okanagan Wines:** You might not have heard of them yet, but the wineries of the Okanagan Valley are producing some highly acclaimed wines and earning top honors in international circles; small batches mean they don't often make their way to U.S. wine stores.

★ **Storm-watching in Tofino:** Its beaches and rain forests make Tofino one of B.C.'s most sublime warm-weather environments; come November, the rampant fury of its coastal storms is an even more extraordinary experience.

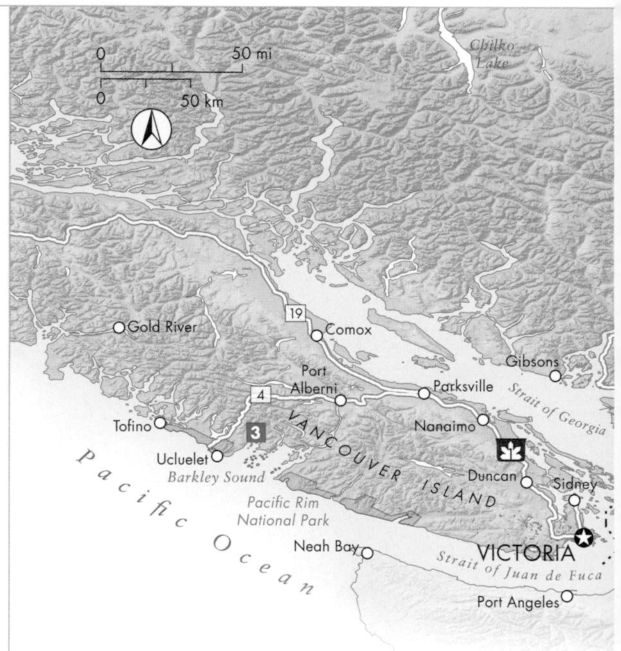

1 Whistler. Just 120 km (75 miles) north of Vancouver, Whistler is easy to get to, and the scenery on the way up will take your breath away. This alpine paradise holds thrills for skiers and nonskiers alike. Attractions like the Squamish-Lil'Wat Centre is just one of the lasting legacies of the 2010 Winter Olympics.

2 The Okanagan Valley. Long known as the fruit-growing capital of Canada, the Okanagan has also become a significant wine-producing area. The Okanagan is about a five-hour drive from Vancouver. Within the Okanagan region, the valley is about 174 km (108 miles) from the gateway town of Vernon, just north of Kelowna, to Osoyoos, near the U.S. border.

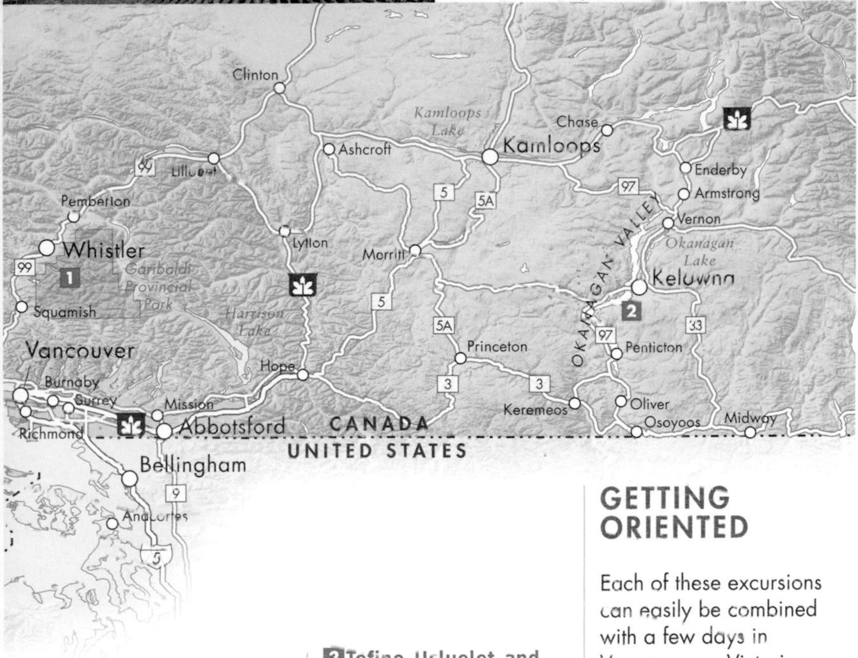

9

GETTING ORIENTED

Each of these excursions can easily be combined with a few days in Vancouver or Victoria. Heading up to Whistler takes only a couple of hours, but traveling by car to the Okanagan or Tofino requires more of a commitment. All three trips promise tremendous scenery and ample places to pause. Taking the BC Ferries to Nanaimo en route to Tofino offers an added bonus of vistas and adventure with a real chance of seeing bald eagles, seals, and whales.

3 Tofino, Ucluelet, and the Pacific Rim. The stretch of open coast along the western edge of Vancouver Island has turned winter storm-watching into an art. And the summers here sparkle. Tofino and Ucluelet are the tourism-oriented towns at either end of the Pacific Rim National Park Reserve.

WHISTLER

Fodor's Choice ★ *120 km (75 miles) north of Vancouver, 58 km (36 miles) north of Squamish.*

With two breathtaking mountains—Whistler and Blackcomb—enviable skiing conditions, championship golf courses, more than 200 shops, 90 restaurants and bars, an array of accommodations, spas, hiking trails, and what experts consider the best mountain-bike park in the world, it's no surprise that Whistler consistently ranks as the top ski resort in North America.

Updated by Chris McBeath

Back in the early 1960s, when Whistler's early visionaries designed the ski resort as a car-free village, they had the 1968 Winter Olympics in mind. That dream was finally realized four decades later when the resort hosted the 2010 Winter Olympic Games. With that came the widening of Highway 99 and other Olympic-size benefits, such as the Squamish-Lil'Wat Centre, a cultural focal point for these proud First Nations who have occupied and explored this wilderness region for millennia.

Whistler Resort, which includes Whistler and Blackcomb mountains, has the largest ski area and two of the longest vertical drops on the continent, as well as one of the world's most advanced lift systems. But there's more to Whistler than skiing and snowboarding; each winter people flow into the resort with no intention of riding a chairlift, preferring to explore the many spas, shops, and restaurants, as well as the varied nightlife. During the rest of the year, they come to play four championship golf courses, race down the world's largest downhill bike park, and hike the hundreds of miles of trails. Then there's horseback riding along mountain ridges, zip-lining across Fitzsimmons Valley, or hopping aboard a helicopter ride to have lunch on one of dozens of nearby glaciers.

The drive into the Coast Mountains from Vancouver is a stunning sampler of mainland British Columbia. You'll follow the Sea-to Sky Highway (Highway 99) past fjordlike Howe Sound, through the historic mining community of Britannia Beach, past the logging town of Squamish, and into Whistler Resort. Once you're in Whistler, you don't really need a car; anywhere you want to go within the resort is reachable by foot or a free shuttle bus. Parking lots ring the village, although as a hotel guest, you may have access to coveted (and often pricey) underground parking.

The bases of Whistler and Blackcomb mountains are just at the village edge. In fact, you can ski right to the door of the many slope-side hotels and condos, though you then miss the fun of the après-ski parade through the pedestrian-only village, a bold urban-design decision that has resulted in an incredibly accessible resort. Families take to the Village Stroll in search of Cows Ice Cream and its racks of novelty, bovine-themed T-shirts. Couples shop for engagement rings or the latest Roots sportswear styles. Skiers and snowboarders shuffle through the crowd, leaning their skis and boards against the buildings to dip into the vibrant après-ski scene on a dozen outdoor heated patios.

The Village warren continues to expand, and Village North (or Marketplace) has all but been absorbed. The petit Upper Village—Blackcomb Mountain's base—remains somewhat isolated, but a wonderful footpath connects the two areas. Whistler Creekside, located 10 minutes south on Highway 99, is the latest shopping and dining development.

Against this backdrop, Whistler has also been building its identity as a progressive, livable, and sustainably green city, with programs for accessible housing and strong schools. Though only 8% of the 100 square miles that comprise Whistler is designated for development, North America's premier four-season resort continues to grow, especially now that the world has visited during the 2010 Winter Games.

PLANNING

WHEN TO GO

Whistler teems with partying Vancouverites, especially during the off-season. Three days provide plenty of time for zipping, skiing, biking, or whatever your alpine adventure may be.

But you'll quickly discover that it's a very happening place almost every day, with open-air concerts throughout the summer and weekly shows in winter with the area's best skiers and riders jumping through blazing rings of fire.

FESTIVALS

FEB.: With **Winterpride Whistler** (*www.gaywhistler.com*), the resort heats up for a week with naughty nightlife, fine dining, fabulous après-ski, and slope-side fun.

APR.: The raucous **Telus World Ski & Snowboard Festival** (*www.whistler.com*) end-of-the-season bash fills 10 days with music, arts, fashion shows, and extreme sports.

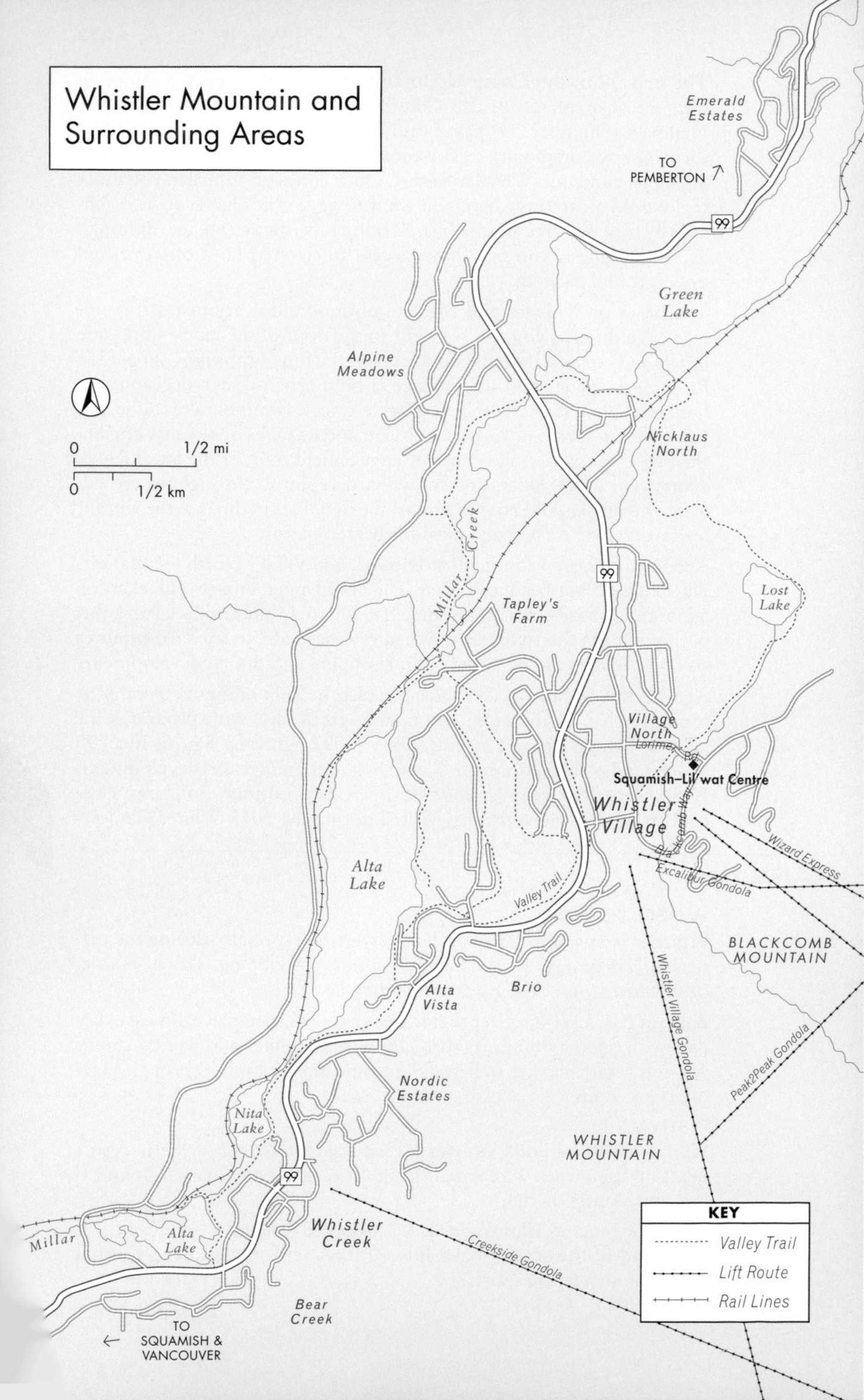

Whistler Mountain and Surrounding Areas
Emerald Estates
TO PEMBERTON
99
Green Lake
Alpine Meadows
0
1/2 mi
0
1/2 km
Nicklaus North
Millar Creek
Tapley's Farm
Lost Lake
Village North
Lorimer Rd.
Squamish–Lil'wat Centre
Whistler Village
Blackcomb Way
Wizard Express
Excalibur Gondola
Alta Lake
Valley Trail
BLACKCOMB MOUNTAIN
Alta Vista
Brio
Whistler Village Gondola
Peak2Peak Gondola
Nordic Estates
Nita Lake
WHISTLER MOUNTAIN
Millar
Alta Lake
Whistler Creek
Creekside Gondola
KEY
Valley Trail
Lift Route
Rail Lines
Bear Creek
TO SQUAMISH & VANCOUVER

MAY: Fitness demonstrations, health seminars, and other events focus on wellness at **Whistler Wellness Week** (🌐 *www.whistlerwellness.com*).

JULY: More than 100 daredevil racers from all over the world hurtle down S-bends at breakneck speeds during **Whistler Longboard Festival** (🌐 *www.whistlerlongboard.com*).

AUG.: The annual **Kokanee Crankworx** (🌐 *www.crankworx.com*) mountain-bike festival showcases the sport's boldest and most talented athletes as they whip down double black-diamond runs; there are also daily concerts and a huge downhill biking scene.

NOV.: There's a little bit of everything at **Cornucopia** (🌐 *www.whistlercornucopia.com*), an annual festival for foodies and oenophiles. The grand gala do is a veritable who's who in the Pacific Northwest wine industry.

DEC.: The annual **Whistler Film Festival** (🌐 *www.whistlerfilmfestival.com*) features world premieres from top directors, industry events, and parties, all with a Canadian focus.

GETTING HERE AND AROUND

Just 120 km (75 miles) north of Vancouver on Highway 99 (Sea-to-Sky Highway), Whistler is easy to get to from Vancouver, depending on your budget. You won't need a car once you're here; even if you choose to stay outside the village, you can get around easily with public shuttle buses or taxis. The closest airport is Vancouver International Airport, about 135 km (84 miles) away.

BUS TRAVEL

Perimeter Whistler Express has daily bus service to Whistler from Vancouver International Airport and from many Vancouver hotels (nine times a day in ski season, five times a day in summer). Fares start at C$80 one way, and reservations are recommended. Greyhound Canada has service to Whistler from downtown Vancouver and from Vancouver Airport. Departing from Vancouver, the Snow Bus is a winter-only luxury coach with snacks and movies. Whistler Direct Shuttle provides year-round service from the airport.

Bus Info Greyhound Canada ☎ *604/482–8747, 800/661–8747* 🌐 *www.greyhound.ca.* **Perimeter Whistler Express** ☎ *604/266–5386, 877/317–7788* 🌐 *www.perimeterbus.com.* **Snow Bus** ☎ *888/794–5551* 🌐 *www.snowbus.ca.* **Whistler Direct Shuttle** ☎ *888/405–2410* 🌐 *www.whistlerdirectshuttle.com.*

CAR TRAVEL

Driving from Vancouver to Whistler takes approximately two hours along the scenic Sea-to-Sky Highway (aka Highway 99). It's recommended to check weather conditions during the winter season; in spite of considerable improvements for the Olympics, rockslides still occur and can cause delays.

AIR TRAVEL

If you've got the money, travel in style. Glacier Air Tours has charter helicopter and airplane service between Whistler and Vancouver International Airport or Vancouver Harbour for anywhere from C$230 to C$3,000. West Coast Air connects Victoria and Whistler, June through September for C$288. Whistler Air runs two daily flights between Vancouver's Coal Harbour and the Whistler area from mid-May to early October; the company also partners with Rocky Mountaineer's Whistler Mountaineer service to offer fly-rail packages for around C$320.

Air Travel Info Glacier Air ☎ *800/208-4421* 🌐 *www.glacierair.com.* **Westcoast Air** ☎ *800/665-0212* 🌐 *www.westcoastair.com.* **Whistler Air** ☎ *888/806-2299* 🌐 *www.whistlerair.ca.*

LIMO TRAVEL

LimoJet Gold runs a stretch limo service from Vancouver International Airport to Whistler for C$320 per trip. Pearl International Limousine Service has limos, sedans, and 10-passenger vans—all equipped with blankets, pillows, bottled water, and videos so you can enjoy the ride. Rates start at about C$300. Vancouver All-Terrain Adventures charters four-wheel drives from Vancouver International or downtown Vancouver to Whistler. Vehicles travel in all weather and will stop for sightseeing. The cost starts at C$350 one way.

Limo Info Limojet Gold Limousine Services ☎ *604/273-1331, 800/278-8742* 🌐 *www.limojetgold.com.* **Pearl International Limousine Service** ☎ *604/732-7897, 877/977-3275* 🌐 *www.pearllimousine.com.* **Vancouver All-Terrain Adventures** ☎ *778/371-7830, 888/754-5601* 🌐 *www.all-terrain.com.*

TAXI TRAVEL

For a cab in the Whistler area call Whistler Taxi. Service is available around the clock.

Contacts Whistler Taxi ☎ *604/938-3333* 🌐 *www.whistlertaxi.com.*

TRAIN TRAVEL

The Whistler Mountaineer is a three-hour, premier train journey from North Vancouver to Whistler. It's an "experience" train trip, providing passengers with commentary and refreshments while taking in the Sea-to-Sky's jaw-dropping scenery. The service runs May to September; fares start at C$235 round-trip, including bus transfers from downtown to North Vancouver.

Train Info Whistler Mountaineer ☎ *888/687-7245*
🌐 *www.rockymountaineer.com.*

WAVE TRAVEL

The Whistler and Valley Express (WAVE) transit system operates a free, year-round public-transit system within Whistler village, as well as paid public transit throughout the Valley and north to Pemberton.

Transportation Contacts BC Transit ☎ *604/932-4020* 🌐 *www.bctransit.com.*

VISITOR INFORMATION

Contacts Tourism Whistler ☎ *800/944-7853* 🌐 *www.whistler.com.*
Whistler Visitor Information and Activity Center ✉ *4010 Whistler Way, Whistler* ☎ *604/932-0606* 🌐 *www.whistler.com.*

ON-MOUNTAIN EATING OPTIONS

Like the world's best ski resorts, Whistler has a great variety of on-mountain eating options. You'll find them all listed on the trail/resort map, but these are the key ones to know about.

Both Whistler and Blackcomb have a day lodge, accessible from the gondola, with a cafeteria that serves an array of soup, sandwich, and hot food options. At the other end of the spectrum, there is fine dining at Christine's in Blackcomb's Rendezvous day lodge and at Steep's in Whistler's Roundhouse. Should you be moving about on one plank or two, don't miss Whistler's Harmony Hut and Blackcomb's Horstman Hut for spectacular views, chili, and other comfort foods. In-the-know skiers head to the Glacier Creek Lodge for a shorter lunch line.

EXPLORING

Squamish-Lil'wat Centre. A collaborative project of the neighboring Squamish Nation and Lil'wat Nation, this cultural center is designed to share and preserve the heritage and traditions of these two peoples. The concrete, cedar, and fir structure melds the longhouse concept of the coastal Squamish people with the traditional Lil'wat pit house. Inside, carvings adorn the walls and displays of art, artifacts, and tools reveal the similarities and differences of the cultures. Try to catch one of the regularly scheduled story-telling sessions. The on site café, which serves contemporary food with a First Nations twist—think Lil'wat venison chili, a "mountain hoagie" with bison salami and wild-boar prosciutto, or a "Caesar" salad of romaine and Parmesan with bannock croutons—is worth a visit itself. ✉ *4584 Blackcomb Way, Whistler* ☎ *866/441–7522* 🌐 *www.slcc.ca* 🎫 *C$18* ⏲ *Daily 9:30–5.*

9

WHERE TO EAT

When Vancouver's celebrity chefs decided to spread their wings and fly out of town, Whistler provided the logical destination. Today, some of the top ski-resort restaurants in the world take advantage of the growing locavore or "slow food" movement—as showcased during four months of Sunday farmers' markets and organic bounty—to provide diners with a surprising array of Northwest cuisine. Foodies will especially enjoy Whistler's Cornucopia Festival, which showcases culinary talents and B.C. wineries every November.

While no one would ever mistake Whistler for a thrifty resort, there are plenty of sandwich and coffee shops scattered around the village. There is also a full-scale grocery store should you land a room with a kitchen.

Prices in the reviews are the average cost of a main course at dinner or, if dinner is not served, at lunch.

$$$$ CONTEMPORARY ★ ✕ **Araxi.** Terra-cotta tiles, well-chosen antiques, and original artwork create a vibrantly chic atmosphere for what has always been one of Whistler's top fine-dining restaurants. Local farmers grow produce exclusively for Araxi's chef, who also makes good use of regional

cheeses, game, and fish. The food is fresh and innovative, best described as Pacific Northwest cuisine with a nod to Italy. Seafood is a specialty, so while you can certainly order a superbly prepared beef tenderloin, it's dishes like alder-smoked arctic char or tagliatelle with clams, scallops, and mussels that steal the show. The multitier seafood tower is a must-try for seafoodies who love to graze and share. Wine aficionados take note: the wine list is 27 pages long. A heated patio is open in summer, and the lounge is a popular après-ski spot. *Average main: C$32* *4222 Village Sq.* *604/932–4540* *www.araxi.com* *Reservations essential* *No lunch Oct.–May.*

$$$$ PACIFIC NORTHWEST Fodor's Choice ★

Bearfoot Bistro. As one of Whistler's top destination restaurants, this elegant bistro never fails to impress. The French-inspired cuisine means that the menu choices, which change daily depending on the availabilty of local products, may include anything from a rack of wild caribou with sweet corn to pepper-crusted elk carpaccio to steamed Dungeness crab with garlic herbed butter. If everything looks too delicious to decide, the chef will customize a tasting menu according to your preferences. Allow the sommelier do the wine pairings for a really masterful meal. *Average main: C$33* *4121 Village Green* *604/932–3433* *www.bearfootbistro.com* *No lunch.*

$$ CANADIAN

Christine's on Blackcomb Mountain. On-mountain dining is surprisingly accessible to those without skis. On Blackcomb Mountain, there's Christine's, offering classic dishes such as a tender osso bucco, or a showy salad with roasted asparagus with candied pecans. The place is also a hot spot for weekend brunch. Once accessible only to skiers, now you can get here via the gondola from Whistler. Because of this, most patrons tend to be decked out in full snow gear. Christine's is open in summer. *Average main: C$20* *Rendezvous Lodge, Blackcomb Mountain* *604/938–7437* *www.whistlerblackcomb.com* *Lunch only.*

$$ CANADIAN

Elements. Nestled in the Summit Lodge, Elements is consistently ranked by locals as having the best tapas in the area. It's a hip eatery where animated thirtysomethings and jet-setting families with young children occupy the comfy suede banquettes and booths. The draw here is the open-concept kitchen that produces locally inspired small plates that are perfect for sharing. Steamed Salt Spring Island mussels with lemongrass, kaffir lime, and coconut green curry are yummy, as are the spicy chicken drumsticks and the signature bruschetta. Pair them with fine Canadian wines. The restaurant is open for breakfast, too, when several variations of eggs Benedict are the stars. *Average main: C$15* *Summit Lodge, 4359 Main St.* *604/932–5569* *www.elementswhistler.com.*

$ BAKERY

Hot Buns Bakery. It's as if this sweet spot has been transported from a rural French town, with its stone floors, vintage skis hanging from the ceiling, and simple wooden tables and chairs. But the reason to come here is not the look of the place: it serves the best *pain au chocolat,* lattes, and crepes in town. And their cinnamon buns? Delicious. Choose a savory Tex-Mex crepe for a quick lunch or a decadent pear-and-chocolate crepe to satisfy your après-ski sweet tooth. Not a bad way to start, or end, the day. The address is a bit misleading, because the main entrance is on Sunrise Alley, behind La Brasserie Des Artistes. *Average main: C$8 4232 Village Stroll 604/932–6883 www.hotbuns.moonfruit.com.*

$$$$ STEAKHOUSE **Hy's Steakhouse.** If beef's your passion, then you don't get much better than Hy's, a hardcore steakhouse that's famous for the quality of its sirloins, filet mignons, porterhouses, and T-bones. Roasted primed rib comes with Yorkshire pudding, and the combos are accompanied by king crab or lobster. This is he-man food, although the menu will appeal to everyone, even vegetarians. The place is dark, moody, and just right for a candlelight dinner, a secret rendevous, or a more formal affair. Service is impeccable and discreet. *Average main: C$45 Delta Whistler Village Suites, 4308 Main St. 604/905–5555 www.hyssteakhouse.com.*

$$ EUROPEAN **La Brasserie des Artistes.** "The Brass," as it's known, has one of the area's best patios, situated in the square where people-watching is as entertaining as the street entertainers and free concerts. With this kind of location the food doesn't have to be outstanding, but it offers reasonably priced bistro fare, from burgers to steaks. It opens for breakfast with an assortment of egg dishes and keeps going until the après-ski crowd finally departs around midnight. As popular as the place is, tables turn over quickly so getting a seat doesn't take long. *Average main: C$20 4232 Village Stroll 604/932–3569 www.labrass.moonfruit.com.*

$$$ ITALIAN **Quattro at Whistler.** Vancouverites in search of fine Italian fare flock here for warming après-ski meals. The dining room exudes a whimsical Venetian style with ornamental ironwork, picturesque tiles, and hand-painted chandeliers. For a splurge try *L'Abbuffata,* a five-course Roman feast (C$70) that comes on family-size platters meant for sharing. Other popular dishes include spaghetti *pescatore* (with prawns, scallops, and clams), pistachio-crusted sea bass, pressed cornish game hen, and a plate of five pastas for two to share (C$25). The cellar is filled with 900 wine varieties and an impressive Grappa selection. *Average main: C$30 4319 Main St. 604/905–4844 www.quattrorestaurants.com No lunch.*

9

$$$$ SEAFOOD ★ **Rim Rock Café.** About two miles south of the village, this restaurant is a local favorite as much for its cozy, unpretentious dining room as for its great seafood. If deciding on only one item is hard, why not go for the samplers: the Rim Rock Trio combines sea bass in an almond-ginger crust, grilled prawns, and rare ahi tuna marinated in soya, sake, and mirin. Although seafood takes precedence on the menu—try the raw oysters with champagne—Alberta beef and local game will satisfy carnivores. If you want a booth or a coveted table near the fireplace, dine on the early side or make a reservation. Otherwise, be prepared to wait. *Average main: C$42 2117 Whistler Rd. 604/932–5565, 877/932–5589 www.rimrockwhistler.com No lunch.*

$$ PACIFIC NORTHWEST **Steeps on Whistler Mountain.** Although it's atop Whistler Mountain, you're likely to see as many non-skiers as skiers in the crowd. That's because Steeps is located inside the enormous Roundhouse Lodge at the top of Whistler Village Gondola, and lots of the visitors are simply sightseers. While other mountain dining outlets tend to cater to the

grab-and-go crowd, Steeps is a stay-a-while, full-service dining affair offering lots of West Coast favorites like smoked salmon chowder and Dungeness crabcakes. *Average main: C$20 Roundhouse Lodge, Whistler Mountain 604/905–2379 www.whistler-blackcomb.com.*

$$ JAPANESE ★ **Sushi Village.** If you don't equate sushi with social buzz, then you haven't been to Sushi Village, one of Whistler's perennial hot spots for everything from après-ski to late-night dining. The chef's choice sashimi is a favorite, as are the dozen different house special rolls, including one tasty combination of shrimp tempura, avocado, scallop, and salmon. There are also teriyaki dinners and hot pots served family-style. A score of sakes (and sake margaritas) accentuate the festive environment. Phoning ahead for take-out orders lets you jump the line. *Average main: C$20 4272 Mountain Sq. 604/932–3330 www.sushivillage.com.*

WHERE TO STAY

For expanded hotel reviews, visit Fodors.com.

Price categories are based on January–April ski-season rates; prices will be higher during Christmas and school breaks, but lower in summer and considerably lower in the shoulder seasons. Minimum stays during all holidays are pretty much the rule. Also, Whistler Village has some serious nightlife: if peace and quiet are important to you, ask for a room away from the main pedestrian thoroughfares, book in the Upper Village, or stay in one of the residential neighborhoods outside the village.

Prices in the reviews are the lowest cost of a standard double room in high season.

Whistler Central Reservations. Tourism Whistler is a good source for information on lodging and often features online discounts at selected hotels. *604/932–4222, 800/944–7853 www.whistler.com.*

$$$$ HOTEL **Adara Hotel.** Whistler's only true boutique hotel is the Adara, sister to Vancouver's Opus Hotel and equally as hip. **Pros:** free boxed breakfast in winter; free Wi-Fi; pet-friendly. **Cons:** no on-site restaurant; no bathtubs, just showers. *Rooms from: C$260 866/502–3272, 866/502–3272 www.adarahotel.com 20 rooms, 21 suites No meals.*

$$$$ HOTEL **Delta Whistler Village Suites.** Not only is the Southwestern-style decor warm and inviting, the apartment-size studio and one- and two-bedroom suites are great choices for families. **Pros:** central location; nice mountain views; free ski and bike storage. **Cons:** rooms are small; some street noise; high parking fee. *Rooms from: C$300 4308 Main St. 416/874–2000, 888/299–3987 www.deltahotels.com/whistler 225 suites No meals.*

$$$$ HOTEL Fodor's Choice ★ **Fairmont Château Whistler Resort.** Just steps from the Blackcomb ski lifts, this imposing-looking fortress is a self-contained, ski-in, ski-out resort-within-a-resort with its own shopping arcade, golf course, and impressive spa. **Pros:** ski-in and ski-out option; a terrific spa; shopping and golf on-site. **Cons:** bustling with guests and kids; not particularly intimate. *Rooms from: C$550 4599 Château Blvd. 604/938–8000, 800/257–7544 www.fairmont.com 550 rooms, 56 suites No meals.*

$$$$ HOTEL Fodor's Choice ★ **Four Seasons Resort Whistler.** This plush nine story hotel gives alpine chic a new twist with warm earth tones and wood interiors, big leather chairs beside the fireplace in the lobby, and amazingly spacious rooms. **Pros:** top-notch spa; great fitness classes; free village shuttles. **Cons:** a long walk to restaurants and nightlife. *Rooms from: C$525 4591 Blackcomb Way, Upper Village 604/935–3455, 888/935–2460 www.fourseasons.com/whistler 273 studios and suites, 3 town homes No meals.*

$$$$ RESORT **Hilton Whistler Resort.** With a wealth of family-friendly facilities, this resort hotel sits at the base of the Whistler and Blackcomb gondolas. **Pros:** steps from the chairlift; huge rooms; pet friendly. **Cons:** small spa; some unremarkable street views. *Rooms from: C$275 4050 Whistler Way 604/932–1982, 806/798–0002 www.hiltonwhistler.com 287 rooms, 24 suites No meals.*

$$$$ HOTEL ★ **Nita Lake Lodge.** Within easy reach of the lifts and amenities of Whistler Creekside, this lovely lodge is Whistler's only lakefront hotel, so it feels a world away from the madding crowd. **Pros:** unique lake location; laid-back lounge; next door to the train station. **Cons:** shuttle required to access slopes. *Rooms from: C$450 2131 Lake Placid Rd. 604/966–5700, 888/755–6482 www.nitalakelodge.com 37 studios, 38 suites, 2 villas Breakfast.*

$$$$ HOTEL **Pan Pacific Whistler Mountainside.** With the very lively Dubh Linn Gate Old Irish Pub on the premises, this hotel tends to attract the younger set, most of whom seem to spend their time on the large deck cheering on skiers as they reach the bottom of the slope. **Pros:** about as close to the ski lift as you can get; on-site pub at your door. **Cons:** gets booked up quickly; common areas can get noisy. *Rooms from: C$500 4320 Sundial Crescent 604/905–2999 www.panpacific.com 120 rooms No meals.*

$$$$ HOTEL **Pan Pacific Whistler Village Centre.** Although it bills itself as an all-suites boutique hotel, the Pan Pacific feels more like a beautiful apartment building with a fabulous concierge service. **Pros:** extraordinarily friendly staff; free breakfast buffet; central location. **Cons:** loud ground-floor rooms; limited services. *Rooms from: C$500 4299 Blackcomb Way 604/905–2999, 888/905–9995 www.panpacific.com 82 rooms Breakfast.*

$$$$ HOTEL **Summit Lodge & Spa.** Tucked away in a quiet part of the village, this friendly boutique hotel offers gracious service and one of the area's best values in luxury accommodations. **Pros:** quiet rooms; quality spa; free shuttle to the Village Gondola. **Cons:** small parking spots; lots of pets (and their dander), so it's not recommended for those with allergies. *Rooms from: C$265 4359 Main St. 604/932–2778, 888/913–8811 www.summitlodge.com 75 rooms, 6 suites Breakfast.*

$$$$ HOTEL **The Westin Resort & Spa.** This luxury hotel has a prime location on the edge of the village and many upscale amenities. **Pros:** boot-warming services; quiet yet central location; excellent spa. **Cons:** expensive extras, especially the parking. *Rooms from: C$525 4090 Whistler Way 604/905–5000, 888/634–5577 www.westinwhistler.com 419 suites No meals.*

SPORTS AND THE OUTDOORS

> **WORD OF MOUTH**
>
> "Whistler: the highlight has to be the trip on the cable cars up the mountain. The "peak to peak" is amazing and the views on a clear day are fantastic."
>
> —Maria_H

Adventurers pour into Whistler during every season and from every corner of the world. In winter, you'll meet Australian and New Zealander skiers and guides who follow the snows around the globe; in summer there are sun-baked guides who chase the warm months to lead white-water rafting or mountain-biking excursions. These globe-trotters demonstrate how Whistler's outdoor sports culture now operates on a global, all-season scale.

The staging of sliding (bobsled, luge, skeleton) and alpine and cross-country skiing events in Whistler during the Olympic Games has yielded a host of opportunities for the adventurous, including a world-class cross-country center (and lodge) operated by the Whistler Legacies Society. The sliding center remains as a professional training facility (the ice is rumored to be the fastest on the planet), as well as a public venue for those who've always wanted to experience the 100 km (62 miles) per hour thrill of a sliding sport. The mountains changed little after the games, other than having some commemorative signage to indicate what happened where.

Hikers and anglers, downhill and touring cyclists, free skiers and ice climbers, kayakers and golfers—there really is something for everyone here. Whistler and Blackcomb mountains are the reason why most people are here, but the immediate environs are equally compelling. Garibaldi Provincial Park, adjacent to the Whistler area, is a 78,000-acre park with dense mountainous forests splashed with hospitable lakes and streams for fishing and kayaking. At Alta Lake, you'll see clusters of windsurfers weaving across the surface, dodging canoeists. At nearby Squamish, the Stawamus Chief, the second largest granite monolith in the world behind Gibraltar, attracts serious rock climbers, although there are milder climbs for novices.

Tourism Whistler. Whether online or in person, Tourism Whistler has information on all aspects of the resort. It also runs an online reservation center for accommodations, guides, and virtually anything else you might need. ✉ *4010 Whistler Way, Whistler* ☎ *800/944–7853* 🌐 *www.whistler.com.*

Whistler Visitor Information and Activity Center. A good first stop for most Whistler outdoor activities, here's where to pick up hiking, biking, and cross-country maps or find out about equipment rentals. They'll help organize your stay and even book activities. ✉ *4010 Whistler Way* ☎ *800/944–7853* 🌐 *www.whistler.com.*

BIKING AND HIKING

The 28-km (45-mile) paved, car-free Valley Trail links the village to lakeside beaches and scenic picnic areas. For more challenging routes, ski lifts whisk hikers and bikers up to the alpine, where marked trails

CLOSE UP

Mountain Biking

Ski resorts everywhere have latched onto the popularity of downhill biking. Whistler-Blackcomb were not only among the first to realize the potential of converting ski runs to fat-tire trails, they also established the best downhill-biking center in the world. Located on lower Whistler Mountain, the trails—more than 200 km (124 miles) of them—are marked green through double diamond and groomed with as much care as their winter counterparts.

Riding custom bikes designed specifically for the Whistler terrain, cyclists bomb down the single-track trails, staying high on the steeply banked turns and taking air on the many tables and jumps. Expert riders might add 30-foot rock drops, leaps over streambeds, and 100-foot platform bridges to their brake-free sprints through the forest. Beginners can find plenty of comfortable dirt lanes to follow, though, and you can keep your fingers ready at the hydraulic brake should the speed become uncomfortable. After their first taste of the sport, most novice riders can't wait to sit back on the specially designed chairlift, transition onto the blue terrain, invite a few bumps, and maybe grab some air before the day is through. Downhill biking provides pure, if muddy, adrenaline-fueled bliss.

Whistler Mountain Bike Park, with experienced instructors, is a great place to learn how to downhill bike.

are graded by difficulty. The Peak Chair operates in summer to take hikers to the top of 7,160-foot-high Whistler. Among the most popular routes in the high alpine-trail network is the High Note Trail, an intermediate, 5-mile route with an elevation change of 1,132 feet and fabulous coastal mountain views. Trails are clearly marked— you take the lift up and choose whichever way you want to come down, just as if you were skiing. The casual stroller can also experience the top of the mountain on the **Peak2Peak Gondola**, the largest free-span gondola expanse in the world: it crosses Fitzsimmons Valley, connecting Whistler and Blackcomb mountains in just 11 minutes. Free trail maps are available from Tourism Whistler and the Whistler Activity Center.

Fanatyk Co. Ski and Cycle. This outfit rents bikes, arranges for repairs, and books bike tours. The staff is passionate and knowledgeable about pedals and wheels. ✉ *6–4433 Sundial Pl.* ☎ *604/938–9452* 🌐 *www.fanatykco.com.*

G1 Rentals. Biking enthusiasts, novice or expert, can get geared up with G1 Rentals, located inside the gondola building and next to the access point for the Whistler Mountain Bike Park. Here's where to find out about lessons, equipment, safety gear, and park passes. ✉ *Whistler Gondola Base* ☎ *604/905–2252* 🌐 *www.whistlerbike.com/rentals/rentals/index.htm.*

Whistler Gondola Base. When ski runs turn into trails for mountain biking, hiking, and walking, the Gondola Base is your base camp for renting a bike, picking up a free trail map, signing up for mountain-bike lessons or a sightseeing, hiking, or walking adventure; the options are aplenty here. ✉ *3434 Blackcomb Way* ☎ *604/905–2252, 604/967–8950.*

Whistler is well known as a ski destination, but many of the trails are also accessible in summer for mountain biking.

Whistler Alpine Guides. This year-round outfitter offers everything from avalanche safety courses in winter to mountaineering in summer. Among its signature activities is a hike named Via Ferrata, Italian for "Iron Way," so named because it's straight up a vertical pathway using fixed cables and metal-rung ladders. Surprisingly, no experience is necessary. Even older children can tackle it. Besides, it's great for bragging rights. ✉ *4314 Main St.* ☎ *604/938–9242* 🌐 *www.whistlerguides.com.*

Fodor's Choice ★ **Whistler Mountain Bike Park.** There's something for riders of every skill level at the Whistler Mountain Bike Park, from gentle rides that satisfy novices to steep rock faces that will challenge the experts. High-season rates range from C$48 for a day to C$139 for a three-day pass. The park is open mid-May to early October, and rentals are available. ✉ *Whistler Gondola Base* ☎ *604/967–8950* 🌐 *www.whistlerbike.com.*

BOATING

Canoe and kayak rentals are available at Alta Lake at both Lakeside Park and Wayside Park. A perfect place for canoeing is the River of Golden Dreams, which connects Alta Lake with Green Lake, both within a couple of miles of the village.

Canadian Outback Adventure Company. Contact this adventure specialist for guided river-rafting trips in the Whistler area. It has easygoing trips for families and those not wanting to tackle rollicking rapids. ☎ *604/921–7250, 800/565–8735* 🌐 *www.canadianoutback.com.*

Wedge Rafting. Specializing in whitewater rafting adventures, this company features two-hour to full-day tours on the Green, Birkenhead, or Elaho-Squamish rivers. Tours depart from the village and include all equipment and experienced guides. Adventures are suitable for all levels. ✉ *218-1293 Mountain Sq.* ☎ *604/932-7171, 888/932-5899* 🌐 *www.wedgerafting.com*

Whistler Jet Boating. Owner-operator Eric Pehota runs three daily excursions from May to September, cutting his jet boat through swirling channels and rushing rapids right up to the base of Nairn Falls. Like many Whistler guides, he operates via cell phone and through the activity center. Meeting points vary depending on water levels and weather. Trips are C$109. ✉ *Whistler Activity Center, 4010 Whistler Way* ☎ *604/905-9455, 604/894-5845* 🌐 *www.whistlerjetboating.com.*

SUMMER SKIING

Whistler is a summer hiking and outdoors destination, but dedicated skiers can still get their fix up on Horstman Glacier. Glacier skiing is recommended for intermediate to advanced skiers. One of the fun perks are the stares you'll get in the village as you walk around in your downhill gear in the summer temps.

CROSS-COUNTRY SKIING

The meandering trail around the Whistler Golf Course from the village is an ideal beginners' route. The 28 km (17 miles) of track-set trails that wind around scenic Lost Lake, Chateau Whistler Golf Course, the Nicklaus North Golf Course, and Green Lake include routes suitable for all levels; 4 km (2½ miles) of trails around Lost Lake are lighted for night skiing from 4 to 10 each evening. Trail maps and rental equipment are available in sports shops throughout the village.

Whistler X-Country Ski & Hike. Operating out of the Whistler Nordic Center at Whistler Olympic Park—the same place you can hitch a ride on a bobsleigh—Whistler Cross Country Ski & Hike and Coast Mountain Guides team up to give lessons or guided cross-country ski tours that are ideal for beginners and advanced skiers. The countryside is considered one of the largest Nordic recreational areas in North America. They have two Nordice-gear retail outlets: here and in Squamish. You can also connect with these folks via the Whistler Activity Centre. ✉ *Whistler Nordic Center at Olympic Park, 5 Callaghan Valley Rd., Whistler* ☎ *604/964-2454, 604/567-2232* 🌐 *www.whistlerski-hike.com.*

DOWNHILL SKIING AND SNOWBOARDING

Blackcomb and Whistler Mountains. When Whistler and Blackcomb Ski Resorts merged in 1997, they created a snow behemoth not seen in these parts since the last sighting of a yeti—the alpine version of the Northwest's infamous Sasquatch. Whistler had already garnered top-notch status, but the addition of Blackcomb left the competition buried in the powder. The numbers are staggering: 410 inches of annual snowfall, more than 8,000 skiable acres, 200 named runs, 12 alpine bowls, three glaciers, and the world's most advanced lift system. Point yourself downward on Blackcomb and you can ski or snowboard for a mile from top to bottom. And there are lots of ways to get to the top, either via the Whistler Village, Creekside, or Blackcomb Excalibur gondolas or by taking one of several chairs from the base up the mountain.

According to the locals, many of whom are world-class competitors, picking the day's mountain depends on conditions, time of day, and time of year. While most residents swear by Whistler's bowls and steeps, some prefer the long glade runs and top terrain park of Blackcomb. You can do both in the same day, thanks to the Peak 2 Peak Gondola, which whisks riders along the 2.7-mile journey in just 11 minutes. ✉ *4545 Blackcomb Way* ☎ *604/932–3434, 800/766–0449* 🌐 *www.whistlerblackcomb.com.*

Ultimate Ski Adventures. Whether your goal is to gain confidence and control on the runs or to tackle the best terrain the mountain has to offer, these folks will show you how with one-on-one instruction or in small groups. ✉ *7273 Fitzsimmons Rd. S* ☎ *604/263–2390* 🌐 *www.ultimateski.com.*

WHY DO BEGINNERS LOVE WHISTLER?

For a primer on the ski facilities, drop by the resort's free Whistler Welcome Night, held at 6:30 every Sunday evening during ski season at the base of the village gondolas. First-timers to Whistler, whether beginners or experienced skiers or snowboarders, may want to try Ski or Ride Esprit. Run by the resort, these three- to four-day programs combine ski or snowboarding lessons, après-ski activities, and an insider's guide to the mountains.

Whistler Alpine Guides Bureau. These expert mountain guides offer group tours, instructional clinics, and customized one-on-one trips to get you shredding untouched backcountry powder. ✉ *19–4314 Main St.* ☎ *604/938–9242* 🌐 *www.whistlerguides.com.*

Whistler/Blackcomb Hi Performance Rentals. Equipment rentals, including some of the best brands on the market, are geared toward intermediate and advanced skiers. It has several outlets in the village as well as at the Whistler gondola base. ✉ *3434 Blackcomb Way* ☎ *604/905–2252* 🌐 *www.whistlerblackcomb.com.*

Fodor's Choice ★ **Whistler/Blackcomb Ski and Snowboard School.** The school offers lessons for skiers and snowboarders of all levels. Whistler Kids remains one of the best children's ski schools anywhere. ✉ *4545 Blackcomb Way* ☎ *604/967–8950, 800/766–0449* 🌐 *www.whistlerblackcomb.com.*

FISHING

Tourists first developed this region for the fishing. All five area lakes—Alta, Alpha, Lost, Green, Nita—are stocked with trout.

Whistler Fly Fishing. These fly-fishing specialists target five species of Pacific salmon, steelhead, trout, and char on dozens of rivers and lakes in the area. They take care of all the details including equipment, licenses, and transportation. The store is jam-packed with tackle, lures, and angling gear. ✉ *117–4368 Main St.* ☎ *604/932–7221, 888/822–3474* 🌐 *www.whistlerflyfishing.com.*

One of the reasons Whistler is so popular is because it's great for avid skiiers, and beginners, too!

GOLF

Few visitors associate Whistler with golf but the four championship courses vie with some of the best in the Pacific Northwest. Golf season in Whistler runs from May through October; greens fees range from C$99 to C$235.

Golf Whistler. You can arrange advance tee-time bookings through Golf Whistler, an online service that also features last-minute specials and accommodation packages. ☎ *866/723–2747* ⊕ *www.golfwhistler.com.*

9

GOLF CLUBS AND COURSES

Fodor's Choice ★ **Big Sky Golf and Country Club.** Facing some impressive glaciers, this links-style course follows the Green River. Located 30 minutes north of Whistler, Big Sky sits at the base of 8,000-foor Mt. Curie. It's a favorite with locals, and for good reason. Check out the imaginative metal sculptures along the way. ✉ *1690 Airport Rd., Pemberton* ☎ *604/894–6106, 800/668–7900* ⊕ *www.bigskygolf.com* *18 holes. 7,001 yds. Par 72. Greens fee: $145* ☞ *Driving range, putting green, golf carts, pull carts, rental clubs, pro shop, golf academy/lessons, restaurant, bar.*

★ **Chateau Whistler Golf Club.** Carved from the side of Blackcomb Mountain, this challenging and breathtaking course was designed by prominent golf-course architect Robert Trent Jones Jr. Make sure to carry plenty of balls, though you can reload at the turn. ✉ *4612 Blackcomb Way* ☎ *604/938–2092, 877/938–2092* ⊕ *www.fairmontgolf.com* *18 holes. 6,635 yds. Par 72. Greens fee: $169* ☞ *Driving range, putting green, golf carts, pull carts, rental clubs, pro shop, golf lessons, restaurant, bar, snack bar.*

Nicklaus North Golf Course. Jack Nicklaus designed this challenging 18-hole track that finishes beside lovely Green Lake. It's the only course in the world that bears the famous golfer's name. ✉ *8080 Nicklaus North Blvd.* ☎ *604/938–9898, 800/386–9898* 🌐 *www.golfbc.com/courses/nicklaus_north* 🏌 *18 holes. 6,961 yds. Par 71. Greens fee: $189* ☞ *Driving range, putting green and bunker, golf carts, pull carts, rental clubs, pro shop, golf academy/lessons, restaurant.*

> **WORD OF MOUTH**
>
> What to do in Whistler if you don't ski? "There are lots of little shops to browse, lots of good restaurants, hiking trails, spa treatments, etc. There's dog sledding and ziplining. There's the Peak to Peak gondola. Great nightlife."
>
> —taggie

Whistler Golf Club. Often overlooked, this Arnold Palmer–designed course is frequently ranked among the best in the country. It's surprisingly challenging, especially around Bear Island, and recent upgrades have created some spectacular practice facilities. ✉ *4001 Whistler Way, Whistler* ☎ *604/932–3280, 800/376–1777* 🌐 *www.whistlergolf.com* 🏌 *18 holes. 6,722 yds. Par 72. Greens fee: $139* ☞ *Driving range, putting green, golf carts, pull carts, rental clubs, pro shop, golf academy/lessons, restaurant, bar.*

HELI-SKIING AND HELI-HIKING

The Coast Mountains of western Canada have more glaciers than almost anywhere else on the planet. The range is bordered by the Fraser River in the south and the Kelsall River in the north. Helicopter adventures consist of skiing, glacier hikes, and picnics.

Blackcomb Helicopters. Sightseeing tours over Whistler's stunning mountains and glaciers are offered year-round: there are heli-hiking, -biking, -fishing, -picnics, -golfing, and even heli-weddings in summer. The company also operates tours out of Vancouver. ✉ *9960 Heliport Rd., Whistler* ☎ *604/938–1700, 800/330–4354* 🌐 *www.blackcombaviation.com.*

Fodor's Choice ★ **Whistler Heli-Skiing.** Intended for intermediate to expert skiers and snowboarders, Whistler Heli-Skiing offers guided day trips with three or more glacier runs. Prices start at C$815 per person. Heli-hiking is available all year long, and guided tours can be tailored to your group's abilities. You can also enjoy a specially prepared picnic lunch in an old-growth forest, pastoral meadow, or on a 12,000-year-old glacier. ✉ *4545 Blackcomb Way, Whistler* ☎ *604/932–4105, 888/435–4754* 🌐 *www.whistlerheliskiing.com.*

HORSEBACK RIDING

The ultimate gentle summer activity, horseback riding in Whistler can take you through alpine meadows, old-growth forests, and along riverside beaches.

Adventure Ranch. Perched alongside the Lillooet River, this 10-acre ranch has vast tracts of wilderness in every direction. It offers two-hour rides (C$79), as well as longer excursions. The facilities include a swimming pool, volleyball court, and a snack bar with a pleasant patio. The ranch is open mid-May to mid-September. ✉ *1641 Airport Rd., Pemberton* ☎ *604/894–5200* 🌐 *www.adventureranch.net.*

SNOWMOBILING, SNOWSHOEING, AND SLEIGH RIDES

★ **Blackcomb Snowmobile.** You can book guided snowmobile trips through the backcountry, learn to mush a dog sled, or follow a First Nations trapper's trail on snowshoes. Snowmobile trips start at C$129 for two hours. ✉ *Hilton Whistler Resort, 4050 Whistler Way* ☎ *604/932–8484* 🌐 *www.blackcombsnowmobile.com.*

Canadian Snowmibile and All-Terrain Adventures. Snowmobiles, dog sleds, and snowshoes are just some of the transportation choices here. After a day in the snow you can reward yourself with a candle-lit fondue dinner in a beautiful log cabin. Seasoned outdoorspeople can take an avalanche skills training course. ✉ *Carleton Lodge, 4290 Mountain Sq.* ☎ *604/938–1616* 🌐 *www.canadiansnowmobile.com.*

TUBING

Coca-Cola Tube Park. Located on Blackcomb Mountain, this fabulous tube park is all about family fun. Features include 1,000 feet of lanes rated green, blue, and black diamond, a magic carpet to get to the top, a fire pit, a play area, and a snack station. There are even minitubes for the little ones. ✉ *Blackcomb Excalibur Gondola, 4010 Whistler Way, Whistler* ☎ *604/935–3357* 🌐 *www.whistlerblackcomb.com.*

ZIP-LINING AND CANOPY TOURS

Wildplay Element Parks. This self-contained adventure center runs skyline zip trekking tours on a forested mountain, 10 minutes north of Whistler Village. There are also tandem tours, which let you fly alongside a friend—or your child. The longest line at Cougar Mountain is 1,500 feet with a 200-foot vertical drop. Each skyline run is connected to the next by a trail, and one 150-foot suspension bridge. Wildplay's other attraction is Monkido, an obstacle "tree course" of rope ladders, swinging platforms, cargo nets, and suspension bridges. ✉ *4293 Mountain Sq.* ☎ *604/932–4086, 888/297–2222* 🌐 *www.wildplay.com.*

Fodor's Choice ★ **Ziptrek Ecotours.** In a rain forest between Whistler and Blackcomb mountains, Ziptrek offers three tours ranging from three hours to nearly five hours. None of them requires any experience, although if you're afraid of heights you should know that the full course includes a heady zip over a canyon far, far below you. (The company claims to have the "longest, highest, and fastest zip-lines in North America.") With runs ranging from 200 to 2,000 feet in length, this is a heart-thumping experience worth splurging on for the whole family. The less adventurous can opt for a Canopy Tour, which takes you from treetop platform to platform via suspension bridges and forest boardwalks. ✉ *4282 Mountain Sq.* ☎ *604/935–0001, 866/935–0001* 🌐 *www.ziptrek.com.*

An inuksuk—a stone landmark—stands sentry over Whistler and Blackcomb mountains.

APRÈS-SKI AND NIGHTLIFE

Whistler has a legendary après scene, and on any given weekend, there may be more nonskiers than skiers filling the patios, clubs, and saloons. Stag and stagette parties wander the pedestrian-only village stroll, and people line up early to get inside Buffalo Bills or the Garibaldi Lift Company, where DJs and bands from Vancouver and beyond come to spin.

The night begins with après, when skiers, bikers, and hikers alike unwind on patios from the Longhorn Saloon & Grill to Citta'—think happy hour for the hyped up—and the clubs usually stay open until 2 am except for Sundays and holidays. The minimum age is 19 and smoking is only allowed outside, although even some patios are smoke-free zones. When the bars close, the local constables lead a (usually) well-behaved cattle drive through the village and back to the hotels.

For entertainment listings, pick up Whistler's weekly newsmagazine, the *Pique,* available at cafés and food stores.

BARS AND PUBS

Black's Pub. You'll find Whistler's largest selection of whiskeys (more than 40 varieties) and 99 beers from around the world at this pleasant pub. The adjoining restaurant is reasonably priced, offering mainly pizzas and pastas. ✉ *4270 Mountain Sq.* ☎ *604/932–6945* 🌐 *www.blackspub.com.*

BrewHouse. Come for the house-brewed ales and lagers and you'll stay to relax in the woodsy atmosphere, complete with fireplaces, pool tables, and a slew of TVs turned to sports channels. Brewery tours are offered

Thursday and Saturday afternoon. The adjacent restaurant and patio are good places for casual meals. ✉ *4355 Blackcomb Way* ☎ *604/905–2739* 🌐 *www.markjamesgroup.com.*

Citta' Bistro. This patio is *the* hot spot for people-watching and microbrew sipping. The place attracts a ton of late-night partiers to crush capacities, but no one seems to mind. It's all part of the conviviality of the aprés-ski scene. ✉ *4217 Village Stroll* ☎ *604/932–4177* 🌐 *www.cittabistro.com.*

Dubh Linn Gate Irish Pub. As its name implies, this place is full of the Irish blarney, with an interior that was actually transported all the way from the Emerald Isle. The staff pours a decent pint of Guinness, and the menu includes solid Irish fare like steak and Guinness pie. Celtic music is a highlight most nights. ✉ *Pan Pacific Hotel, 4320 Sundial Crescent* ☎ *604/905–4047* 🌐 *www.dubhlinngate.com.*

Fodor's Choice ★ **Garibaldi Lift Company.** At the base of the Whistler Gondola, this popular joint attracts a lively crowd to its restaurant, lounge, and club. It's a cozy place to chill out and watch the latest ski and snowboard videos during the day; in the evening, though, things get hopping. Friday night house parties are legendary, in part because the music isn't run-of-the-mill Top 40. In addition to live bands, resident DJ Korik brings in talent from the U.S. ✉ *2320 London La.* ☎ *604/905–2220.*

★ **Longhorn Saloon & Grill.** A veritable institution among Whistler's drinking establishments, the Longhorn has been around for more than 25 years. It still packs them in until the wee hours, with the crowds moving from the saloon to the patio overlooking the base of Blackcomb. The interior calls to mind Steamboat Springs or Crested Butte, but the variety of local brews makes it clear that you're in B.C. The menu is strictly pub food. ✉ *Carleton Lodge, 4284 Mountain Sq., Whistler* ☎ *604/932–5999* 🌐 *www.longhornsaloon.ca.*

DANCE CLUBS

Buffalo Bill's Bar & Grill. Across from the Whistler Gondola, this club features '80s music for the younger crowd, and well known regional bands jam once or twice a month. If you can't get onto the small dance floor, there's a pool table. ✉ *4122 Village Green* ☎ *604/932–6613* 🌐 *www.buffalobills.ca.*

Garfinkle's. One of Whistler's most cavernous clubs, Garfinkle's hosts live rock, hip-hop, funk, and jazz. It's a hangout for a young crowd, many of whom are weekend partiers from Vancouver. It's a high point (literally) on any Whistler trip. ✉ *1–4308 Main St.* ☎ *604/932–2323* 🌐 *www.garfswhistler.com.*

Maxx Fish. Located below Amsterdam Café, this dance club attracts a who's who of DJs from around the world. The crowd is hip and young, the music is eclectic, and the vibe is cool. ✉ *4232 Village Stroll* ☎ *604/932–1904* 🌐 *www.maxxfish.com.*

Moe Joe's. Its hot central location makes Moe Joe's a perennial favorite. Theme nights from Boombox Monday to Ladies' Night Saturday appeal to a diverse crowd. If you're traveling in a group, reserve a party booth or snag a VIP pass to skip the lines. ✉ *4115 Golfers Approach* ☎ *604/935–1152* 🌐 *www.moejoes.com.*

Tommy Africa's. The club's been around forever, and depending on what's happening on any given night it's definitely worth a look. Guest DJs play alternative and progressive dance music, and with so many youthful patrons drinking the club's trademark shooters (shot glasses of undiluted alcoholic concoctions), it's not long before someone is dancing on the stage. ✉ *4216 Gateway Dr.* ☎ *604/932–6090* 🌐 *www.tommyafricas.com.*

SHOPPING

Whistler has almost 200 stores, including chain and designer outlets, gift shops, and outdoor-clothing and ski shops. Most are clustered in the pedestrian-only Whistler Village Centre; more can be found a short stroll away in Village North, Upper Village, and in the shopping concourses of the major hotels.

CLOTHING

Amos and Andes. Amid the endless sweater shops, this one stands out. The handmade sweaters and dresses have offbeat designs and fabulous colors. They're really comfortable, especially those made with silky-soft merino wool. ✉ *2–4321 Village Gate Blvd.* ☎ *604/932–7202* 🌐 *www.whistlersweatershop.com.*

Helly Hansen. Here's where to find high-quality Norwegian-made skiing, boarding, and other outdoor wear and equipment. There's a second location at the Westin Resort. ✉ *4295 Blackcomb Way* ☎ *604/932–0143* 🌐 *www.hellyhansen.com.*

Lululemon Athletica. Best known for its yoga gear, this iconic Canadian retailer carries a wide range of ultracomfortable and flattering athletic wear. ✉ *4293 Mountain Sq.* ☎ *604/938–9642* 🌐 *www.lululemon.com.*

Open Country. There are several upscale clothing shops in Whistler, but here you'll find many designer labels all under one roof: leisure-wear classics for men and women by Tommy Hilfiger, Jack Lipson, Kenneth Cole, Michael Kors, and Ralph Lauren. ✉ *Fairmont Chateau Whistler Resort, 4599 Chateau Blvd.* ☎ *604/938–9268.*

★ **Roots.** This Canadian-owned enterprise is known for its sweatshirts and cozy casuals, and it's something of a fixture in Whistler. It outfits the Canadian Olympic team, and has clothed many American and U.K. Olympians in the past. ✉ *4154 Village Green* ☎ *604/938–0058* 🌐 *www.canada.roots.com.*

GALLERIES

Adele Campbell Fine Art Gallery. This gallery has a broad range of paintings and sculptures, many with wildlife and wilderness themes, by both established and up-and-coming B.C. artists. You'll usually be able to find some affordable pieces. ✉ *Hilton Whistler Resort, 4050 Whistler Way* ☎ *888/938–0887* 🌐 *www.adelecampbell.com.*

Black Tusk Gallery. Specializing in quality regional art, Black Tusk is a showcase for Pacific Northwest Coast Native artists, both from Canada and the U.S. Works include limited-edition silk-screen prints and traditional crafts such as masks, paddles, bowls, jewelry, and totem poles. ✉ *Hilton Whistler Resort, 4293 Mountain Sq.* ☎ *604/905–5540* 🌐 *www.blacktusk.ca.*

Plaza Galleries. The range of artists represented at the Plaza Galleries is inspired. Many, such as acclaimed wildlife artist Robert Bateman, hail from British Columbia, though you're just as likely to see the efforts of international names who are just starting to make their mark in North America. You can also buy art by Hollywood stars like Anthony Quinn and Red Skelton. ✉ *Whistler Town Plaza, 22–4314 Main St.* ☎ *604/938–6233* 🌐 *www.plazagalleries.com.*

Whistler Village Art Gallery. With a focus on contemporary painting, sculpture, and glass, this well-established gallery has earned a loyal following from those looking for innovative work by Canadian artists. There's a second location at the Four Seasons Resort Whistler. ✉ *Hilton Whistler Resort, 4293 Mountain Sq.* ☎ *604/938–3001* 🌐 *www.whistlerart.com.*

SPORTS EQUIPMENT

Can-Ski. With more than 40 years in the business, Can-Ski is synonymous with everything having to do with snow. It has a good selection of brand-name ski gear, clothing, and accessories, and does custom boot fitting and repairs. Can-Ski has other locations at Glacier Lodge and Whistler Creekside (winters only). ✉ *Crystal Lodge, 4154 Village Green* ☎ *604/938–7755* 🌐 *www.whistlerblackcomb.com/stores.*

Fanatyk Co. In winter you can buy off-the-rack skis and boots, as well as order custom-made boots. In summer the shop specializes in top-of-the-line mountain bikes and bike rentals, repairs, and tours. ✉ *6–4433 Sundial Pl.* ☎ *604/938–9455* 🌐 *www.fanatykco.com.*

Showcase Snowboards. Considered by locals to be the town's best snowboard shop, this place is staffed by guys who live for the board: snow, skate, and surf. The 3,500-square-foot shop showcases of all the best gear. ✉ *Sundial Hotel, 4340 Sundial Crescent* ☎ *604/938–7519* 🌐 *www.showcasesnowboards.com.*

9

SPAS

Where there's skiing, there are spas. Whistler has several outstanding hotel spas, such as those in the Four Seasons Resort Whistler, the Westin Resort & Spa, the Fairmont Château Whistler Resort, and the Javanese delight in the Summit Lodge & Spa.

Fodor's Choice ★ **Scandinave Spa.** It's a 10-minute drive north of Whistler Village, but this place is a find. Following the traditions of Scandinavia, these pools and hydrotherapy baths are intended to soothe sore muscles, relax the body, and improve blood circulation. The circuit involves a Eucalyptus steam bath, a Finnish sauna, a soak in the heated outdoor pools—especially wonderful when it's snowing—and then relaxation in a number of lounge areas and solariums. The Bearfoot Bistro is in charge of the café, so you know the food is spa-superlative. Day passes are C$58. ✉ *8010 Mons Rd., Whistler* ☎ *604/935–2424* 🌐 *www.scandinave.com/en/whistler.*

THE OKANAGAN WINE COUNTRY

If you think that "wine country" and "British Columbia" have as much in common as "beaches" and "the Arctic," think again. The British Columbia region known as the Okanagan, roughly five hours east of Vancouver by car or one hour by air, is a significant wine-producing area. It calls itself the "Napa of the North," and although that's stretching the truth somewhat—Okanagan wine production is a literal drop in the bucket compared to that of the Napa Valley—the Okanagan is a magnet for wine enthusiasts, novice and expert alike.

Add to that the region's arid summer climate, lake activities, golf courses, and abundant snow in winter and you have a perfect short getaway from Vancouver and the British Columbia coast.

The Okanagan's wineries are concentrated in three general areas: around the city of Kelowna and north toward Vernon, along the Naramata Bench outside the town of Penticton, and in the area between Oliver and Osoyoos, just north of the U.S. border. If you're planning a short trip, you might want to stick to just one of these areas. Although it's only about 125 km (75 miles) between Kelowna and Osoyoos, it takes about two hours to drive between them. With approximately 200 wineries throughout the Okanagan, each area has enough to occupy several days of tasting.

The Okanagan's sandy lake beaches and hot dry climate have long made it a family-holiday destination for Vancouverites and Albertans, and the region is still the fruit-growing capital of Canada.

PLANNING

WHEN TO GO

The Okanagan hosts a wine festival in May, to open the season, and in early October, to close the season; both weekends are fun and busy times to visit. High season is defined from wine festival to wine festival.

The hot dry summer, especially July and August, is peak season here, and weekends get crowded. May and June are quieter, and most wineries are open, so either month can be a good alternative to the mid-summer peak.

> **WORD OF MOUTH**
>
> "I would head straight for the Okanagan Valley. Lots of wineries, spectacular scenery, wonderful water and mountain views. There are excellent hiking trails, and charming small towns, like Summerland and Penticton at the bottom of the Valley."
>
> —LJ

However, September just might be the best time for an Okanagan wine-tasting trip. Everything is still open, the weather is generally fine, and the vineyards are full of grapes ready to pick. Many wineries release new wines in the fall, so there are more tasting options.

In winter, the Okanagan becomes a popular ski destination, with several low-key but first-rate resorts. If your main objective is wine touring, though, many wineries close or reduce their hours from November through April.

MAKING THE MOST OF YOUR TIME

Three days from Vancouver is barely enough time to enjoy the Okanagan; five days to a week would be optimal.

The best place to start a wine-tasting tour is at one of the two area wine info centers (Kelowna or Penticton). You can get an overview of the area's wines, get help in organizing your time, and usually taste a wine or two.

We've included a selection of the best wineries, but our list is only a fraction of the Okanagan's more than 200 producers. Because new wineries open every year, ask for recommendations at your hotel, or simply stop in when you see an appealing sign.

GETTING HERE AND AROUND

AIR TRAVEL

The main airport for the Okanagan wine country is in Kelowna. There's also a small airport in Penticton.

Air Canada and WestJet both fly into Kelowna from Vancouver. From Vancouver, Air Canada also serves Penticton; flights take about one hour.

Taxis generally meet arriving flights at the Kelowna Airport.

Okanagan Airport Shuttle provides transportation from the Kelowna Airport to local hotels for C$10 per person, to Vernon for C$32, and to Silver Star for C$60, with slight discounts on the return trip. Big White Shuttle runs scheduled service between the airport and resort for C$80 round-trip. You'll need your own transportation to reach Apex Mountain Resort.

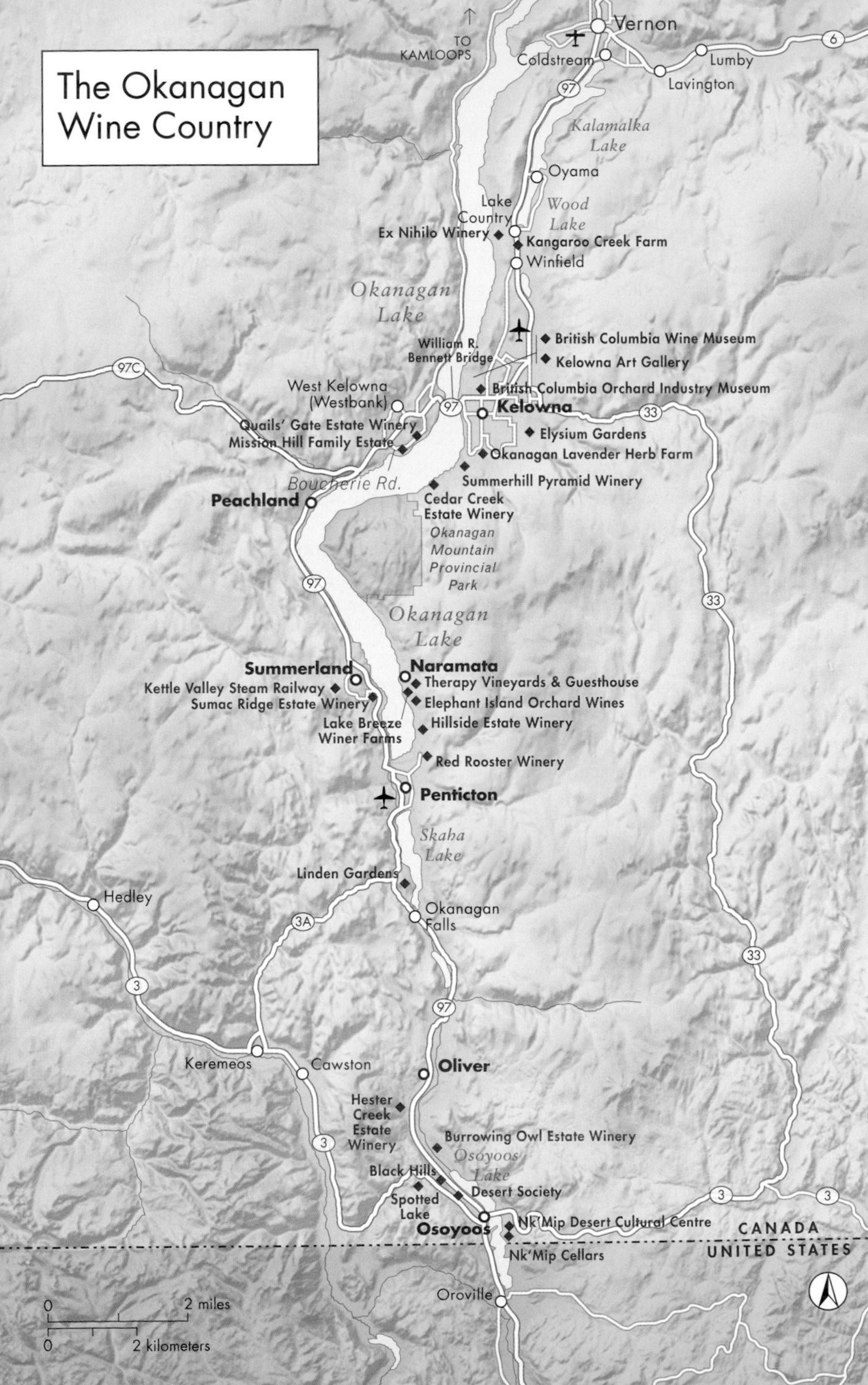

The Okanagan Wine Country
TO KAMLOOPS
Vernon
Coldstream
Lumby
Lavington
6
97
Kalamalka Lake
Oyama
Lake Country
Wood Lake
Ex Nihilo Winery
Kangaroo Creek Farm
Winfield
Okanagan Lake
William R. Bennett Bridge
British Columbia Wine Museum
Kelowna Art Gallery
97C
West Kelowna (Westbank)
British Columbia Orchard Industry Museum
Kelowna
33
Quails' Gate Estate Winery
Mission Hill Family Estate
Elysium Gardens
Okanagan Lavender Herb Farm
Summerhill Pyramid Winery
Boucherie Rd.
Peachland
Cedar Creek Estate Winery
Okanagan Mountain Provincial Park
Okanagan Lake
Summerland
Naramata
Kettle Valley Steam Railway
Sumac Ridge Estate Winery
Therapy Vineyards & Guesthouse
Elephant Island Orchard Wines
Lake Breeze Winer Farms
Hillside Estate Winery
Red Rooster Winery
Penticton
Skaha Lake
Linden Gardens
Hedley
Okanagan Falls
3A
3
Keremeos
Cawston
Oliver
Hester Creek Estate Winery
Burrowing Owl Estate Winery
Osoyoos Lake
Black Hills
Desert Society
Spotted Lake
Osoyoos
Nk'Mip Desert Cultural Centre
Nk'Mip Cellars
CANADA
UNITED STATES
Oroville
0
2 miles
0
2 kilometers

BUS TRAVEL

Greyhound Canada runs buses from Vancouver to Vernon, Kelowna, and Penticton, with connections to smaller Okanagan towns. The Kelowna Regional Transit System operates buses in the greater Kelowna area.

CAR TRAVEL

To get to the Okanagan by car from Vancouver, head east on Highway 1 (Trans-Canada Highway). Just east of Hope, several routes diverge. For Oliver or Osoyoos in the South Okanagan, take Highway 3 east through the winding roads of Manning Park. For the Kelowna area, the fastest route is Highway 5 (the magnificent Coquihalla Highway) north to Merritt, then follow Highway 97C (the Okanagan Connector) toward Kelowna. To reach Penticton and Naramata, you can either take the Coquihalla to 97C, then turn *south* on Highway 97, or take Highway 3 to Keremeos, where you pick up Highway 3A north, which merges into 97 *north*. Allow about five hours of driving time from Vancouver to the Okanagan region.

If you're traveling from Whistler, consider the back route. Highway 99 travels through Pemberton to Lillooet. From here, take Highway 12 to Cache Creek, where you'll join Highway 1 traveling east to Kamloops. Take the Highway 97 exit to Vernon, the northernmost town of the Okanagan Valley. This is not a road to drive in winter, and whenever you go remember that gas stations are few and far between. In summer, the 561-km (350-mile) drive can take about seven to eight hours.

Several major agencies, including Avis, Budget, Enterprise, Hertz, and National, have offices in Kelowna.

Contacts Big White Shuttle ☎ *800/663–2772*. **Greyhound Canada** ☎ *800/661–8747* 🌐 *www.greyhound.ca*. **Kelowna Regional Transit System** ☎ *250/860–8121* 🌐 *www.bctransit.com/regions/kel*. **Okanagan Airport Shuttle** ☎ *250/542–7574* 🌐 *www.okanaganairportshuttle.com*. **WestJet Airlines** ☎ *888/937–8538* 🌐 *www.westjet.com*.

RESTAURANTS AND HOTELS

Like the California wine regions, Okanagan has attracted gourmands and the restaurants reflect that. They also benefit from the amazing fruit harvest here. From summer to fall, every month reaps a harvest of different fruits, from cherries and plums to nectarines, peaches, and several varieties of apples.

The wine industry has added a quiet sophistication with the development of higher-end lodgings and boutique inns geared to wine-and-food lovers. This means that from July to September you need to reserve early, especially if you're planning on visiting on a weekend. The Kelowna region is more urban (and less picturesque), but it has a greater range of accommodations and other services. The Naramata and Oliver/Osoyoos areas are both prettier and more rural.

Prices in dining reviews are the average cost of a main course at dinner or, if dinner is not served, at lunch. Prices in lodging reviews are the lowest cost of a standard double room in high season.

TOUR OPTIONS

Monashee Adventure Tours has full- or half-day bike- and wine-tour combinations, and other tours around the Okanagan. Arbutus Routes also has biking tours of the Okanagan wine country.

With Okanagan Limousine you can tour the wine area in chauffeur-driven style. It offers half-day and full-day tours to wineries in Kelowna, Summerland/Peachland, Naramata, Oliver/Osoyoos, and Okanagan Falls. Okanagan Wine Country Tours offers narrated three-hour, four-hour, and full-day wine-country tours. There's even a floatplane tour over the lush valleys to the Okanagan's Golden Mile near Oliver. Distinctly Kelowna Tours pairs winery visits with walking excursions, ziplining, and other adventures.

Contacts Arbutus Routes ☎ *604/935–7566* 🌐 *www.arbutusroutes.com.* **Distinctly Kelowna Tours** ☎ *250/979–1211, 866/979–1211* 🌐 *www.distinctlykelownatours.ca.* **Monashee Adventure Tours** ☎ *250/762–9253, 888/762–9253* 🌐 *www.monasheeadventuretours.com.* **Okanagan Limousine** ☎ *250/717–5466, 866/336–3133* 🌐 *www.ok-limo.com.* **Okanagan Wine Country Tours** ☎ *250/868–9463, 866/689–9463* 🌐 *www.okwinetours.com.*

VISITOR INFORMATION

The knowledgeable staff at the British Columbia VQA Wine Information Centre will tell you what's new at area wineries and help you plan a self-drive winery tour. The center also stocks more than 500 local wines and offers complimentary tastings daily. It's a good place to stop and find out about places to stay and eat.

Hello BC has information about the province, including the Okanagan. The Thompson Okanagan Tourism Association is the main tourism contact for the Okanagan. Towns like Osoyoos, Kelowna, and Penticton have visitor information centers, though not all are open year-round. Some, like Discover Naramata, are virtual only.

Local Tourist Information British Columbia VQA Wine Information Centre ✉ *553 Railway St., Penticton* ☎ *250/490–2006* 🌐 *www.pentictonwineinfo.com.* **Destination Osoyoos** ☎ *250/495–5070, 888/676–9667* 🌐 *www.destinationosoyoos.com.* **Discover Naramata** 🌐 *www.discovernaramata.com.* **Hello BC** ☎ *800/435–5622* 🌐 *www.hellobc.com.* **Penticton & Wine Country Visitor Information Centre** ☎ *250/493–4055, 800/663–5052* 🌐 *www.tourismpenticton.com.* **Thompson Okanagan Tourism Association** ☎ *250/860–5999* 🌐 *www.totabc.com.* **Tourism Kelowna** ☎ *250/861–1515, 800/663–4345* 🌐 *www.tourismkelowna.com.*

KELOWNA

390 km (242 miles) northeast of Vancouver, 68 km (42 miles) north of Penticton.

The largest community in the Okanagan Valley, with a regional population of more than 180,000, Kelowna makes a good base for exploring the region's beaches, ski hills, wineries, and numerous golf courses. Although its edges are untidily urban, with strip malls and office parks sprawling everywhere, the town's walkable downtown runs along and up from Okanagan Lake. So even though the city continues to expand, you can still enjoy a stroll in the restful lakeside park.

Okanagan Lake splits Kelowna in two. On the east side of the lake is Kelowna proper, which includes the city's downtown and the winery district south of the city center that the locals call the Mission. On the west side of the lake is the community of West Kelowna, which is frequently still known by its former name, Westbank. Several wineries are on the west side, on and off Boucherie Road. The William R. Bennett Bridge connects the two sides of the lake.

EXPLORING

British Columbia Wine Museum. A good place to start your wine country exploration is this museum in a history-filled packing house in the museum district. The staff is knowledgeable and can provide information about local wineries and wine tours. It hosts daily wine tastings and occasional wine-related exhibits. ✉ *1304 Ellis St.* ☎ *250/868–0441* 🌐 *www.kelownamuseums.ca/bc-wine-museum* 🎟 *By donation* ⏲ *Weekdays 10–6, Sat. 10–5, Sun. 11–5.*

British Columbia Orchard Industry Museum. Housed in the same building as the Wine Museum, this museum might be modest, but it's extremely well done. Displays describe the history of the area's fruit industry and puts the entire region into a larger context. ✉ *1304 Ellis St.* ☎ *250/763–0433* 🌐 *www.kelownamuseums.ca* 🎟 *By donation* ⏲ *Weekdays 10–5, Sat. 10–4.*

Elysium Gardens. Carved out of an apple orchard, these gorgeous gardens have lovely views of the lake. The four-acre oasis includes manicured lawns, ornamental grasses, and masses of peonies. Don't miss the simplicity of the Japanese Garden. If you see something you like, there's also a nursery on the premises. ✉ *2834 Belgo Rd.* ☎ *250/491–1368* 🌐 *www.elysiumgardennursery.com.*

Kangaroo Creek Farm. You don't have to go Down Under to catch up with a kangaroo or a wallaby. At this farm you can get up close and personal with these small creatures, and even hold a joey. ✉ *3193 Hill Rd.* ☎ *250/766–4823* 🌐 *www.kangaroocreekfarm.com.*

Kelowna Art Gallery. Works by contemporary Canadian artists make up the majority of the gallery's permanent collection. It's also an elegant venue for temporary local and international exhibits, including many for children (worth noting for rainy days). ✉ *1315 Water St.* ☎ *250/762–2226* 🌐 *www.kelownaartgallery.com* 🎟 *C$5* ⏲ *Tues.–Sat. 10–5, until 9 on Thurs., Sun. 1–4.*

WINERIES

Almost all of the wineries in and around Kelowna offer tastings and tours throughout the summer and during the Okanagan Wine Festivals held in May and October; several have restaurants, and most also have shops open year-round. Many wineries charge a nominal fee (C$2–C$5) for tastings, more if a tour is involved.

■ TIP→ As you plan your tour route, note that Cedar Creek and Summerhill are on the east side of the lake, while Mission Hill and Quails' Gate are on the west.

9

Cedar Creek Estate Winery. South of Kelowna, the award-winning Cedar Creek is in a lovely spot overlooking the lake. Tours of the winery run daily May to October, and the shop is open for tastings year-round. With salads, sandwiches, and other light contemporary fare, the outdoor Vineyard Terrace Restaurant serves lunch mid-June through mid-September, weather permitting. If you like these wines, visit Cedar Creek's sister winery, Greatna Ranch Estates, 9 km (5½ miles) south of Peachland. ✉ *5445 Lakeshore Rd.* ☎ *250/764–8866, 800/730–9463* 🌐 *www.cedarcreek.bc.ca* 🎫 *Tours C$5, tastings C$2–C$5* ⏲ *Tours May–Oct., daily 11, 1, and 3. Wineshop May–Oct., daily 10–6; Nov.–Apr., daily 11–5.*

Ex Nihilo Vineyards. Canada is the world's largest producer of ice wine, a specialty of Ex Nihilo Vineyards, a 10-minute drive north of Kelowna. This small but enterprising winery was among the first in the area to court celebrity endorsements, and struck a deal with the Rolling Stones to label its Riesling ice wine "Sympathy for the Devil." The tasting room is open May to October; tastings are C$5 to C$10, which is waived if you make a purchase. ✉ *1525 Camp Rd., Lake Country* ☎ *250/766–5522* 🌐 *www.exnihilovineyards.com.*

Mission Hill Family Estate. Sitting atop a hill overlooking Okanagan Lake, Mission Hill Family Estate is recognizable for its 12-story bell tower. It was built, as the owner describes it, to resemble "a combination monastery, Tuscan hill village, and French winery." With a vaulted cellar blasted from volcanic rock, the well-established vineyard produces a wide variety of award-winning wines and offers several different winery tours, from a basic 60-minute tour with a tasting of three wines (C$12), to a more in-depth visit that includes wine-and-food pairings (C$85). An outdoor amphitheater hosts art events, music, and theater. The Terrace Restaurant is one of the Kelowna area's best dining options. ✉ *1730 Mission Hill Rd., West Kelowna* ☎ *250/768–6448, 800/957–9911* 🌐 *www.missionhillwinery.com* 🎫 *Tours C$7–C$45* ⏲ *July–early Sept., daily 9:30–7; Apr.–June and early Sept.–early Oct., daily 10–6; early Oct.–Nov., daily 10–5; Dec.–Mar., daily 10–4.*

Quails' Gate Estate Winery. Set on 125 acres above the western edge of Okanagan Lake, Quails' Gate Estate Winery runs tours several times daily from May to mid-October. The winery produces more than a dozen different varieties, although it's best known for its award-winning Chardonnay and Pinot Gris, which were served to the Duke and Duchess of Cambridge during their Canadian visit. Complimentary tastings are offered in the spacious wineshop, and the Old Vines Restaurant is open year-round. The garden patio, open only in summer, is a lovely spot for Sunday brunch. ✉ *3303 Boucherie Rd.* ☎ *250/769–4451, 800/420–9463* 🌐 *www.quailsgate.com* 🎫 *Tours C$5* ⏲ *Tours May–mid-Oct.; call for schedule. Wineshop May and June, daily 10–7; July–early Sept., daily 9:30–7; early Sept.–Apr., daily 10–6.*

Summerhill Pyramid Winery. On the east side of the lake is Summerhill Pyramid Winery, an organic producer best known for its sparkling and ice wines. What startles visitors, though, is the four-story-high replica of the Great Pyramid of Cheops, used to age and store the wine. As a venue

MORE OKANAGAN TIPS

OKANAGAN WINERIES: LARGE OR SMALL?

Is it better to visit large wineries or small ones? It depends. Starting your trip at a larger winery can be a useful orientation. The big ones generally have organized tours, where you can learn about the types of wine they make and the winemaking process, and you can pick up general information about the region as well. They usually have restaurants, too, where you can refuel.

On the other hand, at the smaller producers you may get to talk with the owners or winemakers themselves and get a more personal feel for their wines and the wine-making business. Our recommendation is to include a mix of larger and smaller wineries in your itinerary.

OKANAGAN: NORTH OR SOUTH?

The Okanagan is a large region, with many winding, stop-and-go roads. If your time is limited, consider concentrating on one area:

■ Go to Osoyoos/Oliver if you prefer smaller wineries, a more rural setting, and a dry, desertlike climate.

■ Visit Penticton/Naramata for smaller wineries and if you prefer cycling or other outdoor adventures; there are several biking and hiking options nearby.

■ Head for Kelowna if you're arriving by plane (it has the region's only significant airport), if you prefer a more urban setting, or if you want to check out the largest wineries. Kelowna isn't appealing, though, so if you're envisioning idyllic wine country, go farther south.

WHAT TO DO BESIDES WINERIES?

Before becoming such a hip wine-and-food destination, the Okanagan was a family holiday spot, best known for its "beaches and peaches"—the lakes with their sandy shores, boating and waterskiing opportunities, and waterfront lodges and campgrounds, as well as the countless farm stands offering fresh produce. The beaches and peaches are still there, and the Okanagan still welcomes families. With its mild, dry climate, the region is also popular with golfers, and there are gardens to visit as well as trails for hiking and biking.

The restaurant scene in the Okanagan is evolving, too, and a growing number of high-end eateries emphasize food-and-wine pairings. Some of the best are at the wineries, especially the Sonora Room at Burrowing Owl in Oliver and the Terrace at Mission Hill in the Kelowna area. Surprisingly, outside of Kelowna, it can be hard to find good-quality, cheap eats: your best bet, particularly in the summer and fall, is to stop at one of the many roadside farm stands to pick up fruits, veggies, and picnic fare. Some wineries have "picnic licenses," which means that they're allowed to sell you a glass (or a bottle) of wine that you can enjoy on the grounds, paired with your own picnic supplies or with picnic fare that the winery sells.

for summer concerts, the pyramid's fabulous acoustics are unparalleled. You can tour the pyramid and winery and visit the shop year-round. The Summerhill Sunset Bistro, with a veranda overlooking Okanagan Lake, serves lunch and dinner daily (except from January to early February). If the evening is cool, there's plenty of room inside. ✉ *4870 Chute Lake Rd.* ☎ *250/764–8000, 800/667–3538* 🌐 *www.summerhill.bc.ca* 🎫 *Tours C$5, tastings C$5* ⏲ *Tours May–mid-Oct., daily noon, 2, and 4; mid-Oct.–Apr., daily noon and 2. Wineshop May–mid-Oct., daily 9–7; mid-Oct.–Apr., daily 11–5.*

WHERE TO EAT

$$$ FRENCH ✕ **Bouchons Bistro.** Lots of windows and crisp white-linen tablecloths make this restaurant as bright as a French café, and the menu offers an array of classics. Signature dishes include a mouthwatering bouillabaisse containing everything from fresh salmon and halibut to scallops, shrimp, and mussels; and a hearty cassoulet that includes duck confit, smoked pork belly, and Toulouse sausage over white beans. For dessert, you might opt for a cheese plate or go sweet with classic crème caramel or lavender soufflé served on passion-fruit nectar. The bistro is justifiably proud of its sommeliers and its wine list of roughly 170 bottles, primarily Okanagan and French labels. 💲 *Average main: C$29* ✉ *105–1180 Sunset Dr.* ☎ *250/763–6595* 🌐 *www.bouchonsbistro.com* ⏲ *Closed Jan. No lunch.*

$$$ PACIFIC NORTHWEST ✕ **Old Vines Restaurant.** This contemporary eatery at Quails' Gate Winery is open throughout the year, making it a good choice for off-season visits. When the weather is fine, you can dine on the patio overlooking the lake. Menu choices are a balance of seafood (such as steamed West Coast mussels or steelhead trout served with sauteed mustard cabbage, bacon, and smoked cream) and meat (braised wild boar or duck breast with fennel and hazelnut pearl barley). There's plenty here for vegetarians, and salads like the quinoa and vegetable mix are as colorful as they are tasty. The staff is attentive and knowledgeable about wine pairings. 💲 *Average main: C$26* ✉ *3303 Boucherie Rd.* ☎ *250/769–2500* 🌐 *www.quailsgate.com.*

$$$ MODERN CANADIAN ✕ **RauDZ.** Rod Butters, one of B.C.'s best-known chefs, created this contemporary eatery to deliver a culinarily interesting yet casual dining experience. The restaurant's interior is simple, with an open kitchen, a 21-foot communal table, and exposed brick and beams revealing the historic building's architectural roots. The kitchen emphasizes seasonal, locally sourced fare, and is not afraid to offer chili dogs (made with merguez sausage) or cheeseburgers (topped with artisan cheddar or blue) alongside more innovative dishes. Look for wild boar scallopini or bison meatballs and jumbo scallops paired with a root-vegetable torte and celeriac fondue. If you're into desserts, the "liquid" variety are worth every sip; a favorite is Ripple-icious: buttermilk rippled with espresso, and punched with vodka and Baileys. P.S.: The name is pronounced "Rod's." 💲 *Average main: C$27* ✉ *1560 Water St.* ☎ *250/868–8805* 🌐 *www.raudz.com* ✍ *Reservations not accepted* ⏲ *No lunch.*

$$$$ PACIFIC NORTHWEST ✕ **Summerhill Sunset Bistro.** When the sun cooperates, the skies here become a dazzling array of salmon, orange, pink, and turquoise as dusk approaches. The food is impressive enough, though, that you'll be lingering over every mouthful long after the sun goes down. In

addition to salads and soups—the prawn bisque over dried tomato foam is melt in your mouth smooth—there are expertly prepared dishes like beef bourguinon, chicken breast with lemon-thyme gnocchi, and a coffee-and-pepper-crusted venison strip loin. Make sure to share a plate of artisan cheeses and breads. House-made desserts include a quince mousse served with poached pear, Agassiz hazelnut wafers, and Syrah syrup. Be sure to try the wines named for Robert Bateman, Canada's foremost wildlife artist. Before dinner, try to schedule a tour of the winery's pyramid, fashioned after the one in Egypt. *Average main: C$30 4870 Chute Lake Rd. 250/764–8000 www.summerhill.bc.ca Closed Jan.–mid-Feb.*

$$$$ MODERN CANADIAN ★ **The Terrace at Mission Hill.** With its panoramic views across the vineyards and the lake, this outdoor eatery at the Mission Hill Family Estate is a winner for alfresco dining. It's tough to compete with such a classic wine-country locale, but the innovative kitchen here is up to the task. You might start with a simple salad of perfectly ripe tomatoes and locally made feta cheese, or a tart of duck prosciutto, leeks, and potatoes before moving on to pan-seared sablefish paired with a pea puree, or braised venison with figs. Every item is matched with an appropriate wine. Stay a while to enjoy a tasting plate of cheeses or a decadent assortment of chocolate creations. If the weather's cool, there are heaters and blankets. If the weather's inclement, service stops. *Average main: C$30 1730 Mission Hill Rd., West Kelowna 250/768–6467 www.missionhillwinery.com Closed early Oct.–Apr. No dinner.*

WHERE TO STAY

For expanded hotel reviews, visit Fodors.com.

$$ B&B/INN **A View of the Lake B&B.** Owner Steve Marston and his wife, Chrissy, run this bed-and-breakfast in their contemporary home—he's a former restaurant chef who whips up elaborate breakfasts and offers periodic dinners and cooking demonstrations in his lavish kitchen. **Pros:** lake views; to-die-for kitchen (take a class if you can). **Cons:** guest room furnishings are a bit minimalist for some. *Rooms from: C$130 1877 Horizon Dr., West Kelowna 250/769–7854 www.aviewofthelake.com 4 rooms Breakfast.*

$$ B&B/INN **Apple Blossom Bed & Breakfast.** Set on the western slopes above Okanagan Lake, this cheery B&B offers terrific views and genuine hospitality. **Pros:** warm welcome from owners Jeanette and John Martens; moderate prices. **Cons:** a bit twee—if you need high style, look elsewhere. *Rooms from: C$130 3582 Apple Way Blvd., West Kelowna 250/768–1163, 888/718–5064 www.applebnb.com 3 rooms Breakfast.*

$$$$ RESORT **The Cove Lakeside Resort.** The guest suites at this resort on the western shore of Okanagan Lake have all the comforts of home and then some: fully equipped kitchens complete with special fridges to chill your wine, 42-inch plasma TVs, washer-dryers, and fireplaces. **Pros:** lakeside location; marina and moorage. **Cons:** high season gets busy (and noisy) with young families. *Rooms from: C$339 4205 Gellatly Rd., West Kelowna 250/707–1800, 877/762–2683 www.covelakeside.com 150 suites.*

$$$$ RESORT **Delta Grand Okanagan Resort.** On the shore of Okanagan Lake, this resort is a five-minute stroll from downtown Kelowna, though you may never want to leave the grounds because of all the amenities—there's even a casino and show lounge. **Pros:** a full menu of resort activities for kids and adults. **Cons:** feels like a big convention hotel; pricey parking; not the hippest choice in town. *Rooms from: C$299 1310 Water St. 250/763–4500, 800/465–4651 www.deltahotels.com 260 rooms, 60 condominiums, 70 villas No meals.*

$$$$ HOTEL **Hotel El Dorado.** Combining a 1926 building with a modern addition, this boutiquey lakeside lodging is one of Kelowna's more stylish options. **Pros:** eclectic style; lake views; onsite boat rentals. **Cons:** a short drive from downtown; busy on-site liquor store—a benefit to some, a nuisance for others. *Rooms from: C$275 500 Cook Rd. 250/763–7500, 866/608–7500 www.eldoradokelowna.com 49 rooms, 6 suites No meals.*

$$$$ RESORT **Manteo Resort Waterfront Hotel & Villas.** This striking Tuscan-style resort, painted in vivid reds and ochres, sits on a sandy swimming beach on Okanagan Lake. **Pros:** lots of activities for kids; guest barbecue facilities. **Cons:** rooms are rather generic; a short drive from downtown. *Rooms from: C$270 3762 Lakeshore Rd. 250/860–1031, 800/445–5255 www.manteo.com 48 rooms, 30 suites, 24 villas.*

$$$$ RESORT **Predator Ridge Golf Resort.** Set on two stunning 18-hole golf courses that are part of a vacation-home community, this full-service resort offers a wide range of accommodations, from studio, one-, and two-bedroom units in the modern Craftsman-style lodge to two- and three-bedroom cottages. **Pros:** you can stumble out of bed onto the links; wilderness landscape; proximity to Sparkling Hill Resort. **Cons:** feels understaffed at times; location is rather remote, especially for wine touring. *Rooms from: C$400 301 Village Centre Pl., Vernon 250/542–3436, 888/578–6688 www.predatorridge.com 75 suites, 51 cottages No meals.*

$$$$ RESORT Fodor's Choice ★ **Sparkling Hill Resort.** Carved into a granite hillside, this stunning resort has walls made of glass, so views of the Monashee Mountains and the northern shores of Okanagan Lake are always striking, whether from your beautifully furnished room, the excellent restaurant, the state-of-the-art gym, or the heated infinity pool. **Pros:** a mind-boggling spa; unforgettable views; pet-friendly vibe. **Cons:** no in-room coffee; not a central location, especially for wine-touring. *Rooms from: C$390 250/275–1556, 877/275–1556 www.sparklinghill.com 149 rooms, 3 penthouses No meals.*

SPORTS AND THE OUTDOORS

BIKING AND HIKING

Kettle Valley Rail Trail. This former railroad route runs through some of the Okanagan's prettiest and most dramatic countryside. Bikers and hikers can follow the trail in sections, the most popular being from Brodie (along Highway 5) to just east of Midway (on Highway 3). Other sections run between Penticton and Naramata and through the Kelowna area. Pick up trail maps from the visitor center in Kelowna. *www.kettlevalleyrailtrail.com.*

GOLF

With more than 35 courses in the Okanagan Valley—19 in the Kelowna region alone—golf is a big draw. Several courses have joined forces to create Golf Kelowna (🌐 *www.golfkelowna.com*), a one-stop shop for tee times, accommodation, and visitor information.

Gallagher's Canyon Golf and Country Club. Located about 15 km (9 miles) southeast of downtown Kelowna, Gallagher's Canyon has an 18-hole championship course that meanders among ponderosa pines, as well as a shorter nine-hole course. Greens fees include use of a cart. It's a challenging course, and the vistas of the mountains, orchards, vineyards are a nice bonus. ⊠ *4320 Gallagher's Dr. W* ☎ *250/861–4240, 800/446–5322* 🌐 *www.golfbc.com/courses/gallaghers_canyon* ⛳ *18 holes. 6,802 yds. Par 72. Greens fee: $139* ☞ *Driving range, putting green, golf carts, pull carts, rental clubs, pro shop, golf academy/lessons, restaurant, bar.*

Harvest Golf Club. Surrounded by lush vineyards and orchards (you can pick peaches, apricots, pears, and five kinds of apples while you play), the 18-hole Harvest Golf Club is aptly named. The championship course has bent-grass fairways and multiple tees so you're always challenged. Open mid-March to mid-November, the Harvest Grille serves breakfast and lunches consisting of sandwiches, salads, and other casual fare; more substantial dishes are added to the menu in the evening. ⊠ *2725 KLO Rd.* ☎ *250/862–3103, 800/257–8577* 🌐 *www.harvestgolf.com* ⛳ *18 holes. 7,109 yds. Par 72. Greens fee: C$120* ☞ *Driving range, putting green, golf carts, pull carts, rental clubs, pro shop, golf academy/lessons, restaurant, bar.*

Okanagan Golf Club. With their Okanagan Valley views, the two courses at the Okanagan Golf Course are a feast for the eyes. The Quail Course is a challenging hillside course with dramatic changes in elevation and tight, tree-lined fairways. The newer Bear Course is more forgiving. High-season greens fees are C$139 for either course, including cart. ⊠ *3200 Via Centrale* ☎ *250/765–5955, 800/446–5322* 🌐 *www.golfbc.com/courses/bear* ⛳ *Quail Course: 18 holes. 6,794 yds. Par 72. Greens fee: C$139. Bear Course: 18 holes. 6,885 yds. Par 72. Greens fee: C$139.* ☞ *Driving range, putting green, golf carts, pull carts, rental clubs, pro shop, golf academy/lessons, restaurant.*

SHOPPING

Arlo's Honey Farm. This is a mom-and-pop operation where the bees receive a lot of TLC. A small demonstration area puts glass between you and the bees while honey is harvested. Of course there's a shop filled with honey-related items. ⊠ *4329 Bedford La.* ☎ *250/764–2883* 🌐 *www.arloshoneyfarm.com.*

Carmelis Goat Cheese. The drive to Carmelis is up the side of the mountain, so bring your camera to take photos of the stupendous views. Save some shots for the goats—they're responsible for the array of cheeses you can sample (and buy, of course). Call a week ahead to arrange a tour of the cheese-production facilities and the goat barns. ⊠ *170 Timberline Rd.* ☎ *250/764–9033* 🌐 *www.carmelisgoatcheese.com* 🎫 *Tours C$5.*

Okanagan Grocery. A good place to start if you're assembling a picnic, this first-rate bakery sells a variety of hearty loaves. It also offers a selection of local cheeses and other gourmet items. ✉ *Guisachan Village, 2355 Gordon Dr.* ☎ *250/862–2811* 🌐 *www.okanagangrocery.com.*

SUMMERLAND AND PEACHLAND

Summerland is 52 km (31 miles) south of Kelowna; Peachland is 25 km (15 miles) southwest of Kelowna.

Between Kelowna and Penticton, Highway 97 winds along the west side of Okanagan Lake, past vineyards, orchards, fruit stands, beaches, picnic sites, and some of the region's prettiest lake and hill scenery.

EXPLORING

Kettle Valley Steam Railway. One way to tour the area is aboard the historic Kettle Valley Steam Railway, pulled by a restored 1912 steam locomotive. The 90-minute trips take you along 16 km (10 miles) of a century-old rail line. Several times a year there's a "Great Train Robbery" reenactment with a barbecue dinner and musical entertainment. ✉ *18404 Bathville Rd., Summerland* ☎ *877/494–8424* 🌐 *www.kettlevalleyrail.org* 🎫 *C$22* ⏲ *Mid-May–mid-June and early Sept.–early Oct., Sat.–Mon. 10:30 and 1:30; mid-June–early Sept., Thurs.–Mon. 10:30 and 1:30.*

WINERIES

Sumac Ridge Estate Winery. One of the area's first vineyards, Sumac Ridge has earned a fine reputation for its Merlot, Meritage, and sparkling ice wine. It offers tours combined with tastings, as well as a "founder's tasting" that includes such specialties as lavender crème brûlée, making this a great midmorning or midafternoon stop. The Cellar Door Bistro is open for lunch and dinner. ✉ *17403 Hwy. 97 N, Summerland* ☎ *250/494–0451* 🌐 *www.sumacridge.com* 🎫 *Tours C$7* ⏲ *Tours May–late June, daily at 11, 2, and 4; late June–early Oct., daily at 11, 1, and 3. Wineshop late June–early Sept., daily 9:30–9; early Sept.–late June, daily 10–8.*

WHERE TO EAT AND STAY

For expanded hotel reviews, visit Fodors.com.

$ CAFÉ ✕ **Bliss Bakery and Bistro.** Across the street from Okanagan Lake, this café on Peachland's tiny commercial strip epitomizes the small-is-good philosophy. It's the best place in the area for muffins, pastries, and coffee. The hearty breads are excellent, too, and there's a small selection of sandwiches and soups for lunch. Popular items often sell out, so come early in the day. [$] *Average main: C$9* ✉ *4200 Beach Ave., Peachland* ☎ *250/767–2711* 🌐 *www.blissbakery.ca* ✍ *Reservations not accepted* ⏲ *No dinner.*

$$ MODERN CANADIAN ✕ **Cellar Door Bistro.** Simple dishes take center stage at this bistro in the Sumac Ridge Estate Winery. Salads are made with local greens, and cheese plates feature the best from nearby dairies. The simple charcuterie assortment is designed to share. If you want a more substantial meal, opt for grilled salmon with a vegetable hash or Mediterranean-style lamb shank with a warm lentil-and-olive salad. It's all paired with

Sumac Ridge wines. *Average main: C$17* ✉ *Sumac Ridge Estate Winery, 17403 Hwy. 97 N, Summerland* ☎ *250/494–0451* 🌐 *www.sumacridge.com/cellardoor* ⏲ *Closed mid-Oct.–end Mar.*

$$$$ RESORT **Summerland Waterfront Resort.** Designed for families who like the feel of a summer cottage but want the amenities of a resort, the rooms at this modern lakeside hotel are bright and beachy. **Pros:** prime location on the lake; family-friendly vibe; welcomes pets. **Cons:** not many dining options nearby. *Rooms from: C$280* ✉ *13011 Lakeshore Dr. S, Summerland* ☎ *877/494–8111* 🌐 *www.summerlandresorthotel.com* *115 suites* *No meals.*

PENTICTON AND NARAMATA

16 km (10 miles) south of Summerland, 395 km (245 miles) east of Vancouver.

With its long, sandy beach backed by motels and cruising pickup trucks, Penticton is all about nostalgia-inducing family-vacations. But drive through the city center to the east side of Okanagan Lake and you'll be in the heart of the flourishing Naramata wine country. The route is so peppered with wineries that the seemingly short drive could take all afternoon.

EXPLORING

Linden Gardens. This former family fruit farm has morphed into a breathtaking nine-acre garden of flowers, trees, ponds, and streams. A path winds through a maze of constantly changing colors, passing over footbridges and beside jungles of wildflowers. Benches are strategically placed beneath weeping willows for shade or beside plants that draw butterflies and hummingbirds. The Frog City Café is an excellent stop for a late breakfast or light lunch. ✉ *351 Linden Ave., Kaleden* ☎ *250/497–6600* 🌐 *www.lindengardens.ca* ⏲ *Mid-Apr.–Oct., call for hrs.*

Okanagan Lavender Herb Farm. You can wander through more than 60 varieties at this farm, which has taken a cue from the surrounding wineries and opened to the public. There's a gift shop and a deck where you can enjoy a cool lavender lemonade or lavender ice cream. Arlo's Honey Farm is just around the corner. ✉ *4380 Takla Rd.* ☎ *250/764–7795* 🌐 *www.okanaganlavender.com.*

WINERIES

May through October is high season for the Naramata wineries. Many of the smaller vineyards close or scale back their hours between November and April.

Elephant Island Orchard Wines. Although many vintners take advantage of the nearby orchards, this funky winery makes a specialty out of fruit wine. Using recipes that are generations old, it creates some delightful table and dessert wines from pears, cherries, and black currants. Best of all, tastings are complimentary. ✉ *2730 Aikens Loop, Naramata* ☎ *250/496–5522* 🌐 *www.elephantislandwine.com* ⏲ *May–mid Oct., daily 10:30–5:30; mid-Oct.–Apr., by appointment.*

Hillside Estate Winery. As you drive along the road between Penticton and Naramata, it's hard to miss the 72-foot tower at Hillside Estate Winery.

DID YOU KNOW?

Lake Breeze Vineyards, overlooking Okanagan Lake is an enticing stop for a wine tasting or for lunch at the Patio restaurant.

Its first commercial release was in 1989, and the Old Vines Gamay Noir, Cabernet Franc, Syrah, and Pinot Gris are all award winners. It also produces an unusual white wine called Muscat Ottonel. The Hillside Bistro is open between April and mid-October. ✉ *1350 Naramata Rd.* ☎ *250/493–6274* 🌐 *www.hillsideestate.com* 🕒 *Apr.–Oct., daily 10–6; Nov.–Mar., by appointment.*

Lake Breeze Wine Farms. On the Naramata Benchlands above Okanagan Lake, Lake Breeze Wine Farms is one of the region's most attractively located small wineries. Its white wines, particularly their Gewürztraminer, Pinot Gris, and Pinot Blanc, are well regarded. The tasting room and garden patio have undergone renovations, which have spruced up an already lovely destination. The outdoor Patio Restaurant is open for lunch (weather permitting) between May and mid-October. ✉ *930 Sammet Rd., Naramata* ☎ *250/496–5659* 🌐 *www.lakebreeze.ca* 🎫 *Tastings C$2* 🕒 *Apr., Fri.–Sun. 12–4; May–mid-Oct., daily 11–5.*

Red Rooster Winery. Sampling wine at Red Rooster is a cultural experience. In addition to showcasing the recent vintages, the bright, spacious tasting room sells the work of local artists. If owning a vineyard is your fantasy, Red Rooster's "Adopt-A-Row" program could be the next best thing. You "own" a row of 50 vines for the season and are guaranteed a case of wine. ✉ *891 Naramata Rd., Naramata* ☎ *250/492–2424* 🌐 *www.redroosterwinery.com* 🕒 *Apr.–Oct., daily 10–6; Nov.–Mar., daily 11–5.*

Therapy Vineyards & Guesthouse. With wines that carry such names as Super Ego, Pink Freud, and Freudian Sip, you may feel like running for the analyst's couch. But never fear, this small vineyard combines its whimsical humor with a number of quality wines, especially its Merlot and Pinot Noir. The winery often hosts special weekends focusing on culinary and yoga programs. But with ony two rooms in the guest house, most participants reserve early or stay elsewhere. ✉ *940 Debeck Rd., Naramata* ☎ *250/496–5217* 🌐 *www.therapyvineyards.com* 🕒 *May–Oct., weekdays 10–5, weekends 10–6.*

WHERE TO EAT

$$$ MODERN CANADIAN

✕ **Hillside Bistro.** Hillside Estate Winery's straightforward lunch menu—salads, sandwiches, pizzas, and pastas—is presented with style. The two patios and rustic dining room tend to attract tour groups during the day. In the evening the vibe is more intimate, making this a good choice for traditional favorites like grilled sirloin steak with blue cheese, roasted chicken with grilled peaches, or honey-glazed salmon. $ *Average main: C$25* ✉ *Hillside Estate Winery, 1350 Naramata Rd.* ☎ *250/493–6274, 888/923–9463* 🌐 *www.hillsideestate.com* 🕒 *Closed mid-Oct.–early Apr. No dinner Apr. No dinner Mon.–Thurs. May and June.*

$ CAFÉ

✕ **Bench Artisan Food Market.** In the morning, the smell of coffee is likely to draw you into this foodie-friendly market and café, where just-from-the-oven pastries or homemade granola will tempt you to stay a while. At midday there are soups, salads, and sandwiches. The staff will make picnic platters to go (you can order these the day before), or you can assemble your own from the locally made cheeses, fresh-baked breads, and signature molten-chocolate brownies. $ *Average main: C$12* ✉ *368 Vancouver Ave.* ☎ *250/492–2222* 🌐 *www.thebenchmarket.com* 🕒 *No dinner.*

$$ MODERN CANADIAN **Patio at Lake Breeze.** A seat at this beautifully landscaped patio is one of the hottest tickets in town, so plan on an early lunch if you hope to get a table. Among the wine-friendly dishes you might find a warm seafood salad with a chipotle-lime cream sauce, pan roasted halibut with a prawn and ginger bisque, or a sirloin burger topped with locally made cheese. The tables are outdoors, meaning the restaurant closes in inclement weather. Reservations are accepted for groups of six or more. *Average main: C$18 930 Sammet Rd., Naramata 250/496–5659 www.lakebreeze.ca No dinner. Closed mid-Oct.–Apr.*

WHERE TO STAY

For expanded hotel reviews, visit Fodors.com.

$$$$ B&B/INN **Apple D'Or.** Overlooking Okanagan Lake, this palatial log house has amenities Tom Sawyer could never have imagined: in-room music systems, flat-screen TVs and DVD players (there's a 250-disc lending library), heated bathroom floors, full kitchens, and fireplaces. **Pros:** convenient location in the wine district. **Cons:** two-night minimum. *Rooms from: C$325 2587 Naramata Rd., Naramata 250/496–4045 www.appledor.ca 3 suites Closed Nov.–Mar. Breakfast.*

$$$ B&B/INN **God's Mountain Estate.** Filled with intriguing nooks and crannies, this quirky Mediterranean-style villa has a gorgeous white-washed exterior and sits on 115 rambling acres overlooking Skaha Lake. **Pros:** romantic rooms; dinners are extraordinary. **Cons:** the eccentric style is not for everyone; two-night minimum stay. *Rooms from: C$200 4898 Lakeside Rd. 250/490–4800 www.godsmountain.com 10 rooms, 4 suites Breakfast.*

$$$ HOTEL **Naramata Heritage Inn & Spa.** At this hotel dating back to 1908, many of the Mission-style furnishings, wood floors, and claw foot tubs are original, but plenty of the amenities—heated bathroom floors, fluffy duvets, central air-conditioning—are au courant. **Pros:** great choices at the wine bar; soothing spa. **Cons:** guest rooms are small. *Rooms from: C$225 3625 1st St., Naramata 250/496–6808, 866/617–1188 www.naramatainn.com 11 rooms, 1 suite Closed Nov.–Jan. Breakfast.*

9

OLIVER AND OSOYOOS

58 km (36 miles) south of Penticton, 400 km (250 miles) east of Vancouver.

South of Penticton, between the southern tip of Lake Okanagan and the U.S. border, Highway 97 passes through the country's only desert and runs along a chain of lakes: Skaha, Vaseaux, and Osoyoos. With a hot, dry climate, the lakeshore beaches can be crowded with families in summer; this is also a popular winter destination for snowbirds from the Canadian prairies. The climate makes this a prime wine-producing area, and the roads on both sides of Osoyoos Lake between the towns of Oliver and Osoyoos are lined with vineyards.

Oliver bills itself as the "Wine Capital of Canada" and this sleepy town of about 4,700 does have an ever-growing number of wineries. The community hopes to construct a "wine village" that will include an upscale inn and spa, although the plan has been on the table for the past several years.

CLOSE UP

A Crash Course in Okanagan Wines

GETTING ORIENTED

A great source of information about Okanagan wines is the British Columbia Wine Institute (*www.winebc.com*). The website includes a helpful guide to B.C. wines, as well as detailed itinerary suggestions for Okanagan wine touring. It also includes a calendar of wine-related dinners, tastings, and other events around the province.

A DROP OF HISTORY

Most wine experts agree that back in the dark ages (aka the 1970s), the wine produced in British Columbia was, to put it charitably, plonk. Okanagan Riesling and sparkling Lambrusco were the best sellers. Beginning in the late '70s, however, growers began replacing their vines with high-quality Vinifera varieties to start producing more sophisticated wines. In 1984, B.C. had 13 wineries. Today there are more than 200.

WHAT TO DRINK

In British Columbia overall, the top white varietals are Chardonnay, Pinot Gris, Gewürztraminer, Pinot Blanc, and Sauvignon Blanc. The top reds are Merlot, Pinot Noir, Cabernet Sauvignon, Syrah, and Cabernet Franc. Many Okanagan wineries also produce ice wine, a late-harvest dessert wine made from grapes that have frozen on the vine.

WHAT IS VQA?

British Columbia wines that carry a "VQA" (Vintners Quality Alliance) label must meet certain production and quality standards. A professional tasting panel approves each VQA wine. Participation in the VQA program is voluntary, and there are plenty of fine B.C. wines that have opted not to take part.

TO SPIT OR NOT TO SPIT?

On a day-long wine-tasting excursion, you can taste a good deal of wine. To avoid getting fatigued, or overly inebriated, do as the pros do: sip, swirl, and spit. Most wineries have a bucket on the tasting bar for that purpose, so don't be shy. You'll enjoy your tour more in the long run. And if the sample in your glass is more than you can drink, simply pour it into the bucket.

TRANSPORTING WINE

If you're buying bottles at the wineries, be sure you have some way to keep them cool, particularly in summer when soaring temperatures can spoil them quickly. If you must transport wine in your car, put it in a cooler or keep it on ice.

Most wineries will ship wines for you, but *only within Canada;* they cannot send wine over the border. If you're traveling back to the United States, have your wine packed for travel and transport it yourself.

UH-OH: SOLD OUT?

It's not uncommon for smaller Okanagan wineries to sell out of their wine in a given year. And when there's limited wine left, they generally close or reduce the hours in their tasting rooms. If you have your heart set on visiting a particular winery, check its website or phone in advance to be sure it has wine available.

The southernmost town in the Okanagan region, Osoyoos, has a significant First Nations population among its roughly 5,000 residents. The Osoyoos Indian Band operates North America's first aboriginal-owned winery and also runs an informative desert cultural center that's well worth a visit.

EN ROUTE

If you're approaching the Oliver/Osoyoos area from the west along Highway 3, keep your eye out for **Spotted Lake.** Containing one of the world's highest concentrations of minerals, this 38-acre lake dries up as the summer progresses, leaving mineral deposits in a distinctive "spotted" pattern. The Osoyoos Indian Band, which lives in the area, considers the lake sacred, believing its minerals have healing properties. The lake is on private property, but it's visible from the highway; it's east of Cawston and about 8 km (5 miles) west of Osoyoos.

EXPLORING

Desert Society. The northern tip of the Great Basin Desert is home to flora and fauna found nowhere else in the country. You can learn more about the unique local ecology at this interpretive center, where you can take a one-hour guided tour along a boardwalk leading through the desert. ✉ *146th St., off Hwy. 97* ☎ *250/495–2470, 877/899–0897* 🌐 *www.desert.org* 🎫 *C$7* ⏲ *Late Apr.–mid-May and mid-Sept.–mid-Oct., daily 10–2; mid-May–mid-Sept., daily 9:30–4:30; guided tours mid-May–mid-Sept. at 10, noon, and 2.*

★ **Nk'Mip Desert Cultural Centre.** Run by the Osoyoos Indian Band, this well-designed museum—the name is pronounced "in-ka-meep"—has exhibits about the area's aboriginal community, the region's natural setting, and the animals that make their home in this desert environment. Don't miss "Sssnakes Alive!", a daily show featuring live rattlesnakes and other creatures native to the area. You can also walk to a reconstructed village that includes two pit houses, a tepee, and a sweat lodge. (Bring water, since there's little shade along the trails.) The center's exterior is a striking, environmentally friendly earth wall built of a mix of soil, water, a small amount of cement, and pigment. ✉ *1000 Rancher Creek Rd.* ☎ *250/495–7901* 🌐 *www.nkmipdesert.com* 🎫 *C$12* ⏲ *Early Mar.–early May, Tues.–Sat. 9:30–4:30; early May–June and Sept.–Oct., daily 9:30–4:30; July–Aug., Thurs.–Tues. 9:30–4:30, Wed. 9:30–4:30 and 5–9.*

WINERIES

Wineries line the roads between Osoyoos and Oliver, and continuing north toward the town of Okanagan Falls. Most are fairly small operations, with some notable larger producers. Many wineries close or reduce their operations between November and April, so call first if you're traveling off-season.

Black Hills Estate Winery. On the Black Sage Bench between Osoyoos and Oliver, Black Hills Estate Winery has developed a cult following among Okanagan aficionados, and frequently sells out of its much-admired wines. When the wine is gone, the tasting room closes for the season. It's worth calling to check on the status of its Nota Bene (a blend of Cabernet Sauvignon, Merlot, and Cabernet Franc), Alibi (Sauvignon Blanc with a bit of Sémillon), Chardonnay, or whatever the winemaker dreams up next. May through mid-October, tours of the vineyard and

9

winery depart at 11 am and 1:30 pm and include tastings. ✉ *30880 Black Sage Rd., Oliver* ☎ *250/498–0666* 🌐 *www.blackhillswinery.com* ⏲ *Tours May–mid-Oct. 11 am and 1:30 pm.*

Burrowing Owl Estate Winery. With wines consistently taking home medals in international competitions, Burrowing Owl is one of the area's best-known boutique vineyards. Recent award-winning vintages include a 2009 Pinot Noir and a 2008 Pinot Gris, Cabernet Franc, and Merlot. Winery tours are offered on weekends from May through October, and tastings are available year-round. At the 25-foot tasting bar, C$2 donations go toward the Burrowing Owl Recovery Society. To savor the sweeping views of the vineyards and Osoyoos Lake, enjoy a meal at the terrific Sonora Room Restaurant. ✉ *100 Burrowing Owl Pl., off Black Sage Rd., Oliver* ☎ *250/498–0620, 877/498–0620* 🌐 *www.bovwine.ca* 🎫 *Tours C$5* ⏲ *Tours May–Oct., weekends 11 am and 2 pm. Wineshop May–mid-Oct., daily 10–5; call for off-season hrs.*

Hester Creek Estate Winery. Set high on a bluff between Osoyoos and Oliver, Hester Creek has an inviting bistro called Terrafina and a multipurpose tasting venue that includes a main room large enough to host parties, a private dining room for intimate groups, a patio with a wood-fired pizza oven, and a gourmet demonstration kitchen. There's a grassy picnic area where you can enjoy a snack and a glass of wine—Pinot Blanc, Pinot Gris, Merlot, and Cabernet Franc are all top choices. ✉ *13163 326th Ave., Oliver* ☎ *250/498–4435* 🌐 *www.hestercreek.com* ⏲ *May–mid-Oct., daily 10–5:30; mid-Oct.–Apr., daily 10–4.*

Nk'Mip Cellars. A few minutes east of Osoyoos, Nk'Mip Cellars is the country's first winery operated by a First Nations people. On a ridge overlooking Osoyoos Lake, it's part of a stunningly designed resort complex that is, as odd as it sounds, surrounded by arid desert, a lush golf course, and abundant vineyards. The winery released its first vintage in 2002 and now produces 18,000 cases annually, including an award-winning Pinot Blanc, Reisling, Chardonnay, and Syrah. For every bottle sold of its premium label, C$1 goes to support the Desert Cultural Centre Legacy Fund. In addition to wine, the tasting room sells aboriginal art. Stay to enjoy dining at the Patio Restaurant. ✉ *1400 Rancher Creek Rd.* ☎ *250/495–2985* 🌐 *www.nkmipcellars.com* 🎫 *Tours C$5* ⏲ *Tours May–Oct., daily 11, 1, and 3. Wineshop Apr.–May and Sept.–Oct. 9–5; June–Aug. 9–6; Nov.–Mar. 10–4.*

WHERE TO EAT

$$$ MODERN CANADIAN

✕ **The Patio.** Set on a lovely terrace looking out over the vineyards at Nk'Mip Cellars, this restaurant offers shady respite from the desert heat. The menu includes salads, cheese plates, and other light meals, and dishes sometimes feature aboriginal influences, such as wild salmon or bison steak. Like many winery dining rooms, this one is outdoors and closes when the weather turns. Although it's primarily a place for lunch, it serves dinner on Friday and Saturday evenings in July and August. $ *Average main: C$27* ✉ *Nk'Mip Cellars, 1400 Rancher Creek Rd.* ☎ *250/495–2985* 🌐 *www.nkmipcellars.com* ⏲ *Closed Oct.–Apr. No dinner May–June or Sept; no dinner Sun.–Thurs. July–Aug.*

$$$ MODERN CANADIAN Fodor's Choice ★ **Sonora Room Restaurant.** Start with a picture-perfect backdrop overlooking the vineyards, add a contemporary market driven menu, and top it off with expert service, and the result is one of the Okanagan's finest dining experiences. With its high-beamed ceilings and wood floors, the interior is rustic, but the best seats are on the terrace looking out across the fields. Opt for pan-seared rockfish with organic wild rice and roasted grape tomato risotto, duck breast with cabbage and apple slaw, or a sophisticated vegetarian plate that might include chick-pea-crusted tofu, a salad of quinoa and Brussels sprouts, or roasted cauliflower puree. The restaurant is open for lunch and dinner daily from May through mid-October, but keeps more limited hours off-season. *$ Average main: C$26 ✉ Burrowing Owl, 100 Burrowing Owl Pl., Oliver ☎ 250/498–0620, 877/498–0620 ⊕ www.bovwine.ca.*

$$ PACIFIC NORTHWEST **Watermark Wine Bar and Patio.** Part of the swanky Watermark Beach Resort, this wine bar sits on the water and has terrific views. Guests from other resorts head here for a night out, grazing on more than 30 tapas ranging from Thai-style skewered meats to yam fries with spicy mayonnaise to lamb merguez sausage. More substantial dishes, such as chicken with wild mushrooms, are offered for dinner. Many of the featured wines are limited editions from local wineries, so if you didn't taste them during your afternoon touring, you may find them here. *$ Average main: C$15 ✉ Watermark Beach Resort, 15 Park Pl. ☎ 250/495–5508.*

WHERE TO STAY

For expanded hotel reviews, visit Fodors.com.

$$$$ B&B/INN **The Guesthouse at Burrowing Owl.** You could be forgiven for thinking you're in Tuscany while sitting on your balcony sipping a glass of Chardonnay, overlooking the vineyards, at this romantic inn. **Pros:** great views over the vineyards; excellent service. **Cons:** no resort-style amenities. *$ Rooms from: C$325 ✉ 100 Burrowing Owl Pl., Oliver ☎ 250/498–0620, 877/498–0620 ⊕ www.bovwine.ca ⇨ 10 rooms, 1 suite ⊗ Closed mid-Dec.–mid-Feb. ◎ Breakfast.*

$$$$ RESORT **Spirit Ridge Vineyard Resort & Spa.** At this Southwestern-style resort, all the accommodations—from the one-, two-, and three-bedroom suites to the one- and two-bedroom villas—have gourmet kitchens, living rooms with fireplaces, and expansive balconies. **Pros:** there's plenty to do; family-friendly environment. **Cons:** lake access is a little awkward; away from the center of town. *$ Rooms from: C$290 ✉ 1200 Rancher Creek Rd. ☎ 250/495–5445, 877/313–9463 ⊕ www.spiritridge.ca ⇨ 226 suites ◎ No meals.*

$$$$ B&B/INN **The Villa at Hester Creek.** All the rooms in this Mediterranean-style B&B overlook rows of vines at the Hester Creek Estate Winery. **Pros:** serene environment; spacious rooms. **Cons:** no common areas. *$ Rooms from: C$295 ✉ 13163 326th Ave., Oliver ☎ 250/498–4435, 866/498–4435 ⊕ www.hestercreek.com ⇨ 5 rooms, 1 suite ⊗ Closed Nov.–mid-Feb. ◎ Breakfast.*

$$$ RESORT **Walnut Beach Resort.** With its own sandy beach on the shores of Okanagan Lake, this lovely resort has an away-from-it-all ambience, helped by the fact that it's at the end of a road in a quiet residential neighborhood. **Pros:** relaxed atmosphere; great food; friendly staff. **Cons:** popular

9

wedding venue; a bit awkward to get to; limited evening entertainment. *Rooms from: C$230* ✉ *4200 Lakeshore Dr., Osoyoos, Washington* ☎ *250/495–5400, 877/936–5400* 🌐 *www.walnutbeachosoyoos.com* *112 rooms* *No meals.*

SPORTS AND THE OUTDOORS

BIKING AND HIKING

International Bicycling and Hiking Trail. If you want to travel from winery to winery under your own power, follow the International Bicycling and Hiking Trail. This relatively flat trail begins at the north end of Osoyoos Lake and runs north along the Okanagan River for 18 km (11 miles). To get to the trail parking lot from Osoyoos, follow Highway 97 north for 8 km (5 miles), then head east on Road 22. 🌐 *www.destinationosoyoos.com.*

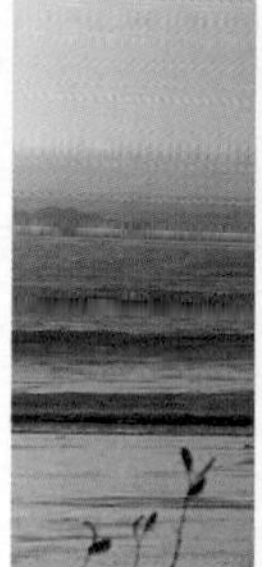

TOFINO, UCLUELET, AND THE PACIFIC RIM

Tofino may be the birthplace of North American storm-watching, but the area's tempestuous winter weather and roiling waves are only two of the many stellar attractions you'll find along the Pacific Northwest's wildest coastline. Exquisite tide pooling, expansive wilderness beaches, excellent surfing, and the potential to see some of the continent's largest sea mammals lure thousands of visitors to Pacific Rim National Park Reserve, sleepy Ucluelet, and quirkily charming Tofino.

No one "happens" upon Tofino; it's literally at the end of the road, where Highway 4 meets the mouth of Clayoquot Sound. As Canada's premier surfer village, Tofino has shed much of its '60s-style counterculture vibe and transformed itself into a happening tourist destination where fine dining, spa treatments, and eco adventures are par for the course. You can enjoy meandering through old-growth forests, exploring pristine beaches and rocky tidal pools, bathing in natural hot springs, and spotting whales, bears, eagles, and river otters in a natural setting.

The harbor towns of Ucluelet and Tofino are chock-a-block with funky shops, services, and eateries—and, in Tofino, there are also fine-dining restaurants. The burgeoning culinary culture on Vancouver Island definitely extends to the Pacific Rim region. Permanent residents include this coast's ancestral aboriginal people, cold-water surfers and adventure-sports types, artists and craftspeople, fishers and loggers, environmentalists—and people who've sought the laid-back life.

PLANNING

MAKING THE MOST OF YOUR TIME

Three full days are about the minimum: once you've made the five-hour trek from Vancouver, it takes a day to unwind and allow the place get into your consciousness. A quick conversation with your host will help you hit the highlights—the best spots to view wildlife, the top trails (some get washed out in stormy weather), when to browse the galleries (some close Monday), and what musicians are playing (if nightlife is on your list).

FESTIVALS

The Pacific Rim has various festivals throughout the year.

MAR.: The **Pacific Rim Whale Festival** (🌐 *www.pacificrimwhalefestival.com*) marks the spring migration of as many as 22,000 Pacific gray whales between Mexico and the Arctic with crafts, food, and cultural events for the whole family. You can try everything from building sand-sculptures to decorating sea creature–cookies.

APR.–MAY: The **Tofino Shorebird Festival** (🌐 *www.tourismtofino.com*) celebrates the thousands of shorebirds that migrate north from Central and South America to tundra breeding grounds in Alaska. The date changes annually, so check with Tourism Tofino.

JUNE: Area lodges and food and wine producers sponsor the three-day **Tofino Food and Wine Festival** (*www.tofinofoodandwinefestival.com*) at Tofino Botanical Gardens.

JULY: The **Pacific Rim Summer Festival** (*www.pacificrimarts.ca*) is a celebration of music, dance, and the arts during the first two weeks of July.

AUG.: Hundreds of imaginatively crafted lanterns make the **Tofino Lantern Festival** (*www.tourismtofino.com*) a sight to behold. It's usually held around Labor Day weekend.

NOV.: The humble bivalve is celebrated during the **Oyster Festival** (*www.oystergala.com*), a three-day gastronomic adventure.

GETTING HERE AND AROUND

AIR TRAVEL

The major airports on Vancouver Island are Victoria International Airport (YYJ), Nanaimo Airport (YCD), and Comox Valley Airport (YQQ); you can fly into one of these, then rent a car (or take a bus) to Tofino-Ucluelet. Only Orca flies regular scheduled flights (on 10- to 18-seat passenger planes) into the tiny Tofino-Ucluelet Airport (YAZ) from Vancouver, Victoria, and Qualicum Beach.

Note that weather can delay and cancel flights; when flights are diverted to other regional airports, alternative transportation is provided. A Tofino shuttle service delivers passengers to major resorts. Pacific Coastal Airlines runs charters to Tofino from Vancouver's South Terminal in summer. Seattle-based Kenmore flies from Washington State to several B.C. communities.

Northwest Seaplanes runs charter flights from its terminal at Renton, near Seattle, to Tofino and Ucluelet. West Coast Air runs seaplane charters from Vancouver, Victoria, Nanaimo, and other B.C. destinations.

Contacts West Coast Air *800/347–2222* *www.westcoastair.com* **Kenmore Air Harbor** *866/435–9524* *www.kenmoreair.com.* **Orca Air** *604/270–6722* *www.flyorcaair.com.* **Pacific Coastal Airlines** *604/273–8666, 800/663–2872* *www.pacific-coastal.com.* **Northwest Seaplanes** *425/277–1590, 800/690–0086* *www.nwseaplanes.com.*

BOAT AND FERRY TRAVEL

BC Ferries has frequent, year-round passenger and vehicle service to Vancouver Island: it's a 1½-hour crossing from Horseshoe Bay (a 30-minute drive north of Vancouver) to Departure Bay, 3 km (2 miles) north of Nanaimo. From here it's a two- to three-hour drive, via Port Alberni, to Ucluelet, and on to Tofino. There's also a two-hour crossing from Tsawwassen (about a 40-minute drive south of Vancouver) to Duke Point, 15 km (9 miles) south of Nanaimo; or a 1½-hour crossing from Tsawwassen to Swartz Bay (a 30-minute drive north of Victoria). Vehicle reservations can be made for any of these ferry routes.

Lady Rose Marine Services takes passengers on a packet freighter from Port Alberni to various points on Vancouver Island's west coast. The MV *Francis Barkley* sails from Port Alberni to the Broken Group Islands and Ucluelet on Monday, Wednesday, and Friday between early June and late September, and to Bamfield and waypoints on Tuesday, Thursday, and Saturday. Sunday stops are Bamfield and the Broken

9

Group Islands, where the company operates Sechart Lodge, a floating base for kayakers. Round-trip fares are C$74 to Ucluelet, and C$70 to Bamfield or the Broken Group Islands.

Contacts **BC Ferries** ☎ *250/381-1401, 888/223-3779 in B.C.* ⊕ *www.bcferries.com.* **Lady Rose Marine Services** ☎ *250/723-8313, 800/663-7192* ⊕ *www.ladyrosemarine.com.*

BUS TRAVEL

Tofino Bus (connecting with Greyhound) provides daily service between Vancouver, Victoria, Nanaimo (Departure Bay ferry terminal), and Port Alberni, Ucluelet, and Tofino. It also runs between Ucluelet and Tofino throughout the year, and provides scheduled summer service to major resorts and beaches to and from Tofino only. One-way fares to Tofino are C$45 from Nanaimo, C$68 from Victoria. Greyhound travels between Vancouver and Victoria to Nanaimo, where it connects with the Tofino Bus.

Contacts **Greyhound** ☎ *800/661-8747* ⊕ *www.greyhound.ca.* **Tofino Bus** ☎ *250/725-2871, 866/986-3466* ⊕ *www.tofinobus.com.*

CAR TRAVEL

Tofino is 314 km (195 miles) from Victoria, about a four-hour drive. If you're coming from Vancouver by ferry (to Victoria or Nanaimo), head north to Parksville via the Trans-Canada Highway (Highway 1) and the Island Highway (Highway 19). From there pick up Highway 4, which crosses the island from Parksville to Port Alberni, Ucluelet, and Tofino. Break up the trip with a lunch or ice-cream break at the Coombs Old Country Market, about 15 km (9 miles) west of Parksville. It's a good stop for picnic supplies.

Budget Car and Truck Rental and Tofino Car Rental rent vehicles at Tofino-Ucluelet Airport.

Contacts **Budget Car** ☎ *250/725-2060* ⊕ *www.bcbudget.com.* **Tofino Airport Car Rental** ⊕ *www.tofinoairportcarrental.com.*

TAXI TRAVEL

Tofino West Coast Taxi provides service to Tofino, including airport pickup. Book in advance for night or off-hours service. The Tofino Water Taxi is a boat shuttle to Meares Island, Hot Springs Cove, and other remote offshore sites.

Contacts **Tofino West Coast Taxi** ☎ *250/725-3333.* **Tofino Water Taxi** ☎ *250/726-5485, 877/726-5485* ⊕ *www.tofinowatertaxi.com.*

TOUR OPTIONS

Thinking about some side trips? Then why not hop onto a boat or floatplane and explore the surrounding roadless wilderness? The most popular day trip is to Hot Springs Cove, where you can soak in natural rock pools. On Meares Island, an easy 20-minute boardwalk trail leads to trees up to 1,600 years old. The remote sand beaches of Vargas Island are popular in warm weather. On Flores Island, a challenging five-hour hike called Walk on the Wild Side leads through the old growth cedar, hemlock, and spruce. These destinations can be reached on various adventure tours.

For boat trips, several companies conduct multiday sea-kayaking trips to the coastal areas of Vancouver Island. Some excursions are suitable for beginners, and many trips are an excellent chance to view orcas, sea lions, and other marine wildlife. Gabriola Sea Kayaking has trips to the Broken Group Islands in the Pacific Rim National Park Reserve and other areas off the west coast of Vancouver Island. Majestic Ocean Kayaking offers guided half-day harbor tours, day trips, and multiday camping trips to the Broken Group Islands.

Remote Passages provides half-day whale-watching excursions as well as trips to Meares Island and to Clayoquot. For hiking and parks information, visit the B.C. Parks website. For West Coast Trail information and reservations, contact Hello BC.

Contacts British Columbia Parks ☎ *604/660–2421* 🌐 *www.bcparks.ca.* **Gabriola Sea Kayaking** ☎ *250/247–0189* 🌐 *www.kayaktoursbc.com.* **Tourism BC** ☎ *800/435–5622* 🌐 *www.hellobc.com.* **Majestic Ocean Kayaking** ☎ *250/726–2860, 800/889–7644* 🌐 *www.oceankayaking.com.* **Remote Passages** ☎ *800/666–9833* 🌐 *www.remotepassages.com.* **Tla-ook Cultural Adventures** ☎ *250/725–2656* 🌐 *www.tlaook.com.*

VISITOR INFORMATION

The Pacific Rim Visitors Centre sells park permits and provides free information and maps on the Pacific Rim National Park Reserve and Tofino-Ucluelet area.

Contacts Pacific Rim Visitors Center ☎ *250/726–4212* 🌐 *www.pacificrimvisitor.ca.* **Tofino Visitor Info Center** ✉ *1426 Pacific Rim Hwy., Tofino* ☎ *250/725–3414, 888/720–3414* 🌐 *www.tourismtofino.com.*

RESTAURANTS

Vancouver Islanders are often credited with starting the "locavore" movement. Wild salmon, Pacific oysters, locally made artisanal cheeses, forest-foraged mushrooms, organic vegetables, local microbrews, and even wines and spirits from the island's family-run wineries and distilleries can all be sampled here. Restaurants are generally casual and few are "late night."

Prices in the reviews are the average cost of a main course at dinner or, if dinner is not served, at lunch.

HOTELS

Prices for lodging and dining are relatively high for such a remote destination. Rates vary widely through the seasons, winter being the lowest: luxury lodge stays during the winter storm-watching season can cost as little as a third of summer rates.

Prices in the reviews are the lowest cost of a standard double room in high season.

9

TOFINO

42 km (26 miles) northwest of Ucluelet, 337 km (209 miles) northwest of Victoria.

Tofino combines the historical roots of the rugged Canadian frontier with the mellow rhythm of a California surf town—think Mendocino in a toque. Old-growth forest meets the relentless surf of the Pacific and explorers from age two to 102 dig into sand, tide pools, and surf. Talk to the locals and you're bound to hear some interesting "How I came to live in Tofino" anecdotes.

> **WORD OF MOUTH**
>
> "The Pacific Rim National Park, Ucluelet and Tofino is a 5 hour drive from Victoria and once there, you'd want at least 3 full days to experience the region. It's truly a magical part of Vancouver Island and would be where I'd steer outdoor/wilderness/nature enthusiasts."
>
> —Carmanah

The district's 1,800 or so permanent residents host about a million visitors every year, but they've made what could have been a tourist trap into an unconventional little town with several art galleries, good restaurants, and plenty of opportunity to get out to the surrounding wilds. Reservations are recommended any time of year. While many outdoor activities are confined to spring through fall, surfing continues year-round, regardless of the temperature. November through February is devoted to storm-watching (best enjoyed from a cozy waterfront lodge).

EXPLORING

Tofino Botanical Gardens. Trails wind through displays of indigenous plant life, and the occasional whimsical garden sculpture may catch your eye at Tofino Botanical Gardens. The 12-acre waterfront site is located about 2 km (1 mile) south of Tofino on the Pacific Rim Highway. The C$10 admission is good for three days. ✉ *1084 Pacific Rim Hwy.* ☎ *250/725–1220* 🌐 *www.tbgf.org* 🎫 *C$10* ⏲ *Daily 9–dusk.*

WHERE TO EAT

$$ ECLECTIC

✕ **Breakers Fresh Food Cafe.** This popular takeout place on Tofino's main drag serves delicious whole-wheat pizzas, salads, wraps, burritos, and all-day breakfasts, all of it hip and ultrahealthy. There's also a gourmet deli with cheeses and other specialty items. [$] *Average main: C$15* ✉ *430 Campbell St.* ☎ *250/725–2558* 🌐 *www.breakersdeli.com/.*

$$$$ CANADIAN Fodor's Choice ★

✕ **The Pointe.** With 180-degree views of the crashing surf, the Pointe is *the* top-notch Tofino dining experience. It's renowned for its Pacific Northwest cuisine, which is superbly presented and excellently paired with options from the award-winning wine list. Ingredients from the water—including oysters, shrimp, salmon, and a variety of other fish—and the land (whatever's in season, such as wild mushrooms and fresh herbs) are used in innovative but not too outlandish dishes. The service is meticulous, formal but friendly. [$] *Average main: C$35* ✉ *The Wickaninnish Inn, 500 Osprey La.* ☎ *250/725–3100* 🌐 *www.wickinn.com/restaurant.html.*

CLOSE UP

Pacific Rim Storm-Watching

No one's really sure when the concept of "bad weather" morphed into "good weather," but on the tourism-friendly Pacific Rim, nasty storms are usually considered quite fine indeed.

November through March is formally storm-watching season, and thousands of people travel from around the world to witness the spectacularly violent weather. Veteran storm-watchers are known to keep an eye on the weather channels and pack their bags quickly for Tofino or Ucluelet when storm predictions are particularly, well, grim.

Throughout the winter, but particularly during the "peak season" of December through February, as many as 15 "good storms" arrive per month. Winds from the ocean exceed 50 kph (30 mph) and teeming rain—even hail, sleet, or snow—arrives horizontally. Massive waves thunder onto the beaches and crash over the rocky headlands and islets, sending spray soaring. Towering evergreen trees crackle and lean; logs are tossed helter-skelter, high onto kelp-strewn beaches. Unusual storm clouds, mists, and rainbows add to the beauty. And as if the sights weren't enough, expect to hear the eerie sounds of a screaming wind, pounding surf—even the rattling of double-paned windows—unless you happen to be behind reinforced triple-glazed windows, in which case the whole show unfolds in near silence. And that's even more surreal.

The hotels and B&Bs love the storm season because it fills rooms in what could otherwise be a bleak time of year. And it must be admitted that most storm-watching takes place in considerable comfort—particularly at the luxury hotels along Cox Bay, Chesterman Beach, and MacKenzie Beach. These and other waterfront properties in the Tofino-Ucluelet region have shrewdly developed "storm-watching packages," in which treats abound (and rates tumble). Champagne on arrival, fashionable wet-weather gear, complimentary nature walks, and gourmet dinners are among the offerings. Perhaps most important, expect a cozy room, often with a fireplace and a soaker tub with an ocean outlook, in which you can relax in security, while the outer world rages on.

Serious thrill seekers take to the beaches and lookouts to experience storms firsthand. That said, conditions can be decidedly unfriendly, and visitors should remember that this is a coastline famed for its shipwrecks. Storm-watchers planning on walking the Wild Pacific Trail, for example, should go with a companion, and preferably with an experienced naturalist or guide. Other notable storm-watching venues include Wickaninnish Beach, with the largest swells and greatest concentration of logs and driftwood; Second Bay, where powerful swells funnel through the rocks and islets; Long Beach, famed for its rolling swells, wave-washed islands, and panoramic views; Cox Bay, said to receive the largest and most powerful waves; and Chesterman Beach, beloved for its varied conditions and outlooks.

$$$ ECLECTIC ★ **RainCoast Café.** This casual-yet-chic village-center restaurant has a stellar reputation for its Asian-inspired take on local seafood. Sustainably harvested or organic entrées include spot prawns sauteed with plum wine and ginger, pan-seared halibut with a sake, mango, and lime sauce, and duck from B.C.'s Fraser Valley. There are also tasty vegetarian dishes. Servings come as main dishes; small tapas-style plates are roughly half price. *Average main: C$23 101–120 4th St. 250/725–2215 www.raincoastcafe.com No lunch.*

$$$ SEAFOOD Fodor's Choice ★ **Schooner Restaurant.** An institution in downtown Tofino, the Schooner's main-floor dining room is comfortable and casually upscale. The seafood dishes change frequently, but ask for the signature halibut fillet stuffed with Brie, crab, toasted pine nuts, and shrimp in an apple-peppercorn brandy sauce. The steaming bowl of island clams, mussels, salmon, halibut, and sidestripe prawns is another winner. The Schooner also dishes up hearty breakfasts and lunchtime sandwiches, burgers, and pastas. The summer patio is a plus, and the evenings-only Schooner Upstairs has exceptional views of Meares Island. *Average main: C$23 331 Campbell St. 250/725–3444 www.schoonerrestaurant.ca.*

$$$ SEAFOOD **Shelter.** Popular with locals and visitors, the centrally located Shelter has a lounge and patio for casual meals and an upstairs dining room. The fare ranges from crispy calamari to pan-seared salmon to grilled rib-eye. Small plates have a coastal theme, and include such favorites as freshly shucked oysters, steamed mussels, and spicy albacore tuna. *Average main: C$23 601 Campbell St. 915/551–0252 www.shelterrestaurant.com No lunch.*

$$$ ECLECTIC Fodor's Choice ★ **Sobo.** The name, short for "sophisticated bohemian," sums up the style here: a classically trained chef serving casual fare influenced by international street food. The off-beat concept started in a purple truck before finding a permanent home in this light-filled café and bistro. The truck's long gone, but the food is still eclectic. Tapas might include halibut cheeks or forest-mushroom risotto bullets. Small plates like coconut masala curry with quinoa, chickpeas, and house-made roti, and mains ranging from cedar-plank wild salmon to mushroom enchiladas never fail to impress. There's a great kids' menu and a deli counter. Call ahead in winter. *Average main: C$22 311 Neill St. 250/725–2341 www.sobo.ca No dinner Oct.–May.*

$$ PACIFIC NORTHWEST ★ **Wickaninnish Restaurant.** Not to be confused with the restaurant at the nearby Wickaninnish Inn, this spectacular wood-beam dining room sits on Long Beach in Pacific Rim National Park Reserve. Commercial signage is, by park regulation, restrained: all you'll see is the word "restaurant," alongside "Wickaninnish Interpretive Centre," on a green park sign on the Pacific Rim Highway, about 11 km (7 miles) north of Ucluelet; turn onto Wick Road and drive to the ocean. Lunch involves hearty soups, salads, and quiches along with more substantial plates like salmon and crab; many of these are repeated on the dinner menu. The wine list includes a selection of B.C. ice wines. *Average main: C$17 Pacific Rim National Park Reserve, Wick Rd., Ucluelet 250/726–7706 Closed Oct.–Feb.*

WHERE TO STAY

For expanded hotel reviews, visit Fodors.com.

$$$$ RESORT Fodor's Choice ★ **Clayoquot Wilderness Resort.** Sleeping beneath canvas never was so elegant, which is why people from around the globe arrive via floatplane or boat to experience one of the top wilderness resorts. **Pros:** escapism at its best, with no phone or other distractions; excellent food; a ton of outdoorsy activities. **Cons:** it's pricey; takes a while to get here. *Rooms from: C$1,800 Bedwell River 250/726–8235, 888/333–5405 www.wildretreat.com 20 tents Closed Oct.–Apr. All meals.*

$$$ B&B/INN **Inn at Tough City.** Vintage furnishings and First Nations art make this harborside inn funky, if a bit cluttered. **Pros:** prime Tofino location; loads of character; restaurant has best sushi in town. **Cons:** the lobby is small and noisy; front-desk staffing friendly but inconsistent. *Rooms from: C$199 350 Main St. 250/725–2021, 877/725–2021 www.toughcity.com 8 rooms.*

$$$$ HOTEL ★ **Long Beach Lodge Resort.** With handcrafted furnishings, dramatic pieces of First Nations art, and a tall granite fireplace, the great room at this luxury lodge offers front row seats to the surf (and surfers) rolling into miles of sandy beach. **Pros:** exceptional beachfront location; terrific restaurant; cozy areas within the great room. **Cons:** no spa or pool; beach gets busy with guests from neighboring resorts. *Rooms from: C$320 1441 Pacific Rim Hwy. 250/725–2442, 877/844–7873 www.longbeachlodgeresort.com 41 rooms, 20 cottages Breakfast.*

$$$ RESORT ★ **Middle Beach Lodge.** Set on a bluff overlooking a mile of private beach, this rustically elegant lodge has several types of accommodations, from spacious rooms and suites reserved for guests 12 and over to self-contained cabins suitable for families with younger children. **Pros:** truly secluded, with an almost exclusive beach; ideal for adults seeking peace and privacy; good dining room with great views. **Cons:** no room service or in-room Wi-Fi. *Rooms from: C$220 400 MacKenzie Beach Rd. 250/725–2901 www.middlebeach.com 35 rooms, 10 suites, 19 cabins Restaurant closed Nov.–Mar. Sun.–Thurs. No lunch Breakfast.*

$$$$ RESORT ★ **Pacific Sands Beach Resort.** Set on 45 marvelous acres along Cox Bay, this resort offers a range of lodge rooms, waterfront suites, and beach villas with full kitchens, fireplaces, and private decks. **Pros:** on prime beachfront; good family destination. **Cons:** no restaurant; no elevators; some suites are on the small side. *Rooms from: C$350 1421 Pacific Rim Hwy. 250/725–3322, 800/565–2322 www.pacificsands.com 22 villas, 57 suites No meals.*

$$$ RENTAL **Red Crow Guest House & Cottage.** Tucked away down a leafy lane, this retreat is a real find if what you're seaching for is seclusion. **Pros:** plenty of privacy; near gardens and beaches. **Cons:** no TV; minimum stay in high season. *Rooms from: C$195 1064 Pacific Rim Hwy. 250/725–2275 www.tofinoredcrow.com 2 rooms, 1 cottage No meals.*

$ HOTEL Fodor's Choice ★ **Whalers on the Point Guest House.** With its harbor-view picture windows and big stone fireplace, this modern seaside inn looks more like an upscale lodge than a budget option for everyone from backpackers to families. **Pros:** unbeatable location in Tofino; ideal for young travelers; sauna. **Cons:** no restaurant; sells out quickly; a bit noisy. *Rooms from: C$65 ✉ 81 West St. ☎ 250/725–3443 ⊕ www.tofinohostel.com ⇨ 7 rooms, 11 dorm rooms 🍴 No meals.*

$$$$ RESORT Fodor's Choice ★ **The Wickaninnish Inn.** On a rocky promontory with open ocean on three sides and old-growth forest as a backdrop, this cedar-sided inn is exceptional in every sense. **Pros:** at the end of a superb crescent beach; the silence of storms through triple-glazed windows is surreal; excellent staff. **Cons:** pricey and posh; no swimming pool. *Rooms from: C$500 ✉ 500 Osprey La., at Chesterman Beach ☎ 250/725–3100, 800/333–4604 ⊕ www.wickinn.com ⇨ 64 rooms, 11 suites.*

SPORTS AND THE OUTDOORS

FISHING

Chinook Charters. At Chinook Charters, Captain Mike Hansen is an independent guide born and raised in the area. His custom-designed 30-foot vessel is well equipped to land a prized coho. Prices are in line with other Tofino operators at around C$600 per day for up to 3 people. *✉ 331 Main St. ☎ 250/726–5221 ⊕ www.chinookcharters.com.*

Cleanline Sport Fishing. Experienced anglers appreciate the expertise of this company. As the only multiboat operator in Tofino, it offers both saltwater and freshwater excursions. Prices are competitive at C$115 per hour in the ocean and about C$500 per day on the rivers. *✉ 561 Campbell St. ☎ 250/725–2700, 888/534–7422 ⊕ www.cleanlinesportfishing.com.*

Weigh West Marine Resort. One of the few fishing resorts accessible by car (most are on remote islands), Weigh West Marine Resort runs charters fishing trips throughout the year. Rates are C$115 per hour for up to six people. It also offers whale-watching and kayaking trips from March to October. *✉ 634 Campbell St. ☎ 250/725–3238, 800/665–8922 ⊕ www.weighwest.com.*

FLIGHTSEEING

Tofino Air. These 20-minute flightseeing tours wing you over outlying forests and beaches to Hot Springs Cove. Other trips take you to the lakes and glaciers of Strathcona Provincial Park. If you can, soar over Cougar Annie's Garden, a century-old wilderness homestead that was once the home of a legendary local character. *✉ 50 1st St. ☎ 250/725–4454, 866/486–3247 ⊕ www.tofinoair.ca.*

KAYAKING

★ **Remote Passages.** No experience is necessary for these relaxed guided paddles in sheltered waters. Also on offer are whale-watch trips and excursions to Meares Island, Hot Springs Cove, and Clayoquot Sound. *✉ 71 Wharf St. ☎ 250/725–3330, 800/666–9833 ⊕ www.remotepassages.com.*

Tofino Sea-Kayaking Company. Tofino Sea-Kayaking Company rents kayaks, runs a kayaking school, and provides day and multiday wilderness kayaking trips. No experience is necessary. *✉ 320 Main St. ☎ 250/725–4222, 800/863–4664 ⊕ www.tofinoseakayaking.com.*

SURFING

The coast from Tofino south to Ucluelet is, despite perpetually chilly waters, an increasingly popular surf destination—year-round.

Live to Surf. You can rent boards and other gear at Live to Surf. Jean-Paul Froment runs the business (founded by his parents in 1984) with his sister Pascale from the funky Outside Break commercial hub south of Tofino, which is conveniently close to the major surfing spots of Long Beach, Cox Bay, Chesterman Beach, and MacKenzie Beach. The shop also sells boards, wet suits, and accessories, and provides rentals and lessons. ✉ *1180 Pacific Rim Hwy.* ☎ *250/725–4464* 🌐 *www.livetosurf.com.*

Pacific Surf School. This company offers everything from three-hour introductory sessions to multiday camps. ✉ *430 Campbell St.* ☎ *250/725–2155, 888/777–9961* 🌐 *www.pacificsurfschool.com.*

Storm. This hip surf shop in downtown Tofino carries all the latest gear. ✉ *444 Campbell St.* ☎ *250/725–3344, 888/777–9961* 🌐 *www.stormcanada.ca.*

Surf Sister. This well-respected school has women-only lessons as well as those for everyone. Check out mother-daughter surf packages, teenager surf camps, and progressive sessions. ✉ *625 Campbell St.* ☎ *250/725–4456, 877/724–7873* 🌐 *www.surfsister.com.*

WHALE-WATCHING AND MARINE EXCURSIONS

In March and April, an estimated 20,000 gray whales migrate along the coast here; resident grays can be seen anytime between March and October. In addition, there are humpback whales, sea otters, sea lions, orca, black bears, and other wildlife. Most whale-watching operators lead excursions along the coast and to the region's outlying islands, including Meares Island, Flores Island, and Hot Springs Cove. Services range from no-frills water-taxi drop-off to tours with experienced guides; prices vary accordingly.

Jamie's Whaling Station & Adventure Centre. One of the most established whale-watching operators on the coast, Jamie's has motorized inflatable boats as well as more comfortable 65-foot tour boats. You can book a whole range of adventures, including kayaking, bear-watching, and trips to Meares Island or Hot Springs Cove. Jamie's operates from mid-February through October. There's also a location in Ucluelet. ✉ *606 Campbell St.* ☎ *250/725–3919, 800/667–9913* 🌐 *www.jamies.com.*

★ **Tla-ook Cultural Adventures.** Led by First Nations guides, Tla-ook Cultural Adventures lets you paddle traditional dugout canoes through traditional native territory on the way to Meares Island and Echachist Island. The all-day trip features a seafood feast in an old village dotted with historic middens. ☎ *250/725–2656, 877/942–2663* 🌐 *www.tlaook.com.*

Tofino Whale Centre. This company has a maritime museum with a 40-foot-long gray whale skeleton that you can study while waiting for your boat. It runs whale watching, bird watching, and bear spotting tours year-round. ✉ *411 Campbell St.* ☎ *250/725–2132, 888/474–2288* 🌐 *www.tofinowhalecentre.com.*

CLOSE UP

Pacific Rim Surfing

Though the water tends to be nippy—full-length wet suits are worn in summer and winter alike—Tofino has skimmed its way onto the international surfing map for several reasons. Framed by rocky headlands, the curvaceous hard-sand beaches are smack on the open Pacific Ocean, guaranteeing long swells and sizable waves year-round; the area is also a rain forest, providing a genuine wilderness experience. What's more, the Tofino region nurtures an easy-going, even mildly anarchic lifestyle. It's no surprise that a distinctive "free style" of surfing has taken root here as local surfers often eschew competitions in favor of doing their own thing. The culture attracts many warm-climate surfers to test themselves in what's considered a more challenging environment. What they find, along 20 miles of rugged shoreline between Ucluelet and Tofino, are at least four spectacular surfing beaches.

The most famous, Long Beach, together with Wickaninnish Beach, is within the Pacific Rim National Park Reserve. The next beach northward is Cox Bay, arguably the most popular—and most challenging—of the surfing beaches located outside the park. This is where the most skilled surfers launch their boards and where competitions, when they're held, take place. That said, there's space for everyone on this long and lovely stretch of forgiving sand, even for beginners. Several lodges, all suitable for families, are located on Cox Bay. Chesterman Beach, the next major beach as you travel towards Tofino, is similarly picturesque and is considered the best beach for those just starting out in the sport. Finally, MacKenzie Beach is conveniently close to the town of Tofino.

Whichever beach you choose, take note that the waves and rip currents present real danger, and first-time surfers are advised to take lessons. Parks Canada employs surf guards at Long Beach in the summer. Wave-hazard signs are posted along the highway and updated daily.

The Pacific Rim Highway, running the length of the Tofino peninsula, includes a separate bike path, and almost any day of the year you'll see surfers, with a skate, skim, or long board under one arm, cycling their way to their preferred destination. It's quite common to pick up surfers hitchhiking from one beach to another. And it's equally normal to see local surfers heading out on stormy days and when it snows. The best surfing is said to take place in spring and fall, when the waves are strong and consistent and the weather more or less cooperates. Lessons and equipment rentals are available year-round.

SHOPPING

Eagle Aerie Gallery. In a traditional longhouse, the magnificent Eagle Aerie Gallery houses a collection of prints, paintings, and carvings by renowned B.C. artist Roy Henry Vickers. ✉ *350 Campbell St.* ☎ *250/725–3235* 🌐 *www.royhenryvickers.com.*

Himwitsa Native Art Gallery. Here's where to find a good selection of First Nations crafts, jewelry, and clothing. The complex also has a seafood restaurant. ✉ *300 Main St.* ☎ *250/725–2017, 250/725–2017* 🌐 *www.himwitsa.com.*

DID YOU KNOW?

The water in Tofino is cold enough (about 50 degrees Fahrenheit) to require a full wetsuit and booties year-round; the upside is that winter surfing is very popular and most surf businesses operate all year.

Reflecting Spirit Gallery. More than 200 local artists are showcased here with a wide range of photographs, paintings, carvings, pottery, and jewelry. There's a second location in Ucluelet. ✉ *411 Campbell St.* ☎ *250/725–2472* 🌐 *www.reflectingspirit.ca.*

Shorewind Gallery. This lovely store specializes in West Coast fine art, including paintings, sculpture, pottery, glass, jewelry, and other handcrafted objects. ✉ *120 4th St.* ☎ *250/725–1222* 🌐 *www.shorewindgallery.com.*

SPAS

Sacred Stone Spa. A small spa above the harbor in downtown Tofino, Sacred Stone specializes in different styles of massages, including hot stone, Ayurvedic, and Thai foot massage. ✉ *421 Main St.* ☎ *250/725–3341* 🌐 *www.sacredstone.ca.*

UCLUELET

295 km (183 miles) northwest of Victoria.

Ucluelet, which in the Nuu-chah-nulth First Nations language means "people with a safe landing place," along with the towns of Bamfield and Tofino, serves the Pacific Rim National Park Reserve. Ucluelet is quieter than Tofino and has a less sophisticated ambience. Despite a growing number of crafts shops, restaurants, and B&Bs, it's still more of a fishing village than an ecotourism retreat, although Black Rock Resort competes with Tofino's upscale dining-and-lodging market.

Like Tofino, whale-watching is an important draw as are the winter storms. Ucluelet is the regional base for fishing and kayaking in the Broken Group Islands, part of Pacific Rim National Park Reserve. Various charter companies take boats to greet the 20,000 gray whales that pass close to Ucluelet on their migration to the Bering Sea every March and April.

EXPLORING

Wild Pacific Trail. Ucluelet is the starting point for the Wild Pacific Trail, a hiking path that winds along the coast and through the rain forest; it's a work in progress that will eventually link Ucluelet to Pacific Rim National Park Reserve. A 2.7-km (1.7-mile) loop starts at He-Tin-Kis Park off Peninsula Road and can also be reached from the Amphitrite Point Lighthouse at the end of Coast Guard Road. Take note of the sea-facing trees, bent at right angles in a face-off against the wild and stormy winds. Another 4-km (2½-mile) stretch starts at Big Beach at the end of Matterson Road and continues to the bike path just outside Ucluelet. 🌐 *www.wildpacifictrail.com.*

WHERE TO EAT AND STAY

For expanded hotel reviews, visit Fodors.com.

$$$ CONTEMPORARY ✕ **Matterson House.** In a tiny 1931 cottage with seven tables and an outdoor deck, husband-and-wife team Sandy and Jennifer Clark serve generous portions of seafood, prime rib, and veal cutlets. It's simple food, prepared well with fresh, local ingredients; everything, including soups, desserts, and the wonderful bread, is made on the premises and

can be accompanied by various local wines. *Average main: C$22* ✉ *1682 Peninsula Rd.* ☎ *250/726–2200.*

$$$$ MODERN CANADIAN **Norwoods.** When this small but cozy wine bar and bistro opened on main street Ucluelet, it was—and still is—an anomaly. It's just so stylish, and with an open kitchen that dominates the scene, that there's a happening vibe here. The food is pretty darn good, with lots of regional fare, including freshly caught seafood and picked today produce. The sticky braised short ribs are succulent, so make sure to add them to your list. The tuna tatake, with a seaweed salad and edamame wasabi purée, hints to the chef's travels around Asia, and the venison chop with blackberry jus and parsnips gives a nod to European cuisine. Everything is paired with predominantly B.C. wines. *Average main: C$30* ✉ *1714 Peninsula Rd.* ☎ *250/726–7001* *www.norwoods.ca.*

$$$$ B&B/INN **A Snug Harbour Inn.** Set on a cliff above the ocean, this couples-oriented B&B has some of the most dramatic views anywhere. **Pros:** friendly vibe; unique location; hot tub. **Cons:** a bit off the beaten track; no on-site dining; no children allowed. *Rooms from: C$300* ✉ *460 Marine Dr.* ☎ *250/726–2686, 888/936–5222* *www.awesomeview.com* *6 rooms* *Breakfast.*

$$$$ HOTEL ★ **Black Rock Oceanfront Resort.** On a rocky ledge at the edge of a shallow inlet, Black Rock Resort is Ucluelet's first upscale, full-service resort, and its modern design and ambience is unexpected in this quiet village. **Pros:** gorgeous views at every turn; chic aesthetic; lovely spa. **Cons:** limited beach access; service can be inconsistent; austere design is not for everyone. *Rooms from: C$550* ✉ *596 Marine Dr.* ☎ *250/726–4800, 877/762–5011* *www.blackrockresort.com* *71 rooms, 62 suites* *Breakfast.*

$ HOTEL **Canadian Princess Resort.** Permanently moored in Ucluelet's marina, this 1932 steam-powered survey ship is a fun, albeit cramped, lodging. **Pros:** ideal downtown Ucluelet location; laid-back character. **Cons:** shared bathrooms; fishing boats sometimes fire up their engines in the early morning; open seasonally. *Rooms from: C$100* ✉ *1943 Peninsula Rd.* ☎ *250/726–7771, 800/663–7090* *www.canadianprincess.com* *46 shoreside rooms, 27 shipboard cabins without bath, 1 suite* *Closed mid-Sept.–mid-May* *No meals.*

$$$ B&B/INN **Majestic Ocean Bed and Breakfast.** Longtime kayaking-business operator Tracy Eeftink and her husband, Ted, have three fetching ground-level rooms opening onto Ucluelet Harbor. **Pros:** On Ucluelet Harbor; hearty breakfasts; picnic lunch on request. **Cons:** a long walk into town; no nearby restaurant. *Rooms from: C$170* ✉ *1183 Helen Rd.* ☎ *250/726–2828, 800/889–7644* *www.majesticoceanbb.ca* *3 rooms* *Breakfast.*

SPORTS AND THE OUTDOORS

FISHING

Island West Fishing Resort. In addition to fishing charters, this company offers floatplane tours around Ucluelet. The staff will clean and ice-pack the fish you caught for your departure home. ✉ *1990 Bay St.* ☎ *250/726–7515* *www.islandwestresort.com.*

KAYAKING

Majestic Ocean Kayaking. Excursions range from three-hour paddles around the harbor to trips to the Broken Group Islands and Barkley Sound, as well as multiday adventures to Clayoquot Sound and the Deer Group Islands. A whale-watching trip for seasoned paddlers is a blast. ✉ *1167 Helen Rd.* ☎ *250/726–2868, 800/889–7644* 🌐 *www.oceankayaking.com.*

SURFING

Ucluelet, like Tofino, is a popular year-round surf destination with waters that are equally as cold, so bring your full dry suit summer and winter.

Relic Surf Shop and Surf School. These guys are cool dudes with a shop packed with surf boards and gear. They offer rentals and private lessons, surf camps, tours to remote beaches, and three-hour sessions for beginners. ✉ *1998 Peninsula Rd.* ☎ *250/726–4421,* 🌐 *www.relicsurfshop.com.*

WHALE-WATCHING

Jamie's Whaling Station. If you don't see a whale on your first trip with this well-regarded company, you can take another at no charge. You can book a range of adventures, including kayaking trips and hot-springs tours. The season runs mid-March through October. ✉ *168 Fraser La.* ☎ *250/726–7444, 877/726–7444* 🌐 *www.jamies.com.*

Subtidal Adventures. This company specializes in whale-watching and nature tours to the Broken Group Islands. Choose between trips on an inflatable Zodiac or a 36-foot former Coast Guard rescue boat. ✉ *1950 Peninsula Rd.* ☎ *250/726–7336, 877/444–1134* 🌐 *www.subtidaladventures.com.*

PACIFIC RIM NATIONAL PARK RESERVE

105 km (63 miles) west of Port Alberni, 9 km (5 miles) south of Tofino.

EXPLORING

Fodor's Choice ★ **Pacific Rim National Park Reserve.** This national park has some of Canada's most stunning coastal and rain-forest scenery, abundant wildlife, and a unique marine environment. It comprises three separate units—Long Beach, the Broken Group Islands, and the West Coast Trail—for a combined area of 123,431 acres, and stretches 130 km (81 miles) along Vancouver Island's west coast. Admission to the park is C$7.80, and visitors must display a permit, available from the visitor center, in their vehicle.

The **Pacific Rim Visitor Centre** (✉ *Tofino-Ucluelet junction on Hwy. 4, 2791 Pacific Rim Hwy.* ☎ *250/726–4212* 🌐 *www.pacificrimvisitor.ca*) is open daily mid-March through August, from 9 am to 7 pm, and until mid-October, 9 am to 5 pm.

Long Beach (✉ *Pacific Rim Hwy.*) gets its name from a 16-km (10-mile) strip of hard-packed sand strewn with driftwood, shells, and the occasional Japanese glass fishing float. When the tide is out, the views seems to stretch forever. As the most accessible part of the park, Long Beach can get especially busy in summer. People come in the off-season to watch winter storms and to see migrating whales in early spring.

A good first stop for many Pacific Rim National Park visitors, the **Wickaninnish Interpretive Centre** (✉ *Off Hwy. 4* ☎ *250/726–7721* ⏲ *Mid-March–mid-Oct., daily 10–6*) sits on the ocean's edge about 16 km (10 miles) north of Ucluelet. It's a great place to learn about the wilderness; theater programs and exhibits provide information about the park's marine ecology and rain-forest environment. Bring your camera: the views are stupendous.

The more than 100 islands of the **Broken Group Islands** archipelago can be reached only by boat. The islands and their clear waters are alive with sea lions, seals, and whales, and because the inner waters are much calmer than the surrounding ocean, they are excellent for kayaking. Guided kayak and charter-boat tours are available from Ucluelet, Bamfield, and Port Alberni.

The third element of the park, the **West Coast Trail,** runs along the coast from Bamfield to Port Renfrew. It's an extremely rugged 75-km (47-mile) trail for experienced hikers. It takes an average of six days to complete, and is open from May 1 to September 30. A quota system helps the park manage the number of hikers, and reservations are highly recommended between mid-June and mid-September. Hiking requires a C$24.75 reservation fee and C$128.75 for a hiker's permit. ✉ *2791 Pacific Rim Hwy.* ☎ *250/387–1642* 🌐 *www.pacificrimvisitor.ca.*

SPORTS AND THE OUTDOORS

Ecosummer Expeditions. The West Coast Trail is one of the world's great hiking challenges, even for seasoned adventurers. If trekking the 74-km (46-mile) route is on your bucket list, Ecosummer Expeditions offers seven-day trips with experienced guides. Most camping equipment is provided, though you'll be expected to help carry it. The number of hikers is limited, so advance reservations are a must. Costs average C$1,800 per person, including park permits. ☎ *250/674–0102, 800/465–8884* 🌐 *www.ecosummer.com.*

Travel Smart Vancouver

WORD OF MOUTH

"You don't need a car in Vancouver; its downtown peninsula is tiny and compact (you could walk from one end the other in 30-40 minutes) and public transit is easier/cheaper than having a car. [Also] parking's limited and extremely expensive."

—BC_Robyn

www.fodors.com/community

GETTING HERE AND AROUND

Most visitors to British Columbia arrive by car via the I–5 interstate highway (called Highway 99 in Canada) or fly into the province's main airport in Vancouver. For visitors who plan to rent a car, well-maintained roads and highways make it easy to drive to destinations such as Victoria, Ucluelet and Tofino on Vancouver Island, Whistler (two hours outside Vancouver), or the Okanagan. Public transportation in Vancouver is accessible and well run.

AIR TRAVEL

Flying time to Vancouver is 5½ hours from New York, 6½ hours from Montréal, 4 hours from Chicago, and 2½ hours from Los Angeles.

Security measures at Canadian airports are similar to those in the United States. Be sure you're not carrying anything that could be construed as a weapon: a letter opener, Swiss Army knife, a pair of scissors, or a toy weapon, for example.

Passengers departing from Vancouver must pay an airport-improvement fee before they can board their plane; however, this fee is now included directly in the cost of tickets, simplifying the process. The fee is C$5 for flights within British Columbia and the Yukon, C$20 for all other flights.

Airlines and Airports Airline and Airport Links.com. Airline and Airport Links.com has links to many of the world's airlines and airports. 🌐 *www.airlineandairportlinks.com.*

Airline Security Issues Transportation Security Administration. Transportation Security Administration has answers for almost every question that might come up. 🌐 *www.tsa.gov.*

AIRPORTS

The major airport is Vancouver International Airport (YVR), in the suburb of Richmond about 16 km (10 miles) south of downtown Vancouver.

Vancouver International Airport is Canada's second-busiest airport, but it's easy to get around this spacious facility. Getting through the immigration process for early-morning departures can add 45 minutes to your travel time, so plan on getting there early. Extensive duty-free shopping, dining, spa, children's play areas, and other services are available, plus free Wi-Fi. Regular courtesy shuttles run between the Main and South Terminals.

Vancouver Island is served by Victoria International Airport. Otherwise, there are domestic airports in or near many towns on the island, including Campbell River, Comox, and Nanaimo. Smaller communities without airports are served by floatplanes.

GROUND TRANSPORTATION

There are many options for getting downtown from Vancouver International Airport, a drive of about 20 to 45 minutes, depending on traffic. If you're driving, go over the Arthur Laing Bridge and north on Granville Street (also signposted as Highway 99). Signs direct you to Vancouver City center.

The fastest and cheapest way to travel downtown or to points en route is via the Canada Line, the newest addition to Vancouver's rapid-transit system, which runs downtown from the Vancouver International Airport in 25 minutes. The station is inside the airport, on level four, between the domestic and international terminals. The trains, which are fully wheelchair accessible and allow plenty of room for luggage, leave every six minutes from the airport and every three minutes from downtown Vancouver. Fares are C$3.75 each way.

Taxi stands are in front of the terminal building on domestic- and international arrivals levels. The taxi fare to downtown is about C$38. Area cab companies include Black Top and Yellow.

Limousine service from LimoJet Gold costs between C$75 and C$95 one way; they also offer service from the airport to Whistler for C$320 each way.

Taxis and Shuttles Black Top and Checker Cabs ☎ *604/681–2181* 🌐 *www.btccabs.ca.* **LimoJet Gold** ☎ *604/273–1331, 800/278–8742* 🌐 *www.limojetgold.com.* **TransLink** ☎ *604/953–3333* 🌐 *www.translink.ca.* **Yellow Cab** ☎ *604/681–1111* 🌐 *www.yellowcabonline.com*

FLIGHTS

Of the U.S. airlines, American, Delta, Northwest, and United fly to Vancouver. Among smaller carriers, Horizon Air (an affiliate of Alaska Airlines) flies to Vancouver and Victoria from many western U.S. cities. Many international carriers fly to Vancouver, including Air Canada, Lufthansa, Quantas, and British Airways. Canadian charter companies Air Transat and Canadian Affair fly to Vancouver, usually at lower rates than the other airlines offer.

Within Canada, regularly scheduled flights to every major city and to most smaller cities are available on Air Canada. WestJet, a regional carrier, serves most Canadian cities.

Airline Contacts Air Canada ☎ *888/247–2262* 🌐 *www.aircanada.ca.* **Alaska Airlines** ☎ *800/252–7522* 🌐 *www.alaskaair.com.* **American Airlines** ☎ *800/222–2377* 🌐 *www.aa.com.* **Delta Airlines** ☎ *800/221–1212* 🌐 *www.delta.com.* **United Airlines** ☎ *800/864–8331 for U.S. reservations, 800/538–2929 for international reservations* 🌐 *www.united.com.* **US Airways** ☎ *800/428–4322 for U.S. and Canada reservations, 800/622–1015 for international reservations* 🌐 *www.usairways.com.* **WestJet Airlines** ☎ *800/538–5696* 🌐 *www.westjet.com.*

BIKE TRAVEL

Despite British Columbia's demanding landscape, bicycle travel is extremely popular. One of the most spectacular routes follows the abandoned 600-km-long (370-mile-long) Kettle Valley Railway through the mountains of the B.C. interior; Tourism Kelowna has details. Gentler options include the 100-km (62-mile) Galloping Goose Regional Trail near Victoria and the rolling hills of the Gulf Islands. Cycle Vancouver Island has information about bike touring on Vancouver Island and the Gulf Islands. Mountain-biking enthusiasts gravitate toward the trails on Vancouver's North Shore Mountains and up at Whistler.

Bike Maps Cycle Vancouver Island ☎ *250/592–4753* 🌐 *www.cyclevancouverisland.ca.* **Galloping Goose Regional Trail** ☎ *250/478–3344* 🌐 *www.gallopinggoosetrail.com.* **Tourism Kelowna** ☎ *250/861–1515, 800/663–4345* 🌐 *www.tourismkelowna.com.* **TransLink** ☎ *604/453–4500* 🌐 *www.translink.ca.*

BIKES IN FLIGHT

Most airlines accommodate bikes as luggage, provided they are dismantled and boxed; check with individual airlines about packing requirements. Some airlines sell bike boxes, which are often free at bike shops, for about $25 (bike bags can be considerably more expensive). International travelers often can substitute a bike for a piece of checked luggage at no charge; otherwise, the cost is about $100. Most U.S. and Canadian airlines charge $50–$100 each way, though fees are increasing steadily. Many also ask that the bike be preregistered when you book your ticket.

BOAT AND FERRY TRAVEL

Ferries play a central role in British Columbia's transportation network. In some areas, ferries provide the only access (besides floatplanes) to remote communities. For visitors, ferries are one of the best ways to get a sense of the region and its ties to the sea. BC Ferries operates one of the largest ferry fleets in the world, serving about 40 ports of call on B.C.'s west coast. The ferries carry all vehicles as well as bicycles and foot passengers.

Reservations are recommended between Vancouver and Vancouver Island and on most sailings between Vancouver and the Southern Gulf Islands, especially on weekends and holidays. Most other companies load vehicles on a first-come, first-served basis.

BC Ferries operates two ferry terminals outside Vancouver. From Tsawwassen (an hour south of downtown), ferries sail to Swartz Bay near Victoria, to Nanaimo on Vancouver Island, and to the Gulf Islands. From Horseshoe Bay (45 minutes north of downtown), ferries sail to the Sunshine Coast and to Nanaimo on Vancouver Island. Vehicle reservations on Vancouver to Victoria and Nanaimo and Vancouver to the Sunshine Coast routes are optional and cost an additional C$15 to C$17.50. There's no charge for reservations on Gulf Island routes.

There are several options for getting to Vancouver Island from Washington State: Black Ball Transport operates the MV *Coho*, a car ferry, daily year-round between Port Angeles, Washington, and Victoria's Inner Harbour. The car and passenger fare is US$57; bikes are US$6.50. The *Victoria Clipper* runs daily, year-round passenger-only service between downtown Seattle and downtown Victoria. Trips take about three hours, and the one-way fare from mid-May to late September is US$92; bicycles are an extra US$10, and reservations are recommended. Washington State Ferries runs a car ferry daily from April through December from Anacortes, Washington, to Sidney (some runs make stops at different San Juan Islands), about 30 km (18 miles) north of Victoria. Trips take about three hours. One-way high-season fares are US$59.85 for a vehicle and driver, and bikes are US$6.

Boat and Ferry Information

BC Ferries ☎ *888/223–3779, 888/223–3779 in B.C., Alberta and Washington State* ⊕ *www.bcferries.com.* **Black Ball Ferry Line** ☎ *250/386–2202, 360/457–4491* ⊕ *www.ferrytovictoria.com.* **Clipper Navigations** ☎ *250/382–8100* ⊕ *www.clippervacations.com.* **Washington State Ferries** ☎ *206/464–6400, 888/808–7977* ⊕ *www.wsdot.wa.gov/ferries.*

BUS TRAVEL

IslandLink Bus operates bus service to most towns on Vancouver Island and connects with BC Ferries in Nanaimo. The same company operates AirportLink, ValleyLink, and WhistlerLink buses, which serve Vancouver International Airport, the Fraser Valley, and Whistler. Pacific Coach Lines operates frequent service between Victoria and Vancouver (both downtown and the airport) on BC Ferries. The Tofino Bus provides daily service from Vancouver, Vancouver Airport, Victoria, Nanaimo, and points en route to Port Alberni, Tofino, and Ucluelet. From May to September, the West Coast Trail Express shuttles hikers from Victoria and Nanaimo to the trailheads of the West Coast and Juan de Fuca trails. All bus companies ban smoking, and most long-distance buses have restrooms on board. Some even play videos.

Greyhound serves most towns in the province and provides frequent service on popular runs. The company's North America Discovery Pass provides unlimited bus travel for 7, 15, 30, or 60 days anywhere in Canada or the United States. These passes are an excellent value for travelers who want to wander the highways and byways of the country, packing many miles into a relatively short period of time. For occasional day trips, however, they're hardly worth it.

Bus terminals in all major cities and many smaller ones are efficient operations with plenty of agents on hand to handle ticket sales. In villages and some smaller towns, the bus station is simply a counter in a local convenience store, gas station, or snack bar. Getting information on schedules beyond the local ones is sometimes difficult in these places.

Most bus lines accept at least some of the major credit cards. To buy a ticket in really small centers, plan on using cash. Pick up your tickets at least 45 minutes before the bus's scheduled departure time.

Contacts Greyhound ☎ *800/661–8747 in Canada, 800/231–2222 in U.S.* 🌐 *www.greyhound.ca.* **IslandLinkBus** 🌐 *www.islandlinkbus.com.* **Pacific Coach** ☎ *604/662–8074, 800/661–1725* 🌐 *www.pacificcoach.com.* **Tofino Bus Island Express** ☎ *250/725–2871, 866/986–3466* 🌐 *www.tofinobus.com.* **West Coast Trail Express** ☎ *250/477–8700, 888/999–2288* 🌐 *www.trailbus.com.*

CAR TRAVEL

Canada's highway system is excellent. It includes the Trans-Canada Highway, or Highway 1, the longest highway in the world—running about 8,000 km (5,000 miles) from Victoria, British Columbia, to St. John's, Newfoundland, using ferries to bridge coastal waters at each end. The second-longest Canadian highway, the Yellowhead Highway (Highway 16), follows a route from the Pacific Coast and over the Rockies to the prairies. North of the population centers, roads become fewer and less developed.

Within British Columbia itself, the Trans-Canada Highway (Highway 1), Highway 3, and the Coquihalla Highway (Highway 5) offer easy access to the Okanagan. Speed limits range from 50 kph (30 mph) in cities to a maximum of 100 kph (60 mph) on highways. The Sea-to-Sky Highway between Vancouver and Whistler is full of twists and turns, and although it was upgraded and widened prior to the 2010 Winter Olympics, drivers should still exercise caution. Landslides occasionally occur along this highway, also noted for its spectacular scenery along Howe Sound.

FROM THE UNITED STATES

Drivers must carry owner registration and proof-of insurance coverage, which is compulsory in Canada. The Canadian Non-Resident Inter-Provincial Motor Vehicle Liability Insurance Card, available from any U.S. insurance company, is accepted as evidence of financial responsibility in Canada. If you're driving a car that is not registered in your name, carry a letter from the owner that authorizes your use of the vehicle.

The main entry point into British Columbia from the United States by car is on Interstate 5 at Blaine, Washington, 48 km (30 miles) south of Vancouver. Three highways enter British Columbia from the east: Highway 1, or the Trans-Canada Highway; Highway 3, or the Crowsnest Highway, which crosses southern British Columbia; and Highway 16, the Yellowhead Highway, which runs through northern British Columbia from the Rocky Mountains to Prince Rupert. From Alaska and the Yukon, take the Alaska Highway (from Fairbanks) or the Klondike Highway (from Skagway or Dawson City).

Border-crossing procedures are usually quick and simple. Most British Columbia land-border crossings are open 24 hours; exceptions are the crossing at Aldergrove and smaller border posts in eastern British Columbia, which are typically open 8 am to midnight. The Interstate 5 border crossing at Blaine, Washington (also known as the Douglas, or Peace Arch, border crossing), is one of the busiest border crossings between the United States and Canada. Weekend and holiday traffic tends to be heaviest; listen to local radio traffic reports for information about wait times, which can sometimes be as much as three hours. The Canada Border Services Agency posts estimated wait times on its website.

Insurance Information Canada Border Services Agency ☎ *204/983–3500* 🌐 *www.cbsa-asfc.gc.ca.* **Insurance Corporation of British Columbia** ☎ *604/661–2800, 800/663–1466* 🌐 *www.icbc.com.*

GASOLINE

Gasoline prices vary significantly from neighborhood to neighborhood in British Columbia. Expect to pay at least C$1.30 per liter (1 gallon = 3.78 liters), with prices slightly higher in Vancouver. In B.C., the price includes federal and provincial taxes, a gradually increasing carbon emissions tax, and in the Greater Vancouver region, 15 cents per liter of local transit tax. The total tax for every liter is more than C$1.

Most gas stations are self-serve and most are automated, so you can pay at the pump using a credit card; major credit cards are widely accepted. A local law requires customers to pay for the gas before it's dispensed, so if you want to pay cash you'll have to estimate how much you'll need. It's not customary to tip attendants.

PARKING

More than 300 parking lots (above- and belowground) are available in Vancouver. Underground parking prices downtown typically run C$3 to C$5 per hour, depending on location. Parking meters are in effect 9 am to 8 pm daily and are strictly monitored. On-street parking can be hard to find downtown, especially during workdays and on weekends. Read signs carefully to avoid being towed or fined; be aware that some spots must be vacated by the time rush hour begins at 3 pm. Fines run between C$30 and C$75, plus the cost of the tow truck.

ROAD CONDITIONS

Snow tires are recommended when traveling the Sea-to-Sky Highway between Vancouver and Whistler or driving on the Coquihalla or Trans-Canada highways during the winter. Keep in mind that speed limits are expressed in kilometers, not miles, in Canada.

ROADSIDE EMERGENCIES

In case of emergency anywhere in B.C., call 911; if you are not connected immediately, dial "0" and ask for the operator. The British Columbia Automobile Association (BCAA) provides 24-hour roadside assistance to AAA and CAA members.

Emergency Services British Columbia Automobile Association ☎ *800/222–4357 roadside assistance* 🌐 *www.bcaa.com.*

RULES OF THE ROAD

In Canada your own driver's license is acceptable. By law, you're required to wear seat belts and to use infant seats. In B.C., babies under the age of one and under 20 pounds must travel in a rear-facing infant seat and not in a front seat with an active air bag; children over one year old and between 20 and 40 pounds need to be secured in child seats, while kids up to age nine or four-foot-nine inches tall (whichever comes first) must use booster seats. Motorcycle and bicycle helmets are mandatory. Right turns are permitted on red signals. Speed limits, given in kilometers, are usually within the 50–100 kph (30–60 mph) range outside the cities.

WINTER DRIVING

In coastal areas, the mild damp climate contributes to roadways that are frequently wet. Winter snowfalls are not common (generally only once or twice a year), but when snow does fall, traffic grinds to a halt and the roadways become treacherous and stay that way until the snow melts. Beware icy roads, especially east of Vancouver.

Tire chains, studs, or snow tires are essential equipment for winter travel in the north and in mountain areas such as Whistler. If you're planning to drive into high elevations, be sure to check the weather forecast beforehand. Even the main-highway mountain passes can be forced to close because of snow conditions. The Ministry of Transportation website has up-to-date road reports.

Road Reports BC Ministry of Transportation 🌐 *www.drivebc.ca.*

CAR RENTAL

When you reserve a car, ask about taxes, cancellation penalties, drop-off charges (if you're planning to pick up the car in one city and leave it in another), and surcharges (for being under or over a certain age, for additional drivers, or for driving across state or country borders). All these things can add substantially to your costs. Request car seats and extras such as GPS when you book.

Rates are sometimes—but not always—better if you book in advance or reserve through a rental agency's website. There are other reasons to book ahead, though: for popular destinations, during busy times of the year, or to ensure that you get certain types of cars (vans, SUVs, exotic sports cars).

TIP→ Make sure that a confirmed reservation guarantees you a car. Agencies sometimes overbook, particularly for busy weekends and holiday periods.

Renting a car is a good option if you're getting out of the cities. If you plan to spend most or all your time in downtown Vancouver, you won't need a car: parking can be difficult to secure and most attractions are within walking distance or a short cab or bus ride away. Downtown Victoria is even more compact. Rates in Vancouver begin at about C$40 a day or C$230 a week, usually including unlimited mileage. Car rentals in B.C. also incur a 12% tax as well as a vehicle-licensing fee of C$1.99 per day. An additional 17% Concession Recovery Fee (also known as a premium location fee), an extra fee charged by the airport authority for retail space in the terminal, is levied at airport locations. Some companies located near Vancouver International Airport offer free customer pick-up and drop-off at the airport, enabling you to avoid the latter fee. Some companies also tack on other fees, such as an Energy Recovery Fee, or a Vehicle Maintenance Fee, of about C$1 per day. If you prefer a manual-transmission car, check whether the rental agency of your choice offers stick shifts; some companies don't in Canada.

Car-rental rates vary by supply and demand, so it pays to shop around and to reserve well in advance. Vancouver's airport and downtown locations usually have the best selection. When comparing costs, take into account any mileage charges: an arrangement with unlimited mileage is usually the best deal if you plan to tour the province.

Additional drivers are charged about C$10 per day. Child seats and booster seats, which are required for children up to age 9, also cost about C$10 per day, so if you need one for more than a few days, it's worth bringing your own or buying one locally.

CAR RENTAL RESOURCES

Local Agencies Lo-Cost Rent A Car ☎ *888/556–2678* 🌐 *www.locostrentacar.com.*

Major Agencies Alamo ☎ *877/222–9075* 🌐 *www.alamo.ca.* **Avis** ☎ *800/230–4898* 🌐 *www.avis.ca.* **Budget** ☎ *800/268–8900* 🌐 *www.budget.ca.* **Hertz** ☎ *800/654–3131* 🌐 *www.hertz.ca.* **National Car Rental** ☎ *800/227–7368* 🌐 *www.nationalcar.ca.*

CRUISE TRAVEL

Vancouver is a major embarkation point for Alaska cruises, and virtually all Alaska-bound cruise ships call here; some also call at Victoria and Prince Rupert. After leaving Vancouver, however, most luxury liners make straight for Alaska, leaving the fjords and islands of B.C. to smaller vessels and expedition ships. Some operators lead sailing trips around B.C.'s islands; independent travelers can explore the coast on BC Ferries or on one of the coastal freighters serving remote outposts.

The small, expedition-style ships operated by American Safari Cruises and Cruise West explore the British Columbia coast on their way to Alaska; some offer cruises exclusively in B.C. Bluewater Adventures has 8- to 10-day sailing cruises of the B.C. coastline, including the Queen Charlotte Islands.

For less traditional experiences, check out the *Aurora Explorer,* a 15-passenger packet freighter operated by Marine Link Tours that weaves in and out of the Broughton Archipelago. Mothership Adventures operates a 10-passenger restored hospital ship dating from 1956 that offers guided kayak paddles to otherwise inaccessible coastal inlets.

Cruise Lines American Safari Cruises ☎ *206/284–0300, 888/862–8881* 🌐 *www.innerseadiscoveries.com.* **Bluewater Adventures** ☎ *604/980–3800, 604/980–3800* 🌐 *www.bluewateradventures.ca.* **Cruise West** ☎ *888/862–8881* 🌐 *www.cruisewest.com.* **Marine Link Tours** ☎ *250/286–3347* 🌐 *www.marinelinktours.com.* **Mothership Adventures** ☎ *888/833–8887* 🌐 *www.mothershipadventures.com.*

TRAIN TRAVEL

Amtrak has service from Seattle to Vancouver, providing connections between Amtrak's U.S.-wide network and VIA Rail's Canadian routes. VIA Rail Canada provides transcontinental rail service. In B.C. VIA Rail has two major routes: Vancouver to Jasper, and Jasper to Prince Rupert with an overnight stop in Prince George. A third route, Victoria to Courtenay on Vancouver Island, is being upgraded. At this writing, service was set to resume in 2012, but delays could well see this edge into 2013. Rocky Mountaineer Vacations operates a variety of spectacular all-daylight rail trips between the Canadian Rockies and the west coast as well as the Whistler Mountaineer between North Vancouver and Whistler. All trains are no-smoking, and they do not run in winter.

WORD OF MOUTH

After your trip, be sure to rate the places you visited and share your experiences and travel tips with us and other Fodorites on www.fodors.com.

If you're planning to travel much by train, look into the Canrail pass. It allows seven one-way coach-class trips within a 21-day period. Sleeping cars are available, but they must be reserved at least a month in advance. In high season (June through mid-October) the passes cost C$1,008, while in low-season rates (October 16 through May) they are C$630.

Reservations are essential on the Rocky Mountaineer and highly recommended on Amtrak and VIA routes. All the train services accept major credit cards, traveler's checks, and cash. VIA Rail will accept U.S. and Canadian currency.

Information Amtrak ☎ *800/872–7245* 🌐 *www.amtrak.com.* **Rocky Mountaineer Vacations** ☎ *604/606–7245* 🌐 *www.rockymountaineer.com.* **VIA Rail Canada** ☎ *888/842–7245* 🌐 *www.viarail.ca.*

ESSENTIALS

ACCOMMODATIONS

In Vancouver and Victoria you have a choice of luxury hotels; moderately priced modern properties; bed-and-breakfasts, both simple and luxurious; and smaller older hotels with perhaps fewer conveniences but more charm. Options in smaller towns and in the country include large, full-service resorts; remote wilderness lodges; small, privately owned hotels; roadside motels; and B&Bs. Even here you need to make reservations at least on the day on which you plan to pull into town.

In addition to Canada's national star-rating system, Canada Select, you can look for a blue Approved Accommodation decal on the window or door of a hotel or motel. Both indicate that the property has met industry association standards for courtesy, comfort, and cleanliness.

Expect accommodations to cost more in summer (except for ski resorts, where winter and spring break are high season). If you're planning to visit in high season, book well in advance. As a rule, hotels in downtown Vancouver are substantially pricier than those located 10 or 15 minutes outside the downtown core. Be aware of any special events or festivals that may coincide with your visit and fill every room for miles around. Note also that many out-of-the-way lodgings are closed during the winter.

The lodgings we list are the cream of the crop in each price category. When pricing accommodations, always ask what's included and what costs extra. Properties are assigned price categories based on the range between their least and most expensive standard double rooms at high season (excluding holidays). *Prices in the reviews are the lowest cost of a standard double room in high season.*

Most hotels and lodgings require you to give your credit-card details before they will confirm your reservation. If you don't feel comfortable emailing this information, ask whether you can fax it (some places even prefer faxes). However you book, get confirmation in writing and have a copy of it handy when you check in.

Be sure you understand the hotel's cancellation policy. Some places allow you to cancel without any kind of penalty—even if you prepaid to secure a discounted rate—if you cancel at least 24 hours in advance. Others require you to cancel a week in advance or penalize you the cost of one night. Small inns and B&Bs are most likely to require you to cancel far in advance. Most hotels allow children under a certain age to stay in their parents' room at no extra charge, but others charge for them as extra adults; find out the cutoff age for discounts.

APARTMENT AND HOUSE RENTALS

Rental houses, apartments, and cottages are popular in British Columbia, particularly on the coast and the islands, and in Whistler. Whistler condos are usually time-share or consortium arrangements and can be booked directly through Tourism Whistler. Vacation rentals elsewhere are usually privately owned and range from simple summer cottages to luxurious waterfront homes. Rates range from C$800 per week to several thousand; popular places book up as much as a year in advance.

Local Agents Chalet Select ☎ *800/741–1617, 800/741–1617* 🌐 *www.chaletselect.com.*
Sojourn Vacation Properties ☎ *250/479–8600, 888/479–8600* 🌐 *www.bcacc.com.*
Tourism Whistler ☎ *604/664–5625, 800/944–7853* 🌐 *www.tourismwhistler.com.*

BED-AND-BREAKFASTS

B&Bs are found in the country and the cities. In Vancouver, many of the top B&Bs are scattered throughout the West End, between Stanley Park and downtown. In Victoria, try in the historic neighborhoods of Oak Bay and Rockland or in James Bay near the Inner Harbour. For assistance in booking these and other B&B lodgings, contact Tourism British Columbia. Room quality varies from house to house as well, so you should ask to see a room before making a choice. Note that many B&Bs require you stay at least a certain number of nights in high season.

Reservation Services (U.S.-based) Bed and Breakfast.com ☎ *800/462–2632* 🌐 *www.bedandbreakfast.com.* **Bed & Breakfast Inns Online** ☎ *800/215–7365* 🌐 *www.bbonline.com.* **BnB Finder.com** ☎ *888/469–6663* 🌐 *www.bnbfinder.com.*

Reservation Services (Canada-based) Hello BC ☎ *800/435–5622* 🌐 *www.hellobc.com.* **Victoria Bed and Breakfast Guide** 🌐 *www.bestinnsofvictoria.com.*

COMMUNICATIONS

INTERNET

As in most North American cities, Internet cafés and Wi-Fi service can be found throughout Vancouver and Victoria. Most hotels and B&Bs also have Internet connections; many of the larger properties have Wi-Fi, which is usually free. It's harder to find Internet cafés in smaller towns in the Okanagan, Tofino, and Ucluelet, but many lodgings have some kind of connection that you can use. Internet and Wi-Fi access are available free at all 22 branches of the Vancouver Public Library. Internet cafés throughout the city charge about C$3 per half hour.

Contacts Cybercafés. Cybercafés lists over 4,000 Internet cafés worldwide. 🌐 *www.cybercafes.com.* **Vancouver Public Library** ✉ *350 W. Georgia St., Downtown* ☎ *604/331–3603* 🌐 *www.vpl.vancouver.bc.ca.*

PHONES

The good news is that you can now make a direct-dial telephone call from virtually any point on earth. The bad news? You can't always do so cheaply. Calling from a hotel is almost always the most expensive option; hotels usually add huge surcharges to all calls, particularly international ones.

> **WORD OF MOUTH**
>
> Did the resort look as good in real life as it did in the photos? Did you sleep like a baby, or were the walls paper-thin? Did you get your money's worth? Rate hotels and write your own reviews or start a discussion about your favorite places in Travel Talk on www.fodors.com. Your comments might even appear in our books.

In some countries you can phone from call centers or even the post office. Calling cards help keep costs to a minimum, but only if you purchase them locally. And as expensive as mobile phone calls can be, they are still usually a much cheaper option than calling from your hotel.

CALLING WITHIN CANADA

Vancouver uses 10-digit calling for local calls (e.g., 604/555–1212). The city's area codes are 604 and 778. Whistler and the Sunshine Coast also use a 604 area code, and for the rest of British Columbia, including Victoria and Vancouver Island, it's 250. Pay phones are easy to find, and new ones accept credit cards and prepaid calling cards. Dial 411 for directory assistance, 0 to reach an operator, and 911 for emergencies. All long-distance calls, including calls to the United States, must be prefixed with a 1.

CALLING OUTSIDE CANADA

The country code for the United States is 1.

MOBILE PHONES

If you have a multiband phone (some countries use different frequencies from those used in the United States) and your service provider uses the world-standard GSM network (as do T-Mobile, Cingular, and Verizon), you can probably use your phone abroad. Roaming fees can be steep, however: 99¢ a minute is considered reasonable. And overseas you normally pay the toll charges for incoming calls. It's almost always cheaper to send a text message than to make a call, since text messages have a really low set fee (often less than 5¢).

If you just want to make local calls, consider buying a new SIM card (note that your provider may have to unlock your phone for you to use a different SIM card) and a prepaid service plan in the destination. You'll then have a local number and can make local calls at local rates. If your trip is extensive, you could also simply buy a cell phone in your destination, as the initial cost will be offset over time.

TIP→ If you travel internationally frequently, save one of your old mobile phones or buy a cheap one on the Internet; ask your cell-phone company to unlock it for you, and take it with you as a travel phone, buying a new SIM card with pay-as-you-go service in each destination.

To avoid roaming charges, you can rent a cell phone in Vancouver. Cita Communications, at the Visitor Information Centre at the Vancouver International Airport international and domestic terminals, offers cell-phone rentals for C$4.99 a day, with local calls costing C$0.49 a minute, and SIM cards for $1 a day with calls costing C$0.35 a minute. Alternatively, cell-phone stores abound throughout downtown Vancouver.

Contacts Cellular Abroad. Cellular Abroad rents and sells GMS phones and sells SIM cards that work in many countries. ☎ *800/287-5072* 🌐 *www.cellularabroad.com.* **Cita Communications** ☎ *604/671-4655, 888/593-2482* 🌐 *www.cita.info.* **Mobal.** Mobal rents mobiles and sells GSM phones (starting at $49; $99 for a phone that works in North America) that will operate in 150 countries. Per-call rates vary, but are typically more than $1 per minute. ☎ *888/888-9162* 🌐 *www.mobalrental.com.* **Planet Fone.** Planet Fone rents cell phones, but the per-minute rates are expensive. ☎ *888/988-4777* 🌐 *www.planetfone.com.*

CUSTOMS AND DUTIES

You're allowed to bring goods of a certain value back home without having to pay any duty or import tax. But there's a limit on the amount of tobacco and liquor you can bring back duty-free, and some countries have separate limits for perfumes; for exact figures, check with your customs department. The values of duty-free goods are included in these amounts. When you shop abroad, save all your receipts, as customs inspectors may ask to see them as well as the items you purchased. If the total value of your goods is more than the duty-free limit, you'll have to pay a tax (most often a flat percentage) on the value of everything beyond that limit.

Visitors may bring certain goods into Canada for their own use as "personal baggage." Camping and sports equipment, cameras, tape recorders, and laptops are considered personal baggage. Your own vehicles, vessels, and aircraft may also be imported. Provided these goods are declared upon arrival and taken back out of Canada when you leave, they will not be subject to any duties or taxes. A visitor's goods cannot be used by a resident of Canada, or on behalf of a business based in Canada.

Visitors may bring in the following items duty-free: 200 cigarettes, 50 cigars, and 7 ounces of tobacco; 1 bottle (1.14 liters or 40 imperial ounces) of liquor or 1.5 liters of wine, or 24 355-milliliter (12-ounce) bottles or cans of beer for personal consumption. Any alcohol and tobacco products in excess of these amounts are subject to duty, provincial fees, and taxes. You can also bring in gifts up to a total value of C$60 per gift as long as the gifts do not include alcohol or tobacco.

Note that handguns and semiautomatic firearms are not allowed in Canada. They will be confiscated at the border, and criminal charges may result. Contact the Canadian Firearms Centre, part of the Royal Canadian Mounted Police, if you intend to travel with rifles and shotguns for hunting purposes.

Information in Canada Canada Border Services Agency ☎ *204/983-3500, 800/461-9999 in Canada* 🌐 *www.cbsa.gc.ca.* **Canadian Firearms Centre** 🌐 *www.cfc-cafc.gc.ca.*

U.S. Information U.S. Customs and Border Protection 🌐 *www.cbp.gov.*

TRAVELING WITH PETS

No longer relegated to boarding kennels during a vacation, pets are now the norm when it comes to travel. You'll find many hotels and inns have set aside dog-designated rooms. If you are bringing a cat or dog into Canada, it must have a certificate issued by a licensed veterinarian that clearly identifies the animal and certifies that it has been vaccinated against rabies during the preceding 36 months. Assistance dogs are allowed into Canada without restriction.

EATING OUT

In Vancouver, where several thousand eateries represent almost every cuisine on the planet, deciding what to eat is as important as deciding what to see and do. Vancouverites are a health-conscious lot, so light, organic, and vegetarian meals are easy to find, and every restaurant and even most pubs ban smoking indoors and out. Good coffee is everywhere—downtown you'll never have to walk more than half a block for a cup of high-test cappuccino.

On-the-go dining, served from mobile trucks, is a relatively new phenomenon and is giving mundane hot-dog vendors a run for their money. Street eats are so good that many locals choose them over sit-down restaurants, especially when they're short on time. Neighborhood pubs, both in and outside cities, are another good bet for casual meals. Many have a separate restaurant section where you can take kids.

In Victoria and on Vancouver Island, the farm-to-fork ethos is particularly strong, in part because the island's bounty is so accessible. Many chefs work directly with organic farmers when they are creating their distinctive regional dishes. You'll be please to find that in addition to top-draw destinations such as Whistler, you'll find excellent food even in the most out-of-the-way places in the province.

Although the Canadian dollar is no longer the steal it once was, dining in British Columbia is still one of North America's great bargains. To be sure, high-end entrées, especially where seafood is involved, can top C$35, but C$20 to C$25 is more the norm. Bargains abound: the densest cluster of cheap eats in Vancouver is along Denman Street in the West End. Another budget option is to check out the lunch specials at any of the small Asian restaurants lining the streets in both Vancouver and Victoria. They serve healthy hot meals for about the same cost as a take-out burger and fries. But beware: alcohol is pricey in B.C., and bottle of wine can easily double your bill.

MEALS AND MEALTIMES

Despite dwindling stocks, wild Pacific salmon—fresh, smoked, dried, candied, barbecued, or grilled on an alder wood plank in the First Nations fashion—remains British Columbia's signature dish. Other local delicacies served at B.C.'s upmarket restaurants include Fanny Bay or Long Beach oysters and Salt Spring Island lamb. Another homegrown treat is the Nanaimo Bar. Once a Christmas bake-sale standard, this chocolate-and-icing concoction has made its way to trendy city cafés.

Most upscale restaurants in Vancouver, Victoria, and Whistler observe standard North American mealtimes: 5:30 to 9 or so for dinner, roughly noon to 2 if open for lunch. Casual places like pubs typically serve food all afternoon and into the evening. Restaurants that stay open late (meaning midnight or 1 am) usually morph into bars after about 9 pm, but the kitchen stays open. In Vancouver, the West End and Kitsilano have the most late-night choices. In Victoria, pubs and a couple of jazz clubs are your best bet.

Unless otherwise noted, the restaurants listed in this guide are open daily for lunch and dinner.

PAYING

Credit cards are widely accepted, but a few smaller restaurants accept only cash. Discover Cards are little known in Canada, and many restaurants outside of Vancouver do not accept American Express.

RESERVATIONS AND DRESS

Regardless of where you are, it's a good idea to make a reservation if you can. In some places, it's expected. In British Columbia, smart casual dress is acceptable everywhere.

At the hottest restaurants in Vancouver, Victoria, and Whistler, you need to make reservations at least two weeks in advance, perhaps more if you want to dine between 7 and 9, or on a Friday or Saturday night. On weeknights or outside of the peak tourist season, you can usually secure a table by calling the same day.

If you want to dine, but not sleep, at one of B.C.'s better-known country inns, such as the Sooke Harbour House or the Wickaninnish Inn, make your reservation as far ahead as possible. Six months ahead is not unreasonable. Guests staying at these inns are given first choice for dining reservations, which means spaces for nonguests are limited. Remember to call the restaurant should you need to cancel your reservation—it's only courteous.

WINES, BEER, AND SPIRITS

Though little known outside the province, British Columbia wines have beaten those from many more established regions in international competitions. A tasting tour of B.C.'s Okanagan wine region is a scenic way to experience some of these vintages, many of which are made in smallish batches and rarely find their way into liquor stores.

British Columbians are also choosy about their beer, brewing and drinking (per capita) more microbrewed ales and lagers than anyone else in the country. You'll find a daunting selection of oddly named brews, since many cottage breweries produce only enough for their local pubs. It's always worth asking what's on draft.

ELECTRICITY

Canada uses the same voltage as the United States, so all of your electronics should make the transition without any fuss. No need for adapters.

EMERGENCIES

Foreign Embassies Consulate of the United States ✉ *1095 W. Pender St.* ☎ *604/685–4311* 🌐 *vancouver.usconsulate.gov.*

HOLIDAYS

Canadian national holidays are as follows: New Year's Day, Good Friday, Easter Monday, Victoria Day (third Monday in May), Canada Day (July 1), Labor Day, Thanksgiving (October 11), Remembrance Day (November 11), Christmas Day (December 25), and Boxing Day (December 26). British Columbia Day (first Monday in August) is a provincial holiday.

MAIL

In British Columbia you can buy stamps at the post office or from many retail outlets and some newsstands. If you're sending mail to or within Canada, be sure to include the postal code (six digits and letters). Note that the suite number often appears before the street number in an address, followed by a hyphen. The postal abbreviation for British Columbia is BC.

Within Canada, postcards and letters cost C$0.61 for up to 30 grams, C$1.05 for between 31 and 50 grams, and C$1.22 for between 51 and 100 grams. Letters and postcards to the United States cost C$1.05 for up to 30 grams, C$1.29 for between 31 and 50 grams, and C$2.10 for up to 100 grams.

International mail and postcards are C$1.80 for up to 30 grams, C$2.58 for between 31 and 50 grams, and C$4.20 for between 51 and 100 grams.

Post Office Canada Post ✉ *Bentall Centre, 595 Burrard St., Downtown* ☎ *604/482–4296, 800/267–1177* 🌐 *www.canadapost.ca.*

SHIPPING PACKAGES

Small packages can be sent via the Small Packets service offered by Canada Post. Rates are determined by weight, size, and method of delivery. You can also use DHL, UPS, or FedEx, or the Canadian shipping companies ICS and Purolator.

Express Services DHL ☎ *800/225–5345* 🌐 *www.dhl.ca.* **FedEx** ☎ *800/463–3339* 🌐 *www.fedex.ca.* **ICS Courier** ☎ *888/427–8729* 🌐 *www.ics-canada.net.* **Purolator** ☎ *888/744–7123* 🌐 *www.purolator.com.* **UPS** ☎ *800/742–5877* 🌐 *www.ups.ca.*

MONEY

Throughout this book, unless otherwise stated, all prices, including dining and lodging, are given in Canadian dollars.

TIP→ Banks never have every foreign currency on hand, and it may take as long as a week to order. If you're planning to exchange funds before leaving home, don't wait until the last minute.

ATMS AND BANKS

Your own bank will probably charge a fee for using ATMs abroad; the foreign bank you use may also charge a fee. Nevertheless, you'll usually get a better rate of exchange at an ATM than you will at a currency-exchange office or even when changing money in a bank. And extracting funds as you need them is a safer option than carrying around a large amount of cash.

TIP→ PINs with more than four digits are not recognized at ATMs in many countries. If yours has five or more, remember to change it before you leave home. ATMs are available in most bank and credit-union branches across British Columbia, as well as in many convenience stores, malls, and gas stations. Major banks include RBC Royal Bank, BMO Bank of Montreal, TD Bank Financial Group, HSBC, Scotiabank, and the Canadian Imperial Bank of Commerce.

ITEM	AVERAGE COST
Cup of Coffee	C$3
Glass of Wine	C$7
Glass of Beer	C$4
Sandwich	C$5
One-Mile Taxi Ride in Capital City	C$7
Museum Admission	C$20

Prices here are given for adults. Substantially reduced fees are almost always available for children, students, and senior citizens.

CREDIT CARDS

Visa and MasterCard are ubiquitous throughout British Columbia. Diners Club, also known as En Route, is less widely accepted. Discover is little known in Canada outside major hotel chains, and many small retailers are reluctant to accept American Express cards because of the high fees charged.

It's a good idea to inform your credit-card company before you travel, especially if you're going abroad and don't travel internationally very often. Otherwise, the credit-card company might put a hold on your card owing to unusual activity—not a good thing halfway through your trip. Record all your credit-card numbers—as well as the phone numbers to call if your cards are lost or stolen—in a safe place, so you're prepared should something go wrong. Both MasterCard and Visa have general numbers you can call (collect if you're abroad) if your card is lost, but you're better off calling the number of your issuing bank, since MasterCard and Visa usually just transfer you to your bank; your bank's number is usually printed on your card.

If you plan to use your credit card for cash advances, you'll need to apply for a PIN at least two weeks before your trip. Although it's usually cheaper (and safer) to use a credit card abroad for large purchases (so you can cancel payments or be reimbursed if there's a problem), note that some credit-card companies *and* the banks that issue them add substantial percentages to all foreign transactions, whether they're in a foreign currency or not. Check on these fees before leaving home, so there won't be any surprises when you get the bill.

■ TIP→ Before you charge something, ask the merchant whether or not he or she plans to do a dynamic currency conversion (DCC). In such a transaction the credit-card processor (shop, restaurant, or hotel, not Visa or MasterCard) converts the currency and charges you in U.S. dollars. In most cases you'll pay the merchant a 3% fee for this service in addition to any credit-card company and issuing-bank foreign-transaction surcharges.

Dynamic-currency-conversion programs are becoming increasingly widespread. Merchants who participate in them are supposed to ask whether you want to be charged in U.S. dollars or the local currency, but they don't always do so. And even if they do give you a choice, they may well avoid mentioning the additional surcharges. The good news is that you *do* have a choice. And if this practice really gets your goat, you can avoid it entirely thanks to American Express; with its cards, DCC simply isn't an option.

Reporting Lost Cards American Express ☎ *800/528–4800 in the U.S., 336/393–1111 collect from abroad* 🌐 *www.americanexpress.com.* **Diners Club** ☎ *800/234–6377 in the U.S., 303/799–1504 collect from abroad* 🌐 *www.dinersclub.com.* **MasterCard** ☎ *800/627–8372 in the U.S., 636/722–7111 collect from abroad* 🌐 *www.mastercard.com.* **Visa** ☎ *800/847–2911 in the U.S. and Canada, 410/581–9994 collect from abroad* 🌐 *www.visa.com.*

CURRENCY AND EXCHANGE

The units of currency in Canada are the Canadian dollar (C$) and the cent, in almost the same denominations as U.S. currency ($5, $10, $20, 1¢, 5¢, 10¢, 25¢, etc.). The C$1 and C$2 bill have been replaced by C$1 and C$2 coins—known as a "loonie," because of the loon that appears on the coin, and a "twonie," respectively.

U.S. dollars are accepted in much of Canada (especially in communities near the border), but you won't get the exchange rate offered at banks. ATMs are ubiquitous in Vancouver and Victoria, and credit cards are accepted virtually everywhere.

In Vancouver and the rest of British Columbia, attire tends to be casual but neat. T-shirts, polo shirts, and slacks are fine at tourist attractions and all but the most upscale restaurants. Waterproof, breathable fabrics are recommended for those planning outdoor excursions. Weather in British Columbia is changeable and varied; you can expect cool evenings and some chance of rain even in summer, so don't forget your umbrella. If you plan on camping or hiking in the deep woods in summer, particularly in northern British Columbia, definitely take insect repellent. In wilderness areas it's also a good idea to carry bear spray and/or wear bells to warn bears of your presence. Both are available in camping and hardware stores in B.C.

SHIPPING LUGGAGE AHEAD

Shipping your luggage in advance via an air-freight service is a great way to cut down on backaches, hassles, and stress—especially if your packing list includes strollers, car seats, etc. There are some things to be aware of, though.

First, research carry-on restrictions; if you absolutely need something that isn't practical to ship and isn't allowed in carry-ons, this strategy isn't for you. Second, plan to send your bags several days in advance to U.S. destinations and as much as two weeks in advance to some international destinations. Third, plan to spend some money: it will cost least $100 to send a small piece of luggage, a golf bag, or a pair of skis to a domestic destination, much more to places overseas.

Some people use FedEx to ship their bags, but this can cost even more than air-freight services. All these services insure your bag (for most, the limit is $1,000, but you should verify that amount); you can, however, purchase additional insurance for about $1 per $100 of value.

Contacts Luggage Concierge ☎ *800/288-9818* 🌐 *www.luggageconcierge.com.* **Luggage Free** ☎ *800/361-6871* 🌐 *www.luggagefree.com.* **Luggage Forward** ☎ *866/416-7447* 🌐 *www.luggageforward.com.* **Sports Express.** Sports Express specializes in shipping golf clubs and other sports equipment. ☎ *800/357-4174* 🌐 *www.sportsexpress.com.*

PASSPORTS AND VISAS

Citizens of the United States now need a passport to re-enter the United States from Canada. Passport requirements apply to minors as well. Anyone under 18 traveling alone should carry a signed and dated letter from both parents or from all legal guardians authorizing the trip. It's also a good idea to include a copy of the child's birth certificate, custody documents if applicable, and death certificates of one or both parents, if applicable. Citizens of the United States, United Kingdom, Australia, and New Zealand do not need visas to enter Canada for a period of six months or less.

TIP→ Before your trip, make two copies of your passport's data page (one for someone at home and another for you to carry separately). Or scan the page and email it to someone at home and/or yourself.

If you're renewing a passport, you can do so by mail. Forms are available at passport-acceptance facilities and online.

TAXES

Most purchases in British Columbia incur a 12% Harmonized Sales Tax, which replaced separate provincial and federal taxes in 2010. The tax so incensed British Columbians that it was overturned in a plebiscite in 2011. It's still being charged on most goods and services as politicians decide how to revert back to the two-tax system.

Prices in this book do not normally include taxes.

TIME

Vancouver, Victoria, Vancouver Island, and the nearby areas are within the Pacific time zone, on the same time as Los Angeles and Seattle. It's 19 hours behind Sydney, 8 hours behind London, 3 hours behind New York City and Toronto, 2 hours behind Chicago, and 1 hour ahead of Alaska.

TIPPING GUIDELINES	
Bartender	C$1–C$5 per round of drinks, depending on the number of drinks
Bellhop	C$1–C$5 per bag, depending on the level of the hotel
Hotel Concierge	C$5 or more, if he or she performs a service for you
Hotel Doorman	C$1–C$2 if he helps you get a cab
Hotel Maid	C$1–C$3 a day (either daily or at the end of your stay, in cash)
Hotel Room-Service Waiter	C$1 to C$2 per delivery, even if a service charge has been added
Porter at Airport or Train Station	C$1 per bag
Skycap at Airport	C$1 to C$3 per bag checked
Taxi Driver	15%, but round up the fare to the next dollar amount
Tour Guide	10% of the cost of the tour
Valet Parking Attendant	C$2–C$3, but only when you get your car
Waiter	15%–20%, with 20% being the norm at high-end restaurants; nothing additional if a service charge is added to the bill

TIPPING

Tips and service charges are not usually added to a bill in Canada. In general, tip 15% of the total bill. This goes for waiters, barbers and hairdressers, and taxi drivers.

TOURS

GUIDED TOURS

Guided tours are a good option when you don't want to do it all yourself. You travel along with a group (sometimes large, sometimes small), stay in prebooked hotels, eat with your fellow travelers (the cost of meals is sometimes included, sometimes not), and follow a schedule.

But not all guided tours are an if-it's-Tuesday-this-must-be-Belgium experience. A knowledgeable guide can take you places that you might never discover on your own, and you may be pushed to see more than you would have otherwise. Tours aren't for everyone, but they can be just the thing for places where making travel arrangements is difficult or time-consuming (particularly when you don't speak the language).

Whenever you book a guided tour, find out what's included and what isn't. A "land-only" tour includes all your travel (by bus, in most cases) in the destination, but not necessarily your flights to and from or even within it. Also, in most cases prices in tour brochures don't include fees and taxes. And remember that you'll be expected to tip your guide (in cash) at the end of the tour.

SPECIAL-INTEREST TOURS

BIKING

AOA Adventures, Rocky Mountain Cycle Tours, and Austin-Lehman Adventures run a variety of comfortable multiday bike trips in Whistler, the Gulf Islands, and the Okanagan.

TIP→ Most airlines accommodate bikes as luggage, provided they're dismantled and boxed.

Contacts AOA Adventures ☎ *480/945–2881, 866/455–1601* 🌐 *www.aoa-adventures.com.* **Austin-Lehman Adventures** ☎ *800/575–1540* 🌐 *www.austinlehman.com.* **Rocky Mountain Cycle Tours** ☎ *800/661–2453* 🌐 *www.rockymountaincycle.com.*

ECO TOURS

British Columbians are known for their green-friendly practices, whether it's protecting endangered species, instituting responsible climate-change initiatives, or running local recycling programs. And it's all fed into tourism as well. Ecosummer Expeditions hosts a number of outdoor adventure trips in B.C., including week-long hiking trips along the West Coast Trail on Vancouver Island, kayaking tours amid orcas in Johnstone Strait, and inn-based kayaking trips in the Gulf Islands.

Contacts Ecosummer Expeditions ☎ *250/674–0102, 800/465–8884* 🌐 *www.ecosummer.com.*

GOLF

BC Golf Safaris specializes in complete, customized golf vacations based around courses in Vancouver, Victoria, Whistler, the Okanagan, and the Rockies.

Contacts BC Golf Safaris ☎ *866/723–2747* 🌐 *www.bcgolfsafaris.com.*

SKIING

Contact Whistler Blackcomb, the host mountain resort of the 2010 Winter Games, to book a complete vacation at one of the world's most popular ski resorts.

Contacts Whistler Blackcomb ☎ *866/218–9690* 🌐 *www.whistlerblackcomb.com.*

VISITOR INFORMATION

Regional visitor information services are available in British Columbia. In addition, Downtown Ambassadors, sponsored by the Downtown Vancouver Business Improvement Association, are easily spotted on Vancouver streets in their red uniforms. They can provide information, directions, and emergency assistance to anyone visiting Vancouver's central business district.

Contacts Aboriginal Tourism Association of British Columbia ☎ *877/266–2822* 🌐 *www.aboriginalbc.com.* **Canadian Tourism Commission** ☎ *613/946–1000* 🌐 *uscw.canada.travel.* **Downtown Ambassadors** ☎ *604/685–7811* 🌐 *www.downtownvancouver.net.* **Tourism British**

Colombia ☎ *800/435-5622* 🌐 *www.hellobc.com.* **Granville Island Information Centre** ☎ *604/666-5784* 🌐 *www.granvilleisland.com.* **Tourism Victoria InfoCentre** ☎ *250/953-2033* 🌐 *www.tourismvictoria.com.* **Vancouver Visitor Centre** ☎ *604/966-3260* 🌐 *www.tourismvancouver.com.*

ONLINE RESOURCES

Information of particular interest to outdoorsy types is on the website for British Columbia Parks (🌐 *www.bcparks.ca*), which outlines recreation, camping, and conservation initiatives at provincially operated reserves throughout British Columbia. At the site for Parks Canada (🌐 *www.pc.gc.ca*), you can learn about the seven national parks that fall within B.C.'s borders. The Great Outdoor Recreation Page (🌐 *www.gorp.com*) is another fount of information for hikers, skiers, and the like.

There are several useful general-interest sites that deal with travel in British Columbia. One good option is the ever-expanding VancouverPlus.ca (🌐 *www.vancouverplus.ca*), which provides tourism tips and travel suggestions for Vancouver. Among alternative newsweeklies, the *Georgia Straight* offers timely features about exploring the province in its "Outside" section (🌐 *www.straight.com*).

For outdoors enthusiasts, in addition to specific sites mentioned in the book, there are several websites that can provide information. These include the Canadian Cycling Association (🌐 *www.canadian-cycling.com*), the Canadian Recreational Canoeing Association (🌐 *www.paddlingcanada.com*) for canoeing and kayaking, the Alpine Club of Canada (🌐 *www.alpineclubofcanada.ca*) for climbing and mountaineering, and the Royal Canadian Golf Association (🌐 *www.golfcanada.ca*).

Safety Transportation Security Administration 🌐 *www.tsa.gov.*

Time Zones Timeanddate.com. Timeanddate.com can help you figure out the correct time anywhere. 🌐 *www.timeanddate.com/worldclock.*

INDEX

K

L

M

N

O

T

U

V

W

Y

Z